■ SUNDAYS IN THE POUND ■

SUND
IN THE POUND:

AYS

The Heroics and Heartbreak
of the 1985–89 Cleveland Browns

JONATHAN
KNIGHT

THE KENT STATE UNIVERSITY PRESS
Kent, Ohio

■

© 2006 by The Kent State University Press,
Kent, Ohio 44242
All rights reserved
Library of Congress Catalog Card Number 2005037574
ISBN-10: 0-87338-866-6
ISBN-13: 978-0-87338-866-5
Manufactured in the United States of America
10 09 08 07 06   5 4 3 2 1

Library of Congress Cataloging-in-Publication Data
Knight, Jonathan.
Sundays in the pound : the heroics and heartbreak of the 1985–89
Cleveland Browns / Jonathan Knight.
p.   cm.
Includes bibliographical references.
ISBN-13: 978-0-87338-866-5 (pbk. : alk. paper) ∞
ISBN-10: 0-87338-866-6 (pbk. : alk. paper) ∞
1. Cleveland Browns (Football team : 1946–1995)—History.
I. Title.
GV956.C6K66   2006
796.332'640977132—dc22
2005037574

British Library Cataloging-in-Publication data
are available.

■

To my dad,
for all those Sundays in the living room.

■

Success is counted sweetest
By those who never succeed.
 —EMILY DICKINSON

Contents

Preface and Acknowledgments

I imagine to everyone but writers, the following can sound cliché. But without a doubt, this book never would have been possible without the love and support of my ever-beautiful wife, Sara, who never protested the countless hours I spent either away from home or in front of a computer. Babe, I promise to someday publish something *you'll* want to read.

I'm also indebted to Mike Baab, Bob Golic, and Marty Schottenheimer, who took time out of their busy schedules to talk with me about their memories of those wonderful days. And thanks to Dino Lucarelli of the Browns for helping me get in touch with them.

Special thanks to the Kent State University Press and its crackerjack staff for providing another downright wonderful collaborative experience.

Tom Cammett came through in a big way, providing some top-notch pictures. Also thanks to Ray Yannucci, not only for directing me to Mr. Cammett but also for doing such a great job on *Browns News/Illustrated* through those years. *BN/I* essentially became the backbone of my research, and I'm not sure if this project would have been possible without it.

Joining Yannucci's wise words in *BN/I* were those of John Delcos, Frank Derry, the legendary Pete Franklin, and Jim Mueller.

Also kudos to the many talented writers who filled the pages of the *Plain Dealer* during this era, primarily Bob Dolgan, Tony Grossi, Bob Kravitz, Bill Livingston, and editor Gene Williams.

And, perhaps most of all, I must acknowledge two men who played such large roles in my life during the time frame covered in this book: my father, Dale Knight, with whom I watched or listened to almost every single one of these games, and Jack Suter, my first "editor," who, thanks to these Browns teams, became a lifelong friend.

Finally, unlike my previous two books, I really can't acknowledge one specific moment when the idea for this one struck me. All I can do is point to a memory that fueled the entire project and I'm sure reflects the emotional involvement of so many at that time.

After Earnest Byner's fumble that lost the 1987 AFC Championship in Denver, my father and I went for an aimless drive into the winter night. Not knowing why and unable to talk about it, we drove country roads and highways, wandered the aisles of a grocery store, and wound up silently eating hot-fudge sundaes at a McDonald's far from home.

Now as an adult, a husband, and a father, I look back and can't imagine being so devastated by something so trivial. It was, after all, just a football game, not life or death. My life would go on just the same as before. So why does that night—as well as all the raucous Sunday-night celebrations in our house after a Browns' victory—burn so brightly in my memory?

Perhaps the answer is also why the following is a story that needs to be told.

Hard as it may seem to believe, the Cleveland Browns used to be fun to watch. You didn't turn on the game and keep a thumb on the remote, ready to flip it off at the first nincompoop play, knowing many, many more would follow. The primary intrigue in following the team didn't surround who was going to get hurt next or who would get arrested for lighting up a police breathalyzer as if it were a party favor.

Now, I don't mean to suggest that football is no longer exciting, nor am I intimating that 73,000 fans don't pack into Cleveland Browns Stadium eight times a year and have a great time.

Still, if you've followed the team at all in the past fifteen years, you know what I'm talking about. While they've still got a long way to go, the new Browns are doing a wonderful job of becoming the old Indians—who, if you remember, went forty-one years between World Series in the second half of the twentieth century.

I write that and sort of feel like an old man telling his grandkids about a time before iPods and the Internet, when men were men and you'd go outside to use the bathroom. In fact, I can envision many folks rolling their eyes just like the kids at their grandfather. In a way, I don't blame you. The cranky-old-man, world-is-going-to-hell-in-a-handbasket shtick makes me crazy, too. Plus, I'm not even thirty yet. I'm too young to be old.

That being said, bear with me for a moment.

Before Carmen Policy, Dwight Clark, and Butch Davis and their decidedly un-Midas touch, before corporate sponsorship all but emasculated the game, the Cleveland Browns, while still a business enterprise, actually resembled a football team. And for a five-year period in the 1980s, they were the most beloved on the planet. No city clung to a football team more than Cleveland clung to the Browns. And perhaps more importantly, no team better represented the growing, changing nature of its city. In a few short years, as Cleveland transformed from a rust-belt hole into a gleaming renaissance town, the Browns mirrored it with a never-say-die, "Yeah-you-want-to-make-something-of-it?" attitude that stood up to the city's critics.

That was twenty years ago. In the past ten years the roles have reversed. As the Browns try and try again to become an elite NFL team (failing dazzlingly at every turn), it's the city that patiently stands by like the two hopeless tramps in *Waiting for Godot*. But instead of sharing a rugged work ethic and gritty personality that tied them together in the 1980s, the Browns and Cleveland now seem to be pantomimed by the antiseptic glass-and-brass palace the team now calls home.

Before artificial crowd noise was pumped through the stadium speakers before key plays, before the team spin machine started patronizing the fans by calling them the "World's Greatest" while not allowing them to hang up signs or banners in the stadium, there was the friendly old sump pump we knew as Cleveland Municipal Stadium. It was there that the teams of the 1980s and the city merged to become one entity. You see clips of games from that era now and can't help but wince. The playing surface was made up of painted dirt, not gourmet Kentucky Bluegrass with a sand-soil root zone and an underground heating system containing nine boilers and forty miles of underground piping. The stands were farther back from the field yet seemed ten times closer. The sight lines were terrible, but somehow you'd still see more. Fans would fork over hard-earned, blue-collar money to sit on long, cracked, wooden bleachers with no backs and scream themselves hoarse (and perhaps throw a few snowballs and batteries) in support of their team. The idea of paying money simply for the right to pay more for tickets or talking on a cell phone during the game while sitting in a fifty-yard-line seat seemed like something out of an apocalyptic Ray Bradbury yarn of the future. Twenty years ago, going to a Browns' game was uncomfortable, inconvenient, and unattractive—none of which is true today. But it didn't matter. You were among family.

Before Tim Couch set a new standard for disappointment, before Kellen Winslow Jr. and his motorbike adventures, the Browns consisted of players that Cleveland adored—players that, while perhaps not saints, certainly weren't public embarrassments. And they were players that represented their team and city, not merely themselves and their agents.

This is not meant to reflect that cranky-old-man tone I alluded to earlier, waxing nostalgic for a simpler time that wasn't really that much simpler, cursing everything modern and all the changes made along the way. Nor is it meant to be a rebuke of the current Browns and their cunning public-relations machinations. Rather, think of this as a celebration of what has come before—the memories of happier days that may well be the only thing standing between today's fans and outright apathy.

Since the 1989 season, the final year covered in the journey you're about to embark on, the Cleveland Browns have made the postseason a grand total of twice. After winning four division titles in five years, they haven't won a single one since. They've posted two winning seasons and eleven losing ones. They've gone through seven head coaches and fifteen starting quarterbacks, missed on countless draft picks, and—oh yeah—lost the team to Baltimore.

Can the team find its way back? I certainly hope so. Will it ever be the same as it was back in those—gulp!—"good old days" of the 1980s? On this, I'm less confident. Wounds may heal but scars usually remain. In the meantime, I prefer to look back. So come with me now, back to a time before fantasy football and the Nextel Halftime Report, when, hard as it may seem to believe, the Cleveland Browns were fun to watch.

Prologue
The Final Play

It was a warm and sunny September Sunday afternoon—ideal football weather. A gentle breeze lilted in off the lake and brushed through the hair of the crowd filtering into Cleveland Municipal Stadium.

At stadiums just like this across the country, fans gathered with tickets burning brightly in their pockets, eager to find their seats and enjoy an afternoon of professional football.

But there would be no football in Cleveland on this day.

Though thousands of fans carried tickets across parking lots and over bridges toward the musty old stadium, they weren't making the trip with any real excitement. They were coming, like you would to a funeral, to say good-bye.

Four months from now, Cleveland Stadium would be gone, just as the team that played there for a half-century had ceased to exist in the wisp of one haunting press conference ten months before. They'd called the events at the Stadium on this summer-like September weekend "The Final Play," and Clevelanders poured downtown to say farewell to the old ballpark they'd come to know so well.

Once inside, organizers tried to create a county-fair atmosphere. One radio station was broadcasting live, another was blaring the broadcast of an Indians' baseball game from up the street. You could line up and kick a field goal at one end of the field and pretend to dive in for a winning touchdown at the other. In between were merchant tables and hundreds of people just walking around aimlessly, looking up at 80,000 barren seats and trying to figure out why football wasn't being played there that day.

It was just ten years before that the team that played there had twice come within inches of playing for a championship. It was just ten years before that this team was more beloved than any civic official, any state politician, any area rock star. It was just ten years before that this city was defined by its football team and—win or lose—the city was just fine with that.

When this team should have been hated, it was still loved. When it should have been ignored, it received attention. And when this team should have stayed in Cleveland, it moved away, leaving thousands of heartbroken and irate fans in its wake.

Nothing would ever be the same after.

By that September Sunday of "The Final Play," everyone knew Cleveland would be getting an expansion team three years later. Most eagerly anticipated its arrival. Some didn't care—and after another half-decade of front-office ineptitude and public-relations nightmares, that group would grow larger and even more disillusioned. This ever-growing pessimism was based on one powerful, inescapable theme: if a team that was so beloved, so adored by a city that had so little else to cherish could up and vanish on a whim, it could and likely would happen again. In baseball, the unthinkable was the Dodgers leaving Brooklyn. In football, it was the Browns leaving Cleveland. But in both cases, the machinations of the sport carried on without pause or apology. It was the ever-loyal fans that were left with nothing but their tainted memories.

By 1996, Cleveland had learned once and for all that professional football was, without a doubt, no more than a business. It was easy to forget that ten years before, easy to get caught up in the excitement and, at the least, be able to ignore the white-collar, occasionally whoring nature of the beast. But come what may in the future, Cleveland would never forget. Their team had been sacrificed for the "greater good" of all the other NFL teams, and seemingly fifteen minutes after it happened, Clevelanders were the only ones who remembered.

Ten years before, Sundays in the Pound weren't like this. The team belonged to Cleveland—*was* Cleveland. It was a storied franchise at its peak, more attuned to the city than any other team had ever been before.

And yet, as in the tragedies of yore, its fall stemmed from its greatest height. In retrospect, it was the team's success and achievement that played as big a role as any in its eventual perish. By the time the final domino fell, on a glorious day for the city of Baltimore, it seemed impossible to trace precisely when the first domino was tipped.

The following is the story of the confluence of the Cleveland Browns' mightiest hour and the beginning of its most devastating. It's the story of the last time Cleveland loved the Browns—and conversely, the last time the Browns truly belonged to Cleveland. And mostly, it's the story of what Cleveland lost when it lost the Browns, and what it may never find again.

Twenty years ago, while the franchise enjoyed unprecedented popularity, the wheels of disaster silently began turning. And slowly, like the softening of a spring sky in the hours before sunset, heartbreak and betrayal drew closer without anyone realizing it.

Yet all the while, there was a spectacular view of the horizon.

1

Bleed
Before You Heal

"You can quote me," Art Modell told a reporter in the summer of 1984. "We're going to have a very, very outstanding team this year. What I expected to happen the last two years I think will happen this year. I expect to be at 9-7 and be in the playoffs. In fact, this might be the best group we've had since the mid-1960s."

Modell, entering his twenty-fourth season as Browns' owner, was never one to sell the team short to the public, but for him to praise a team that much that early was certainly out of the ordinary. True, the Browns were coming off a 9-7 season in which only an inexplicable Week Fifteen loss to the Houston Oilers (who finished 2-14) had kept them out of the playoffs. Head coach Sam Rutigliano had spent the previous three seasons rebuilding and remodeling the team, switching the philosophical emphasis from offense to defense and filling in the gaps vacated by aging players with younger ones, many of whom were full of potential.

The defense had enjoyed a breakthrough year in 1983. The Browns had posted back-to-back shutouts for the first time in thirty-two years and proved they could compete with anyone in the American Football Conference. After a solid draft and some key free-agent signings in 1984, for the first time in recent memory, the Cleveland defense appeared to be stronger than its offense. Thus, the questions surrounding the 1984 Browns were directed at the offense, or more specifically, to the man who would take over its reins: Paul McDonald.

McDonald was no stranger to Cleveland fans. He'd been with the Browns for four seasons, though never as the full-time starter. Since 1980, he'd served as backup and part-time relief man for Brian Sipe, who had departed to the New Jersey Generals of the upstart United States Football League after ten years in brown and orange. There was good reason to believe in that sultry Olympic summer of 1984 that the Browns wouldn't miss Sipe that much. Yes, Sipe had set a handful of team records in his decade in Cleveland and had been the leader of one of the league's most potent offenses for years. But his final three years with the Browns had not gone well. After a fairy-tale 1980 season in which Sipe directed the Browns to the AFC Central Division title and was named NFL Player of the Year, he threw fifty-six interceptions in his final thirty-seven games in Cleveland, as the Browns struggled to an overall record of 18-23 from 1981 through 1983.

Sipe had suffered through long stretches of ineffectiveness and nagging injuries in 1982 and 1983, and McDonald was called on to start five times. He'd taken over in the seventh game of the strike-shortened 1982 season and directed the Browns to two clutch wins that secured a spot in the restructured postseason tournament. Though inexperienced, he'd displayed potential, and it was clear the team considered him the quarterback of the Browns' immediate future.

When Sipe came to head coach Sam Rutigliano after the 1983 season finale and told him he had a guaranteed contract offer from the Generals, Rutigliano could have tried to talk Sipe out of it. Even if Sipe wouldn't be the starter in the future, his presence alone could help, and he could also serve as a handy insurance policy at quarterback. But Rutigliano, as well as much of the Browns' front office, felt McDonald was ready. The morning of Sipe's final game, McDonald had signed a four-year contract. The Browns assumed they had their man.

There were other holes on the offense, but the key to everything in 1984, both offensively and overall, was McDonald. If he could just play at the level Sipe had achieved in his final two seasons, the Browns likely would be no worse than a .500 team. If McDonald could play even better, fans and coaches alike conjectured, the Browns could be a playoff team. Maybe even a Super Bowl team. But even before it began, there were subtle hints that this would be an unorthodox season.

First, offensive coordinator Larrye Weaver mysteriously resigned twenty-four hours before the college draft. The official explanation was "personal reasons," but rumors swirled that Weaver was a Sipe man and did not have as much confidence in McDonald. Then, the Browns' opening game in Seattle on Labor Day weekend was moved from Sunday to Monday afternoon due to a Kingdome scheduling conflict between the Seahawks and Seattle's Major League Baseball team, the Mariners. Around the same time, *Playboy,* certainly not the most respected sports think tank in the magazine business, predicted the Browns to win the division. It was one of the only publications to do so.

Then, in the final week of the preseason, the Browns lost two offensive starters. First right tackle Cody Risien was sidelined for the season when he tore ligaments and cartilage in his right knee with five minutes remaining in Cleveland's final exhibition game. Then wide receiver Dwight Walker was placed on the injured-reserve list after he was hospitalized following a late-night, single-car accident.

Still, Rutigliano was confident that 1984 would be the Browns' year. "We're going to win," he told a gallery at the Cleveland Touchdown Club Kickoff Luncheon the week before the opener. "It's not going to be a long year, and it's not going to be a journey, so don't be patient."

He also concurred with Modell's comment of two months earlier and didn't hope but *expected* the Browns to make the playoffs. "We have the best talent since

I've been here, and that's the key. Now my advice to you is sit back and enjoy, because we're going to win the division."

All was sunshine and lollipops. Then the season began.

At the time, it was unquestionably the worst season opener in Browns' history (only to be topped by the abysmal display in the new Browns' opener against Pittsburgh, a 43-0 drubbing on September 12, 1999). The Seahawks pounded Cleveland, 33-0, as the Browns managed just 120 yards of offense, committed five turnovers, and were zero-for-eleven on third-down conversions. Paul McDonald, the man everyone was hoping would lead the Browns into a new era, completed just one of his first fourteen passes, fumbled once, threw two interceptions, and was sacked five times. Rutigliano, McDonald, and the team tried to shrug off the game as "just one of those days," but permanent damage had been done to the team's psyche.

However, the slaughter in the Kingdome did not truly set the tone for the season. The theme for the 1984 Browns surfaced in Week Two when the Browns stood tall against the playoff-bound Los Angeles Rams and took a 17-10 lead into the fourth quarter. The Rams rallied to tie, then took a 20-17 lead after Browns' kicker Matt Bahr missed a potential go-ahead field goal with five minutes remaining. Time ran out on the Browns before they could threaten to score again. It was the first in a long line of games the 1984 Browns could have, maybe even *should* have won but didn't.

A week later, the Browns roared to a 14-0 lead in the first half over the quickly improving Denver Broncos, who were led by second-year quarterback John Elway. Though Elway was held in check (one of only two times in his career the Browns would do so), Cleveland handed Denver seventeen points on a pair of interceptions and a McDonald fumble. The final turnover came after the Browns marched into Denver territory in the final two minutes, trailing 17-14. McDonald, who had been sacked seven times, tried to fire a pass to rookie wide receiver Brian Brennan, but misjudged the youngster's speed. Denver cornerback Randy Robbins intercepted the pass and returned it for the game-clinching touchdown with thirty-seven seconds left. It would not be the last time a Denver touchdown with that much time remaining on the clock would break the hearts of Cleveland fans.

Not surprisingly, McDonald was loudly booed when he was introduced to the sellout crowd a week later prior to the Browns' battle with the arch-rival Pittsburgh Steelers. He did little to counter the criticism in the early going, throwing an interception for a touchdown for the third straight game that gave Pittsburgh a second-quarter lead. But McDonald bounced back with a fine game, throwing for 293 yards and two scores while the Cleveland defense held Pittsburgh to just 219 total yards. The Browns coasted to their first victory, a 20-10 triumph, and for a week, all was right in Browns Town. Or so it seemed.

Rutigliano, usually jovial and humorous with the media, was beginning to show signs of strain. After the Steeler win, a television reporter asked him if he was a much better coach after beating the Steelers than he'd been before. "That's not true, and I know you're being funny," Rutigliano replied. "I was a good coach a week ago, and I was a good coach when I came here. I don't let anybody evaluate Sam Rutigliano. That doesn't mean a damn thing to me. I believe in myself and there's an awful lot of other people who do also, in spite of people's opinions, as opposed to the facts."

Rutigliano eventually walked out of the room, ending the press conference.

The temporary upswing for the Browns ended the following week when McDonald was sacked a team-record eleven times by the Kansas City Chiefs. The Browns' defense held the Chiefs to just 234 yards, but the Cleveland offense could only manage a mere 186 yards of its own in a 10-6 loss. McDonald, who was the victim of seven dropped passes, threw four interceptions, including one on each of the Browns' final three series, each ending a potential game-winning drive. McDonald had now thrown eleven interceptions and had been sacked twenty-eight times in five games. Risien's preseason injury had crippled the offensive line, but McDonald was also criticized for holding onto the ball too long, then making bad mistakes when he did release it. Though the Browns were 1-4 and the vultures were circling, the worst for both McDonald and Rutigliano was yet to come.

Cleveland raced to a 16-3 lead midway through the third quarter at home the following week against the New England Patriots. Rutigliano entered this contest with a new game plan: play more conservatively on offense to prevent the big mistakes and let the Browns' suddenly dominant defense win the game. For most of the afternoon, it worked. But New England rallied and took a 17-16 lead early in the fourth quarter. Kicker Matt Bahr appeared to have given the Browns back the lead with three minutes left with a 36-yard field goal, but the field judge ruled the kick was wide left. A key stop by the Cleveland defense gave the Browns' offense the ball back with one final chance to win.

McDonald, enjoying the best game of his career, drove his team to the New England twenty-one yard line with twenty-three seconds to go. Most Browns' fans figured Bahr would be called upon to attempt the game-winning field goal. But Rutligliano opted to throw his conservative game plan out the window and decided to go for one more pass. It was an almost identical situation to the infamous "Red Right 88" call nearly four years earlier, when the Browns were in position to attempt a game-winning field goal in the final minute of a frozen playoff with the Oakland Raiders. In that instance, Rutigliano also opted for one more pass play, and Brian Sipe was intercepted in the end zone, ending Cleveland's season.

McDonald fired an out-pass to the New England five yard line for wide receiver Duriel Harris, who had already caught seven passes for 120 yards on the day. But Harris slipped, allowing Patriots' cornerback Raymond Clayborn to intercept the pass and return it 85 yards to the Cleveland seven with seven seconds remaining. It was Red Right 88 all over again.

Browns fans everywhere were stunned. Art Modell called the decision to throw another pass "inexcusable" and said that it "defied comprehension." "Sometimes," a beleaguered McDonald said in the locker room, "I wonder if anything good will ever happen."

Plenty of good had happened on this early October day. Aside from the final pass, McDonald was impressive, completing twenty-three of thirty-seven passes for 320 yards. The Browns had out-gained the Patriots by nearly 100 yards but had nothing to show for it. They were 1-5, and the media and fans were calling for Rutigliano's scalp. "It's about this time of the season when you are 1-5 that the finger-pointing should start and the rationalization should begin," radio personality Pete Franklin wrote in a column. Rutigliano publicly blamed himself for the loss. "You can look at a lot of things in the game, but I want you all to know, in the final analysis, it was my decision," he said afterward. "And very frankly, it was the wrong decision."

After the game, Rutigliano marched into Modell's office and took full responsibility for the loss. Part of him knew he shouldn't open himself up so much in front of the team's brain trust, but his emotions got the best of him. He said he wouldn't hold Modell to the contract extension he'd agreed to prior to the season. If Modell wanted to fire him right then and there, Rutigliano said, he'd understand.

Modell refused the offer. He told Rutigliano they'd get through this tough stretch together. "I intend to make no coaching changes this season," Modell told the media the following week. "I don't believe in coaching changes in mid-term. It has never worked in the NFL, and it's an owner's copout to make changes when things go bad."

But things had not just gone bad, they'd become ridiculous. Three death threats on Rutigliano were phoned in to the Browns' offices at Cleveland Stadium following the New England loss, and extra security had been assigned to protect him. And Rutigliano's relationship with the media was becoming more and more adversarial.

"Let me tell you something," he barked at the Monday press conference following the New England loss, "I am good for the city of Cleveland, both as a coach and as a person, and I think you're all lucky that I'm here. And when we win, it will even be better because I stand for all the things that are right in the National Football League and the things that are important, I frankly believe, in this country.

"And there's absolutely no difference in the guy who was Coach of the Year in '79 and '80, and I would say to you, this too, that's very important. It's very easy to be negative. It's very easy to kick a dog when he's down, and I don't intend to stay down, and I'm not going anyplace. And I think it's *our* team. And we'd all be a heckuva lot better off, with the fans and everybody, if we'd just look at some of the brighter things about this football team in spite of the fact we're 1-5."

It was an impassioned plea for fairness from an emotional coach under a great deal of strain. But to many, it looked like a man cracking under pressure. "The media essentially assassinated Sam Rutigliano," Browns' nose tackle Bob Golic said. "It was my first real exposure to the media having that much strength."

The pressure only became greater the following week when the Browns fell to 1-6 with a 24-20 home loss to the New York Jets. Once again, Cleveland had a lead in the fourth quarter and couldn't hold on to it. They also had a chance to win the game in the final minutes, only to self-destruct. McDonald, having another superb day, drove the Browns from their own twenty-three yard line to the New York thirty with two minutes remaining. But then three straight Jet sacks clinched victory for the visitors. The loss wasted a career performance by tight end Ozzie Newsome, who set team records with fourteen receptions and 191 yards in defeat. The Browns had now lost five games by a total of twenty-two points. "Someone made the statement before this game that it seems like we're getting paid back for what we did in 1980," Newsome said.

The worst, however, was yet to come.

On a dreary, drizzly day in Cincinnati a week later, the Browns and Bengals both tried to avoid dropping to 1-7 at the season's midpoint. In a sloppy contest in which the Browns dropped eight passes and neither team reached the end zone, a Matt Bahr field goal tied the game at nine with two minutes remaining. Then, thanks to an amazing catch of a 42-yard pass by Cincy wide receiver Mike Martin with two Browns all over him, quarterback Turk Schonert drove the Bengals into Cleveland territory. They were soon in position for kicker Jim Breech to boot a game-winning 33-yard field goal as time expired. The Browns had lost another heartbreaker.

It was one of the longer walks off the field in Sam Rutigliano's life. He envisioned the criticism he would no doubt face and realized his job security was in danger. He walked into the lifeless locker room and conducted the usual prayer with the team. Afterward, he realized the players needed encouragement. What was happening to them wasn't due to a lack of effort. "What have we done to deserve what has been happening to us?" Cleveland cornerback Hanford Dixon asked afterward, echoing that sentiment.

Rutligliano then thought of a story he'd heard that might help the players make it through. "Fellas," he said, "when I was walking off the field, I thought of Tony Lema. He became a great golf champion, but he wasn't born a champion. He had to work his way through a lot of disappointments. Early in his career as a pro golfer, Tony had the habit of dropping out of a tournament if he felt he had no chance of winning it. He just quit. He would then go to a practice tee and hit balls to prepare for the next tournament. Ben Hogan went to him and told him he couldn't do that. Tony wanted to know why not. Ben said, 'You gotta finish. You can't quit. You can't be a champion unless you finish. You have to learn how to lose and keep going before you can be a winner.'

"So fellas, regardless of what happens the rest of the season, make sure you finish."

It was the last time Rutigliano would ever speak to the team.

Of course, the media could smell Rutigliano's pink slip coming. After the game, he was asked if the Browns' season was over. "No," he replied, "at least not for me. I'll finish today and I'll finish next week and I'll be here for the rest of the season. I'm just going to keep going."

But Art Modell felt otherwise. When the coaches and players boarded the team bus to the airport afterward, Modell didn't sit next to Rutigliano and made very little eye contact.

Despite his confident statements to the press, Rutligliano knew his job was in jeopardy. The tension was palpable at his home that evening, growing thicker each time the phone rang. Finally, Rutigliano got the call he'd been expecting. Modell asked him to come over to his house. On the short drive over through Waite Hill, Rutigliano felt like a man marching up onto the gallows.

He thought back on his years in coaching. His career had begun at the high-school level in 1956, then he slowly moved up to the collegiate level at Connecti-cut and Maryland before breaking into the NFL as an assistant. He was hired as the Browns' head coach in December of 1977 and quickly turned the team from a tired underachiever into one of the most exciting in the league. The 1980 Browns, the "Kardiac Kids," went 11-5 and won the AFC Central Division title as Rutigli-ano won his second straight United Press International Coach of the Year Award.

But the following seasons had not proved as bountiful. The team collapsed to 5-11 in 1981 then wobbled to a 4-5 finish in the strike-shortened 1982 season and a spot in the expanded playoff structure. Though the Browns had gone 9-7 in 1983, they could have been better and probably should have made the playoffs. Now, despite having constructed the top-ranked defense in the AFC, without Sipe or a bona-fide running game, the offense had dragged the team into the bottom tier of the league.

Was it Rutigliano's fault? Certainly, irrational decisions like the final pass against New England had taken their toll, but intelligent football fans knew that the team wasn't truly this bad. The 1984 season was clearly an aberration. It was nothing a good draft and a few key signings couldn't cure. But intelligence doesn't govern professional sports.

Rutigliano arrived at Modell's thirty-two-acre estate and thought back to the day he'd first come here seven years before, when he was interviewed for the Browns job. He remembered all the times he'd been here since after big wins and heartbreaking losses. He remembered all the times he'd stayed up late eating pizza and watching *Monday Night Football* with Modell in his study.

David Modell, Art's son, greeted Rutigliano at the door and led him back to that study, making as little eye contact as possible. Rutigliano knew he was a dead man walking. "We want to make a change," Art Modell said a few moments later. "We want you to step aside."

Modell went on about wanting Rutigliano to move into the front office, but the coach—*former* coach—wasn't really listening. After decades of fighting to get to this station in his career, it was over. Just like that, on a Sunday night in October.

When Rutigliano left, he couldn't drive all the way home. He pulled over on the side of the road, not wanting to listen or talk with anyone. His NFL coaching career was over.

Just over twelve hours later, Rutigliano and Modell were sitting side-by-side at a table in front of dozens of reporters and photographers. To their left sat Marty Schottenheimer, the Browns' defensive coordinator for the previous four seasons, who would now become Cleveland's permanent, not interim, head coach.

Shortly after the devastated Rutigliano left his home the night before, Modell called Schottenheimer and invited him over. When he arrived, Ernie Accorsi, Modell's top assistant, was also present. They offered Schottenheimer the head coaching position on an interim basis. After a moment, Schottenheimer replied, "Art, I appreciate your offering me the position, but I can't accept it on the basis of interim. I've always believed that interim coaches are doomed to fail because there's no accountability."

Modell and Accorsi excused themselves and left the room. They returned a few moments later and offered Schottenheimer a contract through the 1986 season.

Both Schottenheimer and Rutigliano felt very awkward. It wasn't customary for the fired coach to be present at the press conference announcing his termination. But he was still a part of the team and his presence made the transition a bit smoother. "My only advice to Marty," he said in one final attempt at humor, "is make sure you kick field goals." Schottenheimer, meanwhile, couldn't help but realize the final straw leading up to Rutigliano's dismissal was a loss caused by his defense's inability to stop the Bengals in the final moments of the previous game.

Modell said the choice to fire Rutigliano was "agonizing." He added, "I never have had a more difficult decision." Difficult and contradictory, since just two weeks earlier he said he'd never fire a coach in the middle of the season.

"I felt this move was in the best interests of the organization," he said. "I didn't feel it was two weeks ago, I feel it is now."

This essentially meant that Modell felt Rutigliano was less of a coach than he had been fourteen days earlier. Anonymous reports said that the owner thought his coach was crumbling under the weight of the pressure of the poor start, and that this breakdown was reflected in the way the team was playing. Modell fired Rutigliano for his own good, claimed one story.

"It's not all Sam's fault," Modell added, "but in baseball terms, this move is like shaking up the lineup. Sunday's loss was not a determination. Suffice it to say, the timing was appropriate. This is a new era beginning with Marty."

Though Schottenheimer had worked with Rutigliano for nearly five years, the two could not have been more different in personalities and football philosophies. Rutigliano was outgoing with his players and the media, belting off jokes and one-liners as if he were the headline act at a nightclub. The bespectacled Schottenheimer was more reserved, more careful with his words, and had a more business-like candor. Rutigliano was a gambler, an offensive-minded gunslinger. Schottenheimer was conservative, more of a throwback to the early days of professional football: play good defense, develop a strong running game, and go home. "I believe you can control the game by running the ball," he would say. "I never met Woody Hayes, but I'm sure I'd like Woody Hayes."

Yet Schottenheimer was just as passionate about his players. "I loved the fact that he wore his emotions on his sleeve," Bob Golic said. "He cried when we won and he cried when we lost. When he had tears in his eyes after one game, I asked Clay Matthews, 'Did we win or lose?' But I liked that. That was the type of player I was."

Schottenheimer was born in Canonsburg, Pennsylvania, in 1943. He had played offensive and defensive tackle in high school then moved on to the University of Pittsburgh, where he switched to linebacker. He majored in English in college and planned on going to either dental school or possibly law school. After his senior season (which earned him a spot in the College All-Star Game the following August, at which he played the world-champion 1964 Cleveland Browns), Schottenheimer was drafted by both the Buffalo Bills of the American Football League and Baltimore Colts of the National Football League. After meeting with both teams, he decided to go with the Bills, where he made an immediate impact as a special-teams player.

"My approach as a player was always somewhat cerebral, because I didn't have much talent," Schottenheimer said. "I always approached it from the standpoint of seeing what advantages I might gain, because I knew I might need that."

After playing primarily special teams for five seasons in Buffalo, Schottenheimer was traded to the Boston Patriots in 1969 and played two seasons there. In the summer of 1971, he was traded to Pittsburgh, then after six weeks, was dealt to Baltimore. But the NFL team that had originally drafted him cut him three weeks later. His playing career presumably over, Schottenheimer moved to Miami, where he sold real estate for a year.

But he still had a love for football in his veins. He took a real estate development job in Denver, and spent time with Broncos' defensive coordinator Joe Collier, who had coached Schottenheimer in Buffalo. "I wanted to learn more about the coaching business," Schottenheimer said, "and Joe is one of the best."

Schottenheimer then moved to Portland, Oregon, looking for a job with that city's World Football League team, the Storm. Ironically, the Storm wasn't looking for coaches, but they were interested in former NFL players. Schottenheimer, now in his early thirties, staged a football comeback. But after injuring his shoulder in training camp and then his knee in Portland's opening game, he officially called it quits as a player. He stayed in Portland and helped coach the linebackers for the remainder of the season, after which the team folded.

The following spring, Schottenheimer returned to Denver and told his wife Pat that if he couldn't find a coaching job by April 1, he would go into another field. On March 30 New York Giants' head coach Bill Arnsparger hired Schottenheimer as linebackers coach. When John McVay replaced Arnsparger two years later, Schottenheimer was promoted to defensive coordinator. In 1978 he moved on to Detroit as linebackers coach, where he served for two seasons. When the defensive coordinator position became available, Lions' head coach Monte Clark decided to hire Maxie Baughan from outside the Detroit staff rather than choose between Schottenheimer or defensive line coach Floyd Peters. It turned out to be a great move—for the Browns, at any rate. At the 1979 Senior Bowl, Schottenheimer heard about the creation of the defensive coordinator position with the Browns from Chuck Weber, Cleveland's defensive backs coach who was departing for Baltimore. Schottenheimer threw his hat into the ring, and on February 3, 1980, Rutigliano hired him.

Now, less than five years later, Schottenheimer sat beside the man who brought him in, about to take his place. "This is a bittersweet moment for me," Schottenheimer said at the press conference. "I have always wanted to be a head coach in the NFL, but I feel badly my becoming one has affected someone like Sam. Still, I'm very excited about the opportunity. I'm positive I'm going to be good at what I do. Right now, I'm looking to start a winning streak. I want to get this organization back on winning ways."

Schottenheimer had already done that with the Cleveland defense. When he took over after the 1979 season, the Browns' defense was one of the worst in the league. Part of the reason the Kardiac Kids were so thrilling in 1979 and 1980 was simply because the defense had trouble stopping teams on a consistent basis. In four seasons, Schottenheimer had changed that. He replaced older veterans nearing the end of their careers with smart draft choices, and from 1981 through 1983, the unit gradually improved. In 1984, though still improving, the Browns' defense was ranked number one in the AFC and number two in the NFL in yardage allowed. Plus, most of the squad's key members were young and, it appeared, would be the building blocks for a long run of success.

Schottenheimer admitted he would have to quickly absorb himself in the Browns' offense and make the changes he felt were necessary. By the start of the 1985 season, he'd hired four new offensive coaches, brought in two new quarterbacks and two new running backs—all four of whom would be counted on as starters—and ripped apart the Cleveland playbook. Rather than the gambling, aerial style promoted by Rutigliano for the previous six years, Schottenheimer took a more conservative, ground-oriented approach.

Although the Browns' defense was now one of the best in the NFL, and he'd seen the Cleveland offense at its pinnacle in 1980, Schottenheimer did not want to put a priority on boasting one of the best offenses or defenses in the league. "I don't want us to be the best offensive or defensive team in the league," he said. "I want us to have the best special teams, and in time we will." Further underlining his emphasis on all phases of the game, he changed the way the team watched game films. Rather than splitting into their respective units to break down the previous game, the entire team would watch all game films together.

Despite the awkwardness of his promotion, Schottenheimer took his new job by the horns. In his first meeting with the team that Monday afternoon, he said they all had played a role in what had led to Rutigliano being fired and that they should all feel bad about it. But, he added, the decision had been made, so they had to move forward. The new coach made it clear from the get-go that everybody—from himself on down—was accountable for his performance.

"At his first team meeting, Marty did what was critically important," said Browns' linebacker Eddie Johnson. "When he came into the room, right there we accepted him as head coach." Appropriately, the team's first full practice under Schottenheimer lasted more than four hours.

He also made some difficult decisions that he knew would not be popular but would make the team better. "The first thing Marty did was take a bunch of the older players who were mostly fan-favorite, Kardiac-Kid type people and put them on the bench," center Mike Baab said. But instead of alienating his players, Schottenheimer's straightforward and businesslike handling of a situation that could have torn the team apart earned him their respect. "Marty is going to be a great coach," right guard Joe DeLamielleure said a few weeks later. "He'll take this team to a Super Bowl someday."

But before anyone started talking about the Super Bowl, the Browns had to get through the critical second half of the 1984 season. Were they to finish the season as poorly as they'd started it, they would have to start all over again in 1985. But a strong finish could start the wheels in motion to getting the Browns where they wanted to be.

"I think we've got a good team," Schottenheimer said, "and the thing we have to do is recognize we aren't far from winning consistently. We have shown improvement, but we need to learn how to win. That's the ingredient that's missing, and as that unfolds, we can begin to win consistently."

Six days after the Browns changed coaches and hoped to initiate a fresh start, everything returned to the quagmire of frustration that had been the 1984 season.

Once again, it appeared Cleveland had victory in its grasp in the final minutes, this time at home against New Orleans. Leading 14-13, Paul McDonald hit Brian Brennan for what appeared to be a game-clinching, 40-yard pass to the Saints' five yard line with two minutes remaining. But the completion was called back on a holding penalty, and the Browns eventually punted back to the Saints. New Orleans drove into Cleveland territory in the final minute, and as time expired, Morten Andersen kicked a 53-yard field goal into the wind and rain at the open end of the stadium to propel the Saints to a 16-14 victory. The Browns now had lost seven games by a total of twenty-seven points and dropped four games in the final ninety seconds.

With even more justification to fold, Schottenheimer and the Browns didn't. The following week in a cold, driving November rain in Buffalo, they finally tasted victory upon getting a much overdue good bounce—literally. Trailing 10-6 midway through the fourth quarter of an ugly game with the winless Bills, the Browns were faced with third-and-twenty at their own thirty-two. McDonald completed a pass to wide receiver Willis Adams for a 26-yard gain, but as Adams was being brought down by former Cleveland cornerback Lawrence Johnson, he fumbled the football. Instead of Buffalo falling on it, Browns' rookie running back Earnest Byner, trailing the play, just happened to be in the right place at the right time. He scooped up the football, then bobbled it, recovered it, stumbled, recovered, then ran 55 yards down the sideline for the game-winning touchdown.

While Byner's first NFL touchdown had been the highlight, another Browns' running back had been the star of the game. Boyce Green rushed for 156 yards, sparking Cleveland's 211-yard ground attack and announcing loud and clear Schottenheimer's offensive preference. "We basically took it to them," Dieken said. "I guess we're going back to basics. That's Marty's philosophy. We're just lining up and running the ball, pushing them off the line of scrimmage. In the past we would throw. Now, we're controlling the ball with the run."

The jubilation was short-lived. The following week, the Browns discovered just how far away they were from being a perennial playoff contender, when the Super Bowl-bound San Francisco 49ers came to Cleveland and pasted the home-town team, 41-7. Earnest Byner went from hero to goat when he fumbled first the opening kickoff, then again on the Browns' first possession. The Browns' heralded defense was ripped for 468 total yards. Meanwhile, Browns' receivers dropped nine passes.

A week later, Cleveland picked on someone its own size and proved it was stronger. In a 23-7 triumph in Atlanta, the Browns sacked Falcon quarterbacks eleven times, while Boyce Green turned in another impressive performance, rushing for 121 yards. The Browns then improved to 4-9 with a 27-10 win over the Houston Oilers in Cleveland, holding Houston to a harmless 147 yards of offense. With three victories in four weeks, for the first time all season, the Browns were winning the games they were supposed to. But there were still heartbreaks to come.

Believe it or not, entering Week Fourteen, the Browns were still mathematically alive in the playoff hunt. Only Pittsburgh in the AFC Central was above .500, and if the Browns were to win their final three games (including a Week Fifteen showdown at Three Rivers Stadium) while the Steelers lost their last three, Cleveland would win the division at 7-9. While many in the media pointed to the

Pittsburgh game as the key to what would be an incredible (if not ridiculous) turnaround to the season, first the Browns had to beat the Cincinnati Bengals in their Cleveland Stadium rematch on December 2.

Leading 17-7 with ten minutes to play, then 17-10 with the football at the two-minute warning, it appeared they'd done it. But with just over sixty seconds left, the Browns were faced with a fourth down from the Cincinnati forty-two. Steve Cox was called on to punt, and with the Bengals out of time outs, going the length of the field for a game-tying touchdown in less than a minute would be nearly impossible. But Cox's punt was blocked by Cincinnati tight end Rodney Holman, and the Bengals recovered at the Cleveland twenty-eight yard line. Hanford Dixon was penalized for pass interference in the end zone, giving Cincinnati a first down at the Cleveland one a few moments later. The Bengals tied the game when rookie quarterback Boomer Esiason hit right tackle Anthony Munoz for a one-yard touchdown pass on a tackle-eligible play with one second left. The game went to overtime, when, not surprisingly, a 30-yard Cincy punt return set up a game-winning 35-yard field goal by Jim Breech, giving first-year coach Sam Wyche and his Bengals a season sweep of the Browns.

It was more of the same the following week in Pittsburgh, where the Browns fell, 23-20, on a Gary Anderson field goal with five seconds remaining. Though Paul McDonald threw four costly interceptions, Cleveland actually staged a re-markable comeback from a 17-6 second-quarter deficit to tie the game midway through the fourth quarter. But in the end, it was not enough. The Browns lost for the fifteenth straight time at Three Rivers Stadium.

"I told the team after the game that you have to bleed before you heal," Schot-tenheimer said afterward, "and I'll tell you what, we're bleeding now, but we're going to heal, because we're going to be a good team. There were things that happened today that makes it very easy to make that statement. I'm confident next year we're going to turn this thing around."

The debacle that was the 1984 season ended on a promising note in the Astrodome as the Browns held off the Oilers for a 27-20 victory. Earnest Byner, who had rushed for 103 yards in Pittsburgh the week before, ran for 188 in the finale, including 157 in the second half as the Browns compiled 254 rushing yards.

When it was all said and done, the 1984 Browns had finished 5-11. Not bad, considering they'd started 1-8, then won four of their final seven games to close the season with optimism for 1985. And 1985, figured Browns' officials, coaches, and fans alike, would be incredibly important. "Next season will be critical for this franchise, because the fans no longer will remain patient," wrote Ray Yan-nucci in *Browns News/Illustrated.* "They will turn deaf ears to more hollow promises. As evidenced by all the empty seats (in the final few home games), Browns' fans no longer will tolerate the mediocrity that has infested this club."

Yannucci was right. Since the 1980 division championship team, the Browns had compiled a four-year record of 23-34. Three of the previous four seasons had been losing ones, and twice the team had gone 5-11. Fans could look at it one of two ways: either the Browns had wasted half the decade, or they'd spent half the decade retooling the team for the future. If they believed in the latter, there needed to be obvious progress in 1985, or apathy may just rule the remainder of the 1980s. "They are tired of rhetoric," Yannucci continued, "they want results, results that will make this team a perennial contender, not a one-year flash like the club that pulled off the miracle of 1980."

Changes would be needed, but Art Modell had the right coach to lead the team through the decade.

Now he just needed the quarterback.

2 Bernie Comes Home

Amidst the hoopla and general chaos of the week preceding Super Bowl XIX in January of 1985, the wheels began turning on a major achievement in Cleveland Browns' history—though no one knew it at the time.

NFL commissioner Pete Rozelle announced that University of Miami quarterback Bernie Kosar, albeit only twenty-one years old, would be eligible for the 1985 collegiate draft that spring if he completed the credits he needed to graduate. To most football fans it wasn't exactly earth-shattering news, even though Kosar had clearly made a name for himself in two years as the Hurricanes' starting quarterback. What many didn't realize was that Kosar still had *two* years of eligibility remaining, not just one. He wouldn't simply be coming out early; he would be *graduating* early with a double major in finance and economics and a 3.27 GPA. Most athletes would have stuck around at least one more year to take another shot at the Heisman Trophy or an even bigger NFL contract down the line. But Kosar's priorities were much different.

"College football was not challenging," he said. "With our passing system at Miami, which was head and shoulders above any other college's, after a while it was just too easy.... For me to grow at so slow a pace—what was the point?"

Around the same time, the NFL told young Kosar that if he didn't apply for the NFL draft by its April 15 deadline, he could still enter the supplemental draft in June. The NFL created the concept of a supplemental draft the previous year primarily as an outlet to acquire players who had been "stolen" away by the upstart United States Football League, begun in 1983 as a spring league to rival the NFL. With its draft before the NFL's and the season immediately following, the USFL was able to lure several potential NFL draftees into its fold with promises of big money and immediate playing time. But the NFL, American sports fans, and even some USFL players had a feeling the new league would not last long. Looking ahead to when players would become available the NFL organized a "supplemental draft" in which teams could select the rights to players under contract in the USFL or the Canadian Football League. Also, once the USFL folded, which the NFL believed it eventually would, the deluge of suddenly available talent would already be accounted for, avoiding a free-for-all.

In the first supplemental draft in June of 1984, teams selected players know-ing it would generally be anywhere from two to four years before those players could be signed, either when their USFL contracts or the USFL itself expired. As a result, many teams put little thought and even less energy into the supplemen-tal draft.

A second supplemental draft was scheduled for June of 1985, and though it wasn't designed for a case such as Kosar's, he realized how it could be used to his advantage. The NFL made its statement to Kosar thinking he could have a few extra weeks to decide whether or not he wanted to jump to the NFL or return to Miami for another year. Though unintended, the supplemental draft and the Kosar situation would combine to create one of the great loopholes in NFL draft history.

Kosar, born the day President John Kennedy was buried, was a native of Board-man, Ohio, near Youngstown and had grown up the oldest of three children whose parents both had Czechoslovakian heritage. They were a devoutly catholic, middle-class working family. Kosar's father was an engineer who had served as a foreman in the Youngstown steel mills, and his mother was a nurse. Together, they instilled an intense desire for their three children to succeed academically above all. It was a trait reflected when Bernie came home crying from his first day of school. When his mother asked him what was wrong, he complained that they hadn't taught him to read yet.

The younger Kosar also adopted his father's passion for the Cleveland Browns. And as Bernie Jr.'s high school career began, he followed the adventures of Brian Sipe and the Kardiac Kids. While the Browns were becoming the NFL's most ex-citing team, Kosar was attending Boardman High, where he starred in three sports: football, basketball, and baseball. But it was on the gridiron where he truly made his mark. After missing much of his sophomore season to injury, half of his junior year was wiped out due to a teachers' strike. As a senior he threw for 2,022 yards and nineteen touchdowns, leading Boardman to an 8-2 record in 1981, and was named the Ohio Player of the Year by the Associated Press. Though he'd en-joyed a prosperous prep career, he wasn't heavily recruited by many big-time colleges. In fact, though he would have preferred to stay close to home, he was ig-nored by area schools like Ohio State, Penn State, and Pittsburgh. His final de-cision was among West Virginia, Cincinnati, Florida, and Miami of Florida.

Miami's program, under the guidance of head coach Howard Schnellenberger, was on the rise and had already begun what would become a decade-long line of talented quarterbacks from Jim Kelly to Gino Torretta. Yet when Kosar was set to begin his playing career, Schnellenberger had other plans.

As Kosar sat out his freshman season of 1982 as a red-shirt, he watched Kelly set a handful of school records and guide the Hurricanes to their first bowl ap-pearance in fourteen years. After Kelly graduated, the job was expected to go to either Kyle Vanderwende or Vinny Testaverde in 1983. But Kosar made the choice more complicated. From the first spring practice through the final session before the opener, the curly-haired nineteen-year-old pushed Vanderwende out of the picture and whittled down the choice to him or the athletic Testaverde. Still agonizing over the decision five minutes before it was to be announced, Schnellenberger, who had helped develop Joe Namath and Kenny Stabler at Alabama, chose Kosar primarily for two reasons. First, he felt that Kosar had done a better job moving the second-team offense than Testaverde had, and second, if the Hurricanes lost to Florida in their first game, he felt Kosar would do a better job of keeping the team together. Florida crushed Miami, though Kosar tied a school record for completions in a game. A new era had begun in Miami, one that would end with Kosar winning nineteen of his twenty-five starts and taking the Hurricanes to back-to-back major bowl invites.

But it was the first of those two bowl games that put Kosar on the map. After the loss to Florida, Miami rebounded to win its next ten games and finished the season ranked fifth in the Associated Press national poll, Miami's highest ranking in nearly sixty years. The Hurricanes were invited to the Orange Bowl, played at their home field, against what many were calling one of the greatest college football teams of all time in the Nebraska Cornhuskers, ranked number one and riding a twenty-two-game winning streak. Instead of backing down from Nebraska, an eleven-point favorite, Kosar took it right at the 'Huskers, blasting their heralded defense for 300 yards. Miami won the game when a two-point conversion attempt by Nebraska failed in the final minute. Kosar later admitted he was hoping it had been successful. With forty-eight seconds remaining, he was confident the Hurricanes would have scored again.

Miami was the national champion thanks to what *Sports Illustrated* called "a round-eyed, curly-haired freshman quarterback who talks as if he's thirty, thinks as if he's forty, and may not be spacy but is definitely from another world." After another impressive season at Miami in 1984, Kosar was ready for the next level.

Though his performance was almost always good, Kosar wasn't exactly the model of a prototype quarterback. His passes, though uncannily accurate, were winged sidearm, "like a guy losing a bar of soap in the shower," Jim Murray of the *Los Angeles Times* once wrote. "We worked and worked on it when he was a pitcher in Little League, trying to stretch that long body over the top," Bernie Sr. said. "But he was so effective throwing the way he did, usually from three-quarters, that you just hated to tamper with anything."

Several more times over his career coaches had tried to get Kosar to throw with a "normal," circular shoulder motion, but he always reverted back to what worked best. It didn't hurt that at 6'5" Kosar could get away with flinging passes sideways without their being knocked down at the line of scrimmage.

And despite his unathletic appearance, Kosar was an outstanding multi-sport athlete. He'd also been a star on his high school basketball and baseball teams at Boardman. But when he ran, Kosar often resembled a giraffe galloping across an

African plain. "Yes, I know I have slow feet," Kosar said. "But, God gave me a good mind to make up for that."

NBC broadcaster Bob Trumpy would call Kosar the "ugly duckling of the NFL," who may not be pretty now, but he will someday grow into a swan.

"He's going to be a great one," Browns' tight end Ozzie Newsome would say a few months later. "He has some ingredients that you can't teach, you can't coach. He makes things happen."

Just the idea of Kosar wearing brown and white was enough to get Browns' fans and sportswriters drooling. "It is my judgement," wrote Cleveland radio personality Pete Franklin, "that Bernie Kosar . . . is a franchise quarterback, perhaps comparable to the Marinos and Elways and stars of tomorrow. Art Modell should hawk the furniture and offer any two players . . . if he knows for certain that Kosar is coming out."

After just two years, Kosar knew he was ready for the next level. Yet as the April draft grew closer, a chain reaction of sports-management hysteria resulted in one of the wildest pre-draft dramas in sports history.

Long before the draft, Kosar announced that he would like to play in Cleveland for his hometown Browns. It was a shocking revelation. Here was Kosar, the top-rated quarterback in his class, about to write his ticket to a long, prosperous career in the NFL, saying he wanted to play in what had become the Siberia of professional sports.

Cleveland was the home of the absolutely dreadful Indians of Major League Baseball and the downright embarrassing Cavaliers of the National Basketball Association. The Browns had a rich history through the 1950s and 1960s, but the 1970s and early 1980s had been disappointing. The fan base was loyal, but the venue was terrible. This was a city no one wanted to live in, certainly no one with as much potential as a professional athlete like Bernie Kosar.

That sentiment was reflected by statements made by two other high-profile quarterbacks shopping for a team in the months previous to the Bernie Derby in the spring of 1985. When heralded Canadian Football League playcaller Warren Moon was weighing his options to sign with an NFL team in December 1983, he made a statement about sacrificing money for the right situation, which was less an analogy than a slap in the face. "Say Seattle offered me $800,000 and some other team offered $1 million," he said. "I'd take Seattle over, say, Cleveland."

Then in January of 1985, after rumors swirled about the Browns trying to trade up in the draft to acquire him, Boston College quarterback Doug Flutie signed a $7 million deal with the New Jersey Generals of the USFL (after which, incidentally, the Generals traded quarterback Brian Sipe, whom they'd looted from the Browns a year earlier, to the Jacksonville Bulls). "I evaluated the situation," Flutie stated, "and I would rather be in New Jersey than Buffalo. I would rather be in New Jersey than Cleveland."

Rather be in *New Jersey* than Cleveland? Was there a worse insult?

Yet the simple fact remained: Kosar wanted Cleveland. He even went so far as to say that had the Browns not been interested in acquiring him, and had the possibility of him landing in Cleveland not been likely, he would have returned to Miami for at least one more season.

Thus, the Browns, who held the seventh pick in the NFL draft, had an advantage over several other teams. But while it sounded nice and Browns' fans loved the idea of the hometown kid coming back to lead the team into a new era of success, they knew it was a long shot. There was no way Kosar would slip down to the seventh spot on the board, and trading up would be difficult. The Buffalo Bills had already signed defensive end Bruce Smith prior to the draft with the first pick, and the Houston Oilers, who had just spent a large chunk of money luring Warren Moon out of Canada the year before, didn't need a quarterback. But not wanting to have to face Kosar twice a year, Houston declined six trade offers from the Browns trying to move up. The four other teams between the Oilers and Browns in the draft order desperately wanted a playcaller like Kosar: Minnesota, Atlanta, Indianapolis, and Detroit.

It appeared the Vikings were in the driver's seat. They even swapped their number three spot for Houston's number two in an unorthodox deal. First, Minnesota agreed not to trade the rights to Kosar to any other team in the AFC Central Division (in other words, Cleveland). Second, even if Kosar did not enter the regular draft, the Vikings could not pick Texas A&M defensive end Ray Childress, whom the Oilers wanted to select. It appeared the deal would benefit both: the Vikings were that much closer to getting Kosar, and the Oilers did what they could to keep him out of their division.

Kosar and his family met with Minnesota head coach Bud Grant and assistant coach Marc Trestman, who had been Kosar's quarterback coach at Miami, and were impressed. But the family was reportedly turned off by Vikings' general manager Mike Lynn and his high-pressure pre-negotiation talk. Ultimately, Kosar's choice was the Vikings or the Browns. And since the Vikings had cornered him in the college draft, he opted for the supplemental draft.

"I looked into the situation in Minnesota very deeply and very openly," Kosar said of his choice. "The question, I think, of my being from the area and my commitment toward the Youngstown-Cleveland area, was basically just wanting to go home."

Preparing for that possibility, the Browns swung a deal with the Buffalo Bills, who also had the top supplemental pick. In the crazed weeks prior to the regular draft the trade reportedly gave the Bills the Browns' first-round pick in the 1986 college draft plus a starting linebacker in exchange for the top supplemental selection in 1985.

But the Oilers and Vikings cried foul. They said since Kosar had hired an agent prior to the April 15 deadline to enter the college draft, he'd already forfeited his remaining college eligibility and therefore did not have the option of entering the supplemental draft. They claimed he had to enter the college draft. The "agent" they referred to was Dr. John Geletka, Kosar's dentist.

Thus, whether Kosar could enter the supplemental draft, whether the Vikings-Oilers trade was legal, and whether the Browns-Bills trade was legal all had to be determined by Pete Rozelle before the college draft. He made his decision on April 23, supporting both trades and allowing Kosar to choose which draft he wanted to enter.

"After weighing all the facts in this matter," Rozelle stated, "I have determined to apply the rule as written, and as it applied in the past. In circumstances of this case, I did not feel it was appropriate for the NFL commissioner to make a definitive determination of Kosar's collegiate eligibility status as Minnesota and Houston have requested. The NCAA has informed us that it has not declared Kosar ineligible and would not further consider his status unless Kosar attempts to resume college football participation. We received no clear evidence that would justify a determination that Kosar has lost eligibility."

Though the NCAA washed its hands of the entire process, Rozelle eliminated what the Oilers and Vikings considered to be the smoking gun proving Kosar had forfeited his eligibility and therefore had to enter the regular draft. The commissioner determined that Dr. Geletka's role in the matter was simply that of an advisor, whether financial or tooth-related. The commissioner also pointed out that there was no evidence of an attempt by either Cleveland or Buffalo to encourage Kosar to keep his intentions to enter the supplemental draft secret until after the college draft.

"Indeed, had either Buffalo or Cleveland been so inclined, they could have quietly prearranged such an understanding with the Kosar interests and refrained from making or announcing their trade until after the April 30 draft had passed," Rozelle said. "Instead, they have been forthright about their trade."

Rozelle extended the deadline to midnight on April 25 for Kosar to enter the college draft. The day after Rozelle made his decision, Kosar announced his. He held a press conference at Miami announcing he would bypass the college draft and enter the supplemental draft the week after his June 25 graduation. The day after, the hushed details of the now-legal Browns-Bills deal were released. In exchange for the top supplemental pick, Buffalo got Cleveland's third-round college pick in 1985, its first- and sixth-round selections in 1986, and All-Pro linebacker Chip Banks. But there was a provision in the deal stating that if it appeared Banks would not come to Buffalo, the Bills could opt to take the Browns' first-round pick in 1985 instead. It turned out to be a wise line item.

When Banks heard he had been dealt to the worst team in the NFL, he blew a fuse. He stormed out of Cleveland after Marty Schottenheimer told him the news, returning to his home in Atlanta. He made it clear that he didn't want to go to Buffalo. Bills' head coach Kay Stephenson called Browns' security director Ted Chappelle, concerned that Banks would not report. Art Modell sent Chappelle to speak with Banks in Atlanta, but it didn't do any good. The day before the draft, Banks told Stephenson that not only did he not want to play in Buffalo but that he simply wouldn't. He said he was willing to sit out the entire season if necessary. Stephenson realized it was too risky to pursue the possibility of luring Banks to Buffalo, so the Bills opted to return Banks to the Browns in exchange for the seventh overall pick in the 1985 college draft.

In the meantime, the Oilers were still desperately trying to keep Bernie Kosar from setting up camp in the AFC Central. After Rozelle made his decision, they threatened a lawsuit to hold up the college draft. But when the Vikings failed to stand with them, the Oilers quickly backed down, resigning themselves to accept what had suddenly become a series of coincidences and good fortune that had gone the Browns' way.

Bernie Kosar officially became a member of the Cleveland Browns on July 2, 1985, when the team selected him with the first pick of the supplemental draft. Two hours later, Art Modell announced Kosar had signed a series of five one-year contracts, reportedly worth nearly six million dollars. The arrangement made Kosar one of the five highest paid quarterbacks in the league, along with Dan Marino, Joe Montana, Warren Moon, and John Elway—elite company for someone who wouldn't turn twenty-two for five months. The quick signing was highly unorthodox and further revealed the unique nature of the entire episode. Forbidden by the league to negotiate with Kosar until after he'd graduated, Kosar's representative (who turned out to be Dr. Geletka) met with Browns' vice president of football operations Ernie Accorsi the following Friday. They closed the deal Monday night, and Kosar was drafted the next day.

Accorsi had played a major role in landing Kosar despite rising into the upper echelon of the Browns' front office just a few weeks before. He had been hired in March 1984 as an assistant to Art Modell after serving two years as general manager for the Baltimore Colts. When the Colts moved to Indianapolis, Accorsi, a longtime Baltimore resident, refused to go with them. "The only attraction to that team for me was Baltimore," he said. "If I was going to move, I wanted to move where I wanted to go." His duties with the Browns increased after Sam Rutigliano was fired that fall, and by the spring of 1985 he had been elevated to the second-most visible front-office position behind Art Modell. His first act as VP was to pull off the most impressive acquisition in team history. Accorsi also made the decision to give Kosar jersey number 19, since he reminded him so much of Johnny Unitas, whom Accorsi had seen work magic in Baltimore.

Needless to say, though it was a great human-interest story akin to the return of the prodigal son, many NFL executives were troubled by the circumstances in which the Browns acquired Kosar. (Or, perhaps more accurately, they were troubled that they weren't the ones benefiting from such circumstances.) "The league needs to look into revising these rules," said 49ers' head coach and team president Bill Walsh. "Some changes probably should be made in areas of equitable interests. It could hurt the future of the regular draft. The need for a supplemental draft could happen more in the future, and soon we'd have two annual drafts."

Walsh made a good point, but one had to consider how many NFL-bound athletes would be in Kosar's position, earning a loophole only because of his honed academic compass. "There are those who claim Kosar 'manipulated' league rules in order to play for the team of his choice, the Browns," said Jets' president Jim Kensil. "Whatever ability he had to do so was because of the unique situation he was able to place himself in by graduating ahead of his class. The Jets are not particularly troubled at this time by providing such an incentive to someone who combines superior academic performance and exceptional athletic ability."

"Bernie beat the system by going to school and passing his classes," one Browns' official added. "Maybe there's a lesson there."

It was one of those rare scenarios in professional sports in which both the ownership and the athlete were tickled with the entire situation. Kosar got what he knew he was worth, but more importantly, he got a chance to play for his hometown team. Modell, in turn, got a sure-fire draw at the ticket window for a relative bargain. Kosar wanted to play with the Browns so badly that Geletka later admitted the quarterback would probably have gotten more money had he been drafted by the Vikings or any other team.

"There was a relationship and a closeness between the ownership and the player, and you don't normally have that today," Geletka said. "Bernie's biggest desire was to play in Cleveland. We knew what we thought he was worth, and the Browns knew what they thought he was worth. We got what we were comfortable with."

And because of the manner in which he came to Cleveland, in a bizarre way, Kosar would not have as much negative pressure to perform. Certainly, the expectations would be immense for Kosar to turn the Browns into a playoff team once he became the starter, but he was no ordinary first-round draft pick. Clevelanders adopted him immediately. He was one of their own. He knew the history of the team and the city. He wasn't the usual type of athlete who comes to town from the far reaches of the continent talking about what he could bring to the team, not knowing anything about it or the city he now called "home." The only reason the Browns acquired Kosar was because he wanted to come to Cleveland. Had he been the typical professional athlete, he would have landed in Minnesota for more money.

And it became apparent early that Kosar was not a typical professional athlete. When representatives of *Sports Illustrated* set up a photo shoot with him, they arranged for a limo to pick Kosar up from practice. Kosar agreed, but only if he could meet up with the limo at a nearby gas station out of the sight of his teammates.

Despite numerous reasons not to, Kosar stuck with his commitment and his dream to play for the Browns. True, the cost of acquiring him was substantial,

◄

since the team gave up a handful of draft picks. But interestingly, the Browns lost no players from a young, improving team. The entire acquisition was like a fairy tale, the kind of thing Browns' fans of 1985 had only read about, the kind of thing you'd associate with someone like Lou Gehrig or the kind of fictional athletes in youth readers of yesteryear.

Before Kosar ever put on an orange helmet, he represented something special to Cleveland. He immediately became an icon for a downtrodden city. He *was* the prodigal son returned, a native boy who had left home and achieved greatness. But unlike the scores of natives before him, this one wanted to cash in his success for a chance to come home. "Frankly, it is not often over the years that I've been here that a professional athlete in any sport has said 'I want to play in Cleveland,'" Modell said. "So I think that statement of Bernie's that he wanted to play in Cleveland, near his home, did as much to activate the interest of this community as any other single factor. It created and developed a sense of civic pride and community spirit that has long been missing around here."

With so much hoopla surrounding Kosar's arrival, Schottenheimer called Denver coach Dan Reeves to see how he had dealt with a similar situation two years before when Stanford star John Elway made his NFL debut with the Broncos. In retrospect, Reeves felt that he had rushed Elway into the starting position too early and had regretted it. Some warned of the same happening to Kosar if the Browns succumbed to public opinion and played the youngster right away.

However, Kosar's new teammates saw a mental toughness that didn't appear shakable by the public's opinion of him. Bob Golic remembered, "As much as Marty wore his emotions on his sleeve and you could see the muscles in his jaw clenching with all the tension he had, it seemed that Bernie had the ability to keep himself loose and cool no matter how much was put on him."

Yet considering what he had given up and what he represented, if Kosar struggled, it would take a lot of guts—or insensitive stupidity—to be the first to criticize.

"Whether he performs or not, only time will tell," Modell added. "But the very fact Bernie, with his credentials and his background, chose to come to Cleveland, meant a lot to this community."

And he had yet to throw a pass.

But even the rosiest of optimists couldn't expect Kosar to be an immediate star in the NFL. As with most rookies with potential, it would take time for the youngster to adjust to the increased speed and talent of the NFL. With that in mind, the Browns did not want to throw Kosar to the wolves right away. Such a move, though popular with the fans, could cripple a young player's confidence and retard his growth process.

The Browns wanted to provide Kosar with a mentor, a veteran quarterback who would be expected to start the season and let the rookie learn in practice and on the sideline for much, if not all of 1985. The team still had Paul McDonald, but he wasn't really what they had in mind. True, he was a veteran, with twenty-one starts under his belt. And once upon a time, *he* had been their quarterback of the future. But with so much at stake—developing Kosar as well as what was expected to be an improved overall team—the Browns went shopping.

They considered Bill Kenney, Steve Grogan, and Steve DeBerg before settling on Gary Danielson, a nine-year veteran who'd spent his entire NFL career with the Detroit Lions. After spending two seasons as the Lions' linebackers coach in the late 1970s, Marty Schottenheimer remembered Danielson, who was now expendable after Detroit acquired longtime Buffalo quarterback Joe Ferguson after the 1984 season. The Browns acquired Danielson the day after the 1985 draft for a third-round pick the following year. It turned out to be a bargain and gave Cleveland two contrasting quarterbacks. "Danielson is thirty-three going on twenty-one," wrote Tony Grossi of the Cleveland *Plain Dealer,* "Kosar is twenty-one going on thirty-three."

Interestingly, Danielson also had a connection to the last quarterback the Browns selected as a franchise player. When Danielson was wrapping up his high school career at Divine Child in Dearborn, Michigan, in 1970 he took a visit to Purdue University. On the visit, he was shown around by Mike Phipps, the Boilermakers' star quarterback whom the Browns had traded Hall-of-Fame wide receiver Paul Warfield to draft. Phipps never reached his potential in seven seasons with the Browns, but now fifteen years later, the Browns were hoping Danielson could help ensure that Kosar would not be the same kind of bust.

Danielson turned in a solid career at Purdue and graduated in 1974. But he wasn't selected in any of the twenty rounds of the NFL draft, primarily because the Boilermakers had switched to a wishbone offense that limited his abilities during his senior year. He played in the short-lived World Football League for two seasons with the New York Stars and Chicago Wind then was traded to Portland. But rather than stay in a dead-end league, Danielson decided to return to college to pursue a master's degree in physical education.

Still, he thought he'd give his pro football career one last shot. He wrote letters to every NFL team offering his services, but only the Lions and Pittsburgh Steelers showed any interest. With Terry Bradshaw in the middle of a four–Super Bowl run in Pittsburgh, Danielson decided to go with his hometown Lions. He showed potential but was cut just prior to the end of training camp. Certain his football career was over, Danielson went to work at a sheet-metal firm for $3.50 an hour.

Six weeks later, after a 1-3 start, Rick Forzano was fired as Detroit's head coach, and Tommy Hudspeth was promoted to replace him. Hudspeth wanted to open up the Lions' inept offense and brought Danielson back. Ironically, Danielson's first NFL job was to serve as a backup to Detroit's then-starting quarterback Greg Landry. Now, as he began his last NFL job, Danielson would again be working side-by-side with Landry, who was the Browns' new quarterbacks coach.

After limited action in his first two years in silver and Honolulu blue, Danielson replaced Landry as the Lions' starter in 1978 then he missed the entire 1979 season with a knee injury. Danielson returned with another solid year in 1980 but missed much of 1981 with a wrist injury. He spent the next two years in a drawn-out quarterback derby with youngster Eric Hipple then turned in the finest season of his career in 1984, completing nearly 62 percent of his passes for better than 3,000 yards and seventeen touchdowns on a team that won only four games. Clearly, Danielson was no star. But considering his experience and personality, he was exactly what the Browns needed. Ernie Accorsi likened Danielson to Earl Morral, a wily twenty-one-year veteran who helped mold Bob Griese into a Hall-of-Fame quarterback with the Dolphins in the early 1970s.

Danielson said it succinctly enough that August: "I will make Bernie better."

For some veterans, entering a situation like this would have been a serious blow to their ego. But Danielson, who would turn thirty-four in September, didn't come to Cleveland with any misconceptions. Though he said if he started in place of Kosar it would be "like 60,000 people being here to see Bruce Springsteen and having Andy Williams show up instead," he kept things in perspective when Schottenheimer told him he'd start the season.

"It's not my job," he told Kosar. "I'm just keeping it warm for you a little while."

3 Like Dogs Chasing a Cat

It all started innocently enough.

To pick up the tedious and stagnant practices during the seemingly endless summer sprawl of training camp in 1984, Browns' cornerback Hanford Dixon began energizing his teammates on the defensive line by barking at them between plays. He soon began calling the members of the line "the Dogs," and for some bizarre reason, the name stuck. "I thought we needed something," Dixon said. "I got the idea watching game films. You need guys who play like dogs up front, like dogs chasing a cat."

The local media soon picked up on the nickname and publicized it, but not simply because it was original and sounded good. Dixon's preseason antics weren't really appreciated until the Cleveland defense got off to a great start that fall, suddenly becoming the best unit in the AFC. That's when the "Dog" phenomenon really began. Fans began painting their faces and wearing masks to games. The highest concentration of this creative sect was in the bleachers, where fans were so close to the field, opposing players could hear their barking and howling. "I especially love the little section down at the open end of the Stadium," Dixon said that year. "I call them my 'Dog fans,' and I bark at them, and they bark at me." It didn't take long for the fenced-in bleachers to adopt its own nickname: the Dog Pound, which quickly became *the* place to watch games.

While the nicknames were fun, they represented a major shift in terms of the team itself. No longer were the Browns a young, still-improving defense that had its moments. Now they were a pack of bloodthirsty hellhounds out to turn the team into a playoff contender.

"A dog takes very little from anybody when he's ferocious," said linebacker Eddie Johnson. "That's what we wanted to instill in our defensive line. In order for us to be successful, our defensive line has to play like dogs."

Ironically, the nickname became less associated with the defensive line and more so with the Cleveland secondary, anchored by the Dog originator, Hanford Dixon.

Dixon, born on Christmas Day 1958, was a first-round draft pick of the Browns in a stretch when the team wasn't using its first-round picks very wisely.

After the Browns finished 11-5 and won the AFC Central in 1980, the following spring, Dixon was the team's first pick, the twenty-second overall. He hailed from the suburbs of Mobile, Alabama, where playing football was a mission in itself. "My father didn't want me to play football, and he'd tell me to come home right after school," Dixon said. "I stayed anyway, even though I knew I'd get a whipping when I got home. I'd tell my friends to go on home, not to come in the house, because I knew what was coming." Eventually his mother convinced his father to let Hanford play, and by the time he made the varsity high school team as a freshman, the confident youngster knew he'd someday play in the NFL.

He had attended Southern Mississippi and, as a freshman, aimed at becoming a fifth-round NFL draft choice. By the time he was a senior, he wanted to go in the first round, and with good reason. He had become one of the top defensive backs and arguably the best cornerback in the country. After veteran Browns' corner Ron Bolton took the young Dixon under his wing, he replaced Lawrence Johnson at right cornerback in the third game of the 1981 season. Dixon started the remainder of that year, then forty of his next forty-one games over the following two years.

Though he played well, it took Dixon almost two whole seasons to snag his first interception. However, he turned the day of his first interception into a memorable one. In a December showdown with the Pittsburgh Steelers in 1982, Dixon tied a team record by picking off Pittsburgh quarterback Terry Bradshaw three times in a 10-9 Browns' win. After another solid campaign in 1983, Dixon enjoyed the best season of his career in 1984, thanks in part to a key acquisition in the secondary that put the defense over the top.

Frank Minnifield, born on New Year's Day 1960, was not quite as highly touted as Dixon coming out of Louisville following the 1982 college season. Many draft experts projected Minnifield, who had 4.45 speed in the 40-yard dash, as a second- or third-round pick. But before the draft, Minnifield opted to go another route. He signed a two-year contract with the Chicago Blitz of the new United States Football League then dislocated his knee in his first game that spring. It was during the recovery period that Minnifield realized what he really wanted to do was play in the NFL.

"It was all in my game plan," he later said. "I knew I only wanted to play two years in the USFL. I knew the money the NFL was putting up front would still be there in two years. The third year would then be the year in which either the USFL would succeed or go down. That was my strategy, to play two years, build a reputation, then come back to the NFL and try to get some type of bidding war between the NFL and USFL."

As it turns out, Minnifield got his bidding war. The Blitz franchise moved to Arizona and became the Wranglers for the 1984 USFL season, for which Minnifield returned. Once the season was over, Minnifield assumed he was a free agent and signed a series of four one-year contracts with the Browns on April 3. The Wranglers, however, claimed Minnifield was still their property until November 30, and he therefore could not play or even practice with the Browns until then. The Wranglers also argued that Minnifield's contract had an option year that they wanted to exercise. Minnifield's agent said there had been an option year in the original contract, but both sides had orally agreed to delete it. Throughout that summer, his agent tried in vain to work out a deal with the Wranglers that would allow the cornerback to participate in the Browns' training camp.

Minnifield showed up to camp on time, but with the legality of his services still a question mark, he was sent home to Louisville until the mess could be straightened out. A month later, the Browns filed a temporary restraining order to prevent anyone (the Arizona Wranglers) from interfering with Minnifield's contract with the Browns. Cleveland had defeated the Wranglers, earned Minnifield's services, and had successfully landed a former USFL player for the first time. It would not be the last.

Though the dispute gave Minnifield some extra time to heal a strained arch suffered in his final USFL game, he would still have to put his body through the rigors of two full football seasons in nine months. Once he got the hang of the Cleveland defensive schemes, Minnifield made an immediate impact.

He made his first start in Week Four against the Pittsburgh Steelers, and for the first time, the Cleveland defensive coaches decided to let Dixon and Minnifield dictate the style of the Browns' defense. They used primarily bump-and-run coverage, a defensive tactic where the corners play up on the line of scrimmage opposite the wide receivers and pound them for the first five yards off the snap. Most teams don't use the bump-and-run because the corners can get easily burned after contact. This was not such a risk with the speedy Dixon and Minnifield. "Beating them on the side of the head, whacking them, that's intimidation itself," Dixon said. "You're telling them, 'You better not run this route anymore, 'cause if you do, I'm going to tear your butt off." The Browns' defense dominated the Steelers that day and clinched their first victory of the season. Dixon and Minnifield pounded Pittsburgh's potent wideouts Louis Lipps and John Stallworth and had begun a beautiful relationship. "With Hanford and myself we have two cornerbacks who play the bump-and-run very well," Minnifield said afterward, "and that gets the defense fired up."

Unfortunately, Dixon and Minnifield's shenanigans also tended to fire up their opponents and some felt they should tone down their act. Marty Schottenheimer may have agreed with that, but he did nothing to try to shorten the leash on his two corners. "I'd be afraid they'd bite me, and I'd get rabies," he once joked.

"Our antics ain't taunting," Minnifield explained as 1985 training camp opened. "With our bump and run, we stand up there, and we talk to those receivers. We talk about their shoes, their uniforms. Then we got out there, and we bump 'em."

For better or worse, Dixon and Minnifield gave the Browns' defense a personality, a first in team history.

The unit continued to hum along through the 1984 season, though Minnifield began to deteriorate under the strain of two-seasons-in-one. A nagging hamstring injury would not go away and he missed portions of several games over the second half of the season. But as the 1985 training camp began, Minnifield had had seven months to rest his aching body and would be able to give the Browns his full effort for the first time.

Though the "Dog" moniker had originally been directed at the defensive line, by the time camp rolled around in 1985, it was the secondary that had truly adopted the nickname, becoming better position-by-position. Exemplifying this improvement was second-year free safety Don Rogers, the Browns' first-round pick of the 1984 draft. Rogers had earned the well-deserved reputation of a hard-hitter while at UCLA, and longtime Bruin followers were quick to compare him with Ken Easley, another Bruin safety who had gone on to a prosperous career with the Seattle Seahawks in the early 1980s. Rogers was also drafted by the USFL's San Antonio Gunslingers, who then traded his rights to the Arizona Wranglers, who were already battling the Browns for the services of Frank Minnifield. Despite the Wranglers' efforts to enact revenge by stealing Rogers away, he stuck with the NFL and the Browns, making an immediate impact as a rookie in 1984. He started fourteen games despite separating his shoulder at midseason and collected 105 tackles, earning the respect of his peers. He was eventually named Defensive Rookie of the Year by the NFL Players Association and appeared to have a long, prosperous career ahead of him.

Al Gross would start the 1985 season at strong safety after slowly working his way up the ranks from the waiver wire, from which the Browns plucked him in August of 1983. Backing up Gross to start 1985 would be Chris Rockins, drafted by the Browns in the second round in 1984. Following the 1985 draft, the Browns signed Felix Wright, a former Houston Oiler cornerback who had gone on to stardom in the Canadian Football League, and he challenged Rogers for his starting spot during camp.

After nearly a decade of mediocre (or worse) play in the secondary, by 1985 the unit had become arguably the strength of the team, in terms of talent and depth. Though Dixon had been a mainstay throughout the early part of the decade, it wasn't until 1984 with the additions of Minnifield and Rogers that the squad truly improved. Interestingly, the secondary was the final of the three phases of the defense the Browns focused on as they looked to improve the unit as a whole following the post-1980 fallout.

"We started building the defense with linebackers a few years ago and upgraded that, then addressed the defensive line," Marty Schottenheimer said as the team broke camp in 1985. "We began to upgrade that as the linebacking continued to improve. After that, we went to the secondary, and that showed some improvement. All of a sudden, you've got a pretty good defense."

The Browns turned their attention to the linebacker position in a big way in 1982, adding what appeared would be two dominant players in the same week.

The first, like Bernie Kosar would be three years later, was a native Northeast Ohioan returning to his roots. Tom Cousineau had been a football and wrestling star at Lakewood St. Edward High School then started for three years for Woody Hayes's Ohio State Buckeyes in the late 1970s. A two-time All-American selection, Cousineau was the first player selected in the 1979 NFL draft, taken by the Buffalo Bills. But three months and several failed negotiations later, Cousineau opted to sign with the Montreal Alouttes of the CFL, where he played for three years. Then, at the age of twenty-five, he decided to jump back to the NFL. The Browns were immediately interested.

Cousineau entertained offers from Houston, but Buffalo had the right to match any offer presented to him. The Browns didn't want to see Cousineau in Oiler blue (much like the Oilers later didn't want to see Bernie Kosar in orange and brown), thus they intensified their negotiations. After appearing out of the running, the Bills traded Cousineau to the Browns for several draft picks, including Cleveland's top selection in 1983—with which the Bills selected Kosar's precursor at Miami, Jim Kelly. Expectations were high from the start for Cousineau, who would play left inside linebacker. Fans expected him to become the team's first dominant defensive player since lineman Jerry Sherk in the 1970s. But three days later, the Browns acquired another linebacker who also demanded lofty aspirations.

With their first pick, the third overall, of the 1982 college draft, the Browns selected William "Chip" Banks from USC. He was a monstrous, 6'5", 235-pound linebacker who had twice made the All-PAC-10 team. Browns' coaches and officials whispered that Banks could have as big an impact on their team as another rookie had in New York the year before: a young man named Lawrence Taylor.

Banks did make an immediate impact, collecting three sacks in his NFL debut in a Browns' win in Seattle. He was selected to the Pro Bowl that year and was chosen as the Associated Press Rookie of the Year. After another Pro Bowl season in 1983, Banks had another solid campaign as the defense came of age in 1984. In many ways, he felt he was the heart of the Cleveland defense and was clearly upset when he was dealt to the Bills as a part of the Bernie Kosar saga. "I couldn't determine what was going on and exactly how I was going to react and respond to what events were going to happen," Banks said. "It was a traumatic time for me, I must say."

He was also unhappy with the way the Browns appeared to limit his playing time in 1984, taking him out in third-down situations and replacing him with a defensive back. The move also puzzled fans. As a part of the training-camp reconciliation in 1985, Marty Schottenheimer and Banks reportedly worked out their differences, and Banks would be on the field more for third downs—if not as an outside linebacker, then possibly as a fourth lineman.

With Banks back in the fold, the Browns' talented pair of bookend linebackers remained intact. Clay Matthews would return for his eighth season at right outside linebacker coming off of the best season Schottenheimer said he'd ever seen from a defensive player. He racked up twelve sacks in 1984, a team record for linebackers, and was named to both *The Sporting News* and *Sports Illustrated's* All-NFL teams. Strangely he was not selected to the Pro Bowl. In fact, despite already amassing an impressive career, Matthews had never been invited to Honolulu.

He was the Browns' first draft pick in 1978, and the former USC Trojan won the starting right outside linebacker position over veteran Gerald Irons a year later. Matthews had switched from offensive line to inside linebacker at USC, and then he made another position switch at the professional level before hitting his stride in the Browns' magical season of 1980. In 1981 he was voted the MVP of the defense by the Cleveland Touchdown Club. After missing almost all of the strike-riddled 1982 season with a broken ankle, Matthews rebounded to lead the team in sacks and forced fumbles in 1983.

The 1984 season was also a red-letter year for the Browns' fourth starting linebacker, left-inside man Eddie Johnson. A 134-pound linebacker at Daugherty High School in Albany, Georgia, Johnson turned down scholarship offers from Florida State and Oklahoma, both of which wanted him to play defensive back. Instead, Johnson went to Louisville, where he started four straight years for the Cardinals and collected 100 or more tackles in his final three seasons. Johnson was drafted by the Browns in the seventh round in 1981 and slowly worked his way into the lineup, bringing an immediate intensity to the club. He shaved his head prior to each training camp and lived up to a nickname given to him in college: "Assassin." His play mirrored that image. "You see Johnson coming and you promptly take anti-terrorist measures," Bill Livingston once wrote in the *Plain Dealer.* "You dead-bolt the doors. You make the moat wider. . . . You start boiling the oil."

He filled in nicely in 1983 when Dick Ambrose was sidelined in October with a broken ankle, then earned a starting position when complications from the injury forced Ambrose to miss the entire 1984 campaign as well. With Johnson now the incumbent and the Browns loaded at linebacker, Ambrose's comeback attempt in 1985 was unsuccessful. A teary-eyed Marty Schottenheimer announced Ambrose's release the last week of August, concluding a valiant nine-year career in Cleveland.

Up front, the Browns also appeared strong, but many pundits felt they still lacked a "dominant" pass rusher. Left defensive end Reggie Camp had certainly enjoyed a dominant 1984 season, collecting fourteen sacks, nine-and-a-half in the final eight games. Selected in the third round of the 1983 draft out of the University of California, Camp won the starting job on the left side in his first camp, beating out incumbent Marshall Harris. Camp's immediate success helped ease the suffering caused by the bust of defensive end Keith Baldwin, drafted by the Browns in the second round a year earlier. In three seasons in Cleveland, Baldwin had only collected six-and-a-half sacks, less than Camp picked up in the final two months of 1984 alone.

On the other side of the line was the oldest player on the Browns' defense: nine-year veteran Carl Hairston, who had blazed an unlikely trail to NFL success. Hairston had put together an impressive prep career at Martinsville High in Virginia, but he wasn't quite good enough to warrant college scouts' attention. After graduating in 1970, Hairston enrolled at Southern University in Baton Rouge, Louisiana, but didn't like it and quit after two weeks. He returned home to Martinsville and entered the workforce, driving an eighteen-wheel furniture truck for two years.

After work one day in the summer of 1972, Hairston stopped off for a beer and to shoot some pool at a local bar. A customer recognized Hairston from his high school playing days and asked him if he'd be interested in trying out for the University of Maryland-Eastern Shore football team. The patron was an alumnus and was certain Hairston could make an impact on the team. Hairston was interested, and a few days later, the patron told him when and where to report to training camp. A good performance got him a spot on the team, and he enrolled at the school.

He worked his way through four years, starting at linebacker and defensive end. Unlike his high school experience, this time Hairston was noticed and was selected by the Philadelphia Eagles in the seventh round of the 1976 draft. A long-term NFL career seemed unlikely, considering the Eagles had drafted two other defensive linemen ahead of Hairston. Even Philadelphia head coach Dick Vermeil knew Hairston was a long shot. "You know," Vermeil told the rookie one day during training camp, "it's going to be tough for you to make this football team."

But make the team Hairston did, and three games into the 1976 season, he moved ahead of Will Wynn at the right defensive end spot and started the next 106 games. He became one of the defensive leaders on a strong Eagles club that reached the postseason four straight years from 1978 to 1981 and won the NFC in 1980. As Philadelphia's fortunes rose, so did Hairston's. He led the NFC with fifteen sacks in 1979 and collected fifty-five-and-a-half in eight years with the Eagles, who selected him as a team captain for his final five seasons in Philly.

Hairston became a Brown in February 1984, when the Eagles dealt him to Cleveland for the bargain-basement price of a ninth-round draft pick in 1985. At the age of thirty-one, Hairston, who'd been hampered for much of 1983 with a knee injury, made an immediate impact on a defense desperate for a pass rush. Though he didn't start a game in 1984, his presence as a substitute gave depth to a line that spearheaded a jump from thirty-two sacks in 1983 to forty-three in 1984. With Keith Baldwin suffering from an offseason injury, Hairston won the starting right defensive end job in the 1985 preseason. He also entered the season with a new nickname. Because of his experience and imposing presence, Browns' strength coach Dave Redding started calling Hairston "Big Daddy."

Two days before the final exhibition game, the Browns had also added some depth to the line when they traded a seventh-round draft pick in 1986 to Seattle for Sam Clancy. The 6'7" Clancy had played both football and basketball at the University of Pittsburgh and was drafted by the Seattle Seahawks (eleventh round in 1982) and the NBA's Phoenix Suns (third round in 1981).

Certainly, with Hairston and Camp on the ends, the Browns' defensive line looked to improve upon its 1984 performance. But the heart of the line, as is the case in most 3-4 defenses, is the nose tackle, who generally sacrifices his body by taking out the center and guards with little statistical reward. For the previous three seasons, the Browns had turned to another native Clevelander to occupy this role, a man who would wind up becoming one of the most memorable players in team history: Bob Golic.

Long before his professional career began, many Clevelanders were familiar with Golic. He attended St. Joseph's High School in Cleveland, where he starred on the gridiron as an inside linebacker. His father, Louis, had played defensive tackle for seven seasons in the Canadian Football League, and his younger brother, Mike, was also bound for an NFL career, getting drafted as a defensive end by the Houston Oilers in 1985. Another brother, Greg, played offensive tackle at Notre Dame with Mike in the early 1980s. This glutton-for-punishment family tendency was exemplified after Bob Golic's first pee-wee football game. After his parents picked him up, he laid sprawled in the back seat, so sore he was unable to move. His mother asked if he wanted some aspirin. "No, Mom," he replied, "let me enjoy this for a while."

Despite his gridiron lineage, Bob Golic's strong suit was wrestling. He was a star at St. Joe's, winning a state title in 1975. Along the way, he matched up with future teammate Tom Cousineau of St. Ed's on the mat four times in his high school career, winning twice and tying once. (Even more interesting, their fathers were roommates together for a year at Indiana University.)

Golic continued both his football and wrestling careers at Notre Dame, where he compiled a 54-4-1 mat record and finished third in the nation in his weight class as a junior. Almost as a side note, Golic also earned All-American honors as a linebacker for the Fighting Irish, setting a school record with 479 career tackles. He was Notre Dame's defensive MVP of the now-legendary "chicken soup" Cotton Bowl in which Joe Montana led the Irish to a stunning comeback victory over Houston.

Highly touted coming out of Notre Dame, Golic was selected by the New England Patriots in the second round of the 1979 draft. In New England, he saw limited action at linebacker in three seasons. Finally, in 1982, new Patriots' head coach Ray Meyer wanted to move the defense in the direction of younger, faster players, and Golic didn't exactly fit that mold at linebacker despite dropping nearly thirty pounds. Though he had talent, he was a bit bigger and a bit slower than what the Patriots had in mind. They released Golic on September 2, 1982, in the team's final wave of cuts prior to the season. The Browns immediately picked him up, and the local boy was thrilled at the prospect of coming home.

"I knew the history of the Browns," he said. "When I put that uniform on for the first time, I couldn't believe it. It was like I was a kid. I had watched the orange helmets and the brown jerseys, and I just thought it was the coolest uniform out there. It was an amazing feeling."

The Browns had no intention of inserting Golic at linebacker, especially since the team was already loaded at the position. But the Browns, specifically Allan Webb, the team's director of pro scouting, envisioned Golic as a nose tackle. In fact, Cleveland had Golic ranked as a possible second-round pick as a nose tackle in the 1979 draft but only a late-rounder as a linebacker. He'd played some nose tackle at Notre Dame, but it was essentially a brand-new position to him. But Browns' director of player personnel Bill Davis took a chance based on two factors: first, Golic was a native Clevelander, and second, his wrestling background would make him a valuable asset. The Browns' coaches made it simple enough to understand: he was told to "occupy" opposing centers—and sometimes guards and tackles. "Of course, at the time they didn't mention the two-on-ones and three-on-ones," Golic said. "It was conveniently omitted."

When Henry Bradley went down with an injury in the sixth game of the 1982 season, Golic took over at nose tackle and made an immediate impact, racking up two sacks in a loss in Cincinnati. Bob Golic had finally found his calling. "It reminds me so much of wrestling, taking a guy one-on-one," he said. "It's a thrill, that one-on-one. That's what I liked about wrestling so much. Team sports are nice, but in one-on-one, you really test yourself."

And over the next three seasons, Golic found himself in several one-on-one battles. Yet even when he was victorious, usually only his coaches and teammates knew it. When Golic did his job, it meant, for example, that Chip Banks or Tom Cousineau was able to make a good play.

"Linebackers are supposed to make tackles, but a lot of times you're flowing, and other people make the tackles," Golic said. "At nose tackle, every time the ball is snapped, you're right in the middle of everything."

Often going against bigger and stronger offensive linemen, the relatively small Golic (6'2", 248 pounds when the Browns acquired him) used the scientific thinking that had made him all but unbeatable on the wrestling mat. "When one of those big guards would come out at me, I had the knowledge of body control and was able to get rid of him," Golic said. "It gave the illusion I was overpowering him. When I'd hear about how strong I was, I'd laugh."

A key factor in his success was the way he reinvented the position. "I lined up about a yard-and-a-half off the ball, as opposed to most people who lined up with an inch between helmets. A lot of times they called me the nose-backer. I wasn't as far away as the linebacker but wasn't as close as a nose man.

"When I tried to line up like a regular nose tackle up close, I felt like when we were hitting I was still balled up. My legs were still underneath me and had no power."

As the defensive line watched films the week after one game, Golic asked his position coach, Tom Pratt, why he never critiqued him. "Bob," Pratt replied, "to be perfectly honest, I don't know what to tell you. I've never seen anybody play it like this."

Nor did most players take the beating Golic would week-in and week-out. Playing at a position that, by his own admission, was "like being inside a pinball machine," Golic would be physically drained and beaten to a pulp by the end of each game. He would often lie on the floor of the locker room after a game and fall asleep. Writers would gather around him, waiting for him to wake up to be interviewed. "Some of the guys would already be out at the nightclubs," Golic said, "and I was still sleeping in a clothes hamper."

With Golic as the sparkplug, a cadre of talented linebackers, and a secondary foaming at the mouth, the 1985 Browns' defense appeared ready to lead the team into the dawn of a new age of Cleveland football.

Unfortunately, by sunset on opening day, the new age looked a bit too much like the old one.

Despite rallying from a fourteen-point fourth-quarter deficit in a thunderstorm to take a 24-17 lead with thirty-eight seconds remaining, the heralded Browns' defense couldn't stop the St. Louis Cardinals from tying the contest and forcing overtime. Nor could they stop them from driving right down the field to kick the winning field goal moments later.

"I am going to tell you this right now, and I'm going to nip it in the bud," an emotional Marty Schottenheimer told the press afterward, "don't anybody think for a minute that this is 1984 revisited. Because I guarantee you, it is not."

But most had to agree that in rallying from behind against a potential playoff team in less-than-ideal conditions, the 1985 Browns had taken a huge step.

"Unfortunately," Schottenheimer said, "it was sideways."

The Cleveland defense, fresh off a huge disappointment in Week One, was under the gun again eight days later as the two-minute warning of Week Two's Monday-night showdown with the Pittsburgh Steelers neared.

The Browns held a precarious 10-7 lead, but the Steelers had the ball at their own nineteen with three minutes left. The Dogs had redeemed themselves before a packed house of better than 79,000 at Cleveland Stadium by stuffing Pittsburgh all night long.

But now all the chips were down. Despite Cleveland's defensive domination through the first fifty-seven minutes, it would once again come down to the last three. Yet this time, the Dogs would come through. Veteran linebacker Curtis Weathers intercepted a Mark Malone pass to set up the game-clinching touchdown run by Earnest Byner. The Cleveland defense had officially redeemed itself and kept the 1984 comparisons away—at least for another week.

The naysayers returned six days later when the Browns were chewed up and spit out by the Dallas Cowboys at Texas Stadium. The Cowboys scored on their first two possessions and controlled both lines of scrimmage all day, making the Cleveland defense look average once again. Meanwhile, the Browns' offense couldn't muster anything until it was too late, scoring its only touchdown with five minutes remaining, making the final 20-7.

The message to Browns' fans seemed to toll loud and clear: don't expect too much from the 1985 Browns, and you won't be disappointed. This team, now 1-2, was a young team, a team still putting it all together, a team that didn't have what it took to become a serious playoff contender.

Or so it seemed.

4

The Die Is Cast

It was as if Kevin Mack knew his NFL career had gotten off to a rough start and he needed to make up for it. So rather than make fans wonder if he was ever going to break through with a big game and showcase the talent he'd hinted at in the preseason, the first-year running back decided to answer the question on the first play of his fourth game.

Gary Danielson took the initial snap of the Browns' Week Four game with San Diego and pitched to Mack, who was racing toward the left side. Mack, showing remarkable quickness for a man his size, exploded through a hole and steamed toward daylight down the left sideline. He was finally dragged down at the San Diego nineteen yard line after a 61-yard run that immediately put the Browns in scoring position. The tone for the game and the remainder of the season had been set on a warm, overcast afternoon in southern California.

Mack was a rarity in professional football. While most players are brimming with confidence—either legitimately or by faking it—Mack was the opposite. For years, he had been the kind of player who would wonder what he was doing on the field with all these talented athletes.

In Kings Mountain, North Carolina, he'd grown into a considerate but extremely quiet young man, one who used silence as a shield to defend his fear of getting close to people. Despite having fun and playing well on the gridiron in middle school, Mack didn't even try out for his high school team as a freshman or sophomore, thinking everyone there was bigger and better than him. He had played some football but quit the team when his coaches decided he was only suited to return kicks. Luckily, the coach had Mack's sister persuade him to give it another shot. He rushed for 1,585 yards as a senior and soon had scholarship offers from North Carolina State, North Carolina, and Clemson. Mack opted to become a Tiger and saw a lot of time as a sophomore fullback on Clemson's national championship team in 1981. Mack then led the team in rushing two years later with 862 yards, a school record for a fullback, which ranked him fourth in the nation in rushing yardage. Yet despite his on-field success, Mack still didn't entirely believe in himself.

"I always had a problem with my self-confidence," he said. "The thought was always in the back of my mind, there's someone out there bigger, faster, stronger, better than me."

Though he was projected as a potential late first- or early second-round choice in the 1984 NFL draft, Mack decided to play it safe. He signed a contract with the Los Angeles Express of the USFL two months before the NFL draft simply because they offered first, and he wasn't confident he'd get an offer from any NFL team. It was a virtually ridiculous line of thinking, but in the long run, it worked to the Browns'—and probably Mack's—advantage. Even Eddie Lambert, the head coach of the Express, noticed Mack's habit of selling himself short. "I don't think Kevin realizes his ability," he later said.

Three months later, the NFL held its first supplemental draft. The Browns, like they would a year later, would use this exercise to their full advantage. On the second day of the NFL's college draft that spring, they pulled off one of the craftiest moves in franchise history. As the draft neared its conclusion, Browns' vice president of personnel Bill Davis spun together a plan. He wanted to pick running back Earnest Byner with one of the team's two tenth-round selections, but he figured he could get more out of the team's remaining four picks than bottom-of-the-barrel college-draft talent. He had director of pro personnel Chip Falivene get on the phone to try to deal the Browns' remaining four draft choices in rounds nine through twelve for a team's top three choices in the supplemental draft that summer. Falivene called seventeen teams before the Chicago Bears agreed to it. It marked the first time a team had traded for additional choices in the supplemental draft.

At the time, the Browns may have looked a bit foolish, though the entire deal was essentially an afterthought transaction that went largely unnoticed. The Bears would have four more young players to bring into camp, and the Browns would have four less. And it appeared Chicago essentially gave up nothing for the privilege, considering there was only a *chance* that any of the players it acquired in the supplemental draft would be on the roster in the next three years. The Browns had traded minimal talent now for the possibility of major talent later. "I'm banking on it being a good bet for the future," Davis said. "I don't think any other team thought ahead that far." It was a gamble that would pay off in spades.

In the supplemental draft five weeks later, with the Bears' first-round pick, eleventh overall, the Browns drafted the rights to Kevin Mack. With their own selection seven spots later, they picked linebacker Mike Johnson of the Philadelphia Stars, and with the Bears' second-round choice, Cleveland snagged wide receiver Gerald McNeil of the Houston Gamblers. With their four extra college picks, the Bears did acquire defensive back Shaun Gayle, who would be a mainstay with the team for eleven seasons. But they also drafted a running back who would contribute just 70 yards in one pro season and two guys who never played a down in the NFL.

"We have a very, very strong feeling that was a good idea," Davis said after the 1984 supplemental draft. "If we can get one or two or three of the players we picked in the future, they're going to be much better players than whom we could've gotten in the later rounds of the regular draft."

Three years later, it was clear the Browns got the bigger piece of the wishbone. In the long run, this would go down as one of the best and most cunning moves the team ever made.

Still, the Browns had to wait for Mack. He rushed for 330 yards in an abbreviated 1984 season with the Express. As the Browns suffered through the first half of their 5-11 season in 1984 with a nonexistent running game, fans and team officials dreamt about how much they could use the powerful young running back.

Then the Browns either got lucky or their strategy began to pay off. The Express, like many USFL teams, were suffering financial problems after their second season and began cutting costs. On January 31, 1985, Los Angeles waived Mack, whose contract would not have expired for another year. The Browns signed him the next day and immediately began the mission of making Mack a self-believer. "I guess I may lack confidence," Mack said that summer. "I realize that I need to be pushed. And they are doing just that here."

Now, finally at the pinnacle of the game he loved, Mack slowly began to gain some confidence. When the Browns selected Greg Allen, a running back from Florida State, in the second round of the college draft three months later, Mack took that as a challenge rather than a blow to his confidence. Prior to the Browns' annual rookie scrimmage with Buffalo, Marty Schottenheimer pulled Mack aside. "Kevin, you might be better than 90 percent of the players on this field right now," he said. "The only thing you have to do is believe it."

He was still reserved and not very talkative ("I have to poke him with a stick to make him talk to me," center Mike Baab once said), but he started to believe he belonged at this level. In training camp, Mack said he had two goals: rush for 1,000 yards and be named Rookie of the Year. He got off to a great start in the preseason and won the starting halfback job with a combination of determined power running and surprising speed.

"When Kevin showed up, he was dramatically out of shape, and we didn't know anything about him," Baab said. "I remember us looking at Kevin and saying, 'Who the hell is this guy?' But he got together with [strength coach] Dave Redding, and Dave completely changed everything about the way Kevin went about his business. And he hooked him up with the greatest example in the world: Earnest Byner."

Ironically, the player who benefited the most from the Browns' "big Mack attack" was Byner, another running back. Rather than watching his stock drop, Earnest Byner became an integral part of the Cleveland offense.

What a difference a year made. Little was thought of Byner as he went into the 1984 season. And with good reason, since he was just a tenth-round draft choice out of East Carolina, not exactly a football hotbed. Byner, just 5'10", 215 pounds, didn't even expect to be drafted that spring, but sixteen hours after the draft began, he got a call from the Browns. The team had discovered Byner by accident. Scout Dave Beckman was visiting East Carolina to take a look at a few other players. When Pirate coaches asked him about some specific blocking rules, they wound up some film to use as an example. In the clips they happened to cue up of the offensive line, Beckman couldn't help but notice Byner, who looked unstoppable. He eventually took the films to Bill Davis, and though the Browns had no time to arrange any agility or speed tests for Byner, they remembered his name and eventually drafted him.

Some were surprised Byner even made the team, especially considering the team's fifth-, sixth-, and ninth-round picks did not. "I've got speed, I can catch, and I can block," Byner said that summer. "I'll contribute with everything I have." And he did, though once the season began he had little chance to show it.

Even with the Browns' offense (particularly its running game) struggling, Byner remained on the bench. Through Cleveland's first eight games, seven of which the team lost, Byner carried the football just eight times and caught five passes. He had become the team's kickoff-return man, but it wasn't the best use of his talent.

But everything changed when Sam Rutigliano was fired on October 21. Byner soon became a much more prominent figure in the Cleveland offense under Marty Schottenheimer. He made his first real contribution by accident two weeks later on a rainy afternoon in Buffalo. He was in the right place at the right time when he scooped up a fumble by Browns' wide receiver Willis Adams and raced 55 yards for the winning touchdown. "That play was made by a young man we feel has a tremendous future with this team," then left tackle Doug Dieken said. For the rest of the season, Byner continued to prove that sentiment.

He topped the century mark for the first time in Week Fifteen in Pittsburgh, and then he set a franchise rookie record when he scampered for 188 yards on twenty-one carries in the season finale in Houston. In the final eight games of the season, Byner rushed for 398 yards on sixty-four carries, an average of 6.2 yards per rush. He had leapfrogged past Mike Pruitt, Charles White, and Boyce Green on the depth chart and started to look like one of the bigger draft steals in franchise history. "When I came to camp I just wanted to make the team," Byner said. "Anything after that I considered a bonus."

The Browns, like the Pirates of East Carolina before them, considered Byner's contributions an unexpected bonus. After completing a stellar prep career at Baldwin High School in Milledgeville, Georgia, Byner had been recruited by Ed Emory, the defensive line coach at Georgia Tech, to become a Yellow Jacket. But when Emory took the head coaching position at East Carolina, he convinced Byner to follow him. In the next four years, Byner rushed for better than 2,000 yards and was named honorable mention All-American by the Associated Press his senior year.

"He's tough," Schottenheimer said shortly after taking over as head coach. "He's really tough. He's got excellent acceleration and quickness. He catches the ball very well. He's also very bright and aware for a rookie."

In his first season, he reminded many longtime fans of another rookie who graced the Cleveland sports scene exactly twenty years earlier: future Hall-of-Famer Leroy Kelly. Byner may not have been as talented as Kelly, but he had more heart and more desire than most professional football players. And he had the on-field presence of a junkyard dog—a trait that carried over from his childhood. In elementary school, Byner was a bully, picking on other kids and starting fights left and right. He also had a terrible temper. "I was going nowhere with the type of attitude I had when I was little," Byner said, "and I'd probably been a serious troublemaker if it wasn't for the sports I got involved in."

However, some of that fury and fire would still spill out onto the playing field. "We knew Earnest was going to be great if we could just keep him from fighting," Mike Baab said. "I don't know how many pileups I pulled him out of and how many times I got punched in the head pulling Earnest out of fights."

With the structure and discipline of football there to help him learn self-control and two older brothers who made him tougher, Byner soon had all the ingredients of a top-notch gridiron warrior. He was incredibly versatile on his high school team, playing linebacker, cornerback, safety, and even quarterback before making a permanent switch to tailback as a junior. Unfortunately, Byner's versatility led to a problem that would rear its ugly head at the professional level. "I'd never had people teach me the mechanics of running with the ball," he said. "Over the years, all they did was hand me the ball and tell me to run. They never taught me how to protect the ball."

As a result, Byner had problems with fumbling—not often enough to be benched and rob the team of his talent, but frequently enough to earn him a reputation. But as the 1985 season wore on, Byner earned another reputation—that of one of the best young all-around running backs in the NFL.

"Earnest Byner is a complete back," Schottenheimer would say after the 1985 season. "He is an excellent blocker, as good a blocker as I've seen in the National Football League. He is a very good pass receiver. As a runner, he is a good runner. I don't say he's a great runner, he doesn't have great speed. But he's the type of runner that always makes positive yardage. And he has a certain excitement about him when he runs with the ball that has a positive effect on our football team."

But before the 1985 season began, Byner had his own doubts about his value to the team. "We had a dialogue on the practice field at Lakeland Community College," Schottenheimer recalled. "He wasn't sure if he was going to make the team, and he was looking for some reassurance that everything was okay. I told him, 'Look, Earnest, you don't have anything to worry about. You're a part of this football team.'" And by the end of that season, he may have been the most integral part.

Even by the time the 1985 regular season began, he'd already had a positive influence on the phlegmatic Mack. "Earnest sort of made me his project," Mack said. "I'd go through spurts when I'd get lazy. He wouldn't let me."

"Kevin became Earnest's pull toy," Baab said. "Everywhere Earnest went, Kevin was right behind him."

And with Byner and Mack together in the backfield, the Browns suddenly had a kind of positive effect they'd never had before.

Mack's long run set the tone for a 21-7 Browns' victory highlighted by a whopping 275 yards on the ground, highlighting the Cleveland offensive line for the first time in 1985.

It was actually quite remarkable that this Browns' line had managed to put together any kind of identity at all. It was, after all, not only a unit in transition but one that would be riddled by injury from training camp to the end of the season.

The 1984 season had been a last hurrah for four Browns' linemen, a quartet of the finest athletes ever to don the brown and orange. Left tackle Doug Dieken and center Tom DeLeone both retired after the season, Dieken's fourteenth and DeLeone's thirteenth. Then, in mid-August 1985, the Browns waived thirty-four-year-old right guard Joe DeLamielleure, who'd been a mainstay with the team since it had traded for him prior to the 1980 season. Left guard Robert Jackson, a Brown since 1975, would remain on the team in 1985 but would see limited playing time, primarily as a backup in his final NFL season. Marty Schottenheimer had made it clear in the second half of the 1984 season that his team was going to run the ball early and often. He eventually made the decision to build this ground-oriented offense around primarily young, up-and-coming linemen.

But the anchor of this new era of offense would be sixth-year tackle Cody Risien. Though not selected until the seventh round, the 6'7" Risien became the centerpiece of the Browns' 1979 draft, winning the starting left guard position from George Buehler seven games into his rookie season. He returned to right tackle, the position he'd played at Texas A&M, for the 1980 season and stayed there through 1983. Risien earned a reputation as one of the league's best linemen—This just a few years after twice thinking he might never play the game again.

His high school years were riddled with medical problems. As a sophomore, he caught spinal meningitis. The following year he slightly tore a ligament in his knee, then suffered a detached retina and needed three eye operations to correct it. For a while, it appeared as though Risien's days on the gridiron were over, but he recovered to earn a scholarship to A&M, the school he'd grown up rooting for. Then, during his first training camp with the Browns, Risien's father passed away after a battle with cancer. Risien considered sitting out the entire season, but changed his mind. He would be tested again in 1984. He was forced to sit out the entire season after tearing ligaments and cartilage in his right knee in the closing minutes of the preseason finale, and the Browns' line wasn't the same without him. Bill Contz spent much of that season at right tackle, while youngster Paul Farren saw time there as well.

The Browns drafted Farren from Boston University in the twelfth and final round in 1983, thinking he primarily would play center. He saw little action as a rookie but filled in admirably for Risien in 1984. He would see considerable time at left tackle in 1985 and over the next few years would earn the nickname "Mr. Fix-It" from Schottenheimer for his valuable ability to fill in wherever he was needed on the line.

Also splitting time at that position was Rickey Bolden, who'd taken an odd and winding path to the Browns' offensive line. He was drafted by the team in the fourth round in 1984 with a selection acquired when the Browns dealt wide receiver Dave Logan to the Denver Broncos. Bolden had played tight end at Southern Methodist and the Browns worked him into their offense primarily as a blocker to complement the receiving skills of Ozzie Newsome. But at 6'5", 250-plus pounds, it was just a matter of time before the coaches decided to try to turn Bolden into a lineman.

Sharing the right guard spot with Bolden was a "rookie," Dan Fike. The Browns signed Fike as a free agent in March of 1985 while he was still a member of the Tampa Bay Bandits of the USFL. Following Frank Minnifield and Kevin Mack, Fike became the Browns' third USFL defector as well as the largest guard in team history at 6'6", 280 pounds.

At left guard, the Browns would employ another young journeyman who'd once donned New York green: George Lilja, signed midway through 1984 after being cut by the New York Jets. He would start every game of the 1985 season, one of only three offensive players to start every game at the same position.

Interestingly, center Mike Baab wound up in the NFL by doing something no one else wanted to do. As a youngster growing up in Euless, Texas, Baab volunteered to play center on the school team because he knew nobody else wanted to and because he knew it was the only way he'd get to play. It turned out to be one of the best decisions of his life. He wound up getting a scholarship to Texas, where he broke in as a starter at guard as a freshman, then started every game of his junior and senior seasons at center.

Baab was a fifth-round selection of the Browns in the 1982 draft. "I used to sit in the offensive line meetings and crow at the other guys that I was the highest draft choice," he said. What's more, Baab was only the second center the team had ever drafted. Baab was known as a versatile lineman who could play any position and also long-snap on punts and field goals. He slowly gained attention as the strike-riddled 1982 campaign wore on, eventually getting his first NFL start in the Browns' playoff loss in Los Angeles. In training camp the following year, Baab beat out incumbent center Tom DeLeone and started fifteen games. By 1985, he had become an anchor on the line and also a fan-favorite for his personality and perfect offensive-lineman attitude.

"We don't need the adulation a running back or a quarterback gets," he once said. "If you do something well and someone like Robert Jackson turns to you and says, 'Good job,' you know you did what you were supposed to, and that's all you need. We don't make a big deal about it."

But Browns' fans were starting to make a big deal about Baab, specifically because of a unique hobby of his. While waiting for a haircut in a barber shop one day in college, he picked up a *Conan the Barbarian* comic book and started reading. He was instantly hooked and soon became an avid collector and Conan fan. Browns' backers started referring to him as the "Baabarian," and with his long hair, earring, and unforgettable starring role in a team video for charity in 1986 called "Masters of the Gridiron," he fit the role perfectly. He even shared a special connection with a group of personal fans, pretending to pull an imaginary sword from his belt as he entered the huddle during games and pointing it toward his followers in the stands. They, in turn, would hoist their own wooden swords toward him.

It seemed almost fitting that the heart of the Cleveland line had earned such a nickname. As the season wore on, this group would prove to be true warriors.

And after its sterling performance in Week Four, the Browns were back to .500. It wasn't pretty, and it wasn't terribly exciting. Yet in its own way, that September afternoon in San Diego set the tone not only for the remainder of the 1985 season but for the remainder of the decade as well.

There didn't appear to be much different about October 6 to Browns' fans. Yes, Cleveland was hosting the 2-2 New England Patriots with a chance to move over the .500 mark for the first time in almost two years. And yes, a Browns' win and a Pittsburgh loss in Miami would propel the former alone atop the AFC Central standings. Still, there was a subdued aura around this game.

Only 62,139 came out to Cleveland Stadium on a brisk, gray afternoon to watch the Browns and Patriots, both widely considered to be in the "mediocre" category of the AFC.

But as the Browns began their 500th NFL game, there were signs that this would be no ordinary football game. Cleveland took the opening kickoff, drove right down the field and took a 7-0 lead. They then missed a chance to make it 10-0 minutes later when Matt Bahr hooked a short field goal.

It was an unusual letdown from Bahr, who had taken over the Browns' precarious kicking spot in 1981 after David Jacobs had failed in his attempt to replace retired veteran Don Cockroft. After a horrible opening month, Jacobs was released, and the Browns traded a ninth-round draft choice to San Francisco for Bahr, who two years earlier had won a Super Bowl with Pittsburgh. The lifelong soccer player, whose father had played on the U.S. World Cup team in 1950 and whose brother had played in the 1972 Olympics, grabbed hold of the job and didn't let go. He entered the 1985 season with the highest field-goal percentage in team history.

But even after Bahr's uncharacteristic miss, it appeared Cleveland still held the momentum. Things changed when Clarence Weathers fumbled a punt return and New England recovered in the end zone to tie the game. Midway through the second quarter, the Browns took back the lead on a trick play that saw Brian Brennan snag a lateral from Danielson, then loft a pass downfield that tight end Ozzie Newsome caught for a 33-yard touchdown.

Cleveland's next possession was halted when New England cornerback Raymond Clayborn intercepted Danielson and returned it to the Cleveland eighteen before Danielson made the tackle. Not only was the turnover damaging (it resulted in a field goal that cut the lead to 14-10) but it cost the Browns their play-caller. On his tackle of Clayborn, Danielson had injured his right shoulder. After receiving medical attention on the sideline, he tried to take a few practice snaps but realized he couldn't stay in the contest.

Thus, following the New England field goal and kickoff, Bernie Kosar entered the game.

The crowd rose to its feet and roared as it realized the historical implication of what was about to happen. Bernie Kosar, the savior of the franchise, was about to take his first snap in the NFL. All the potential, the promise, and the hope that so many had invested in the twenty-one-year-old curly-haired quarterback was about to be realized. The new era of Browns' excellence was set to begin.

Kosar called the play in the huddle and marched up to the line of scrimmage, flapping his arms up and down, requesting the crowd to simmer down a bit so that the offense could hear his signals. He barked them out, and then Mike Baab hiked the football to Kosar for his historic first play. He fumbled the football, and the Patriots recovered at the Cleveland forty-eight.

"I just dropped the ball," Kosar said afterward. "Quite honestly, I was just thinking too far ahead; I was thinking about my reads because it was going to be a pass play. The fumble brought me back to Earth and made me realize I had to take it a step at a time."

When Kosar returned to the sideline, the injured Danielson came up to him, wanting to make sure he didn't get down on himself. "Hell," he said, "I started better than that when I was a rookie."

With humility and irony coursing through the early autumn air, the Patriots cut the lead to one on another field goal late in the half. After the kickoff, Kosar successfully handled three straight Baab snaps, but handed the ball off to Kevin Mack on all three as the Browns ran out the first-half clock. Fans would have to wait a bit longer to see Kosar fire his first pass.

On Cleveland's first possession of the second half, Kosar finally got the chance. On second down, he dropped back and zipped a pass to Brian Brennan on a simple out pattern to the left sideline. It only gained eight yards, but the crowd once again became electrified, rising to its feet and cheering. The Bernie Kosar era was officially under way.

Things got even better as the drive marched on. A play later, Kosar completed his second pass, a 17-yarder to Clarence Weathers, then on the next snap hit Brennan again for 11 more. After a blown draw play, Kosar dumped a short pass to Ozzie Newsome for five yards to the New England twenty-eight, which set up Matt Bahr's 45-yard field goal. The Browns led, 17-13, but not for long. On the ensuing drive, the Patriots took their first lead on a Tony Eason–to–Stanley Morgan touchdown pass.

In the opening minute of the fourth quarter, the Browns recovered a muffed New England punt return then Kosar hit Brennan on the right sideline for 33 yards. It was Kosar's seventh straight completion to begin his career and set up the go-ahead touchdown by Mack a play later. But the Patriots would have two more chances to win the game. First they failed to cash in on a first-and-goal situation at the Cleveland five then faced fourth-and-three at the Cleveland twenty-two with 1:49 left. Carl Hairston stuffed Craig James a yard short of a first down, and the Browns successfully ran out the final seconds of a thrilling 24-20 victory—the first of Bernie Kosar's NFL career.

As the crowd cheered, it also celebrated a score that had just flashed on the boards moments earlier: the Miami Dolphins had scored a last-minute touchdown to defeat the Pittsburgh Steelers, 24-20, in the Orange Bowl. For the first time in two years, the Browns were in first place—and all thanks to a brand of victory Cleveland fans weren't used to seeing.

Kosar fought back to complete nine of fifteen passes for 104 yards in his debut. It was unclear how long Gary Danielson's shoulder injury would keep him sidelined, but Kosar certainly looked like he was ready to take on the challenge. "Bernie really took control," Ozzie Newsome said. "When he was in the huddle, it was Bernie Kosar's huddle."

"I'll either be out one week," Danielson said, "or fifteen years, depending on how Bernie does."

With Kosar filling in on an offense that racked up more than 400 yards for the second straight week, anything seemed possible. The Browns were now in first place all alone for the first time this late in a season since the magical year of 1980. "A game like this can be contagious," Bob Golic said. "Winning can be as contagious this year as losing was last year."

If winning was indeed contagious, then the Browns proved they were infected seven days later in Houston with a hard-earned 21-6 win in Kosar's first NFL start. The lone highlight was the rookie's first touchdown pass: a 68-yard bomb to wideout Clarence Weathers midway through the third quarter to give the Browns their first lead.

While Weathers would prove to be a vital downfield threat for much of 1985, two other members of the Browns' receiving corps promised to be much larger factors for the remainder of the decade.

While Weathers provided the speed and flash the Browns had been waiting the entire decade for, his counterpart across the field supplemented consistency and dependable hands. The Browns selected Brian Brennan in the fourth round of the 1984 college draft after the tiny wideout (5'9", 178 pounds) had set career receiving records at Boston College: 115 catches, 2,180 yards, and 14 touchdowns—all of this despite missing seven games in his junior year with a broken collarbone. In his senior year alone in 1983, with quarterback Doug Flutie firing away, Brennan caught sixty-six passes for 1,149 yards and eight scores.

When he arrived in Cleveland, he immediately impressed his coaches with his receiving and kick-return skills. Sam Rutigliano said he had "the guts of a burglar," adding, "just hold your breath when you watch Brian Brennan. I'm not going to say anything, but he's going to be a helluva player." Brennan, whose grandparents were born in Ireland, also earned an early reputation as a glue-fingers type of receiver—quite an accomplishment considering he didn't become a receiver until he got to college.

After playing quarterback and defensive back at Brother Rice High School in Bloomfield Hills, Michigan, Boston College recruited Brennan as a defensive back. One day after he arrived, he was playing catch with one of the Eagles' quarterbacks, and head coach Jack Bicknell noticed the way Brennan was running crisp patterns. He asked his young recruit if he would like to play wide receiver instead. "Would I play sooner?" Brennan asked. "Right away," Bicknell replied. Brennan took the job and became one of the finest wideouts in school history.

"Catching the football is something that's just natural for me," he said after joining the Browns. "It's been natural ever since I was growing up. If it's thrown my way, I'm going to catch the football. It's mine. That's the way I feel."

Yet Brennan did not seem to have the same bluster or swagger most NFL receivers carried, which made him all the more noticeable. "In the NFL's world of cocky, arrogant Fonzies," reporter John Delcos would write, "Brennan is a Richie Cunningham."

Brennan caught thirty-five passes as a rookie in 1984, the most by a Browns' rookie since Paul Warfield twenty years earlier. In just one season, Brennan had become the best young receiver the Browns had had in years. In his first four professional games alone he caught more passes than Willis Adams, the team's first draft pick in 1979 and long-hoped-for star wideout, had in his first four *seasons*. Along the way, Brennan tried to model himself after his professional idol, Seattle Seahawks' star wide receiver Steve Largent. Longtime Cleveland fans couldn't help notice the similarity between Brennan and a previous Brown who wore the same number 86: Hall-of-Famer Dante Lavelli.

"In times of crisis you think of players, not plays," Schottenheimer said. "Brian is someone we think about in those important third- and fourth-down situations. He's one of those tough Irish guys—feisty and confident."

Because Brennan began the 1985 season on the injured-reserve list with a separated shoulder, he spent a great deal of practice time working with the second team during his recovery. At the time, the second-team quarterback was Bernie Kosar. The two made an immediate connection that would last the rest of the decade.

But in 1985, Brennan was still only a secondary target in the Cleveland passing game. The top honor went to tight end Ozzie Newsome, entering his eighth season. Newsome had been the second of the Browns' two first-round draft picks in 1978 (Clay Matthews was the other). Newsome made an immediate impact as Sam Rutigliano took over the team and implemented his pass-happy scheme. Newsome had been a wide receiver at Alabama, where he set a school record with 2,070 career receiving yards and earned the nickname "Wizard of Oz." Head coach Paul "Bear" Bryant called Newsome the best receiver he ever coached. When Newsome arrived in Cleveland, the Browns already had a pair of outstanding wideouts in Reggie Rucker and Dave Logan. But Rutigliano had a plan.

He persuaded Newsome to switch to tight end, and he almost instantly became one of the finest professional players ever to play the position. He tallied nearly 2,000 yards in his first three seasons and topped the 1,000-yard plateau in 1981. He hit 970 in 1983 then went over the four-digit mark again in 1984, catching eighty-nine passes in each season. From 1979 to 1984, Newsome caught 402 passes, more than any other player in the NFL. By the start of 1985, Newsome was already a Cleveland legend.

He was born in Muscle Shoals, Alabama, where he would often pick cotton in a field behind his backyard after school and on the weekends. Newsome won nine varsity letters at Colbert High in Leighton in football, basketball, and baseball. In fact, his stellar concentration when it came to receiving was partly due to his baseball background. As a Little League player, he was often thrust behind the plate to play catcher. Because of it, Newsome developed an eye for the ball and was able to follow it as it moved through the air. After catching a spinning baseball, snagging a football was easy.

Still, he didn't exactly go down the path that one would expect to lead to stardom as an NFL pass catcher. Both his high school and college teams ran ground-oriented offenses. And had it not been for the Browns switching him to tight end, it's doubtful Newsome would have been as successful in the NFL as a wide receiver. It's doubtful Newsome would have gone to Cleveland at all had it not been for the urging of his close friend and future Cleveland teammate. Just before the 1978 draft, Browns' receivers coach Rich Kotite was sent to Alabama to interview Newsome and decide if the team wanted to select him. Newsome had been out late at a party the night before and when morning rolled around, he didn't feel like going to the meeting. But Johnny Davis, an Alabama fullback whom Kotite also wanted to interview, convinced Newsome to go. Had Newsome skipped the meeting, the Browns may not have selected him. Ironically, Newsome and Davis were reunited when the Browns signed Davis as a free agent in 1982.

With Newsome now on the back side of his career in 1985, he knew his role on the team was changing. He would be depended on less as a receiver and more as a blocker, which was fine by him. "I don't have the quickness or speed I had when I came in the league," he said, "one reason being I'm bigger now than I was then. But I make up for that with mentality and intellect." Both of those factors also translated into consistency. Newsome entered the 1985 season having caught a pass in eighty-two consecutive games. He had not been held without a reception since October of 1979.

With Newsome providing the experience and Brennan representing young potential, the Browns' 1985 receiving corps was deceivingly talented.

With Weathers leading the way in Houston, collecting 146 yards on three catches, Kosar tossed for 203 yards, though he completed just eight of nineteen passes—several under extreme pressure. "He took a lot of pops," Bernie Kosar Sr. said after the game. "But he's tough, like his mother."

More importantly, the Browns were 4-2 and had a two-game lead on both the Steelers and Bengals in the AFC Central. It was cause for celebration.

Unfortunately for the Browns and their fans, it would be premature.

5 Backing In

The win in Houston had sparked a sports enthusiasm not seen in Cleveland since the 1980 Browns. It wasn't nearly at the level of the Kardiac Kids, but there was enough enthusiasm for its arrival to be obvious.

Therefore it was perhaps appropriate that that excitement was spiked by the same team that closed the curtain on the Kardiac Kids. The seasoned Los Angeles Raiders waltzed into Cleveland in Week Seven and broke the Browns' hearts, much as they had done in the 1980 playoffs, handing the home team a last-minute 21-20 defeat and dropping the Browns to 4-3.

Things got worse the following week when Bernie Kosar, still starting for an injured Gary Danielson, was abused by the Washington Redskins in a 14-7 defeat before a wired Stadium crowd. After Kosar handed Washington two early touchdowns that turned out to be the difference, a sore Danielson was inserted in the second half and nearly rallied the home team to victory. Not only did he fall short but now Marty Schottenheimer had a full-blown quarterback controversy on his hands.

Despite the back-to-back losses, the Browns still managed to hang on to a one-game lead over the rest of the AFC Central. But storm clouds loomed.

The coach's hand was forced the following Wednesday when Danielson re-aggravated his shoulder in practice, causing more pain than before. Doctors feared he might have rotator cuff damage and said he'd be unable to play for at least two or three more weeks. Thus, Schottenheimer, who through his comments to the press appeared to be leaning toward Danielson, threw his support behind Kosar—not that he really had any choice.

And maybe the curly-haired rookie was exactly what the Browns needed to break what had become known as simply "The Jinx." Since the opening of Three Rivers Stadium in 1970, Cleveland had not won a game there. Granted, for much of the 1970s, the Steelers were clearly the better team in the midst of a long decade of championship-caliber football, while the Browns were mired in a mediocre-at-best era of disappointment. Yet on several occasions, Cleveland had been poised to win and could not pull it out. But the Steelers, as if guided by an unseen force, always managed to come away with victory.

That week, Cleveland radio station WERE-AM tried its hand at breaking the Steelers' Three Rivers spell. On Thursday, Halloween, the station brought in a witch (a good witch) named Elizabeth to perform an on-air incantation with a Steeler pennant, a bobble-head doll, and a media guide that would break The Jinx. But perhaps the station should have remembered how successful Elizabeth the Witch had been when she came in two years earlier to try to turn the Indians' two-decade slump around, with no success.

Was it goofy? Yes. A publicity stunt? Sure. But considering what the Browns' front office was up to that week, it wasn't altogether crazy.

For the first time, the team would fly the 200 miles from Cleveland to Pittsburgh, rather than taking the bus. It would cost the team an extra $15,000, but no one thought the price was too high for what it might bring. Once the team landed following its brief flight, it was transported to a new hotel, one the Browns hadn't stayed at for four years. Of course, the last time the Browns stayed there they'd also lost, but there were only so many hotels in the greater Pittsburgh area.

But in the most brilliant display, public relations staffers Chuck Fisher and Kevin Byrne brought some dirt from Cleveland Stadium and sprinkled it on the Three Rivers Astroturf in front of the Browns' bench before the game. It's hard to believe no one had thought of this sooner.

Whether it was the plane ride, the hotel, the dirt, or maybe just that for the first time in recent memory the Browns were clearly the better team, they dominated the Steelers throughout the first half as the teams played through a cold, steady rain. But for their superiority, they had little to show for it: just a pair of field goals. It was a good start, but the lead could have been bigger, and Jinx believers knew without a doubt that the team would eventually suffer for not scoring a touchdown on either drive. And of course, that lack of opportunism came back to bite the Browns.

Battling crowd noise, Kosar let a third-quarter shotgun snap sneak past him for a huge loss, a play that swung the momentum to Pittsburgh. The Steelers promptly took a 7-6 lead on the game's first touchdown. Still, the Browns hung tough and took a 9-7 lead on another Matt Bahr field goal with four minutes left. However, a slow and steady Pittsburgh drive ended, predictably, with a Gary Anderson field goal with nine seconds remaining to give Pittsburgh a 10-9 win and extend The Jinx to sixteen years. Elizabeth the Witch had let down Cleveland sports fans again.

The Browns' two-game division lead had evaporated in three weeks, and now all four teams were tied with 4-5 records. The logjam was broken the following Sunday when the Browns lost their fourth straight, 27-10, to the Cincinnati Bengals at Riverfront Stadium.

Now the early momentum and optimism were only a distant memory. The 1985 season was going down the tubes. "We've got to get back what we had when we were 4-2," said linebacker Eddie Johnson, "and get it quickly."

Step one to regaining that early-season momentum came in Week Eleven when a second-half charge prevented an outright disastrous defeat to the 2-8 Buffalo Bills and secured a 17-7 win that, if nothing else, stopped the bleeding.

Now, for the second time in three weeks, the Browns would have to face the Bengals, who had humiliated them in Cincinnati. If they could barely squeak past Buffalo, how were the Browns going to knock off the team with the best offense in the AFC?

Adding to the impending intrigue was a pending quarterback controversy. Gary Danielson had begun throwing in practice the week before and had experienced no pain. Kosar went the distance against Buffalo, but with another so-so performance, many wondered who would start against the Bengals in what would be a must-win game.

"This is our home playoff game," Danielson said. "If we have any serious thoughts about the playoffs, we have to win. And even a win doesn't guarantee anything."

Though Schottenheimer would not publicly reveal his starter, the veteran got the call to start against the Bengals at damp and chilly Cleveland Stadium, where the game-time wind chill was fourteen degrees. The temperature was not as cold as the Cleveland defense, which came out of the locker room blitzing and harassing Cincinnati quarterback Boomer Esiason. Literally from the game's first snap, the Browns sent the house at the blonde-haired, second-year playcaller. "I knocked him on his butt the first play of the game," Eddie Johnson said afterward. "We wanted him to know we weren't taking any shit today."

They didn't, winning 24-6 and bringing them back to .500 at 6-6 and into a first-place tie with Pittsburgh.

The Browns renewed an old rivalry the following week in the Meadowlands, taking on the playoff-bound New York Giants. The visitors jumped to a surprising 21-7 lead, but the experienced Giants recovered and took control at 33-21 in the fourth quarter. After re-injuring his shoulder in the Cincinnati win, Danielson didn't start but was inserted in the second half to try to spark the Cleveland offense. It worked, as the veteran cut the margin to five with a touchdown pass to Clarence Weathers. As the clock ticked down, Danielson's throbbing shoulder sparked another gutsy drive, but at the Giants' nine yard line, his shoulder finally gave out. Kosar came in, and a play later, Earnest Byner gave the Browns a 35-33 lead.

And it held up after Giants' kicker Eric Schubert missed a 34-yard field goal that would have won the game as time expired. The Browns were 7-6 and all alone in first place after a welcome twist of fate. It was the Browns' fourteenth game in two seasons decided in the final two minutes. Unfortunately, it was only their second victory in such a game. "I figured the world owed us one," Frank Minni-field said in the jovial Cleveland locker room.

The Browns had now won three straight games, but they were very much a 7-6 team: mediocre as mediocre can be. Good one week, bad the next. Which is exactly what happened in the first two weekends of December. After the emotional and impressive win over the Giants, they were throttled by the Seahawks in Seattle, 31-13. With Cincinnati pulling off an upset over Dallas, the Browns and Bengals were now tied for first.

Despite the loss, the Browns still controlled their own destiny. If they defeated the Oilers at home the following Sunday and the Jets in New Jersey in the season finale, they would be division champs. If they could just beat the Oilers, they would finish with a 4-2 record in the division and ensure themselves the tie-breaker over either Cincinnati or Pittsburgh. Thus the only way they would lose the title would be a three-way tie.

Adding some intrigue to the bizarrely important upcoming contest was Houston's coaching swap that Monday. Hugh Campbell, under the gun all year, was finally axed, and colorful defensive coordinator Jerry Glanville took over the reins. The Oilers now had new leadership that would eventually spark a turn-around that would last into the next decade and wanted nothing more than to start the new era with a victory that would foil the playoff hopes of their division rival.

Granted, the wind-chill factor was below zero—so cold that some of the loge toilets backed up because of frozen pipes. And, the 5-9 Houston Oilers, who hadn't enjoyed a winning season in five years, weren't exactly the greatest draw in the world. But some outside observers were still surprised at the size of the crowd for the Browns' home finale. Only 50,793 braved the icy temperatures, snow flur-ries, and high likelihood of a bland game, even though the hometown team could take a huge step toward capturing its first AFC Central title in a half-decade.

Even if their fans weren't quite prepared for this game, the Browns were. To counter an expected barrage of blitzes by got-nothing-to-lose Jerry Glanville in his first game at the helm, the Browns came out of the locker room running the football and grabbed a 14-0 lead in the second quarter. Up by seven at the half, the Browns broke the game open in the third. A pair of Kosar touchdown passes made it 28-7, and the Browns hung on for a 28-21 win. And their playoff hopes were buoyed by word of a Bengals' loss in Washington. The 1985 AFC Central Division race now came down to the Bengals and Browns going into Week Sixteen.

The Browns were the heavy favorite. They would have three chances to clinch the title the following weekend: 1) if the Steelers lost to the New York Giants in the Meadowlands on Saturday afternoon; 2) if the Browns beat the New York Jets on the same field the following day; and 3) if the Bengals lost in New England. Since the Giants and Patriots both had to win to make the playoffs themselves, it was highly unlikely that both the Steelers and Bengals would be able to pull road upsets and force a three-way tie, the only way the Browns could lose the title. So it appeared as though the Browns wouldn't even need to win in the final week to win the division. In fact, if the Steelers lost Saturday afternoon, the Browns would know they'd won the division without even pulling on their jockstraps. It wasn't exactly a storybook scenario—especially since the likelihood of the Browns beating the Jets, another veteran team that had to win to make the post-season, was slim.

And as it happened, the Browns won the 1985 AFC Central Division title not on the football field but while returning their seats to the upright position.

As their flight approached the Newark Airport on Saturday afternoon, the pilot announced over the speakers that the Giants led the Steelers, 28-10, with less than a minute to go. Ironically, the plane had passed over Giants Stadium on its final approach.

Rather than celebrate, there was little reaction at all. Sure, the Browns were happy—"relieved" might be the better word—but they felt they still had some business to take care of. They figured they needed to beat the Jets not only to legitimize themselves but to capture some much-needed momentum going into the playoffs. Plus, they did not want to make history by becoming the first NFL team to win its division with a .500 record. They talked and acted like they had something to prove. But they didn't play like it.

The Jets rolled, 37-10, though it wasn't even as close as the lopsided score suggested. The newly crowned AFC Central champions, determined to earn some respect, had been humiliated by a Wild Card team. And just for good measure, the Bengals lost in Foxboro, proving that the Browns needn't have even shown up to clinch the division. And for all intents and purposes, they hadn't.

Still, there was some excitement in the final moments. Earnest Byner entered the contest with 901 rushing yards. With Kevin Mack already over the four-digit mark, the team really wanted Byner to join him, to become only the third team in NFL history with a pair of backs to each rush for 1,000 yards in the same season. But with fourteen seconds left, Byner only had 75 yards on fourteen carries. "I didn't think it would be that important to me coming into the game," Byner said. "But when I thought I wasn't going to get it I realized how much it meant to me. I was crying."

With the game well out of reach, the Browns' mission in the final moments was to get Byner over the 1,000-yard mark. They appeared well on their way when Byner broke loose on a shotgun draw for an 18-yard run and ran out of bounds with seven seconds remaining. But the race appeared over on the next play when he fumbled out of bounds as time expired. Luckily, Jets' defensive lineman Joe Klecko had been penalized for being offside, so since the game cannot end on a defensive penalty, the teams lined up for one more play with no time showing. And naturally, Byner took a direct snap from center, swept right, and broke through the line again, getting the seven yards that he needed and two more for good measure as the 1985 regular season came to a close.

Byner and Mack joined the elite company of Mercury Morris and Larry Csonka of the 1972 Miami Dolphins and Franco Harris and Rocky Bleier of the 1976 Pittsburgh Steelers. Not that any Browns' fans really wanted to hear it afterward, but both of those other teams had gone on to win the Super Bowl. Making the accomplishment even more impressive was that it was done with an injury-riddled offensive line still in transition. However, the celebration in the locker room, both for the 1,000-yard accomplishment and winning the division title, was quite subdued. "When you get your butts handed to you like we did today," Bob Golic said, "there's no reason to celebrate."

Nor was there reason to celebrate becoming the league's first 8-8 playoff team. With the customary week off granted to a division champ, the national snickering and proverbial finger pointing would now officially begin.

Even the Browns' front office was blushing a bit. Though they would play their divisional playoff game on the road, there was a possibility if the Browns won and a Wild Card team advanced twice that Cleveland could host the AFC Championship. As required by league rules, the Browns' ticket office sent out this notification to season-ticket holders. "We're kind of embarrassed by it," said Kevin Byrne, vice president of public relations, "but the notices are in the mail."

Yet Marty Schottenheimer was not embarrassed. "We're 8-8, we're in the playoffs, and we make no apologies for it," he said. "Everybody knew the rules at the outset of the season."

When the team arrived back in Cleveland on Sunday night, a small, almost pathetic crowd greeted its champions at Hopkins Airport. It was almost a parody of the throng that awaited them after the season finale in Cincinnati in 1980 from which they also returned as division champions.

The 1985 season had its share of good times, and even though it wasn't officially over yet, many Browns' fans were left wondering what this whole year had meant. Yes, their team was in the playoffs, but it really didn't deserve to be. Their franchise quarterback had never looked terrible but never really looked good. The defense was loaded with talent, but was still a liability, only seeming to play well down the stretch half the time. And sure, it was great to have two guys rush for 1,000 yards, but shouldn't that mean that the offense was dominant, capable of controlling a game? Clearly not in this case. The biggest question: Had the team really taken a step forward or had it just managed to avoid some of the bad luck that had plagued it the year before?

As the calendar neared its close and the holiday season descended upon Cleveland, Ohio, the 1985 Browns' season was hanging in limbo, with no real purpose or meaning. Fans wondered if it was all just an aberration or the start of something special.

A few days later, they got their answer—in no uncertain terms.

6 Party Crashers

Football fans across the nation were irate that the blasphemous Browns had weaseled their way into the playoffs. The following week, HBO's weekly *Inside the NFL* program held a call-in poll asking who better deserved to be in the playoffs: Cleveland or 11-5 Denver, who failed to qualify. Sixty-three percent of respondents said the Broncos, while only 30 percent voted for the Browns. One could only wonder how Showtime subscribers felt.

Still, most fans weren't overly concerned. The Browns would quickly get what was coming to them. Cleveland would have to face the Miami Dolphins, the defending AFC champions, in the Orange Bowl in a divisional playoff on Saturday, January 4, 1986. Everyone assumed the Dolphins, ten-and-a-half-point favorites, would make quick work of these party crashers.

The year before, Miami had gone 14-2 behind the mythical arm of quarterback Dan Marino. In his second year in the NFL, Marino had thrown for forty-eight touchdowns and better than 5,000 yards as the Dolphins put together the most exciting pass offense in football. They'd cruised to Super Bowl XIX, where they were soundly defeated by the San Francisco 49ers.

But the 1985 season was not quite as sunshiny in Miami. Marino threw for "only" 4,137 yards and thirty touchdowns. In early November, the Dolphins stood at just 5-4 and were looking up at the Jets and Patriots in the AFC East. Marino and the passing game were struggling (at least compared to their 1984 standard), and the Miami defense, which had never been particularly strong, was even more suspect. But a Marino touchdown bomb to Mark Duper in the final minute clinched a critical Week Ten victory over the Jets, and the Dolphins rolled from there. They won their final seven games of the regular season, including a 38-24 thumping of the 12-0 Chicago Bears on *Monday Night Football* in the Orange Bowl, as Marino and company carved through the NFL's best defense.

Miami's late thrust had given them a 12-4 record and the AFC East title over Wild Card entries New York and New England. After a week off, they would host the momentum-less Browns with a return trip to the AFC Championship on the line. Even Art Modell seemed braced for disaster. "I just hope we don't get embarrassed," he said the day before the game.

"What's done is done," Marty Schottenheimer said following the season finale loss in the Meadowlands. "Everyone's 0-0 now. Everyone's even, just like in July."

For two weeks, the players talked about winning the game—not being happy to be there, not just wanting to prove they belonged, but winning. In some ways, their confidence was justified.

Though the Browns' offense was not a unit that would keep defensive coordinators awake at night, its strength was Miami's weakness. The Dolphins had allowed four yards or more per carry in thirteen of their sixteen games in 1985, and the defense as a whole ranked twenty-third in the league. The Browns, meanwhile, had the NFL's eighth-best rushing offense and were averaging 143 yards per game on the ground. Marino and his cadre of offensive weapons were fantastic and capable of dominating a game, but they couldn't do anything without the football.

When the Miami offense was on the field, it would be up to the Browns' defense to stop it—or at least slow it down, something the mighty Bears had not been able to do a month earlier. The key, Schottenheimer felt, was putting pressure on Marino. This would be no easy task against an offensive line that had allowed just eighteen sacks all year. Many teams just dropped back six, sometimes seven defensive backs and hoped for the best. But when given time, Marino would almost always find an open man. The 49ers had proven in the Super Bowl that if you could pressure the Dolphin quarterback, the secondary wouldn't be under the gun as much.

But at the same time, Hanford Dixon and Frank Minnifield were in for their biggest challenge of the season. They would be matched up with Miami's marvelous "Marks Brothers": Mark Clayton and Mark Duper. The Browns' defensive backs would also have to keep an eye on Nat Moore, the twelve-year veteran who had collected 701 receiving yards during the regular season. The Miami running game was nothing to write home about, but halfback Tony Nathan had proven himself a worthy receiver out of the backfield.

Was an upset impossible? No. But it would take dominant performances by both the Browns' running game and secondary to put Cleveland in a position to win. "We don't have to play like supermen," Clarence Weathers said. "We just have to play mistake-free football."

"Nothing's been easy for us all year," Chip Banks added. "We've scratched and bitten our way here. Now we're going to be shooting all our bullets."

Things started naturally enough.

Under a sunny sky and with the temperature hovering around eighty degrees, the Browns, wearing brown, cut-off mesh jerseys, set the tone early by running on their first three plays. But when Kevin Mack was stuffed for no gain on third-and-one at the Cleveland twenty-nine yard line, it was not a good sign. Things looked worse when the Dolphins drove into Browns' territory and took a 3-0 lead on a Fuad Reveiz field goal.

After an exchange of punts, the Browns began one of their most impressive drives of the season. Mixing handoffs among Earnest Byner, Kevin Mack, and Curtis Dickey, who saw his first legitimate action as a Brown after being picked up as a free agent in late November, the upstarts marched right down the favorites' throats. They got to the Miami sixteen before facing a third down, and then crossed up the weary Dolphin defense. After eight rushes in nine plays, Kosar dropped into the shotgun and hit a wide-open Ozzie Newsome streaking over the middle at the Miami seven. Newsome quickly cut upfield and into the end zone for the go-ahead touchdown with just over a minute left in the first quarter. The Browns looked like a playoff team—for one drive anyway.

But their momentum just kept building. They stopped the Dolphin offense on three straight plays and forced a punt, then halted a potential Miami scoring drive when Don Rogers intercepted a Marino pass at the Cleveland goal line and raced up the right sideline before getting tripped up at the Miami forty-five yard line. A perfect opportunity for the heavily favored Dolphins to seize the game's momentum had gone awry. And the Browns' confidence continued to thrive.

With four minutes remaining in the half, the Browns wanted to keep things close to the vest and prevent the Dolphins from scoring again before intermission. But the Cleveland running game just kept pounding through the Miami defense. Mack crashed up the middle for 11 yards to the Miami thirty-three, and Dickey swept around the left side for 10 more. Two plays later, the Browns faced third-and-eight at the twenty-one, and from the shotgun, Kosar handed off to Byner, who twisted and turned his way into the end zone for a 14-3 Browns' lead that held to halftime. As the teams marched off the field toward their respective locker rooms, Hanford Dixon and Browns' special teams coach Bill Cowher exchanged a vibrant high-five at midfield.

What exactly was going on here? The Browns, the team HBO viewers had voted out of the playoffs, were dominating the darlings of the AFC on their home field. The team Las Vegas thought would lose by eleven points was now winning by eleven. The pro football world had been turned upside down. And things would only get nuttier.

The Browns stuffed the Dolphins on their first possession of the second half then took over at their own twenty. Kosar hit Clarence Weathers on the right side for a 12-yard gain to the Cleveland thirty-four yard line on third-and-eight to keep the drive alive. But the drive would only last one more play. On the next snap, Earnest Byner took a handoff on a trap and exploded through a hole and ran untouched into the end zone to complete a 66-yard touchdown run, the longest of the Browns' season and longest in the team's postseason history.

Browns' fans across the nation were pinching themselves. Was this real? Everything the Browns had wanted to do they were doing. The running game was gargantuan. The defense was confusing Dan Marino. Frank Minnifield and Hanford Dixon were dominating Clayton and Duper, neither of whom touched the ball in the first half. "By the second half, Marino didn't even bother to look their way," Minnifield said. "He knew we had taken away their home-run hitters." They were playing with heart and showing the sports world not only that they deserved to be in the playoffs but that they just might be one of the best teams in the NFL.

The Miami crowd was, to say the least, stunned. The large Browns' contingent was going bonkers, as much from sheer surprise as joy. With 11:22 to play in the third quarter, Cleveland was twenty-six minutes away from pulling one of the biggest upsets in NFL history.

It was too good to be true. So, considering the history of Cleveland athletics, it couldn't last.

Things looked even better for the upstarts a few moments later when the Dolphins found themselves stuck in a second-and-fourteen hole at their own twenty-two yard line. Marino's next pass for Clayton fell incomplete, and for a moment it appeared Miami would have to convert on third-and-fourteen or give the football back to the red-hot Cleveland offense. But Don Rogers was penalized for hitting Clayton in the head after the play, moving the Dolphins to the thirty-seven and giving them a first down. It was the break Marino needed—even if it wasn't the correct call. "It was a bad call," Rogers said afterward. "The official said he called it because I tried to go for his head. Clayton got the call because he whines a lot. It wasn't called immediately. I think I made a great play."

Marino connected on five of his next six passes, driving his team to the Cleveland six yard line. There, on third-and-goal, Nat Moore fooled Browns' safety Felix Wright with a cut in the end zone, and Marino hit him with a bullet pass for a score. The Browns' lead was cut to 21-10, and the momentum had begun to shift with five minutes left in the third.

The dazed Miami crowd was reenergized, knowing that if Marino and the Dolphin offense could stay hot, there was still plenty of time left to pull out a victory. Their optimism grew stronger when the Dolphins forced a punt. A pair of short Marino completions moved Miami to the Cleveland thirty-one, and then he handed off to fullback Ron Davenport, who sprinted around the left side. Don Rogers read the play and crashed into Davenport at the twenty-five. But rather than forcing the running back onto the seat of his pants, as Rogers had done several times in 1985, it was Rogers who was thrust backward as Davenport broke free and glided down the sideline untouched for a 31-yard touchdown run. "I made a mistake," Rogers said later. "I was too aggressive and tried to hit him too high. Next time I'll play it smarter." Unfortunately, there would be no next time for Rogers, either on this afternoon or thereafter.

Just as quickly as the Dolphins had fallen behind, they were now back in it. It was now 21-17 with less than two minutes remaining in the third quarter, and the Browns' offense had to do something quickly. Instead, Cleveland went backward on its next series, hampered by a holding penalty and a Kosar sack. The Browns punted back to Miami, and the crowd anticipated the go-ahead score. But the Cleveland defense snapped its string of ineptitude and stuffed the home team on three straight plays to force another punt. The Browns had slowed Miami's momentum and were still in good shape, with the lead and the ball with less than thirteen minutes to play.

An illegal-use-of-hands penalty pushed the Browns back to their own nine yard line, and the Dolphin faithful growled to life once more. Runs by Byner and Mack propelled Cleveland to the twenty-nine where a 15-yard facemask foul on the Dolphins advanced the football to the forty-four. The Browns were out of the hole and on a roll. They quickly dug back into a hole, however, when George Lilja was penalized for a false start on the next play. Byner cut the distance with runs of six and seven yards on the next two plays, setting up third-and-two at the Miami forty-eight with just over eight minutes remaining. A Browns' conversion would give them a new set of downs and, if nothing else, a chance to run another minute or two off the clock after they'd already melted nearly six minutes. It was officially crunch time.

As Byner hobbled back to the sideline after his second-down run, the coaches told him to get back to the huddle, he was needed on the next play. Byner, nursing a bruised knee suffered on the previous play, did as he was told, but got to the huddle late and missed the playcall. A teammate told him what it was— "Pitch-28"—and he lined up to execute it, but Byner was admittedly confused. He'd heard the play, but it hadn't registered. The call was a pitch to Curtis Dickey, who would follow Byner around right end and sprint toward the first-down marker. It was a play that had worked several times in the first half.

But when the ball was snapped, Byner ran to his left, not his right. Kosar turned to pitch the football to Dickey and saw that the play was broken. He hesitated then pitched the ball to Dickey anyway, and predictably, Dickey was tripped up by defensive end Mack Moore at the Cleveland forty-five yard line for a seven-yard loss with 8:03 to play.

The Orange Bowl throng roared louder than it had all day. The Miami defense had come up big when it needed to, and as a result, the entire season would rest on the shoulders of Dan Marino and the Miami offense. Or so it seemed. The Dolphins fumbled the ensuing punt and there was a huge pileup of Browns and Dolphins at the Miami twenty-eight, as both teams fought to recover the most important fumble of the season. If the Browns recovered, they would already be in field-goal range and could run some more time off the clock. If the Dolphins recovered, they had more than enough time to travel the field for a touchdown that would give them the lead.

Browns' linebacker Scott Nicolas, in for an injured Tom Cousineau, originally had the football. But by the time the officials uncovered everyone, they said Miami's Tom Vigorito had recovered the fumble, and the Dolphins had a first down with 7:21 to play. "I don't understand how they gave them the ball," an upset Nicolas said later. "Somebody needs glasses. There is no doubt I had the ball, and nobody was going to get it from me."

"I felt like the fat lady was going to sing if they had given us that call," Minnifield said, "and I thought we deserved the football."

After an incompletion, Marino hit Tony Nathan with a short pass over the middle. Nathan juked past Eddie Johnson, then made another move to elude Chris Rockins and angled toward the left sideline. He sprinted across midfield and reached the Cleveland thirty-four yard line before Al Gross finally brought him down after a 38-yard gain. It was not a proud moment for the Dog Defense.

A play later, Marino hit tight end Bruce Hardy for 14 yards to the Cleveland eighteen. The Dolphins then turned to their running game. Davenport sprinted up the middle for eight yards then Nathan picked up a first down with a four-yard run to the Cleveland six. Another pair of rushes brought Miami to the one yard line at the two-minute warning, and though the Browns still had the lead, everyone in the stadium knew that was about to change.

Davenport pummeled through the right side and into the end zone on third down, making it 24-21 with 1:57 to play. They'd come all the way back. The Browns' offense, not designed to score quickly, hurriedly crept to midfield before time expired. The Orange Bowl crowd counted down the final seconds aloud, and when the clock hit zero, the Dolphins were triumphant—and relieved.

Despite a storybook effort, the Browns hadn't had it when they needed it most. "Give them credit," Bob Golic said in a beleaguered locker room. "They're a great team. It wasn't so much that we played bad in the second half, it's that they played great, and that's the bottom line."

It was hard to criticize the Cleveland defense, even though it had allowed three touchdowns on Miami's final four possessions when it needed to be at its best. Had the Browns' coaches known before the game the Dolphins would score only twenty-four points, they would have thought they a had a good chance to win the game. Marino was held to a modest 238 yards and completed just over 50 percent of his passes. The defense, playing without injured linebackers Tom Cousineau and Clay Matthews, had been dominant for the first half, then shaky for the second. "We had them, we had them," mumbled a despondent Bob Golic in the locker room. "To play as well as we did and have it taken away like that was an emotional roller-coaster ride." It was the perfect end to an up-and-down season for the Dogs.

It also would have been unfair to blast the Browns' offense. The rushing attack piled up a team-playoff-record 252 yards and was never truly shut down by Miami. The offensive line had been dominant, consistently knocking the Dolphins on their tails.

Kevin Mack and Curtis Dickey both made substantial contributions, but the only reason the Browns were in the game at all was Earnest Byner, who picked up

161 yards on sixteen carries and scored two touchdowns. "I showed a lot of people around the nation what type of back Earnest Byner really is," he said. And he had. This game had become Earnest Byner's coming-out party.

But the primary reason the Browns could not hold the lead, many felt, was the Browns' lack of offensive variety. By the middle of the third quarter, the Dolphins were able to plug many of the holes that had been open in the first half by blitzing their linebackers. After collecting 141 rushing yards in the first half, the Browns could manage just twenty-one in the fourth quarter. After all, there was no fear of the Browns hurting Miami through the air—a point many fans would bring up in the following weeks.

The primary critic, however, was Bernie Kosar. "We're just not able to get after things well," he said. "We just don't take advantage of certain defensive situations. That's what we've been doing all year. Whenever we get ahead, we become as predictable as you can get."

Bernie's stats backed him up. He completed ten of nineteen passes for a mere 66 yards. Not bad for a high school quarterback, but nowhere near good enough to win an NFL playoff game. "We're going to have to improve our passing philosophy," he said. "It's not up to a professional level."

He was right. And the Browns would.

Despite the sour taste of the loss in Miami, there were plenty of positive feelings coming out of the 1985 season. As Pete Franklin would forecast, the Browns were about to enter a run of glory not seen in nearly twenty years.

"Browns' fans, you now can wear the team colors," he said. "You can put the stickers on the car. You can come to the game with banners waving. You can actually start attending games in Cleveland. You can even tell your in-laws and outlaws you live in Ohio, in the Cleveland marketplace.

"The Browns' days, the good days, are here and ahead of us."

7 Identity Crisis

The Browns went into the offseason following the 1985 campaign feeling pretty good about themselves, and with good reason. They weren't fantastic, but they'd won the division and were essentially a young team filled with players entering the prime of their careers. There was much reason for optimism that summer.

Don Rogers was a part of that team optimism, with his career and his personal life about to take off. He'd followed up a sterling rookie season with a solid second year and had become one of the anchors of a Cleveland defense with high expectations. He was just at the start of something big professionally. "I think I'm as good as anyone in the league at my position," Rogers said in 1985. "I'm just as aggressive, I'm smart, and I have the durability and ability to play the position. Besides that, I'll get better as the years go on."

"Rogers had an excellent season, worked very hard and has only begun to scratch the surface," Marty Schottenheimer said after the 1985 season concluded. "In 1986, Don is going to surface as one of the top safeties in the NFL."

And to top it off, he was to be married on June 28 in Sacramento. Several friends and teammates had gathered that week to celebrate the occasion. Things could not get much better for Don Rogers.

"I'm a low-key individual who likes to go out and have an outstanding time no matter what it takes," he said during his rookie season. "I like to party, go where the crowd goes, but still keep everything in perspective."

But for at least one day, he lost all perspective.

Rogers' bachelor party was scheduled for June 26. He and several friends, including Hanford Dixon and a few other Browns' players, began the evening with a get-together at a Sacramento hotel. Later, the group left the party and went to a nightclub, then even later returned to the hotel.

At about 2:30 A.M., his friends noticed Rogers was gone. About a half-hour after that, Rogers showed up at his mother's house. The following morning, he spoke to Browns' director of player relations Paul Warfield on the telephone. Warfield said Rogers sounded in good spirits, much like a man who was getting married the next day.

Three hours later, Rogers collapsed. He went into a coma and was taken to the hospital. He was pronounced dead at 4:31 P.M., Pacific Daylight Time.

Before the coroner's report was ever released, it was fairly obvious what had happened to Don Rogers. Twenty-three-year-old, well-conditioned athletes don't just drop dead for no reason. Though Dixon said there had been no drugs at the party, at some point that evening, Rogers had taken a murderous overdose of cocaine. The post-mortem toxicology report said Rogers had 5.2 milligrams of cocaine per liter of blood in his body, five times the amount considered to be the lethal level. He died of heart failure due to the overdose.

The timing was incredible on several levels. Just eight days earlier, Len Bias, a basketball star at the University of Maryland who had just been drafted by the NBA's Boston Celtics, had died of a drug overdose before ever playing a professional game. On the day the coroner's report was released on Rogers, the Browns' tenth-round pick in that spring's college draft, tight end Willie Smith was arrested in Miami for cocaine possession. Also that June, Browns' defensive end Sam Clancy would be arrested twice in one day for drunk driving. The ultimate indiscretion of substance abuse, which had run rampant in the NFL throughout the decade, had finally hit home resoundingly for the Cleveland Browns.

Ironically, though the Browns lost the NFL's first drug casualty, the team was years ahead of its peers in terms of constructing an in-house rehabilitation program. Founded by then head coach Sam Rutigliano in the early 1980s, the Inner Circle wound up changing the lives of nearly a dozen Browns, many of whom would go on to have stellar careers for the remainder of the decade. Rutigliano had taken a personal interest in the Inner Circle and was heavily involved with it, to the point that some callused fans complained that he should spend less time trying to save lives and more time trying to win football games. But now Don Rogers was dead.

Shock overcame Rogers' teammates and coaches as the word filtered across the country. Browns' vice president of public relations Kevin Byrne found Marty Schottenheimer watching a baseball game in Strongsville and told him that Rogers had died. "I was absolutely dumbfounded," Schottenheimer said. "I couldn't believe it. I'll never forget it as long as I live." Dan Fike and Mike Baab were having a beer at a bar in downtown Cleveland when they heard. They figured it had been a car crash—that was the only reasonable explanation. "Whatever Donnie had going on, he sure had it going on all by himself because none of us knew anything about it," Baab said.

"I didn't believe it when I heard it," said linebacker Eddie Johnson. "I'm speechless. I'm so hurt. I don't know what to do, what to think. All I know is I hurt."

"This really hits home," said Bob Golic. "You see this guy every day, and all of a sudden he's not around. It's scary in a way."

It *was* scary. Especially since the coroner's report said there had been no evidence of previous drug use. Teammates said Rogers had not been a part of the

Inner Circle. There was a possibility that this had been the first time Rogers had ever used drugs in his life. Whether or not it was his first, it turned out to be his last.

Rogers' death sent shockwaves across the nation, affecting those close to him as well as those who had never before heard of him. The day after he died, his grief-stricken mother suffered a heart attack and was still in the hospital the day of his funeral. Former UCLA teammate and current Seattle Seahawk Ken Easley had traveled to Sacramento to be a groomsman in Rogers' wedding. He wound up being a pallbearer at his funeral.

A memorial service was held at Sacramento's Arco Arena, as well as another at Old Stone Church in downtown Cleveland. Several Browns were present, either in Cleveland or California. Dixon, who was questioned by Sacramento police and swarmed by the media, and Chris Rockins joined Easley as pallbearers.

Once the shock and sorrow wore off, Art Modell made it clear he'd had enough. "I tell you this, we're going to get tough," he said. "We are not going to tolerate offseason and in-season indiscretions. And you can put that word in quote marks because I consider it worse than indiscretion. . . . We don't want those kinds of people around here. You can't win with them. I don't expect them to be choirboys, but we're not running a halfway house, either."

It was essentially the exact opposite sentiment that inspired Rutigliano to start the Inner Circle. Rutigliano didn't want players to be afraid of confessing their addictions because they thought they would be cut or ostracized. He wanted the players to come to him for help, to get rehabilitation and earn a second chance on life. But by 1986, the NFL's drug problem, as well as the substance-abuse problems in other professional sports, had grown worse, and Modell and commissioner Pete Rozelle decided to crack down.

Four days after Rogers' funeral, Rozelle announced the league's new drug program, which would cost $1 million per year. Players would submit two random tests during the regular season for cocaine, marijuana, heroin, amphetamine, and alcohol. If a player tested positive once, he was put under medical care for at least thirty days but would still receive half his salary. A second offense and the player would re-enter rehab with no pay. Upon a third offense, the player could be banned from the game for life.

It was a dramatic change from the league's previous stance, which, thanks to the steering of the NFL Players Association, had opposed random drug testing, considering it an invasion of privacy. "Invasion of privacy?" Modell said. "Don Rogers has the ultimate privacy now."

Certainly, the Browns had a lot to overcome emotionally before taking the field for training camp a month later. But Rogers' teammates hoped that his death could not only bring the team together but also serve as an example for the rest of the NFL and the sports world.

"Most definitely this can draw the team closer together," Ozzie Newsome said. "There's always some good that can come out of something bad. Don's death can draw us closer together, making us more accountable in our personal lives and on the field."

"Tragically, in death, Don Rogers may have made more of a contribution to society than he could have on the playing field," Modell said. "Let's hope his passing serves as a warning to those who want to try or have used drugs."

Sadly, though Rogers should have been the ultimate martyr in the battle between professional athletes and drugs, it would not be the final time a Browns' player's life and career would be forever altered by cocaine.

The USFL and its eventual disbanding in the summer of 1986 benefited many NFL teams, but probably none as much as the Cleveland Browns. By the time the 1986 season was set to begin, the Browns had a handful of former USFL players on the roster, including several in the starting lineup. Cornerback Frank Minnifield and running back Kevin Mack were the most notable, but Dan Fike had also stepped into a starting role in 1985 on the offensive line, and as the start of the season neared, the Browns signed a pair of USFLers they'd held the rights to since the 1984 supplemental draft: wide receiver Gerald McNeil and linebacker Mike Johnson.

The USFL officially folded just a few weeks before its highly anticipated 1986 season, its fourth. The USFL planned to go head-to-head with the NFL in the fall. But the writing was on the wall that summer (and for some time before that) when the league was awarded just three dollars in damages following its antitrust suit victory over the NFL. It turned out there wasn't room for a second professional football league in America. There was, however, room for USFL players on NFL rosters, and that July and August saw several teams backed against the wall trying to get reps for dozens of extra players who flooded into the NFL.

This tidal wave did not affect the Browns, whose scouts had determined before the USFL folded which players were worth looking at and which weren't. Rather than bringing in a handful of new players all at once, the Browns stuck with the guns they had, including new ones in McNeil and Johnson, and prepared for the 1986 season.

But for all the talented athletes the Browns acquired via the USFL, probably their greatest acquisition from the doomed franchise was a silver-haired, pass-happy forty-five-year-old coach named Lindy Infante.

Infante had been the head coach of the USFL's Jacksonville Bulls for the 1984 and 1985 seasons until the franchise merged with Denver's and there was one too many head coaches. In Jacksonville, he'd worked with former Browns' quarterback Brian Sipe, who had been traded from the New Jersey Generals to the Bulls to make room for Doug Flutie. Sipe had been the last quarterback to spark the Cleveland offense into one of the best units in the league. After his departure, the Browns' passing attack floundered for two years, finishing twenty-fifth in the NFL in 1985. But in February 1986, the Browns hoped Sipe's last coach could bring back some of the magic Sipe had created.

As Marty Schottenheimer assembled his coaching staff for his first full season at the Browns' helm in 1985, he wanted one of three men to serve as offensive coordinator: former Cleveland quarterbacks coach Paul Hackett, Jerry Burns, or Infante. He got none, and had to settle for Joe Pendry. The following winter, Schottenheimer realized the Browns had to become more multi-dimensional to be successful.

"As we as a football team are able to do certain things, then we will expand," he said at the conclusion of the 1985 season. "We did what we did best this year, because it was the thing we did best. I've always been a strong believer that it doesn't make any sense to ask people to do things they're not prepared to do. What we've done is establish the ability to run the ball. Now, through the experience gained by our quarterback and the development of the offensive line, we are going to be able to expand into throwing the ball, because you have to be able to do both if you want to win."

That winter, Schottenheimer found out that Infante was interested in returning to the NFL, where he'd served as the Cincinnati Bengals' offensive coordinator in 1981 and 1982. Schottenheimer informed Modell, who learned that Infante already had offers from at least three other teams. Modell sensed this was something the Browns needed and quickly got involved in the bidding process. He won, and the Browns got Infante's name on a contract—something they'd failed to do twenty-three years earlier.

The Browns had selected Infante, an All-Southeastern Conference running back and defensive back from Florida, in the twelfth round of the college draft in 1963, but he decided to play in Canada instead. After a short-lived career with the Hamilton Tiger Cats, Infante got into coaching in 1965 at the high school level in Miami then returned to his alma mater of Florida a year later as head freshman coach. A year after that, he was promoted to the varsity squad, where he coached the defensive backs for five years. He served as offensive coordinator at Memphis State in 1972 and 1973 then joined the Charlotte Hornets of the World Football League for one season in 1975. The following year, he was named offensive coordinator at Tulane and then finally cracked the NFL in 1977, when he became receivers coach for the New York Giants. It was in New York that his path first crossed with Schottenheimer, who at the time was the Giants' defensive coordinator. He returned to the collegiate level at Tulane as offensive coordinator in 1979 and made one final leap to the professional level.

Infante joined Forrest Gregg as he took over the Cincinnati Bengals in 1980 and served as quarterbacks and receivers coach. The Bengals sloshed to a 3-9 start, but with Infante's input the offense began to show signs of life late in the season. Through the first twelve games of the season, the Bengals had averaged less than thirteen points per game. But over the final four, they averaged more than twenty-three and won three straight before taking the Browns down to the wire in the grand finale to their Kardiac Kids campaign.

In the offseason, Infante was promoted to become Cincinnati's first-ever offensive coordinator, and the Bengals entered a short but memorable string of success as one of the best offensive clubs in the NFL. In 1981, guided by veteran quarterback Ken Anderson, the Bengals averaged better than twenty-six points per game and marched to a 12-4 record and an AFC title before falling just short to the 49ers in Super Bowl XVI. The beat went on the following year as Infante's offense sparked the Bengals to a 7-2 mark in the strike-shortened season and another postseason berth.

But five days before the team's 1983 training camp was to begin, Infante was fired. He had signed a contract with the Jacksonville Bulls to take over as their head coach on February 1, 1984. Rather than happily accepting Infante's services for one final year, the Bengals sued him for breach of contract and showed him the door. With tight ends coach Bruce Coslet now in charge of the offense, Cincinnati averaged five less points per game that fall than the previous two seasons and struggled to a 7-9 record. Many observers blamed Infante's departure for the Bengals' collapse, and the statistics backed it up. After winning twenty-two of twenty-nine games with Infante controlling the offense, the Bengals would compile an overall mark of just 22-26 in the following three years.

Though Infante's arrival was a welcome one, it caused quite a shakeup in the Browns' coaching staff. Joe Pendry was demoted to running backs coach, a position held by Steve Crosby in 1985. Crosby quit and returned to Atlanta, where he had served as quarterbacks and receivers coach in 1983 and 1984. Though Pendry had held the title of coordinator the previous year, in fact there had not been a true leader to the Cleveland offense. Pendry and Crosby were the primary two involved in the offensive decision-making, but as expected, the philosophy lacked a real direction and had no true authority.

"We decided it's in our best interests to have one guy's philosophy as to which way we want to go," Schottenheimer said. "Now the root of it all will be the offense Lindy has brought with him. The most perceptible difference from a year ago is we will be more involved in throwing the ball."

It was music to Bernie Kosar's ears. It appeared the front office had been listening to his postgame comments after the playoff loss in Miami. "I'm not too sure quarterbacks are any different from any other position," Infante said upon his arrival. "A running back who is not given the ball is not going to have a lot of impact—same with a wide receiver. A quarterback who's not given things that allow him to express himself is going to have trouble. . . . We try to do things that best suit the players we have."

Kevin Mack and Earnest Byner were wonderful backs, but for the Browns to take the next step, they would have to broaden their offensive horizons. Lindy Infante was exactly what this team needed to broaden it. "Lindy was the kind of coach who would walk in and say, 'Boys, we got these guys,'" Mike Baab said. "And he'd laugh. He'd say, 'When they do this, we'll do this, and we're going to score.' And he was completely right. He would prove himself time and time again.

"We had ultimate confidence in everything he said. From the very first few practices, we were aware we were on a completely different path. We had gone from a little prop plane to the space shuttle."

"He had a very unique approach," Schottenheimer said. "Every Wednesday, the offensive players would be going into that meeting trying to figure out what new wrinkle he had for them this week. . . . I think there was this sense of intrigue, if you will, on the part of the players as they came in every Wednesday. Lindy always said you need to have enough change in there that they're curious as they approach the plans so it doesn't become routine and mundane."

The secret to Infante's success was an option-route pass system that had turned the lowly Bengals into Super Bowl contenders. "It gives receivers a great deal of flexibility," Infante explained. "It lets them express themselves on the field. I would describe it as a thinking man's offense. It spreads the load around. We believe strongly in having route adjustments on every down."

In theory, it sounded great. But the 1985 Browns had not had much in the receiving department. But Infante was flexible and creative. As training camp wore on that summer, he occasionally used Earnest Byner and fellow running back Herman Fontenot as wideouts. And the installation of his new system coincided with the arrival of rookie wide receiver Webster Slaughter, the Browns' second-round draft pick that spring, and second-year man Reggie Langhorne, who had played primarily special teams in 1985.

Many media pundits were surprised when the Browns selected Slaughter with the forty-third overall pick of the draft. The team had no first-round selection as a result of the trade that earned it the right to acquire Kosar the previous summer, and clearly wide receiver was one of the Browns' primary needs. Many expected the Browns to select John Taylor out of Delaware State or Hawaii's Walter Murray. But instead, they took Slaughter, a wideout who had garnered some attention by draft experts, but generally hadn't been considered one of the top ten pass-catchers in the draft. He had, however, been highly recommended by former Browns' Hall-of-Fame wide receiver Paul Warfield. "Slaughter might not be a blue-chipper like Eddie Brown," Ray Yannucci wrote in *Browns News/Illustrated,* "but he can play."

That he could. Slaughter had been fourth in the nation in receptions his senior year at San Diego State, catching eighty-two for 1,071 yards with ten touchdowns in the Aztecs' pass-happy offense. For his efforts, he was named second-team All-America by the Associated Press. At 6'0", 175 pounds, he was small and somewhat scrawny for an NFL wideout, but he'd shown the speed and quickness necessary to survive at the professional level.

Slaughter didn't play organized football until his senior year of high school, instead spending much of his youth performing on his saxophone as a member of a jazz band in Stockton, California. All through high school, Slaughter, who had excelled at basketball and track, never even considered playing football until his gym coach suggested it.

"I'm not sure why I agreed to try," Slaughter said. "He was a nice man, and I guess I didn't know how to say no. My first day of practice they had to show me where to stand. I didn't even know how to line up."

As it turned out, Slaughter would owe a great deal to that gym teacher. In his only year of prep competition at Franklin High School, he became a force. He had planned on enrolling at Cal State-Stanislaus before a solid performance in an area high school all-star game pointed him to nearby Delta Junior College, where he continued his brief football career. At Delta, Slaughter racked up 1,300 yards in two years and was recruited by several major Division I programs. He narrowed it down to Illinois, Pacific, and San Diego State before settling on the Aztecs.

His collegiate career got off to a rocky start when he fumbled the opening kickoff of his first game, but he soon made up for it, cracked the starting lineup, and found his niche. As a junior, Slaughter caught forty passes for 576 yards in San Diego State's pass-option offense—the same aerial scheme Lindy Infante would bring to the Browns. "The thing that puts him above most other receivers," said Aztec quarterback Todd Santos, "is his courage."

Around the same time Slaughter was being introduced to football, fellow receiver Reggie Langhorne was considering beginning a career based on courage. As he completed high school in Smithfield, Virginia, Langhorne planned on joining the U.S. Army. But he eventually decided to attend Elizabeth City State University because his high school coach had gone there and had convinced him to try it for one year. At NAIA ECSU, Langhorne had too much fun to quit and continued a sterling gridiron career. He excelled as a wide receiver in a ground-oriented offense, gathering better than 1,500 yards in his collegiate career.

Still, the leap from Elizabeth City State to the NFL was a giant one, and accordingly, Langhorne received little notice from pro scouts. But prior to the 1985 draft (after receiving an honorable discharge from the ROTC), he garnered some attention at a combine in Tempe, where he outperformed several highly acclaimed receivers from bigger schools. As a result, the Browns took a chance on him, selecting Langhorne in the seventh round. Immediately, though, they sensed something special about Reginald Langhorne, the name he first went by.

"I don't want to make comparisons," said Browns' personnel director Bill Davis that day, "but it is the same type of thing as we had with Earnest Byner last year. We got late exposure on Earnest, and this kid is the same way."

Like Byner, Langhorne spent much of his rookie season either on the bench or on special teams. But when Clarence Weathers and Glen Young both suffered injuries late in the year, Langhorne cracked the starting lineup three times. He caught just one pass all year but came alive in Infante's new offensive scheme in training camp the following summer. Marty Schottenheimer called Langhorne the biggest surprise of training camp on offense, and Langhorne made the team. It would not take long for him to make an impact.

With youngsters Slaughter and Langhorne rising and Brian Brennan and Ozzie Newsome already in place, the Browns' receiving corps was suddenly strong going into the 1986 campaign. "It's no secret that my true love is the passing game," Infante said. "That does not mean, however, we'll be throwing on every down. You've got to do both well to be effective." Schottenheimer added, "Our objectives on offense are to upgrade our ability to throw the ball effectively while not compromising our ability to run."

As the regular season drew closer, it appeared Cleveland would have the first truly potent offensive attack since the days of Sipe and the Kardiac Kids six years before. Through the preseason, all the pieces but one seemed to fall into place.

Though Bernie Kosar had showed promise as a rookie, he was not going to be handed the starting job for 1986. Gary Danielson had made a lightning-fast recovery from rotator cuff surgery in January and made it clear he was still a candidate for starting quarterback. Plus, that June, the Browns had traded a 1987 ninth-round draft choice to Indianapolis for playcaller Mike Pagel, who had shown potential playing for some very bad Colts teams. Pagel's numbers in four seasons were comparable to those of Paul McDonald, whom the team released shortly after acquiring Pagel. Kosar hit his stride in the third preseason game and led the Browns to a victory in Atlanta. Then, after Kosar again played well in the preseason finale in Los Angeles against the Raiders, Danielson was lost for the season when he fractured and dislocated his left ankle. All the work he'd done to come back from his shoulder injury was tragically flushed away.

With Pagel still a bit of an unknown, the success of the Browns' 1986 season now rested solely on the shoulders of Bernie Kosar. There would be no safety net in the form of Gary Danielson to come in and save the day as he had in 1985. The Browns' franchise quarterback, with a new playbook in his hip pocket, would now have to earn every penny of his salary and live up to the expectations of an adoring yet demanding hometown crowd.

The Bernie Kosar era was set to begin.

While the Browns' offense was going through a philosophical overhaul, the Cleveland defense was also experiencing some growing pains.

In a mild surprise, linebacker Tom Cousineau was released in the final week of camp. Schottenheimer justified the decision by saying Eddie Johnson, Mike

Johnson, and newcomer Anthony Griggs, for whom the Browns had traded an eighth-round draft choice to Philadelphia the previous spring, were all better than Cousineau. It brought a disappointing end to Cousineau's four-year stay in Cleveland. Cousineau had never truly played poorly, but he also had never become the dominant player many had expected him to be. He certainly had not made as much an impact as Chip Banks.

And Banks, still not happy with his lack of usage on third downs, was a hold-out from camp for the second straight year. This time, Banks, entering the final year of his contract, skipped mini-camp in June, then sat out all of the preseason. For good measure, he also added that he'd lost respect for the organization and Schottenheimer as a coach. After the Browns made it clear they would not trade Banks, he eventually ended his holdout after twenty-six days and signed a two-year, $1.3 million contract just prior to the start of the season.

Adding to the intrigue of the Browns' defense was a change at the top. After being promoted to defensive coordinator after Dave Adolph resigned for personal reasons after the 1984 season, Tom Bettis informed Schottenheimer that he wanted to pursue other job offers. Schottenheimer figured who better to fill the vacated position than the man it was originally intended for? He talked Adolph into returning as coordinator and linebackers coach.

Interestingly, as the Browns' defensive coaching staff took a more hard-nosed stance, several of the players themselves backed off a bit. Feeling somewhat morose and contemplative following the death of Don Rogers, Hanford Dixon attempted to "muzzle" the Dog craze in training camp. They'd still bark, he said, but the days of taunting and showmanship were over. It was time for the Dogs to grow up. "I've been getting a lot of letters and a lot of people are asking me, 'What the hell's wrong with the Dogs?'" he said. "I just want people to know the Dogs are intact, but in a positive way, not the old negative stuff."

Even though the 1985 season hadn't exactly been one of the highlights of Browns' history, fans and the media were bubbling with expectations for 1986. The Browns would get a serious test on opening day: the defending world champion Chicago Bears at Soldier Field, where the Bears had won eight regular-season games and a pair of playoff contests in 1985 on their way to a 15-1 season. Kosar and the Browns' offense would be tested right away by what was considered by many to be one of the best defenses of all time. Ironically, it was the Browns' defense, not offense, that would be the primary cause for concern in Week One.

Things actually started off with a bang, as the Browns' defense was involved in NFL history. On the third snap of the game, a Bears' fumble rolled into the end zone and the Browns' Al Gross recovered while diving toward the sideline. The question was whether Gross had been in bounds or not. If so, it was a Browns' touchdown. If not, it was a safety. Though referee Ben Dreith thought Gross had landed in bounds when he caught the ball, he was afraid to make a call. For a few seconds, it was unclear what had happened.

A year earlier, Dreith would have simply raised his arms to signal touchdown and that would have been that. But opening day 1986 marked the beginning of a new era in NFL history: the instant-replay era. And Gross would be the subject of the league's first review. High above Soldier Field, a group of NFL officials watched the play from several angles on monitors then phoned down to the field crew on the sideline to let them know what the correct call was—in theory. After taking a look, the replay officials concurred with Dreith's original instinct (and his hesitancy to make a call, whether it be right or wrong, foreshadowed dark moments ahead). Gross was in bounds, and the Browns had scored a touchdown. Dreith announced the decision, and the Browns' defense galloped triumphantly off the field. Though the Browns' first interlude with replay was a good one, this moment marked the beginning of what would become a rocky and ultimately fateful relationship with the technology.

And for all the hassle, the Browns' lead lasted all of sixteen seconds. On the ensuing kickoff, Bears' wide receiver Dennis Gentry scampered 91 yards for the game-tying touchdown. The tone had been set for what would be a wild day in the Windy City, a day that would end with a 41-31 Bears' victory.

While the Cleveland defense struggled, Bernie Kosar thrived against the league's best. In many ways, the Browns felt better than the victors as they returned to the locker room. They had lit up the heralded Chicago defense for twenty-four points and 349 total yards, totals that would have taken two weeks to match against the Bears in 1985. Kosar finally had looked like the type of leader the fans expected him to be, completing twenty-three of forty passes for 289 yards. Ten of his completions went to wide receivers, quite a statement considering the Browns' lack of talent at the position the year before. "That Kosar kid is going to win a lot of games," one longtime Chicago sportswriter said after the game. The Browns' offensive line also did a marvelous job against the Bears' vaunted pass rush, and Kosar was sacked just once.

In defeat, the Browns had proven that, for better or worse, 1986 was going to be a very different season.

After the offensive euphoria in Week One, the Browns' momentum did not come west with them to Houston seven days later.

For more than three quarters of the Browns' Astrodome clash with the first-place Oilers, Kosar and company could muster nothing. With Mack sidelined because of a bruised shoulder and Curtis Dickey still hampered by a nagging hamstring injury, the Cleveland rushing attack was non-existent. As a result, the air attack suffered from predictability and inefficiency, as the gambling Oilers blitzed the hot-dog vendors at Kosar. The Browns trailed 7-3 at halftime, and Kosar completed just one of his first six passes in the second half. After a miscommunication between Kosar and Webster Slaughter on a third-down incompletion in the third quarter, the pair exchanged frustrated words.

Had it not been for a barrage of Houston turnovers, the Browns would have been on the wrong side of a blowout. A pair of Warren Moon interceptions led to a pair of field goals in the third quarter that gave the Browns a 9-7 lead. But the Oilers responded with two field goals of their own to take the lead back 13-9 with just 3:26 remaining.

It was do-or-die time for the Cleveland offense, which had accumulated minus-four total yards and no first downs in the second half. With the clock ticking toward the two-minute warning, Kosar knew it was going to take a big play for the Browns to win. They'd stalled too many times on the afternoon to count on a sustained drive.

Kosar called a play that Lindy Infante had inserted into the gameplan at halftime: "Two Flip-Wide 75 Lock." It was a play the Browns hadn't practiced all week, thrown in simply because nothing else was working. Reggie Langhorne was covered by safety Bo Eason, who didn't have the speed to keep up with the Browns' second-year receiver. Langhorne knew it and broke wide open. Kosar found him and lofted a perfect pass that Langhorne caught at the Houston twenty-five yard line, then angled down the sideline and ran untouched into the end zone for a 55-yard touchdown pass with 2:10 remaining. The score gave Cleveland a 16-13 lead.

The Browns' bench exploded out onto the field. A frustrating cacophony of a game had been broken open on a sweet symphony of a play. As his teammates ran to swarm him, Langhorne and Slaughter ran up to each other and exchanged an airborne high-five for the first time: it was a moment that would be repeated often in the next few years and would become a team trademark.

On the ensuing kickoff, Matt Bahr placed the ball near the sideline and froze Houston's Willie Drewery long enough for the Browns' D. D. Hoggard to recover it. After an afternoon in which nothing had gone right, suddenly everything was working. An Earnest Byner touchdown and a last-gasp scoring drive by Houston made the final 23-20. The Browns were 1-1 after an impressive gut-check victory.

Unfortunately, the Browns had very little time to enjoy their comeback victory in Houston. Four days later, they would host the Cincinnati Bengals on a nationally televised Thursday-night tilt at Cleveland Stadium. Though it was only the third game of the season, it would be huge for both teams.

An immense crowd of 78,779 packed into the Stadium for the home opener, hoping to see the Browns flex their muscles and dominate the Bengals defensively, as they'd done the previous November. The tenants of downtown office buildings were instructed to leave their lights on that night, and the result was a stunning skyline glowing in the September night on national television. Downtown was lit up at kickoff, and soon after, so were the Browns, victims of a 30-13 pounding.

Browns' fans everywhere were scratching their heads. Hadn't they just been a competent offense away from becoming one of the NFL's elite teams over the past two years? Now they had a solid offense, and the defense had taken a powder. "The Browns are reminding me of my house," wrote Ray Yannucci in *Browns News/Illustrated*. "I finally get the hot-water tank fixed then find out the plumbing needs replaced."

Through the first three games, the Browns had allowed an average of twenty-six points and 390 yards per game, including a horrifying 197 on the ground. They looked helpless against the Bengals, who racked up 212 rushing yards. Somehow, the defense appeared to have regressed from its dominating 1984 season and was now no better than anyone else's.

The 1986 season was quickly turning into a disaster.

8 Lemons
Into Lemonade

In case getting blown out at home by a division rival wasn't bad enough, the Browns would not play again for ten days. That meant the media and fans had nearly two weeks to rake the team over the coals and analyze just what was wrong with it. And by halftime against the lowly Detroit Lions in Week Four, there appeared to be plenty wrong.

Modest boos were filtering out of the stands as the Browns continued to play uninspired football in the third quarter in a 7-7 game. Then, with just under ten minutes to play in the period, Lions' punter Mike Black booted a low, line-drive kick deep into Browns' territory.

Tiny Gerald McNeil caught it at the Cleveland sixteen yard line and scampered to his right. Then, following a key block at the twenty-five, McNeil cut back inside through a horde of Lions and found daylight. After a stutter-move near midfield left Black in the dust, McNeil sailed into the end zone at the closed end of Cleveland Stadium, completing a team-record 84-yard punt return for a tide-turning touchdown. For the first time in 1986, the Stadium crowd went crazy. "You haven't seen the last of that young man in that regard," Schottenheimer said after the game. Once again, he was right.

McNeil had been forcing things a bit in his first games as a Brown, trying to reach the expectations that the team had for him and the long wait it had endured for his services. Selected by the Browns in the second round of the 1984 supplemental draft as a part of their cunning trade with Chicago, McNeil played one more dazzling season in the USFL with the Houston Gamblers, catching fifty-eight passes for 1,017 yards and six touchdowns. But where he truly made his mark was on punt returns. He led the league with a 12.9-yards-per-return average and scored two touchdowns in the USFL's final season. The Browns very nearly had an opportunity to sign McNeil prior to the 1985 NFL season, when the Gamblers' franchise was suffering from major financial problems. Had the team not been able to meet payroll in late July, McNeil would have been released, and the Browns could have brought him into training camp. But at the last moment,

Houston merged with the New Jersey Generals' franchise, and the combined team decided to keep McNeil. His NFL debut would have to wait. But that was something McNeil was used to.

Growing up in Killeen, Texas, just outside Houston, McNeil, the son of a career Army man, watched his older brother Pat excel on the gridiron in high school and longed for the day when it would be his turn. When that time came, his brother's success carried over. Pat had gone on to play in college at Baylor then had brief NFL stints with the Kansas City Chiefs and New England Patriots before completing his career in the Canadian Football League. Gerald McNeil's high school coaches overlooked Gerald's small size (he was just 5'7", 145 pounds in his first year in Cleveland) and focused on the talent that they hoped ran in the family. That philosophy carried over to the collegiate level, and McNeil followed his brother to Baylor and landed a scholarship. If Gerald could mirror Pat's success, it appeared the sky was the limit.

But his career hit a major obstacle upon his first medical examination at Baylor. He was diagnosed with scoliosis, curvature of the spine, a condition that his hometown doctors had missed all his life. The problem did account for some of McNeil's diminished size. Without it, he probably would have been two inches taller. Had it been caught when McNeil was twelve or thirteen, it could have been corrected. But by the time he was in college, it was a much more serious problem. He was sent to Houston for X-rays and warned he may never again play football.

But the problem was eventually corrected, and he returned to the gridiron. He was relegated solely to returning punts his freshman year and proved to be good at it. "I've loved returning kicks since I was a little kid," he would say. "It is a fascinating experience because it gives you time to showcase your talents. Every time there is a punt, everybody in the stands looks back there. I love that feeling."

In his final college season, McNeil set Baylor single-season records with sixty-two catches for 1,034 yards and led the conference in receiving for the second straight year. Rather than trying to catch on with an NFL team, McNeil opted for the USFL. Despite the near-miss opportunity to jump to the NFL in the summer of 1985, Pat McNeil, now Gerald's agent, said his brother was still interested in Cleveland, and the deal wasn't done yet. They unsuccessfully tried to buy out McNeil's contract with the Gamblers/Generals but finally got their chance when the team released him in August of 1986, just before the league collapsed. He signed with the Browns less than a week later.

He quickly gained notoriety as the NFL's smallest player. Because of his presence, the Browns released Glen Young, who had led the AFC in kickoff returns in 1985, and McNeil beat out Herman Fontenot for the return jobs in training camp. In a slight parody of the Bears' mammoth William Perry, nicknamed "The Refrigerator" in 1985, Browns' punter Jeff Gossett nicknamed McNeil "Ice Cube." Partly because of his fractional size in comparison to Perry but also because "He's cool, he's slick, and he's small," according to Gossett.

"Every time Gerald gets his hands on the ball, I feel like we have a chance to go the distance," Schottenheimer said the week before the Detroit game. "He's very exciting and a tough, aggressive player with the ball in his hands."

It was just a matter of time, Browns' coaches figured, until the Ice Cube broke out of his tray. They were right, and it couldn't have come at a better time.

The first person to greet McNeil wasn't a teammate or even an official. It was Browns' special teams coach Bill Cowher, who had run alongside McNeil down the Cleveland sideline, then leapt over a band of photographers to embrace his returner in the end zone. It was just a typical reaction for the fiery twenty-nine-year-old coach from Pittsburgh who was just beginning what would become an outstanding coaching career.

After putting together solid careers as a linebacker at Carlynton High School and North Carolina State (where he played under Lou Holtz his first three years), Cowher cracked the NFL when he was signed as an undrafted free agent by the Philadelphia Eagles in 1979. After being the last linebacker to get cut in training camp, Cowher sat out the 1979 season, then he was signed by the Browns in 1980 and played a key role as backup linebacker on the Kardiac Kids division-champion team. A preseason knee injury wiped out Cowher's 1981 season, but he got a chance for more playing time a year later when Clay Matthews broke his ankle in the 1982 opener and was shelved for most of the season. The fifty-seven-day players' strike, however, wiped out much of Cowher's opportunity, and the Browns traded him to Philadelphia the following year for a ninth-round draft choice.

Cowher made a big impact on the Eagles' special teams in 1983 and was even named the unit's MVP at season's end. But a serious knee injury limited his playing time in 1984 and eventually brought his career to a close. Looking back, the injury may have actually been the best thing that could have happened to Cowher.

"When Bill played here," Marty Schottenheimer said, "I told him that if I were ever in the position to hire someone, and he was available, he would be one of the first people I contacted. There was a lot of joking and kidding about it at the time, but I meant it."

There was no joking about Cowher's dedication and intelligence as a player. He had scars on his chin from splitting it open several times in college, and he always played with reckless abandon. Off the field, though, he was intelligent and articulate. He played chess with teammates on long flights. During the players' strike, he put his education degree to use and worked as a substitute teacher. Even then, it was clear Cowher's future was not on the field, but on the sideline.

True to his word, when Schottenheimer was looking to fill the Browns' special teams coaching position after the 1984 season, he called Cowher. He took the job and became the second-youngest assistant coach in the NFL. His task would be a daunting one: take one of the worst special teams units in the league and turn it into the best. Yet he made immediate strides in his first year. The 1985 Browns went from worst to first in the NFL in kickoff coverage, and the kickoff-return team became one of the most consistent in the league. In the season finale, Brian Brennan became the first Brown to return a punt for a touchdown in eighteen years, and the Browns did not have a punt or field goal blocked all season.

This success was due not only to Cowher's intelligence and teaching skills but also because of his passion and enthusiasm for the game. During his first *preseason* game as a coach, Cowher paced up and down the sideline barking instructions and encouragement to his players. "I just gave Bill one rule," Schottenheimer said, "'Don't ever run over me on the sideline, or you're going to be in trouble.'" When a play ended, Cowher would sprint out onto the field to praise or correct. He told the members of Cleveland's "kamikaze squad" that playing on special teams was like wearing a badge of honor. "The players have great respect for Bill, because he's been there," Schottenheimer said.

Because of Cowher's passion and McNeil's talent, the Browns had saved the 1986 season.

McNeil's touchdown seemed to breathe life into the Browns, both offensively and defensively. The running game, which had been invisible in the first half, finally got going, and the defense got hot. The Browns hung on for a much-needed 24-21 win to even their record at 2-2. It wasn't pretty, but compared to falling to 1-3 and 0-2 at home, it was a masterpiece.

Now the Browns would try to experience that winning feeling for the first time ever at Three Rivers Stadium. Thwarted there sixteen straight times, including losses by last-minute field goals each of the previous two seasons, many Browns' fans thought this was the year.

The Steelers, now clearly in a swoon after its Steel Curtain dynasty from 1972 through 1979 and its aftermath of contending teams from 1980 through 1984, were 1-3, had been outscored 98-39, and were going nowhere fast. "Indeed, if the Browns don't win at Three Rivers this year, they never will," *Browns News/Illustrated* editor Ray Yannucci wrote, "because this has to be the worst Pittsburgh team since the doors opened at that dreaded stadium."

But perhaps the primary reason for this newfound confidence was Cleveland radio personality Pete Franklin. In June, he told Marty Schottenheimer he had nothing to worry about this year. Franklin would be attending his first Browns-Steelers game in Pittsburgh, and the week before, he guaranteed the Browns would win. "Since everything else has failed, I believe it's my duty for the good of the team and the good of the city," Franklin said. "I will allow my presence to infiltrate and add to the confidence of the team." He pointed out the only other time he'd made such a prediction, it had worked. In 1977, Franklin hyped up an Indians' doubleheader with New York as "I Hate the Yankees/Pete Franklin Day." The Tribe soundly swept the Yankees.

Adding to his entertaining heroics, Franklin endorsed a rap song written to inspire the Browns to victory titled, appropriately, "Break the Jinx." He played it over and over on his daily talk show. At the least, it was better than switching hotels or throwing dirt on the field or consulting Elizabeth the Witch.

Cleveland took an early 10-0 lead, and then let it slip away. A pair of fumbles led to two Pittsburgh scores and a 14-10 Steeler lead. With momentum clearly in the Steelers' favor and their previously sour home crowd now rocking, it was starting to look like a typical Browns' game at Three Rivers.

But for the second straight week, Gerald McNeil changed everything. He took Gary Anderson's ensuing kickoff at the goal line and sprinted forward, angling to his left. He got key blocks near the twenty-five and exploded through the subsequent hole. After that, it was just a matter of avoiding the kicker. Anderson made a diving attempt at McNeil near midfield but missed, and the Ice Cube sprinted the final 50 yards untouched. The Cube had iced the Steelers for a 100-yard kickoff return, the Browns' first for a touchdown since Greg Pruitt had done it in 1974. The Browns held their 17-14 lead to halftime.

But as quickly as McNeil became a hero, he turned into a goat, fumbling a punt early in the third quarter. The Steelers cashed in to take the lead back and hung on to a 24-20 advantage early in the fourth quarter. But a Steeler fumble led to an Earnest Byner touchdown and a Cleveland lead.

With time running out, Bahr was called on for a chip-shot, 24-yard field goal that would at least prevent the Steelers from tying the game with a field goal in the final minutes. Somehow, though, Bahr missed the kick. It was his first miss inside of 30 yards in four years, after making forty straight. "Just par for the course for this place," Ozzie Newsome would say later. High above the field in the press box, a stunned Pete "The Prophet" Franklin vocalized what Browns' fans had believed for sixteen years: "This place is haunted."

The Steelers seemed to be following the Three Rivers Jinx script, driving into Cleveland territory. Yet the Browns had a feeling that something was about to happen. For the veterans, it was time to change the "Oh-no-not-again" mentality. "After the missed field goal and when they started getting some first downs, you didn't mean to, but were just kind of looking around like, 'God, this is the way it's happened in the past,'" Cody Risien said. "But we just kept saying, 'No, no, not this year, not this year.'"

"It seemed like they were going to the same end zone as the last five years," Clay Matthews said. "It was time for a change. We were going to do something big to stop what they have done for so many years." Appropriately, Matthews, who had lost at Three Rivers more than anyone else on the defense, would be involved in the play that ripped the script in half.

On a bizarre playcall that saw Mark Malone running the option, the Pittsburgh quarterback was pounded at the line of scrimmage by Sam Clancy and fumbled. Ernest Jackson tried to pick the ball up, but as he did, he was hit violently by Matthews, and the ball came loose again. This time, Browns' safety Chris Rockins recovered at the Cleveland twenty-nine yard line. And after a gutsy 38-yard completion from Kosar to Reggie Langhorne, Kosar knelt out the final thirty-one seconds, and, at 4:12 P.M. on October 5, 1986, the Three Rivers Jinx officially ended.

A sixteen-year burden was suddenly gone from the Browns' backs. It was a victory not only for the 1986 team but for all the good Browns' teams and players who had fought so hard and come so close at Three Rivers in the past, only to come up short. "The feeling will hit when I wake up in the morning," said Ozzie Newsome, a victim of eight losses in Pittsburgh. "That's when the losses would always hit me."

After his radio broadcast was over, Doug Dieken, who lost at Three Rivers fifteen times as a member of the Browns, found Art Modell, cracked open a beer and handed it to him. "We're going to have a toast," Dieken said.

And with good reason. The Browns had gone down to Three Rivers and, as Pete Franklin's rap song predicted they'd do, finally beat those finks.

Riding the emotional coattails of their historic victory in Pittsburgh, the Browns obliterated the Kansas City Chiefs seven days later, 20-7. The angry Browns' defense, ranked dead last in the NFL in rushing yards allowed, put together its finest game not only of the season but of recent history. Five weeks of mediocre play erupted into a sterling performance, holding Kansas City to a mere 126 total yards of offense, 83 passing and 43 rushing, the best day for a Browns' defense since 1973.

With all three facets of the team contributing, it was the best game of the season for the Browns, who completely dominated a team that would wind up going 10-6 and making the playoffs. "I think finally coming up with an easy win like today means this team is starting to mature a little bit," Newsome said afterward. Most importantly, everyone involved with the team breathed a sigh of relief as the defense finally played up to the level expected of it for the past two years.

And that week, Browns' fans were once again beginning to think about the realistic possibilities of a division championship. Cleveland had endured what was thought to be the toughest stretch of the schedule and come out of it at 4-2, tied with the Bengals for first place. With "easy" games coming up against sub-par clubs like perennial also-ran Minnesota, winless Indianapolis, struggling Miami, then the Steelers and Oilers again in Cleveland, many fans envisioned a double-digit victory total by the end of November. And to kick off this cupcake parade, the Browns would host what was widely viewed as the worst team in the NFL, the 0-6 Green Bay Packers.

Everything seemed to be unfolding naturally on a cool, sun-splashed autumn afternoon on the lakefront. The Browns, thirteen-point favorites, built a 14-3 halftime lead on a pair of Kosar touchdown passes. With the Cleveland defensive line dominant for the second straight week, a blowout appeared imminent. But storm clouds were gathering. In addition to several missed opportunities, Earnest Byner was carried off the field just before the half with a severely sprained ankle. Early reports didn't indicate with certainty how serious the injury was, but with the Cleveland running game struggling before Byner left, it simply imploded afterward.

The tone for the second half was set on the Packers' first possession, as they drove 84 yards and made it 14-10. Two series later, speedy wideout Phillip Epps split a seam down the middle of the Cleveland secondary and caught a 47-yard touchdown pass from Randy Wright to give the Packers a 17-14 lead with a minute left in the third quarter.

Though it had been out-coached, the Cleveland defense was not the team's primary problem. The offense was non-existent in the second half. Without Byner to worry about, the Packers zeroed in on Mack, and he finished with just 41 yards on sixteen carries. As a team, the Browns accumulated just 32 rushing yards for the game on twenty-two carries, a downright embarrassing one-and-a-half-yards-per-carry average. Yet despite their troubles running, the Browns never opened up the offense and allowed Kosar to air it out. His longest completion of the second half was 12 yards. Consequently, the Browns' first four possessions of the second half ended in punts. The last two were no better, both ending when the Browns failed on fourth down in Green Bay territory. The Packers melted the clock to clinch their first victory of the season.

The Browns, and the 76,438 who had paid hard-earned money to witness this game, were stunned. A cacophony of boos and derogatory remarks flowed from the stands down to the team as it exited the field. It appeared the Browns' three-game winning streak and all the optimism that the fans had held were simply mirages. "The Browns didn't do anything overwhelmingly stupid or disgraceful," the *Plain Dealer*'s Bob Dolgan wrote. "They simply are not that good a football team."

If nothing else, they appeared to be a miserably coached football team. Even with Byner out, the Browns seemed hell-bent on running the football. Kosar completed twenty-eight of thirty-six passes, but only for 222 yards, evidence of a short and ineffective passing game. "I'm a believer you have to throw [upfield] to stretch the defense," Kosar said. "Today we didn't do that. It was in the game plan, but we just didn't get to it."

With the running attack dead as a doornail and the passing game locked in the closet, the Browns' offense had suddenly become the stuff of Greek tragedy.

And the future, which had looked so bright such a short time before, now appeared as bleak as a Cleveland November. The 4-3 Browns trailed the 5-2 Bengals in the Central Division and would now have to hit the road for two straight dome games. Next up were the Minnesota Vikings, once a milquetoast also-ran but now 5-2. The Vikings had defeated the last two Super Bowl champions (San

Francisco and Chicago) in back-to-back weeks. And after losing to the Packers at home, the "easy" game in Indianapolis a week later now seemed anything but, and division games against Pittsburgh and Houston, whom the Browns had been lucky to beat early in the year, loomed afterward.

Once again, the bottom was about to fall out on the 1986 season.

Hard as it was to believe, by halftime the following Sunday, things were even worse. In a case of football nature taking its course, the blundering Browns trailed the red-hot Minnesota Vikings in the Metrodome, 17-3.

From the get-go, the game was a living nightmare. Bernie Kosar, whom the Vikings were poised to draft eighteen months earlier only to be rebuffed when he chose to go to the supplemental draft, was booed loudly during the player introductions. The Cleveland defense looked sluggish. Conversely, without Earnest Byner, Cleveland's already-struggling running game managed just 39 rushing yards in the first two quarters, and the Browns compiled a mere 55 total yards of offense as Bernie Kosar was sacked four times. Worse, it appeared this would be a trend the team would have to get used to. After further examination earlier in the week, Byner's injury was deemed more serious than initially thought. Rather than just a sprained ankle, doctors discovered Byner had suffered ligament damage and would miss the remainder of the season. Doctors conjectured he might be able to return for the second round of the playoffs if the Browns made it that far—a downright laughable theory by halftime in Minnesota.

With the Browns apparently about to drop back to .500 at the midpoint of the season, it appeared the team was running in place. With a loss in Minnesota, the Browns would fall to 4-4 on the season, 12-12 over the past two seasons, and an even 16-16 in Marty Schottenheimer's tenure. The overall team statistics at the midpoint of 1986 were no better than they'd been halfway through 1985. The defense was arguably worse and the one thing the Browns were good at in 1985—running the ball—they could no longer do. As the third quarter began in the Metrodome, you could hear taps being played in the background for the 1986 Browns.

But as they had done twice before, the Cleveland special teams once again stepped in to salvage the season. After the Vikings were stopped on their first possession of the third quarter, Frank Minnifield blocked a punt and Felix Wright returned it 30 yards for a touchdown. Bill Cowher's kamikaze unit had once again turned a game that had been sliding out of control back into the Browns' favor. And they weren't done yet.

With 8:34 to play and Minnesota ahead 20-13, the Browns' D. D. Hoggard downed a Jeff Gossett punt at the Minnesota two yard line, putting the home team in a field-position hole it couldn't get out of. Moments later, after a bad punt, the Browns took over at the Minnesota thirty-seven with just over five minutes to play. Four plays later, Curtis Dickey, finally getting the playing time he

the week before, cut back inside for a 17-yard touchdown run that tied
t at twenty with 4:23 remaining. Things got even better on the ensuing
en Travis Tucker stripped Rufus Bess of the football, and Felix Wright
gain in the right place at the right time to recover the football at the
twenty-one yard line. Thanks solely to their special teams the Browns
were suddenly in a position to win a game in which they'd been completely outplayed. The Cleveland offense kept things close to the vest, handing off six straight
times and melting the clock. The Browns then settled for a 22-yard Matt Bahr field
goal to take the lead with 1:46 left. But naturally, the game wasn't over yet.

The Vikings drove from their own twenty-four yard line to the Cleveland
twenty-eight in the next minute-and-a-half. With twelve seconds remaining, the
Vikings called on Chuck Nelson to attempt a 45-yard field goal that, if good,
would send the contest to overtime. But instead, Frank Minnifield once again
broke through the line from the left side and got four fingers on the kick. It spun
wildly over the line of scrimmage and landed 20 yards short of the goalpost, seal-
ing a desperately needed Browns' victory.

Dominant special-teams play was becoming a trademark of the 1986 Browns,
echoed by the fact that seventeen of the Browns' twenty-three points on this day
came directly from the third unit. "I think the team has taken on the character of
the special teams," Bill Cowher said. "When you look at what happens after the
special teams make a big play, it changes the momentum."

"In my eighteen years of playing football," Ozzie Newsome said after the
Vikings game, "I have never seen a special team contribute so much." Without the
special teams, the Browns never would have been able to overcome their 396-199
deficit in total yards, nor their seventy-four-to-fifty-four offensive-play disadvantage. "I think what we do is a tribute to Bill Cowher," Wright said. "He keeps us
motivated, and he never lets us let down. We perform for him because we like
him."

It did appear that once again, the 1986 Browns had turned a corner. If nothing
else, they forced a tie atop the AFC Central with the Bengals, who had been
blown out in Pittsburgh. "If the Browns go on to important things this season,"
Bob Dolgan wrote in that Monday's *Plain Dealer*, "they will remember yesterday's
game as the fork in the road which made it possible."

As it happened, Marty Schottenheimer would one day call the victory in Minnesota the turning point not only for 1986 Browns but also for his head coaching career.

Sure, the Browns had come from two touchdowns down to defeat an up-and-
coming playoff contender on the road, but their next game appeared to be an
even greater challenge. For the second time in three weeks, Cleveland would have
to play a team that had yet to win a game. At 0-8, the Indianapolis Colts were
having a nightmarish, mind-numbing season.

Ironically, many felt worse when the Browns surged to a 14-3 halftime lead at the Hoosier Dome, the same advantage they'd held over the Packers at the intermission. But the difference between the second half against Green Bay and the second half in Indianapolis was the outcome of the first series of the third quarter. The Packers drove right down the field and scored to set the tone for the second half. This time, Browns' safety Ray Ellis stripped Colts' tight end Pat Beach of the football on the third play of the third quarter, and linebacker Anthony Griggs recovered at the Indy thirty-eight yard line. Six plays later, Kosar hit Ozzie Newsome for a nine-yard touchdown pass, and the Browns were in the clear for a 24-9 victory. They remained tied for first with Cincinnati, victors in Detroit.

For the next seven days, revenge was all the Browns could talk about. Their next game was a rematch with the floundering Miami Dolphins, who had rallied from an eighteen-point deficit to ruin the Browns' impossible dream of a playoff upset ten months earlier. This time, Dan Marino and the Dolphins would travel north to Cleveland for a showdown on *Monday Night Football,* and the game consumed Cleveland sports fans all week. Hanford Dixon eschewed his preseason commitment to toning down the whole "Dog" thing and asked the fans to come out barking. Just before kickoff on what would become a chilly November night, Dixon and several of his defensive teammates ran over to the bleachers and energized the Dog Pound. Like any Monday-night game in Cleveland, there was electricity in the air, felt by the sellout throng of 77,949. And for the first time in a long time, Browns' fans weren't disappointed with the result of a big game.

For the first time, Schottenheimer and Lindy Infante decided to let their young quarterback loose. With Byner out and the Cleveland running game virtually non-existent, Infante opened up the playbook and structured the game plan around the passing attack, including starting the game with a four-wideout formation. But as the first quarter rolled on, Infante made some changes. The air attack was so successful, Kosar wound up throwing even more often than intended.

The first half was an offensive clinic put on not by the heralded Miami passing attack but by the suddenly unstoppable Cleveland offense. By halftime, the Browns had accumulated 351 yards, an astounding total considering their season-high total for a *game* to that point was only 356. Kosar had completed twenty of thirty-three passes for 275 yards, already his best game of the season, and the Browns led, 16-10. Despite their receivers dropping four potential touchdown passes, the Browns coasted in the second half, thanks to a red-hot Kosar and an inspired defense playing like it had something to prove after letting the Dolphins come back to win the playoff game.

The Browns were victorious, 26-16, and stood at 7-3, all alone in first place after the Bengals had fallen in Houston the day before, and had gained some valuable self-confidence along the way. "People around the league have to respect us now," said linebacker Eddie Johnson. "And we want respect. Everyone now will realize how good we are and how good we're capable of being."

The final score may not have been overwhelming, but the Browns' offensive statistics were. Cleveland racked up 558 total yards, including a season-high 168 on the ground, paced by Curtis Dickey's 92 yards on fifteen carries. "If this were a fight," MNF broadcaster Frank Gifford said at one point, "they might have stopped it." Make no mistake, the home team had both earned revenge and sent a message. "It was as if the Browns were thumbing their noses at the world," Ray Yannucci wrote.

The obvious star of the day was Kosar, who completed thirty-two of fifty passes for 401 yards, including six completions of 15 yards or more and three for more than 20. It was just the third time in team history a quarterback had topped the 400-yard mark, and the performance tied Kosar with Otto Graham for the second-best passing yardage day in Browns' history. Kosar, who would be named AFC Offensive Player of the Week, hit eight different receivers. After two months of trying to find an identity, the Browns had discovered it in no uncertain terms. "For one night anyway, they seem to have realized that telling Kosar to hand off is like telling Pavarotti to sing in the shower," Bill Livingston wrote in the *Plain Dealer*. Bob Dolgan added: "He may be at the point Albert Einstein was while studying arithmetic at age eight, a prodigy headed for immortality."

And the Browns were looking more and more like a team headed for the playoffs. "The next couple weeks will be interesting to see what happens," Kosar said. "We started something special Monday night."

It didn't come as a surprise to many Browns' fans that something special was delayed for a week. After an emotional Monday-night victory at home, which alone can be a recipe for a lousy performance the following week, the Browns would have to travel across the continent to face the Los Angeles Raiders six days later. What followed only seemed natural. Cleveland, nine-point underdogs, played hard, but was just outclassed by a veteran team that had to win to stay alive in the playoff chase. Spearheaded by a bloodthirsty pass rush that beat up Kosar all afternoon, the Raiders won, 27-14, dropping the Browns to 7-4, tied with Cincinnati for first.

Five games remained, and the Bengals had the tougher schedule going into the Browns' highly anticipated December 14 showdown in Cincinnati. All things considered, the Browns were in good shape.

But over the next five weeks, they would get even better.

9 Storming In

The Browns would now have a chance to do something they hadn't done in seventeen years, something they hadn't done since Bernie Kosar was six years old: sweep the hated Pittsburgh Steelers.

But it wouldn't come easy. The Steelers had improved since their first meeting, and defensive coordinator Tony Dungy studied what the Los Angeles Raiders had done to Kosar and the Cleveland offensive line the week before and planned to do the same: blitz like crazy and hope to beat Kosar to a pulp.

It wasn't a bad idea. It was just that Kosar spent much of the afternoon making it look like one.

The Steelers stunned the wired crowd of 76,452 by marching 75 yards on their first possession and taking a 7-0 lead. The Browns tied the game on a short Curtis Dickey touchdown run then took the lead after a Mark Harper interception that led to a Kevin Mack score. But two minutes later, the Steelers pulled back into another tie when running back Walter Abercrombie took a pitch around right end and escaped for a 38-yard touchdown run. The shootout was on.

Kosar, two days shy of his twenty-third birthday, was heating up and burned a desperate Pittsburgh blitz from the Steeler twenty-one by hitting a ridiculously wide-open Ozzie Newsome over the middle for perhaps the easiest touchdown in NFL history. The Browns' 21-14 lead held up until halftime.

Despite Kosar's ability to consistently make the Pittsburgh defense look silly, both teams seemed to be on the same wavelength. The Browns' offense was afire, but Mark Malone and Pittsburgh were hanging in there. Both defenses were underachieving. All the elements were in place for one of the most memorable matchups in the history of one of the NFL's fiercest rivalries.

The Steelers tied the game again on their first possession of the second half, but as he had all day, Kosar answered with a drive of his own, capped by a Dickey touchdown late in the third quarter. The Steelers rallied to tie the game at twenty-eight, and with just over eight minutes to play, the sellout crowd was beginning to get nervous. The Browns allayed their fears with a Matt Bahr field goal with 1:51 to play. Little did anyone know it would be a year before Bahr kicked another.

On the ensuing kickoff, Pittsburgh's Lupe Sanchez found daylight, and it was up to Bahr to prevent a touchdown. The Browns' tiny kicker, a lifelong soccer player, did the right thing by getting in front of Sanchez and knocking him down, but Bahr didn't lead with his shoulders on the tackle. Instead, he just threw himself at Sanchez sideways. Sanchez ran into Bahr's right leg and lost his balance. Sanchez went down at the Pittsburgh thirty-nine, but his return had changed the complexion of the game. The Steelers now had good field position to begin a potential game-winning or game-tying drive. On top of that, the collision tore cartilage in Bahr's right knee. His season was over. The Browns now found themselves with a precarious three-point lead with less than two minutes to play and no kicker. The plot would continue to thicken.

As he had all day, Mark Malone moved his offense when he needed to. With eleven seconds remaining and Pittsburgh at the Browns' twenty-three yard line, Chuck Noll called on Gary Anderson, who calmly hit a 40-yard field goal to tie the game once again at 31-31 with seven ticks left. The Browns and Steelers were going to overtime—one with one of the best kickers in NFL history, the other with no kicker at all.

The Browns won the coin toss, and as they took the field for the kickoff, backup tight end Harry Holt began warming up on the sideline wearing a large, black, square-toed shoe on his right foot. Looking like a combination of Lou Groza and a rhinoceros, the 240-pound Holt, who had handled kickoff duties in his days in the Canadian Football League, practiced kicking straight-ahead style into a net. Browns' fans across the nation held their heads in their hands and hoped it wouldn't come down to the foot of their backup tight end.

After an exchange of punts to open overtime, Kevin Mack pushed the Browns into Pittsburgh territory, and a key third-down completion to Herman Fontenot kept the drive alive.

On the next play from the Pittsburgh thirty-seven, as he had done all day, Kosar waltzed up to the line of scrimmage, read the defense, and called an audible, signaling to Webster Slaughter that he should forsake the route he was going to run and simply go deep.

Kosar pump-faked, then lofted a high, arching pass down the sideline. Slaughter caught it at the Pittsburgh ten, and coasted into the end zone. Just like that, the Browns had won, 37-31. The sellout crowd reveled in an eruption of sound not heard since the storybook days of the Kardiac Kids.

And why not? The Browns' offense had just put on a clinic. Cleveland racked up 536 total yards, the most ever gained against a Pittsburgh defense. They picked up thirty-five first downs. Nine different receivers caught passes, an astounding number considering the Steelers generally had five linebackers on the field. But with a bevy of talented wideouts, the Browns won the chess match. Combined, the teams threw seventy-four passes and collected 880 total yards and fifty-five first downs. It may not have been a football purist's cup of tea, but for fans, it was everything you could possibly ask for.

But the most impressive individual performance was the show put on by Bernie Kosar. Somehow, he'd made his career night against Miami two weeks before look inferior. He completed twenty-eight of forty-six passes for 414 yards and two touchdowns. It was the second-best passing yardage day in Browns' history, trailing only Brian Sipe's 444-yard performance in 1981, and marked the first time in NFL history a quarterback had two 400-yard passing games before his twenty-third birthday.

Marty Schottenheimer called Kosar's performance "remarkable." Dungy's game plan had been shattered by what many now considered to be the most intelligent quarterback in the NFL. "If they wanted to blitz, Bernie made them pay," Ozzie Newsome said. "You just can't disguise coverages against Bernie. He's incredibly intelligent for twenty-two years old."

And he'd now done something that no Browns' quarterback had done in nearly two decades—he'd led the team to a season sweep of the Pittsburgh Steelers, eliminating Cleveland's bitter rival from playoff contention with the second-best quarterback performance in team history.

It wasn't a bad twenty-third birthday for Bernie Kosar.

Before the Browns could even turn their attention to their next game—another AFC Central showdown in Cleveland Thanksgiving weekend with a struggling team, the Houston Oilers—they had to find a kicker. By the time the Steelers' game had ended, Marty Schottenheimer had been informed that Bahr would be out for the year. Now a team fighting for a division title and playoff berth would need to go kicker shopping.

The Browns eventually signed Mark Moseley, who was nearing the end of what had been an amazing NFL career. In fifteen seasons, thirteen with the Washington Redskins, Moseley had made 294 field goals and 469 extra points. He held NFL records for most consecutive field goals made (twenty-three), highest made percentage in a season (.952) and most points in a season (161). The first two records had been set in 1982, when Moseley became the only kicker to ever be named NFL MVP.

But for all his charm and all the records he held, could the Browns depend on Moseley?

"No matter how many years of experience you have, coaches have to feel comfortable with you," he said that week. "A playoff-contending team needs someone who won't choke. I'm not going to kick 60-yard field goals, but I'm not going to choke."

History backed up that statement. Another record Moseley held was most game-winning field goals: seventeen in the final four minutes with the game on the line, including four in overtime.

Ironically, Moseley would get a chance to add to that record right off the bat.

It was a typically cold day in Cleveland the last day of November, but it was also very windy. So much so that quarterbacks often released the ball simply hoping, not knowing, it would get to their receivers. Conversely, receivers felt like a baseball catcher behind the plate with a knuckleball pitcher on the mound. They had no idea which way the ball would spin or twist while it was in the air battling the Lake Erie winds. New kid on the block Mark Moseley called them the worst conditions he'd ever seen in Cleveland. Obviously, there would be no 400-yard passing games on this day.

It was as frustrating a game as either team had played all year. Both offenses were crippled by the wind and weren't always opportunistic when they did have scoring chances. The Oilers took an early 3-0 lead, but the Browns surged ahead on a Kosar-to-Brian Brennan touchdown pass early in the fourth quarter. Moseley's first Cleveland field goal made it 10-3 with 5:46 to play. Victory seemed probable.

But the Oilers drove 73 yards and tied the game with fifty seconds remaining. Incredibly, for the second straight week, the Browns were headed for overtime. But this week, it was the Cleveland defense that saved the day. Twice Frank Minnifield halted a Houston drive with an interception, the second of which set up Cleveland's final chance to win in a long, fruitless overtime. The Browns drove to the Houston nine yard line, melted some clock, and then called on the field-goal unit with sixteen seconds remaining. The league's oldest kicker calmly walked out onto the field, lined up, and booted the game-winner. Welcome to Cleveland, Mark Moseley.

Capitalizing on his chance, he had helped the Browns become just the second NFL team to win overtime games in back-to-back weeks. Cleveland was now 9-4, and after the Denver Broncos hung on for a 34-28 triumph over the Bengals later that afternoon at Mile High Stadium, the Browns had first place all to themselves. As hard as it was for some to believe, the Browns were on the brink of clinching a playoff spot.

They took another step a week later with a gritty 21-17 victory in Buffalo, a game played through a cold winter rain. Meanwhile, the Bengals' hearts were in Foxboro, Massachusetts, where they slapped around the red-hot New England Patriots in a 31-7 triumph. The Browns still had a shot to make the playoffs as a Wild Card, but their best and most direct route to the playoffs would be to win the division by beating the Bengals, ensuring a week off before entering the postseason and possibly a home game.

After the game, former college teammates Jim Kelly, now the Bills' starting quarterback, and Bernie Kosar shook hands at midfield and caught up. Kelly asked Kosar if he was going to the Fiesta Bowl on January 2 to watch the Hurricanes play Penn State for the national championship. "I think I'll be busy," Kosar replied.

The 10-4 Browns could now completely concentrate on the biggest regular-season game for the franchise in six years. In fact, the similarities between this big game and the franchise's last one were eerie.

On December 21, 1980, the Browns played the Cincinnati Bengals at Riverfront Stadium in the season finale with everything at stake. A Cleveland victory, which would be the team's eleventh of the season, would give it the AFC Central Division title and a playoff berth. A defeat would end its season. On December 14, 1986, the Browns would once again travel south to face the Bengals, though this time in Week Fifteen. Again, a Browns' win (their eleventh) would give them the division title and a playoff berth. While a loss may not necessarily eliminate the team's postseason hopes, it would severely cripple them. The main difference between 1980 and 1986 was the caliber of competition. In 1980, the Bengals were improving, still a year away from being a Super Bowl team, but stood at just 6-9. In 1986, with a high-powered offense, Cincinnati was 9-5 and already a championship contender.

Another difference was the fervor in Cleveland itself. In 1980, the city was intoxicated with the Browns, living and dying on every snap of the charismatic and entertaining-as-hell Kardiac Kids. But, seeming to remember the heartbreak that team eventually produced and the five years of mediocrity in between, battle-tested Cleveland fans were still waiting to be convinced that the 1986 Browns were legitimate. "The 1980 gang won with sabres and daggers between their teeth," Bob Dolgan wrote in the *Plain Dealer*. "These guys do it with a pick and a shovel."

Fans of both teams had pointed to this game for weeks. Even the city's respective mayors got into the act. If the Bengals won, Cincinnati's Charles Luken would receive a case of kielbasa ("Whatever that is," Luken remarked) from Cleveland's George Voinovich, and if the Browns won, Luken would provide two cases of Skyline Chili.

It was, without a doubt, the biggest game for both teams in the sixteen-year history of the Battle of Ohio. "War," Hanford Dixon replied when asked what the game would be like. "It's going to be a war."

"Call it a showdown, call it whatever you want," Marty Schottenheimer added. "This is what it's all about."

The seventeen-point loss to Cincinnati on national television in September had become something of a rallying cry for the Browns, who claimed to have improved more than the Bengals since then, winning nine of their next eleven games. "That's what pissed me off more than anything," Dixon continued. "They came to our place and totally embarrassed us. But I guarantee you, that's not going to happen again. We owe them something."

Bengals' coach Sam Wyche begged to differ. Thanks to Wyche's wide-open offensive philosophies, Cincinnati boasted perhaps the most potent attack in football. But there was a down side to that ingenuity. Wyche had become a bit of a time bomb in the Bengals' locker room. After the Bengals' loss in Denver two weeks earlier, he'd ripped a microphone out of the hand of a radio reporter then later claimed he didn't remember doing it. He had on ongoing feud with his starting quarterback, Boomer Esiason, and was criticized for using a no-huddle, surprise-based offensive philosophy rather than just relying on his superior offensive talent. Rumors swirled in the Cincinnati media that Wyche might not return as coach for 1987, even though the Bengals had already clinched their first winning season in four years. Although both had enjoyed success in the NFL, Wyche and Marty Schottenheimer were as different as oil and water. And their teams reflected their respective pros and cons.

"Who would you really rather have as your general going into a big show-down?" The *Plain Dealer*'s Gene Williams asked. "Would you rather have an Eisenhower, a calm, cool, collected man whose glasses never fog up? Or would you prefer Patton, a wild and crazy guy who likes to play tricks with his talented offense and who just might lose his composure at any moment?"

Riverfront Stadium was ready. The sellout crowd of 58,062 (nearly 6,000 of which was made up of Browns' fans) was wired. A local radio station had handed out small cardboard megaphones with Bengal stripes on them called "Browns Blasters," encouraging the Cincinnati faithful to be as loud as possible. It was a clever idea that turned out to be nothing more than a tragic waste of trees.

Still, the Cincinnati faithful put their lungs to use as the Browns took the field for the first play of the biggest game of the season for both teams. They screamed and hollered at the Browns' goofy looking quarterback and their overrated offense. They chanted "Who dey think gonna beat dem Bengals?" They reveled in the memory of four straight Cleveland losses at Riverfront Stadium. This was their day.

Through the ruckus, the Browns broke the huddle and marched to the line of scrimmage. Kosar took the snap, dropped back to pass, then lofted a pass as soft as a Cincinnati sunrise down the right sideline for a wide-open Reggie Langhorne, who had blown past an unsuspecting Louis Breeden. Langhorne caught the pass over his shoulder at the Cincinnati twenty-seven yard line and glided down the sideline. Breeden finally caught up and dragged him down at the Bengals' two, but only after the play gained 66 yards.

The majority of the crowd hushed, stunned. But about 6,000 dressed in orange and brown exploded in a wave of surprise and relief. A play later, Kevin Mack scored to make it 7-0. With one play, the Browns had proven they'd come to win. The pressure would be on the Bengals to match it. The Cincinnati offense responded on its first possession, driving from its own nineteen to the Cleveland four. But the Browns' defense stiffened inside the five and forced the Bengals to settle for a short Jim Breech field goal. A shootout appeared imminent.

Instead, the offenses stalled. After an exchange of punts and a missed Moseley field goal, the Browns picked up a first down at the Bengal forty-five. Kosar pumped and lofted a long pass, this time down the left sideline, and Webster Slaughter caught it streaking into the end zone for a 46-yard touchdown. Moseley's extra point made it 14-3, Browns, with just over a minute to play in the first quarter. Cleveland could not have scripted the first fifteen minutes any better. And matters improved when the Bengals' offense still couldn't get going in the second period. A late Moseley field goal made it 17-3 at the half. George Voinovich could already taste his Skyline Chili. True enough, the second half was simply a refrain of the first.

The Browns added to their lead when a Felix Wright interception led to another Mack touchdown. The margin swelled to 31-3 after Slaughter recovered a Curtis Dickey fumble in the end zone. "This is the point they'd stop it on a TKO," NBC television announcer Don Criqui told his audience.

Another interception of Esiason, this one by Hanford Dixon, set up the Browns' final points, a 20-yard field goal by Moseley with 8:28 left in the game to make it 34-3. But most of the Bengals' faithful never saw it. The stream to the parking lot began forming late in the third quarter. By late in the fourth, only Browns' fans remained.

By virtue of the team's most lopsided big-game victory in decades, the Browns were AFC Central Division champions for the second straight year. "I can't remember, except for the 27-0 blowout of the Colts in the '64 championship game, a more convincing Browns' win in a game this meaningful, a game with so much on the line and against a quality opponent," Art Modell said. By contrast, it made the performance by the 1980 Browns in the season finale in Cincinnati pale just a bit. "I have never played against a more ferocious pass rush since coming to Cincinnati," Esiason said. "It's the most physical game I've played in as a pro."

"It was billed as the Battle of Ohio," wrote the *Cincinnati Enquirer*'s Mike Dodd. "For the Bengals, it was their Waterloo." Accordingly, the same radio station that handed out the "Browns Blasters" selected Ken Anderson as the Bengals' player of the game. Anderson entered the game on Cincinnati's last possession and completed one pass.

"We were out-hit, out-muscled, and out-played," Sam Wyche said. "I don't know how to explain it. We simply got our tails kicked all afternoon." The Browns had "legitimized themselves as (say this slowly, folks) Su-Su-Su-Super Bowl contenders," wrote Bill Livingston.

"We saved our best for last," Marty Schottenheimer said, then caught himself. "Well, not for last, but near last."

Just as had been the case after winning in Cincinnati six years earlier, the Browns had a bit of a welcome wagon waiting for them at Hopkins Airport that night. More than 3,000 crazed fans greeted their division champions and began what would become a month-long stretch of Browns' frenzy. "It was one small step for a team," Tony Grossi wrote in the *Plain Dealer*, "one giant leap for a franchise." Cleveland's general hesitation was gone. It was the Kardiac Kids, Part Two.

"I don't smoke," the often-critical Pete Franklin wrote in *Browns News/Illustrated.* "I don't drink. Folks, I'm high on the Browns."

Much was written and even more said about the Browns' resounding blow-out victory in the following days. But perhaps no one summed up the situation any better than Browns' strength coach Dave Redding. As a gaggle of reporters gathered outside the Cleveland locker room, waiting to enter to interview the triumphant division champions, Redding stopped before them on his way in.

"We kicked their ass!" he shouted.

That they had.

Consequently, the Browns' season finale at home against 4-11 San Diego a week later had the feel of the last day of school. With the Denver Broncos losing in Seattle on Saturday, the Browns had clinched home-field advantage throughout the AFC playoffs without buckling up their chinstraps. Players, coaches, and fans alike came to Cleveland Stadium more to have a good time and to celebrate the wonderful season they'd just experienced than to watch a football game. The Browns could rest their starters, get some bench players in, and win or lose, look forward to a week off and a home game in the divisional playoffs. Little did the fans know the Cleveland coaches had some holiday surprises in store.

The players received a standing ovation during the introduction of the starting lineups. A man dressed up as Santa Claus standing along the sideline received an ovation. The only time the crowd booed was when the attendance for the game was announced—a modest 68,505.

Rather than locking up the playbook and benching all their key players in fear of revealing something to their playoff foes, the Browns' coaches did the opposite. They opened up the playbook as it had never been opened before—and nearly split the binding in the process. There was a fake reverse on a kickoff return, a rarely-used five wide-receiver formation on offense, a fake wide-receiver reverse, and an end-around. Even the less-than-nimble Bernie Kosar broke loose for a 17-yard scramble. But the most pleasant surprise came on Cleveland's second possession of the game. Herman Fontenot took a handoff on a sweep around right end, then stopped and launched a pass for a wide-open Webster Slaughter at the goal line. Slaughter caught it for a 46-yard touchdown and a 7-0 lead. It was the first of many Cleveland trips to the end zone.

The Browns grabbed a 13-10 lead in the second quarter and were driving for more in the final minute of the half when Bernie Kosar was rushed out of the pocket at the Cleveland forty-three yard line. He rolled to his left then fired a long pass down the sideline for Brian Brennan. Brennan caught the pass and hit the ground at the Charger seven. But San Diego safety Vencie Glenn and cornerback Kevin Wyatt, whom Brennan had just burned to get open, had not touched Brennan while he was down. Realizing the play wasn't over, Brennan simply got back up and scampered the seven extra yards into the end zone, completing another unorthodox touchdown with six seconds left in the half. It was the play that symbolized the season for Brennan, who tallied a season-high seven catches for 176 yards on the day and finished his third season with fifty-five receptions for 838 yards, both team bests.

By the end of the third quarter, the game was well out of reach. Seventeen more Browns points made it 37-10, making the fourth quarter the football equivalent of a last-period study hall. The Browns added ten more points, including Mark Moseley's 300th career field goal, and won by a final count of 47-17. It was the most points the Browns had scored in eighteen years, with the team racking up 462 total yards of offense. Kosar, receiving nearly flawless protection once again from his line, completed twenty-one of twenty-eight passes for 258 yards, giving him 3,854 on the season, third-most in team history behind only Brian Sipe's totals in 1980 and 1981. And in case the Cleveland offensive line didn't already have motivation to protect Kosar, that week he'd given them another. He'd presented each member of the line with a case of imported champagne, a small thank-you for their efforts all season.

As the clock ticked down to zero, several Browns jogged toward the Dog Pound and made a victory lap in front of the bleachers, high-fiving fans as they went. Bob Golic even went airborne for an unforgettable high-five with a man dressed as Santa Claus. All things considered, it was the kind of day most football players never get to experience: a day full of fun, with the players publicly appreciating the fans and vice versa.

Once the streamers and confetti had settled on the Browns' Christmas party, several inspiring realities remained. The team had clinched a conference-best 12-4 record, the most wins in a season in team history. "The day I retire," Carl Hairston said, "I'll always remember being a part of the winningest Cleveland team in history."

Unlike a year before when the Browns stumbled backward into the playoffs, in 1986, they'd kicked in the postseason door like John Wayne entering a saloon. The Cleveland offense was on fire, and Bernie Kosar was beginning to look more and more like one of the league's finest quarterbacks. The defense had come around, the coaching was superb, and best of all, any AFC team wanting to get to the Super Bowl would have to win along the shores of Lake Erie to get there. "We're capable of greatness," Kosar said. "We're on a roll," Brennan added. "We feel unstoppable."

"It sounded impossible at the beginning of the year," Pete Franklin wrote, "but this team can make it to Pasadena."

There were few doubters of the Browns' legitimacy now. There may have been teams with more talent and teams that received more media attention. The Browns simply punched their time card, took the field, and won. They may have won ugly, they may have struggled against poor teams, but only one NFL team had a better record than they in 1986. In less than two years after starting the 1984 season 1-8 and firing their head coach, then twice changing their offensive phi-losophy with three different starting quarterbacks and four different starting run-ning backs, the Cleveland Browns had quietly and amazingly become a bona fide Super Bowl contender.

"The one thing that's important to me is we're always well-prepared," Schot-tenheimer said. "We may not be flashy, but we get the job done."

Clearly, this was a team for the city of Cleveland.

10 One Play at a Time

The differences between the Browns and the team they would face in the divisional playoffs were almost laughable. Not so much because the Browns were that much better, but because entering the month of January the teams were stark opposites in almost every imaginable way.

In mid-November, the New York Jets were the best team in football. They'd started the season 10-1 and were coasting toward the Super Bowl on a nine-game winning streak, during which the Jets outscored teams by a total of one hundred points. New York's offense was hot, demonstrated by its 51-45 overtime victory over the Miami Dolphins in Week Three, and its defense was also strong, led by the "New York Sack Exchange" on the line: Mark Gastineau, Marty Lyons, and Joe Klecko.

But the Jets fell apart—big time. They went into the Orange Bowl for a Week Twelve Monday-night showdown with the Dolphins that would have all but clinched the AFC East title for New York. Instead, Miami cleaned the Jets' clock, 45-3, and sent the team into a demoralizing, somewhat legendary tailspin. They lost their last five games by a combined score of 183-61, giving up more than forty-five points three different times, including a combined ninety-seven in the season's final two games. Not once in this stretch did the Jets finish within two touchdowns of their opponent.

Conversely, the Browns had shaken off a wobbly start to the season. While New York was losing its last five, Cleveland was winning its final five. Rather than contemplating yanking its starting quarterback, Bernie Kosar was looking more and more like one of the NFL's best with each passing week. And rather than collapsing because of a handful of key injuries, the Browns seemed to only get better, finding solutions elsewhere.

Despite the collapse, New York became the first NFL team to lose its final five games yet still make the playoffs. The Jets forfeited the AFC East title to New England (who clinched the division and prevented the Cincinnati Bengals from making the postseason with a victory in Miami in Week Sixteen), but secured the first Wild Card spot. The Jets' twenty-eighth-ranked pass defense earned a reprieve when it got to face the NFL's twenty-eighth-ranked offense in Kansas City in the first round of the playoffs. New York head coach Joe Walton benched ineffective quarterback Ken O'Brien for backup Pat Ryan, and Ryan directed the Jets to an impressive 35-15 triumph that led them to the Browns' doorstep.

Before even knowing which team the Browns would play, Cleveland fans were psyched for the team's first home playoff game since the infamous "Red Right 88" deep freeze with Oakland six years earlier. More than 40,000 tickets went on sale two days after the regular-season finale and were snatched up in less than two-and-a-half hours—a rate of 250 sold per minute. It was the hottest ticket in town since a Bruce Springsteen concert in August of 1985. The previous hesitancy of Clevelanders to jump on the Browns' bandwagon was long gone.

"Cleveland desperately needs a love affair that it hasn't had for some time," Art Modell said. "Once the affair starts, the fans respond. What has been the experience of this city is there have been tremendous letdowns."

Most notably the previously mentioned loss to Oakland that halted the dreams of the 1980 Kardiac Kids. "Red Right 88 was grounds for divorce in what had become one of sports' all-time romances," wrote Ray Yannucci. "The hurt would linger for years, wounding the heart like someone who had just been jilted by his high school sweetheart."

Naturally, comparisons were being made between this Browns' team and that one. The consensus seemed to be that while the Kardiac Kids were lightning in a bottle, the 1986 team was something more like a power plant. "There has to be a three-to-five year difference between the age of this team and the age of the 1980 team," said tight end Ozzie Newsome, a stalwart on both. "In 1980, guys had been around awhile. I think there is more talent on this team overall and definitely more depth. This team has endured more adversity. I would characterize 1980 as a Hollywood team. This is a blue-collar team. We just get it done."

And most expected they would once again get it done against the Jets. Las Vegas had made the Browns a seven-point favorite to advance to the AFC Championship to face either New England or Denver, who would lock horns in the other divisional playoff. On paper, the Jets were clearly in over their heads.

The first upset of the NFL postseason wasn't pulled off by a team, but rather by Mother Nature. Nearly six years to the day after the Browns and Raiders battled through a wind-chill factor of thirty-six below, the Browns and Jets took the field to sunny skies on a downright balmy thirty-four-degree afternoon. What's more, the oft-notorious field at Cleveland Stadium was in superb condition after two weeks of tender-loving care by groundskeepers. Whatever happened on Saturday, January 3, 1987, neither the weather nor the field would be a factor.

After the Browns were introduced to a nearly Richter-scale caliber ovation, they kicked off to the apparently overwhelmed Jets and succinctly forced a three-and-out. A short punt gave the Browns their initial possession at their own forty-four yard line, and they quickly marched into New York territory, but Mark Moseley missed a 46-yard field goal short. No matter, most of the capacity crowd of 78,106 thought. The first two possessions seemed to set the tone for what would be a Browns' Saturday on the lakefront.

But after the teams exchanged punts, the Jets begged to differ. After reaching the Cleveland forty-two, they dusted off the kind of trick play that had worked like a charm over the first eleven games of the season. Ryan pitched to Freeman McNeil on the right side, and McNeil stopped and tossed a lateral back to Ryan across the field. Ryan then flung a pass deep down the middle that Wesley Walker reeled in the end zone for a dipsy-doodle touchdown pass and a 7-0 New York lead. Things looked even better for the visitors when a blown kickoff coverage resulted in the Browns taking over at their own two yard line moments later.

But Bernie Kosar didn't even blink. He marched his offense into New York territory and at the thirty-seven, faked a handoff to Kevin Mack then a reverse to Reggie Langhorne, dropped back, and lofted a touch pass down the right sideline for Herman Fontenot. Fontenot caught it at the New York ten, then broke a tackle and toppled into the end zone for a 37-yard touchdown pass to tie the contest. The apparent shootout was on. But nether team could muster anything on their next few possessions. In fact, along the way Ryan aggravated a groin pull and was forced to the sideline, done for the day. The Jets were forced to turn back to their original quarterback, Ken O'Brien.

The Browns took over at midfield on their next possession and cashed in on the fortuitous field position when Moseley connected on a field goal to make it 10-7. The Jets, thanks in part to a 17-yard O'Brien scramble on fourth-and-five, tied the game just before halftime on a 46-yard field goal by Pat Leahy. The teams went into the locker room just as they'd come out: all knotted up.

After the Browns were unable to move on their first possession of the third quarter, the Jets took over at the Cleveland forty-one and drove for a Leahy field goal that put the Jets back on top, 13-10, five minutes into the third quarter. The Browns spoiled an opportunity to tie the contest on their next possession when Moseley missed a 44-yard field goal wide left, then crossed midfield but were eventually forced to punt on their next two series.

The Cleveland defense was hanging tough, not permitting the Jets to add to their lead. After a Carl Hairston sack sabotaged another New York drive, the Browns drove to the New York ten yard line. A pair of Mack runs brought the Browns to the two for third down. Rather than try to plow Mack forward for the final six feet, Lindy Infante called for a quick pass. Kosar didn't see anyone open and tried to toss the ball out of bounds but was hit as he whipped the pass. It floated short and was picked off in the end zone by Jets' cornerback Russell Carter. It was Kosar's first interception in 133 attempts.

The city of Cleveland groaned with a nauseous sense of déjà vu. High above the field in the press box, a frustrated Ray Yannucci shouted, "This damn team can't win a playoff game!" Browns' fans had been here before. And in case they had forgotten, when it returned from commercial, NBC reminded them, running a clip of Brian Sipe's infamous interception by Oakland safety Mike Davis in the opposite end zone, ending the Kardiac Kids' magnificent 1980 campaign. The network cameras then settled on a banner hanging from one of the Cleveland Stadium concourses which read: "No Red Right 88."

While the interception certainly hurt, costing the Browns a chance to at least tie the game, there was still plenty of football to play. The Browns would almost certainly get the ball back, and if the defense could just hang tough one more time and prevent the Jets from scoring, the home team would still have an excellent shot at pulling out a victory in what had become a surprisingly difficult game.

The Cleveland defense did its part, but not until the Jets had driven into Browns' territory and melted precious time off the clock. The Browns took over at their own seventeen with 4:31 to play, plenty of time for a final drive to clinch the team's first playoff victory in seventeen years.

Kosar dropped back to pass on first down and spotted Herman Fontenot in the right flat. He fired a pass toward him, but before Fontenot could reel it in, New York cornerback Jerry Holmes stepped in front of him, intercepted it, and hit the ground at the twenty-five. As the officials ran over to mark the spot, Holmes got up and, holding the football above his head, jogged down to the bleachers behind the end zone to taunt the Dog Pound.

Browns' fans had to feel like this was a signal proclaiming the end of the world. Kosar, who had not been picked off in his previous four games, had now thrown two on consecutive snaps, and the Browns were suddenly in serious trouble. The clock read 4:22. Their only hope was for the Cleveland defense to force the Jets to settle for a field goal quickly and get the ball back to Kosar and company with enough time to drive for the winning touchdown. The tension was getting thick at Cleveland Stadium.

The Jets didn't really surprise anyone with their first-down call. O'Brien handed off to McNeil over right tackle. He broke outside and squirted through a hole in the line. Then Guy Bingham threw a key block that took out both Frank Minnifield and Chris Rockins, and McNeil had daylight. He sprinted into the clear, angling toward the end zone with only Hanford Dixon, coming across from the other side of the field, to beat. Dixon caught up to McNeil inside the five and gave him a dramatic shove toward the sideline, but he was too late. McNeil sailed over the goal line for a 25-yard touchdown run that instantly turned Cleveland Stadium into a mausoleum.

Much like following Red Right 88 six years before, the silence was deafening.

Hanford Dixon, after unsuccessfully trying to shove McNeil out of bounds, took off his helmet and flung it to the ground then wandered off the field.

Back in the press box, Ray Yannucci didn't have any editorial comments. He simply gathered up his material and stormed out, starting the long journey down to the field and then the locker room for a series of losing interviews. The Browns, after a thrilling and satisfying regular season, had once again broken Cleveland's collective heart. Accordingly, thousands of fans got up from their seats and headed for the Stadium exits, grumbling curses under their breath at this team of chokers.

The Jets' five-game losing streak was ancient history, and the players wandered on their own sidelines, beaming, almost unable to believe what was happening. They were going to the AFC Championship.

Technically, there was still enough time for a Cleveland comeback. A quick drive, onside-kick recovery, and another quick drive could get the Browns back in it, but that series of events seemed incredibly unlikely. The Cleveland offense had enjoyed modest success against the horrible New York pass defense, but certainly not as much as it should have had. The Browns' triumphant trio of wide receivers—Brian Brennan, Webster Slaughter, and Reggie Langhorne—had been held to a combined total of seven receptions. As a team Cleveland had gained just 21 yards rushing on fifteen carries. The Browns had only managed one touchdown drive all day, and Mark Moseley had missed two field goals. Three of Cleveland's six possessions in the second half had ended in punts, another on a Moseley miss, and the last two on interceptions. After racking up 139 total yards of offense in the first quarter alone, in the entire second half to this point the Browns had accumulated a mere 134. The Browns would now have to score as many points in four minutes as they'd been able to score in the previous fifty-six.

The shell-shocked Browns' offense took the field at their own thirty-one yard line with 4:08 remaining after a squib kick. "I remember standing in the huddle when Bernie was over talking to the coaches and thinking, 'Somebody's got to say something,'" Mike Baab said. "Ozzie didn't talk. Cody didn't talk. So I grabbed everybody's facemask and pulled them together and I said, 'We need to decide if we're going to be heroes or if we're going to be losers. Who wants to be a hero?' I looked every guy in the face and asked, 'Are you going to be a hero?' By the time Bernie ran on the field, we were just roaring. We were ready to be heroes. I remember Bernie having to tell us to shut up about five times because we were ready."

But the spark was slow to ignite. On first down, Kosar completed a short eight-yard pass to Langhorne, but Baab was penalized for holding, setting the Browns back to the twenty-one for first-and-twenty.

On second down, Kosar dropped back and was immediately swarmed by energized Jets' defensive lineman Mark Gastineau for a four-yard sack at the seventeen yard line. The wild Gastineau immediately got up and waltzed toward the bleachers, screaming and taunting the Dog Pound. With the Browns facing second-and-Shaker Heights, the Jets were three plays away from clinching a shocking playoff victory and silencing thousands of fans who had been giving the cocky Gastineau a hard time all afternoon. "They were chanting some pretty ugly remarks at Gastineau," Browns' tackle Cody Risien said. "The Jets were up by ten, and he was obviously playing hurt. I don't blame him for egging them on."

Kosar's second-down pass for Herman Fontenot was knocked away, but a holding penalty on the Jets and a facemask foul on Paul Farren of the Browns forced a replay. On second-and-twenty-four, take two, Kosar tried to flip a pass into the right flat, but it was knocked down at the line of scrimmage, setting up third-and-twenty-four. Or so it should have been.

Just after Kosar released the pass, Gastineau came crashing through the line on the left side like a mountain ram. Though Kosar no longer had the football, Gastineau kept charging, head-first, right into Kosar's back. The quarterback crumbled to the ground, but before Gastineau could get back up and explain to the Dog Pound how wonderful a football player he was, referee Ben Dreith spiked a penalty flag on the ground right in front of Gastineau's face.

The long-haired wild man was penalized for roughing the quarterback, a 15-yard infraction that also gave the Browns an automatic first down at the thirty-two, digging them out of what appeared to be an insurmountable hole. What was left of the Cleveland Stadium crowd roared with satisfaction, possibly for the last time all season. They may lose the game, but at least they'd have the last laugh on Gastineau.

However, the gift first down seemed to light a fire under Bernie Kosar. "I saw a look in his eyes I'd never seen before," Ozzie Newsome said later. "He was not going to be denied. He was going to find a way to win that football game."

But the Browns couldn't do much with their stay of execution at first. Kosar's first- and second-down passes fell incomplete over the middle, both to the wrong side of Clarence Weathers. With 3:16 remaining, on third down, Kosar flipped a pass to the right sideline for Langhorne, which he caught, then dragged a Jet defender to the marker before hitting the turf. The good news for the Jets was that Langhorne was downed in bounds. The bad news was he was close enough for a measurement, which stopped the clock. Even worse, he got the first down. The Browns were still breathing, though barely.

Kosar hit Langhorne again for 13 yards to the New York forty-five, and this time the second-year wideout got out of bounds to stop the clock with 2:52 showing. On the next play, Kosar finally connected with Brennan over the middle for 23 yards to the twenty-two. The clock ticked down. The Browns hustled to the line, where Kosar took the snap and winged another pass for Brennan down the left sideline which he caught at the Jets' three. The Browns quickly called their first time out with 2:14 remaining.

On first-and-goal, Kosar tossed a quick-out pass that Curtis Dickey reeled in at the one, but he couldn't quite make it over the goal line before being tackled. The

Browns rushed up to the line to try to get another play off before the two-minute warning but were unable to do so. They paused again to collect their thoughts for second-and-goal at the Jets' one yard line.

On the next play, Mack took the handoff and vaulted over the line and into the end zone for a touchdown with 1:57 left. Moseley connected on the extra point to make it 20-17.

Several of the thousands of fans who had departed Cleveland Stadium had now heard of what was going on either on their car radios or from other tailgating fans with televisions. Some turned back. Others paused, in true Cleveland-sports-fan fashion, not going back or continuing their departure, to wait to see what happened next.

The Browns really needed to recover this onside kick. If they didn't, and if the Jets were able to pick up a first down, the game was over. Cleveland could only stop the clock twice. A three-and-out for New York might give the Browns about a minute to drive down the field, but they would most likely have miserable field position. Though there was finally life inside the Stadium for the first time in nearly an hour, the chances of the Browns coming back were still slim to none.

The chances grew longer when Marion Barber recovered Moseley's spiraling onside kick at the Cleveland forty-five. Any chances Cleveland had of coming back now rested with its defense.

On first down, Carl Hairston and Bob Golic were in the Jet backfield so quickly it was as if there was no offensive line trying to stop them. They collared McNeil for a three-yard loss at the forty-two yard line and called their second time out with 1:52 left. Tony Paige got back the three yards McNeil lost on second down as Cleveland took its final time out with 1:48 remaining. It brought up third and ten at the forty-five. With a Jet first down, they would be able to run out the remaining hundred seconds. The Browns had stymied New York on third down all afternoon, limiting them to two conversions in fourteen attempts. But a third conversion here and no one would remember the twelve stops.

Ken O'Brien dropped back then tried to surge forward on a quarterback draw. Instead, the New York offensive line collapsed like a line of dominos, and a handful of Browns crashed through. Sam Clancy officially brought down O'Brien at the forty-eight for a three-yard loss on what was deemed a sack by the officials, thus stopping the clock until the ball could be reset and preserving perhaps eight to ten seconds on the clock.

The Jets hurried their punt team onto the field then stood by while they melted the clock down as much as they could before the playclock expired. Dave Jennings took the snap with 1:15 left and lofted a high kick down the middle of the field that bounced inside the Cleveland fifteen and rolled to the seven, where the Jets downed it with 1:03 to play. It appeared the Browns would have to go 93 yards in sixty-three seconds with no time outs—until they saw the flag. Marion Barber, the same man who had recovered the onside kick, was penalized for holding, pushing the Jets back to their own forty-one and forcing them to kick again. Jennings' punt was less impressive this time, and Gerald McNeil fielded it at the Cleveland twenty-two yard line. He split through the Jets' coverage for ten yards to the thirty-two, where the Browns would take over with fifty-three seconds to play. Barber had essentially committed a 25-yard penalty. Ever so slowly fans began to trickle back into Cleveland Stadium.

On first down, Kosar went back to his bread-and-butter, firing a strike down the middle for Brennan. Carl Howard of the Jets was positioned correctly, except that his back was to the football and that he ran into Brennan at the New York forty-two. The penalty flag landed at Howard's feet. Brennan saw it, turned toward the closed end of Cleveland Stadium the Browns were driving toward, clapped his hands, and thrust his arms in that general direction.

With forty-seven seconds remaining, Kosar dropped back again, and this time cashed in on Brennan's success. Because of the three previous big plays to Brennan in the last two minutes, the Jet defense was overly concerned with covering him over the middle. Thus, when Webster Slaughter ran a fly pattern down the left sideline and had New York cornerback Russell Carter beat, there was no safety there to help. Kosar recognized this and whipped a lofty pass down the sideline for Slaughter. The rookie pinned the football against Carter's helmet, then, as Carter reached up to get a hand on the ball, Slaughter pulled it away with just his right hand and tumbled to the ground while securing it on his chest. He was down at the New York five.

Cleveland Stadium erupted in an explosion of giddy shock and joyful disbelief. The Browns, whom they had all pronounced dead twenty minutes ago, now somehow had a chance to win the game.

Slaughter leaped up and was immediately embraced by Clarence Weathers. Gerald McNeil joined them and hugged his teammate. Several other Browns began congregating in that corner of the field, reveling in the beauty of Slaughter's play.

The only problem: the clock was still running.

Though Slaughter had made the catch along the sideline and had wound up out of bounds, he had landed in bounds, and the side judge correctly kept the clock moving. Slaughter and his teammates thought the clock had stopped at thirty-nine seconds, the moment at which he'd made the catch. So as they celebrated, the seconds kept ticking down to the offseason for the Browns. "They're going to celebrate themselves right out of a football game," NBC's Don Criqui told his television audience.

Bernie Kosar was the first on the field to realize what was happening. He sprinted down the field, screaming at his teammates to knock it off and quickly line up. When he reached the passel, Slaughter, still not aware of what was going on, threw his arms around his quarterback. Kosar shoved him off and grabbed Slaughter's jersey, pulling him back out onto the field. The players who had come from the sideline returned to it, and the ones who were supposed to be on the field quickly scattered back to their position. It was absolute pandemonium.

With the line basically intact with eighteen seconds left, Kosar literally shoved Mike Baab down into position and took the snap for what everyone in the 216 area code figured would be the obligatory pass out of bounds to stop the clock. Instead, Kosar had one more surprise in store for a dizzy Stadium crowd. He took two quick steps back and zipped a very catchable pass toward the left corner of the end zone, again shooting for Slaughter, who was open on the side. But Russell Carter, the man Slaughter had beat on the 37-yard pass moments earlier, was between Kosar and his receiver. Five yards in front of Slaughter, Carter made an athletic angling leap backward, reached up with his right hand, and caught the football in mid-air. As he returned to Earth, Carter dragged the ball into his chest, where it bounced off his pads and then to the ground with eleven seconds remaining. It was probably the most dramatic incomplete pass in Browns' history and way too close to Red Right 88 for comfort.

As Cleveland fans coast-to-coast performed CPR on one another, Marty Schottenheimer decided there would be no more fooling around. Though there was time to take at least one more shot at the end zone, he sent out Mark Moseley and the kicking team to attempt to tie the game on a 22-yard attempt on second down. "All I was thinking was 'get the tie,'" Schottenheimer said. "Everything was going our way. It didn't make any sense to go for the win right then."

Fitting for the insanity of the final two minutes, holder Jeff Gossett was late in coming onto the field, and sensing the pinch, Brian Brennan quickly took the field to take his place. Luckily, Gossett arrived in time, and Brennan sprinted back to the sideline. Meanwhile, Schottenheimer was a few steps out onto the field physically counting the number of players on the line. It was Chinese Fire Drill time at Cleveland Stadium, not a good sign with the kick of the year upcoming.

Moseley had been here before. He'd kicked seventeen game-winning field goals previously in his career, including one that sent the Washington Redskins to the Super Bowl four years earlier. It was just a divisional playoff, right? No big thing. Just trying to win a playoff game for a team that hadn't won a playoff game in seventeen years for a group of fans who felt they were cursed in a city where nothing had gone right for two decades. No problem.

But Moseley had been here for none of that. And perhaps as a result, he calmly took two steps forward and kicked the ball through the uprights.

Cleveland Stadium nearly collapsed under the tidal wave of screams and cheers. The fans who had remained (or the ones who hadn't gone far and had made it back in time) had just witnessed one of the greatest short-term comebacks in NFL playoff history. And their reward would be more football.

After Moseley's ground-ball kickoff was returned by JoJo Townsell to the New York thirty-nine yard line, the clock hit zero, and the Browns and Jets were going to overtime for the first time ever in the postseason for either club. Or as NBC's Bob Trumpy called it, "sudden-offseason overtime."

What might have been the strangest sight of the day occurred over the next few minutes. With sudden-death overtime about to begin, many fans and re-porters who could see outside Cleveland Stadium noticed thousands of fans marching toward the ballpark. It would have been a natural scene a half-hour before gametime, but it was downright bizarre with the fourth quarter ending. Those who had left, assured the 1986 Browns were done and were trying to beat traffic, now realized something of great social and historic importance was taking place, and they still had a ticket.

With the crowd still roaring like a tornado in the background, the Jets won the coin toss and elected to receive. From the Jet thirty-five, Ken O'Brien's first-down pass for Wesley Walker fell incomplete, then Freeman McNeil was pummeled by Bob Golic and Reggie Camp for a four-yard loss on second down. On third down, O'Brien swung a screen pass on the right side for McNeil, who caught it and scampered toward the first-down marker, but Mark Harper stuck to fundamen-tals, grabbed hold of McNeil's legs, and brought him down at the forty-one, four yards short of a first down. Dave Jennings punted to the Browns' twenty-six, and the triumphant Cleveland offense marched back onto the field amidst the ador-ing roar of the once-again-capacity crowd.

The Browns' offense picked up right where it had left off, picking up a quick first down on a short pass and a Kevin Mack run, then another on two more com-pletions to the New York forty-nine. After a nine-yard toss to Mack on first down to the forty, Kosar shuffled back on second down and lofted a pass down the right side which Reggie Langhorne leapt up and caught at the Jet five for a 35-yard gain. It was the same call that led to Langhorne's 55-yard touchdown reception in the waning moments in Houston in Week Two. As that play silenced the Astrodome, this one caused a roar so loud, the network television cameras were shaking.

Marty Schottenheimer would later deny Red Right 88 ever crossed his mind. Be that as it may, many Browns' fans sighed with relief when they saw Mark Moseley trotting out onto the field for a 23-yard field-goal attempt on first down. There would be no "one more pass" this time. Moseley and the Browns would end it right here and head to the AFC title game, completing one of the finest comebacks and most memorable overall games in the annals of playoff football. What less than an hour before had appeared to be one of the worst days in Cleve-land Browns' history would now become one of the best.

The snap and hold were good. Moseley once again took two steps forward, just as he had mere minutes before, and kicked the football toward the same up-rights from essentially the same distance he had to tie the contest. But this time, the kick hooked dramatically right, no good.

For the second time that afternoon, Cleveland Stadium had the wind knocked out of it. Stunned silence swelled through the near-manic crowd. At bars through-out the Flats there were screamed obscenities, tables were overturned, and patrons literally fell to the ground. Many fans couldn't help but remember what Moseley had said the day he signed with the Browns: *I may miss, but I won't choke.* Now, on the biggest kick of the year, Moseley had evidently gotten something caught in his throat.

"I don't know what happened," he said later. "For some reason I ended up all off-balance when I hit the ball. I just barely hit the ball."

This ordained moment, the moment in which the Browns would shrug off seventeen years of frustration and heartbreak, had just been destroyed. Mark Moseley had just missed a field goal—a kick just four yards longer than an extra point—and the Browns had missed an opportunity to win a game that they had seemingly gone through the bowels of Middle Earth to reclaim.

The New York Jets had received a stay of execution. There would be more football.

Though most Browns' fans would now require serious psychological help, Marty Schottenheimer was unfazed. As he watched Moseley's quacker of a kick flummox wide right, there was one instant of dismay. Then, before he could even raise his hands to his head, he snapped back together and ordered the defense back onto the field as if nothing had happened. "I remember the disappointment that crossed my mind," he would say later. "But almost instantaneously I knew that if I gave evidence of that to the players on the sideline, they might respond in kind. So I immediately turned it into a positive. The whole idea was, 'Hey, this is a part of the game and let's just continue doing what we're doing, and we'll find a way to win it later.'" It was as fine an example of leadership as there has ever been in professional sports.

Still, many Cleveland fans began sweating bullets again when the Jets converted their first first down since the five-minute mark of the fourth quarter. An O'Brien toss to Al Toon moved New York to its own thirty-eight, and the Jets were only two more first downs away from considering a field goal of their own. But once again, the Browns' defense came through. On first down, Sam Clancy tipped a pass out of O'Brien's hand, and it sailed up into the air. Reggie Camp reached out for it at the New York thirty but saw the football go right through his hands and fall incomplete. The Jets had dodged yet another bullet. O'Brien couldn't dodge Carl Hairston on second down, and Big Daddy nailed him for a six-yard sack, the Browns' eighth of the day. Playing conservative on third down, Tony Paige picked up five yards on a draw, and Dave Jennings once again punted back to the Browns.

But for the first time since Kosar's second interception, the Browns did not threaten to score. They dodged a bullet of their own when Kevin Mack fumbled the football on first down, but Paul Farren pounced on it at the Cleveland forty-two yard line. A play later, Herman Fontenot was tagged for a one-yard loss on third-and-one, and Jeff Gossett booted the ball back to what had become a terrified Jets' offense.

From the New York nineteen, Reggie Camp brought Freeman McNeil down for a five-yard loss then O'Brien hit McNeil for an 11-yard pickup on second down. On third-and-four, O'Brien was sacked by Sam Clancy for an 11-yard loss, the Browns' ninth sack of the afternoon. As he left the field, Carl Hairston shook his head and said to a passing Jet, "Damn, this is a great football game." Jennings again took the field for his NFL playoff-record fourteenth punt.

The Browns took over at their own thirty-one with just under three minutes remaining in overtime and began marching methodically. Kevin Mack picked up two first downs then the Browns caught a break when Jets' safety Lester Lyles dropped an interception at the New York twenty-eight. It was yet another scary moment for Cleveland, and not surprisingly, it was the final pass Bernie Kosar would throw on the day.

After Fontenot exploded up the middle for eight yards on second down, the clock hit zero, putting the teams in an odd predicament. Unlike basketball, the clock expiring in overtime of a playoff game did not mean the teams simply started over. It was treated as a regular quarter-change, the teams would shift direction, the clock would be reset to fifteen minutes, and play would resume.

Sudden-death overtime was born in the NFL in 1977, with the rule that if the teams reached the end of one fifteen-minute extra period, the game ended in a tie. But since playoff games can't end in a tie, in the postseason, the teams simply play until someone scores. ("This may last till Thursday," beleaguered NBC color man Bob Trumpy remarked as the first overtime drew to its conclusion). Though it was the seventh overtime game in league playoff history, it marked only the second time in NFL history that a game would go to a second overtime. The other was the longest game in league history, an eighty-two-minute Christmas Day divisional playoff between the Miami Dolphins and Kansas City Chiefs in 1971. The 1962 American Football League Championship between the Dallas Texans and Houston Oilers had also gone to two extra frames. Now, so would the Browns and Jets as the sun began to set on a wild Saturday afternoon in Cleveland.

On the first play of double overtime, third-and-two from the New York thirty-five, Mack burst up the middle for 15 yards to the Jet twenty. For a moment, Browns' fans began to feel that ticklish sensation of near-victory, then remembered Mark Moseley's last field-goal attempt. The crowd was electrified, yet cautious—in classic Cleveland form.

Mack plowed up the middle through an exhausted New York defense on the next two plays, picking up four, then seven yards to the Jet nine. Ironically, despite things going so well, Marty Schottenheimer was now in a pickle of a situation. He could keep plugging away and order a few more attempts at the end zone (à la Red Right 88) or play it safe and call on Moseley to attempt a short game-winning field goal (à la a half-hour earlier). On this day in this town, it was almost a no-win situation.

But Schottenheimer had to do one or the other, and he opted to go with Moseley. "You make it, you make it," the coach said later. "You miss it, you miss it. I don't say that in a cavalier way, but it's true. There was no doubt in my mind we'd find a way to win. That was my only thought."

As Moseley began to make his way onto the field, Schottenheimer pulled his kicker aside. "Go make it," he said. "It's time to go home."

The Browns' kicking team took the field, and the Jets took a time out, hoping to give Moseley another couple minutes to think about how awful his last kick had been. As it turned out, he didn't. He simply focused on what he had to do and put the past behind him. Still, he felt just a smidge of pressure. "It was as if 80,000 people were riding on my shoulders," Moseley said, "every one of them with a knife behind his back."

It was a symbolic moment. Not only would Moseley be kicking to rinse away the memory of his previous mistake but he would be kicking into the bleachers, the same direction Don Cockroft would have been kicking on that cold January day six years earlier had he been given the chance.

Moseley had spoken with Cockroft just the week before, and naturally, the discussion turned to Cockroft's lousy day in the Oakland playoff (three missed field goals and an extra point) that had cost the Browns a chance to win. People remember that game, Cockroft told Moseley, but not all the kicks he made that won games before that. Moseley would now get a chance to right the wrong Cockroft never had the opportunity to.

Scott Nicolas's snap was perfect, Jeff Gossett's hold was right on, and this time, at 4:41 P.M., Moseley calmly pushed the football through the uprights and into Cleveland history.

It's hard to describe exactly what happened next. Perhaps the simplest way to describe it is that after four hours and eleven minutes of tension, nearly 70,000 people collectively almost lost their minds. The Browns' bench exploded out onto the field, screaming, jumping, embracing and celebrating the team's first post-season victory since 1969. "Trumpy, I'm ready to hug you at the end of this one," Don Criqui told his partner in the NBC booth. What's more, Cleveland was now just one win away from the Super Bowl, and it would get to play the decisive conference title match on its own home field. "If this doesn't get us to Pasadena," Browns' safety Al Gross yelled during the celebration, "nothing will!"

It was hard to argue with that sentiment. Without question, the Browns were now a team of destiny, rallying for an impossible victory in arguably the most thrilling game in team history. "I've been on teams that made better comebacks on the sandlots just before dark," said Ozzie Newsome, "but I've never been on one like this in professional football."

"I've never experienced or seen a comeback like that," Schottenheimer concurred. "After it was over, just before we said our prayer in the locker room, I told the players to listen. You could still hear the people cheering for us. This is a victory, a game, a moment all of us will remember the rest of our lives."

Mark Moseley had redeemed himself and kept his career alive, at least for one more week.

And was it not appropriate these Browns won a playoff game in a fashion the previous beloved Browns' club could not? "Not even the Kardiac Kids ever came back like that," Cody Risien said. "They won in a fashion which made the famed Kardiac Kids finishes look like hum-drum affairs," Frank Derry wrote in *Browns News/Illustrated*. It was as if an exorcism had taken place on the haunted soil of Cleveland Stadium, reflected by Ray Yannucci's comment, "To hell with Red Right 88!"

In closing a chapter of the Browns' past, they also seemed to pave the road for the future. Specifically, for Bernie Kosar, who had somehow escalated his already-impressive status among the Cleveland faithful to now legendary proportions.

It was easy to forget Kosar was only twenty-three years old. Had he wanted to, had he not graduated early with a desire to play for his hometown team, he could have stayed at the University of Miami. If so, he, not Vinny Testaverde (who was actually ten days older than Kosar) would have started for the Hurricanes in the national championship on Friday night rather than for the Browns on Saturday. And there were few who believed Kosar would have emulated Testaverde's five-interception performance in a 14-10 loss to Penn State.

It had only been Kosar's twenty-fourth career start and only his second playoff game. Yet he looked as cool and as calm as a Hall-of-Fame-bound veteran in willing the Browns to their finest clutch performance in decades. "Bernie comes into the huddle and says, 'We're going to take this game,'" Paul Farren said. "It's incredible the way he brought us together as a unit, one play at a time."

"Bernie took the offense aside and said, 'We can win this game. Don't give up,'" Brian Brennan said. "I'll tell you, now that it happened, it almost brings tears to my eyes."

Kosar's confidence even transcended to the defense. "I just felt that they wouldn't score no matter how long we played," Frank Minnifield said. "I knew all we had to do was get the ball back to Bernie."

And that's exactly what the Dogs did in the final two minutes and throughout overtime in a downright frightening display of dominating defense. "I've never seen the kind of push and penetration from a defensive line that we had in overtime," Schottenheimer said. "It was unbelievable, frankly. Obviously it was an indication when you get emotion working with the ability of the things you can accomplish."

On New York's final four series, the Jets compiled a total of 15 yards on fourteen non-punting plays. They picked up just one first down, rushed the football five times for minus-four yards, and Ken O'Brien was sacked three times for a combined loss of 20 yards. Schottenheimer said it was the best his defense had ever played, and only a fool would argue with him. Part of it was conservative playcalling by Joe Walton and the New York coaches, playing not to lose rather than for victory, but the superiority of the Cleveland defense in crunch time could not be denied.

The Browns, meanwhile, racked up an amazing 558 yards of offense and dominated time of possession by nearly thirteen minutes. Both advantages were due mostly to Bernie Kosar, who set NFL playoff records with thirty-three completions in sixty-four attempts for 489 yards—three of eight league records set that day. Seven more records were tied.

Surprisingly, Ozzie Newsome was Kosar's most dangerous target, snagging six receptions for 114 yards, while Kevin Mack brushed off early troubles to rush for 63 yards, 37 of which came on the final drive.

"I think we all had an opportunity to experience one of the finest games in the history of the sport," Schottenheimer said. "Midway through the first quarter of overtime, I thought to myself, 'This is a great football game.' Of course, the way it ended up confirmed my suspicions."

And those who had experienced it would never forget it.

Even before regulation was over and it appeared the Jets had won, bummed-out Browns' fans began piling into bars in the Flats, hoping to drown their sorrows of another football heartbreak. But as the afternoon turned into evening, the event changed from a wake to one of the greatest celebrations in Cleveland history. "It was like the biggest wedding you've ever been to combined with New Year's Eve and the end of the war," one *Plain Dealer* article declared.

Cars plowed through snarled traffic on Old River Road, horns blaring. Strangers hugged and exchanged high-fives. Bars filled up and stayed packed well into the winter night. "This team has Cleveland in the palm of its hand," wrote the *PD*'s Lou Mio, "and they did it in a game that will be rehashed a few hundred thousand times wherever armchair quarterbacks gather for a beer."

At one point during the seemingly endless barrage of interviews after the game, Bernie Kosar winked at a reporter. "Just another day at the office," he said.

Yet there was a deeper meaning to this victory, one that would last longer than the two days the Browns and their fans basked in its afterglow before setting their sights on the AFC Championship. Two years later, Reggie Langhorne would put that feeling into words.

"I think about that game a lot," he said. "I think about that game when things look bad. I think about it, and it motivates me. I will always tell stories about that game."

And he wouldn't be the only one.

11 Alfred Hitchcock Time

As the following week wore on, it was hard to imagine there was a time when the citizens of Cleveland were lukewarm in their enthusiasm for the 1986 Browns.

The city was absolutely intoxicated with its football team, demonstrating a passion not seen since the Kardiac Kids had won the division title in 1980. But this was different. With the win over the Jets, "the city of Cleveland simply went over the psychic brink, and Ohio's north coast lapsed into perfect ecstasy," wrote Denver sportswriter Russell Martin. It was as if winning a playoff game for the first time in seventeen years had awakened something in the city—an off-the-charts level of zeal and love for the Browns that manifested in dozens of varying ways.

Mayor George Voinovich declared an "orange-and-brown" day during that week, when the residents were requested to don the Browns' colors in tribute to their heroes. Browns' symbols turned up everywhere, from Baskin Robbins desserts to atop stone statues downtown. The radio airwaves were clogged with songs about the team, from the rap take-off "The Browns Are Too Cold" to the kingpin of the genre: "Bernie, Bernie" by the Bleacher Bums, sung to the tune of the Kingsmen's classic "Louie, Louie" ("If I had to hear that one more time," Bob Golic remembered, "I was going to go down to the station and rip the antennas off the building"). Videos and records of "Masters of the Gridiron," the team's music video for charity played out to a song by Michael Stanley, were hard to find. The Browns had transcended their medium.

"It was an amazing time to see the city," Golic said. "From the time we got up in the morning to the time we went to bed at night, it was all about us. It was one of the most amazing feelings I'd ever had."

At the end of its Saturday-night performance, the members of the Cleveland Orchestra began barking. Bridal shops offered specials on brown-and-orange gowns. A "Go Browns" banner was strung atop the control tower at Hopkins Airport, signaling to all visitors to Cleveland just where they were and what mattered here. While adopting about seventy immigrants as United States citizens, a district judge spent much of the ceremony holding up the Browns as an example to the new Americans of what this country was all about. Proving his point, on the wall behind him hung an American flag bookended by a pair of Browns' pennants.

The Browns' return to glory wasn't just the talk of Cleveland. The entire nation was sitting up and paying attention. When Browns' public relations director Kevin Byrne came into the office Monday morning, he had more than two hundred phone messages waiting for him—a prelude to the 650 media representatives that would attend Sunday's game. "Can you believe it?" Johnny Carson said during a monologue on *The Tonight Show* that week. "The Cleveland Browns in a championship? The last time the Browns were in the playoffs, Cleveland wasn't a city. It was a president."

When tickets for the AFC Championship went on sale at 8:30 Monday morning, they sold out in less than two hours, mostly because hundreds of fans camped outside the Cleveland Stadium ticket office Sunday night. For the rest of the week, scalpers sold them for anywhere between $85 and $150 apiece. "I have not been to a city that has been this crazy about the playoffs," said Ahmad Rashad, who spent the week in Cleveland preparing a story for NBC's pre-game show. More than just crazy, Cleveland was resuscitating its national image.

"I don't think this town can be made fun of again," said WKYC news director Ron J. Bilek. "Yes, it doesn't solve poverty, but it certainly gets people revved up. It has nothing to do with trivialities. It's solidified the fact that Cleveland's on the rebound."

Win or lose, most felt the city had turned a corner—and almost everyone expected a win. On Saturday morning, a Cleveland Stadium employee hoisted a tall ladder out onto the field and began to coat the goalposts with furniture polish to make them so slick stampeding fans couldn't tear them down. "If the goddamn Jets couldn't stop them with a ten-point lead late in the fourth quarter, then no one could," Russell Martin wrote. "The Browns, it seemed certain, would bowl over the Broncos, then smash the hell out of whatever NFC team dared to show up for the Super Bowl, and all of America would at long last get off Cleveland's case. It was going to be beautiful."

Indeed it was. In theory.

Though to most fans it didn't matter who the Browns played next, their players and coaches knew better. The Denver Broncos were the last hurdle standing between Cleveland and its first trip to the Super Bowl, and Dan Reeves' club would symbolize an even greater challenge than the Jets had provided.

The Broncos, who had never won a playoff game on the road, were coming off an up-and-down regular season in which they'd started 8-1 but lost four of their last seven games to finish 11-5. Thanks to a late-season collapse by the Los Angeles Raiders, they'd captured the AFC West title and just eked past the New England Patriots at home in the divisional playoff, 22-17. Their defense was solid, led by lineman Rulon Jones (the AFC's Defensive Player of the Year) and linebacker Karl

Mecklenberg. Their offense was also potent, though inconsistent. Quarterback John Elway was the catalyst of the Denver attack, but most Bronco backers felt he hadn't lived up to his lofty expectations in his first four seasons. Certainly Elway was good and could take over a game with his rifle arm and uncanny scrambling ability, but sportswriters and other coaches were questioning whether the Stanford product had what it took to be a winning NFL quarterback—especially mentally.

"In truth, Elway is overrated," wrote the *Plain Dealer*'s Bob Dolgan. "He has not yet arrived as a first-class operator. The voters must have been dreaming when they put him into the Pro Bowl as Dan Marino's substitute."

Elway was highly regarded coming out of Stanford in 1983—both as a quarterback and a baseball player. He was drafted by Baltimore that spring but refused to play for the hapless Colts and earned an immediate reputation as a troublemaker. Threatening to sit out the season, Elway eventually forced the Colts to trade him to Denver for offensive tackle Chris Hinton and quarterback Mark Herrmann. Thrust into the starting position almost immediately, Elway struggled as a rookie, completing just 47.5 percent of his passes with seven touchdowns and fourteen interceptions for a dreadful quarterback rating of 54.9. He improved over his next three seasons, but not dramatically, with his rating never topping eighty. He finished the 1986 regular season as the twelfth-best quarterback in the NFL, throwing nineteen touchdown passes and thirteen interceptions.

That week Browns' defensive lineman Sam Clancy said he felt Bengals' quarterback Boomer Esiason was better than Elway, a view shared by many Cleveland writers. Though the Broncos had won the previous Sunday, Elway's numbers had done little to sway his critics. He threw for 257 yards, but completed just thirteen of thirty-one passes, often showing little touch—"He throws the football ninety miles an hour whether his receiver is 50 yards away or five yards away," Dolgan wrote—or grace under pressure. "Elway is open-faced, excitable, more likely to get flustered when things go wrong," Dolgan continued. Exemplifying that point was a silly tantrum Elway threw in the New England win, spiking the football after a questionable call by the officials. It earned him a penalty and cost the Broncos a touchdown.

Naturally, the media made comparisons all week between Elway and the heir apparent to the throne of NFL quarterback stardom, Bernie Kosar. Cleveland and national writers alike agreed that the Browns were better off with Kosar than Denver was with Elway. While Elway was emotional and occasionally frazzled, Kosar was careful, suspicious, and guarded. Dolgan said Kosar "reminds you of a lethal poker player, with his tight lips and flat eyes," while Elway "looks like the trusting boy next door going out for a malted milk."

And if Elway couldn't carry the Broncos to victory, most assumed they couldn't win. With Sammy Winder leading a mediocre rushing attack, Denver certainly wasn't going to dominate time of possession. And while good, the Broncos' defense clearly wasn't dominant—perhaps not even as good as Cleveland's. In an interesting sidebar, Marty Schottenheimer would get to match wits with his former mentor, Denver defensive coordinator Joe Collier. Ironically, Collier also had a history with Lindy Infante: Collier had cut the Browns' offensive coordinator when he tried out for the Buffalo Bills in the 1960s.

Probably the most important Browns' advantage of all was that for the first time in seemingly ages, they appeared to be a team of destiny. They'd rescued victory from the jaws of certain defeat against the Jets and would now play before a delirious crowd at home for a trip to their first Super Bowl. Even Miami head coach Don Shula, moonlighting as an NBC analyst during the playoffs, admitted after Denver's win over New England that while the Broncos were good, this was simply the Browns' year. What's more, Earnest Byner, the heart of the team, was reactivated on Saturday and would see limited action.

"I see a Browns' team that simply does not believe it can be beaten," wrote Bill Livingston in the *Plain Dealer*. "It was said during the Steelers' Super Bowl years that they loved nothing more than facing a team from some posh, trendy place like Dallas or L.A. I think the Browns are like that. I think the Dogs can't wait to fasten their teeth on Johnny E's cuffs."

Accordingly, the *Plain Dealer* printed the predictions of twenty-nine sportswriters from around the country. All but seven said the Browns, three-point favorites, would win, including every football writer on the *Plain Dealer* staff. Even Sam Wyche predicted a Cleveland victory. But Pete Franklin was a bit more cautious.

"This matchup has the setting for another great game," he wrote. "I don't know if it is possible to surpass what we saw last week. But the ingredients are there for one fantastic finish. I do see it as Alfred Hitchcock time, with the Browns winning. Maybe even in overtime again. It will be that close."

After a week of irrational yet jubilant behavior that served little purpose other than to create and release excitement, on Saturday night, several Browns' fans figured out a way to try to parlay their enthusiasm to make an impact on Sunday's game.

On Friday, Cleveland radio stations had announced the Broncos would be staying at the Stouffer's Hotel downtown. When they arrived, dozens of Browns' fans were there to jeer and harass them. But the following night, they took it a step further. Well past midnight, a few fans piled into their cars and circled the hotel, blaring their horns and screaming out the window, hoping to make enough ruckus to keep the Broncos from getting a good night's sleep. Another group somehow managed to slip past hotel security and ran up and down the hotel hallways yelling and hollering with the same motivation.

While successful in its immediate goal, the plan would have no impact on the game. This was the AFC Championship. The Broncos showed up bright-eyed and bushy-tailed for what would turn out to be 1986's game of the year, in a perfect football backdrop. "Who needs domes?" Bob Costas asked during NBC's pre-game show. "Who needs artificial turf? It's cold. It's dark. It feels like a football game."

On a day when the sun would not fight through the embers of a foreboding January sky, the wind off Lake Erie made the thirty-degree temperature feel more like six. Snow flurries would swirl through the Stadium several times on the day, adding another twinkle to an already electric afternoon on the lakefront. In addition to a gentle layer of January snow, the field was blanketed with dog biscuits by kickoff, thrown by anxious Dog Pound inhabitants. Yet another source of excitement was the presence of the Ohio State University marching band, which designed a makeshift "Script Browns" formation just for the occasion.

As is usually the case in big games, the tension and anticipation surrounding the game led to a sloppy beginning. Both teams went three-and-out on their first possessions and looked bad doing it. But the Browns adjusted quickly and got rolling with their second possession. Taking over at their own fourteen yard line, they marched deep into Denver territory. On third-and-goal from the six, Kosar dropped back and swung a screen pass for Fontenot to the right side. Fontenot caught it at the nine, but Denver safety Tony Lilly was between him and the end zone. The wily Fontenot made a stutter-step move and got Lilly to dive at him at the five. Fontenot then simply hurdled over Lilly and pranced untouched into the end zone for a 7-0 Browns' lead. The capacity crowd of 79,915 (incredibly, there were only fifty-eight no-shows) roared with satisfaction.

The din grew even louder when the Browns forced a Denver punt on the next possession. Cleveland took over at its own thirty-six with a chance to push their lead to double digits. But after a three-yard run by Mack on first down, Kosar made a crucial mistake. Under pressure from Rulon Jones, he tried to fire a 15-yard pass to Webster Slaughter across midfield. Slaughter was open, but Kosar hadn't seen Denver linebacker Ricky Hunley in between them. Hunley picked off the pass at midfield and rumbled to the Cleveland thirty-five. The Broncos were in position to capture the momentum. The Browns' defense rose to the occasion, however, forcing a punt. As the second quarter began, the Browns had apparently weathered their first storm.

A seven-yard toss from Kosar to Brian Brennan gave Cleveland a first down at its own twenty-seven a play later, but on the next play Kosar made another uncharacteristic mistake. Flushed out of the pocket, he tried to glide a soft pass upfield to Ozzie Newsome. Denver linebacker Jim Ryan, who on the play before had been fooled badly by Kosar's ability to look one way then throw the other, had Newsome covered and picked off the pass at the Cleveland thirty-five yard line. He hit the ground untouched, then got up and raced to the nine before being knocked out of bounds by Cody Risien. Kosar, who had the lowest interception ratio in the NFL and had only been intercepted ten times in 531 attempts in the regular season, had now thrown two in his first ten attempts on the day.

Counting the two bad decisions late in the fourth quarter against the Jets, four of Kosar's last thirty-two passes had been caught by opponents.

But once again, the Cleveland defense held. The Broncos settled for a 19-yard Rich Karlis field goal to cut the lead to 7-3. While frustrated, Browns' fans were still relieved. Two turnovers in their own territory had only resulted in three Denver points. If the Browns could quit shooting themselves in the foot, the game was theirs for the taking. Unfortunately, the chamber wasn't empty.

After a nice kickoff return by Gerald McNeil to the Cleveland thirty-seven, on first down, Kevin Mack ran into left tackle Rickey Bolden (just activated for the game after missing three months to injury) and fumbled the football. Denver linebacker Ken Woodard recovered at the thirty-seven. The Browns had now turned the ball over three times in their last five plays. This was not how you got to the Super Bowl.

And this time, the mistake cost the Browns dearly. On first down, Elway scrambled out of the pocket and down the left side for 34 yards. The Cleveland defense stiffened, forcing fourth down from the Cleveland one yard line. Rather than playing it safe and calling on Rich Karlis and the kicking team, Denver coach Dan Reeves would roll the dice and go for it on fourth down. Whatever happened, the decision made an impact on the Bronco players. Even if they didn't score, Reeves had sent a clear message that Denver was here to win.

The gamble paid off, though only with the assistance of another Browns' mental breakdown. Eddie Johnson, seeing limited playing time after injuring his knee in the Jets game, reaggravated his knee on the third-down incompletion. He hobbled off the field and backup Mike Johnson ran in to replace him. But in the confusion of that replacement and the few moments of mystery surrounding Reeves' decision, Browns' linebacker Brad Van Pelt thought Denver was going for a field goal. He sprinted off the field, thinking the special-teams replacements would come in. Naturally, they didn't, so when Elway and the Broncos lined up for fourth down, they only had ten Cleveland defenders to contend with. Marty Schottenheimer realized what had happened and was screaming and frantically motioning for a time out, but with the roar of the crowd, neither his players nor the officials heard him.

Elway handed off to running back Gerald Willhite on a sweep toward right end. At the two, he vaulted into the air and into the arms of Browns' safety Chris Rockins. But Willhite's twisting momentum was enough to carry him across the goal line, and he landed in the end zone to give Denver its first lead at 10-7. Presumably, Van Pelt would have been right around where Willhite crossed the goal line, and may have made a seven-point difference.

The Browns were now losing and had no one to blame but themselves. Three straight turnovers had led to ten Bronco points and had softened the intensity of the capacity crowd. Though they managed to hang onto the football and pick up a couple of first downs, the Browns could not turn momentum back in their favor. They reached the Denver forty-five before being forced to punt. The Cleveland defense, plagued with poor field position all day, stepped up again and held the Broncos at their own twenty-seven. With the second quarter waning, Cleveland needed a spark.

On third-and-seven from the Cleveland thirty-eight, Kosar looped a long pass down the right side for Clarence Weathers, who caught it at the Denver twenty yard line for a 42-yard gain. The Browns' only receiving threat of 1985, who had virtually vanished through all of 1986, had brought the worrisome crowd back into it.

The Browns crept inside the Denver ten at the two-minute warning then Mark Moseley came on and connected on a 29-yard field goal to tie the game at ten with twenty seconds remaining in the half. The teams returned to the locker room tied.

The teams exchanged punts on the first two possessions of the third quarter then Cleveland cornerback Mark Harper interrupted a promising Denver drive when he intercepted an Elway pass at the Browns' thirty-one yard line. But Cleveland could do nothing with the windfall and punted back to the Broncos, who drove right back into Browns' territory. Denver wound up with a 26-yard Rich Karlis field goal that gave the Broncos a 13-10 lead with 2:50 remaining in the period.

But just as Denver had done when challenged in the first half, the Browns responded. Taking over at their own seventeen, Kosar and Co. quickly began marching down the torn-up Cleveland Stadium turf. They reached the Bronco eight before stalling, and Moseley booted a 25-yard field goal to tie the contest at thirteen with 12:38 remaining.

Knowing that the game was now down to its final few minutes, the Browns' defense again rose up, stuffing Denver and forcing a three-and-out. The Browns took over at their own forty-one. After a Rulon Jones sack of Kosar and an 11-yard completion to Brian Brennan, Kevin Mack was stopped a yard short of a first down on third-and-two.

For the second straight possession, the Denver offense was pinned deep and was no match for the Cleveland defense. After three plays, Mike Horan punted to the Cleveland thirty-eight yard line, and Gerald McNeil returned it to the Browns' forty-eight, where the home team took over with 6:40 remaining and the tension as thick as frozen peanut butter.

A first-down Kosar pass for Mack fell incomplete then Herman Fontenot snuck through the right side of the line for a four-yard rush on second down. It brought up third-and-six from the Denver forty-eight as the clock ticked down under six minutes. As Kosar came up to the line, he recognized that the Broncos were going to blitz. He also noticed that would put Denver safety Dennis Smith, who had not played the previous weekend with a knee injury, on the crafty Brian Brennan. Before taking the snap, Kosar knew where his pass was going.

"Kosar backpedaling . . ." Nev Chandler, the voice of the Browns, described from the radio booth.

He dropped back four steps and lofted a high-arching pass down the left side-line for Brennan, who had gained a step on Smith right off the line. But since Smith was six inches taller, the advantage was negated.

". . . he's firing the home-run ball for Brennan . . ."

Regardless, Kosar's pass was underthrown, and Brennan realized it before Smith did.

". . . turns one way, turns another . . ."

He slowed down, crouched beneath Smith as he flew by, and caught the football.

". . . HE'S GOT IT!"

Completely turned away from Brennan, Smith then hit the ground as Brennan motored past him.

"AT THE FIFTEEN! TEN! FIVE! TOUCHDOWN BROWNS!"

He ran untouched into the end zone and sent Cleveland Stadium into a level of hysteria never before felt in the building's fifty-five-year history.

"Brian Brennan has done it for the umpteenth time!"

And in doing so, Brennan apparently had sent the Browns somewhere for the first time.

In one instant, Cleveland's long history of sports woe evaporated. The death of Indians' shortstop Ray Chapman after getting hit by a pitch in 1920. The Tribe's shocking sweep at the hands of the New York Giants in the 1954 World Series. The firing of Paul Brown. The death of Ernie Davis. The sudden retirement of Jim Brown. The disappointment of Mike Phipps. The long, miserable post-1950s summers of the Indians. The annual winter embarrassment that was the Cava-liers. Red Right 88. And the heartbreaking evaporation of a 21-3 lead in Miami 372 days before.

The Cleveland Browns were going to the Super Bowl. There was no doubt.

"You may have just seen," Jim Mueller told his radio audience, *"the straw that broke the Broncos' back."*

Five minutes and forty-three seconds remained when Mark Moseley's extra point sliced through the uprights, sending the now-delirious home crowd into another level of ecstasy. The Browns led, 20-13, but they may as well have been up by thirty points. After a generation of clobbering their hopes and dreams, destiny was finally smiling on Cleveland sports fans. Brennan's touchdown was "a vivid canvas to be placed in the Cleveland Museum of Art," Rick Telander would write in *Sports Illustrated*. "I was literally shaking," Brennan would say, "knowing I had made the play that was going to put us in the Super Bowl."

As Cleveland began to prepare for what would be the greatest party in the city's 190-year history, most of the Broncos realized the game wasn't over. Sure, they were down, but there was plenty of time left. They still only needed one touchdown. Awaiting the kickoff, Dan Reeves even mentioned to Elway that the Broncos didn't necessarily need to score on this drive. There was enough time left that even if Denver punted, it could still probably get the ball back with enough time left to try to tie the game. It was not quite backs-to-the-wall time.

Then Mark Moseley kicked off.

"All right, here's Moseley's kickoff," Nev Chandler continued. *"It's a floater that hits at the fifteen . . ."*

"Floater" is one way to describe it. Even better would be "knuckleball." By the time Moseley's kick—which traveled west, toward Pasadena—was descending, it had no spin on it at all. It simply hung in the air with no rotation or movement, like the knuckleballs Indians' pitcher Tom Candiotti had entranced batters with on this same field the previous summer. Denver's Gene Lang was in the position of having to predict how the ball would bounce off the turf.

". . . it skips inside the five!"

The only chance Lang had was to have caught the ball before it hit the ground. And to do that, he would have had to sprint ten yards forward and perhaps make a diving catch—not the ideal way to field a kickoff. The football hit at the Denver fifteen and skipped past the oncoming Lang at the ten, too low for him to reach down and get it. Lang was now experiencing the nightmare of every kickoff-return man: running backward to pick up the football.

"It's all the way back at the two!"

Which is where Lang caught up to it and then made his second crucial, though forgivable, mistake. At this point, the ball still had enough momentum that it would have carried into the end zone. As long as Lang didn't touch it before then, if the ball reached the end zone, and he covered it, it would be a touchback, and the Broncos would start at their twenty. But Lang was already in a crisis situation and didn't know how close the Browns' defenders were behind him. Unlike punts, on kickoffs the football is live and it becomes anyone's football once ten yards downfield. Lang didn't have time to stop and wait for the ball to roll into the end zone before recovering it.

"The Broncos can't recover it, and now they do at the one-yard line!"

Lang finally covered up the football on his knees and within a second was pulverized by Al Gross as Browns' fans at the Stadium and around the world looked at each other in amazement. Few had ever seen a football bounce that way. None had seen their team in a Super Bowl.

"A big mistake by the Denver Broncos!"

Technically, the ball was between the one and the two, essentially as far as it could possibly be from where the Broncos needed to go. Not surprisingly, Denver's mentality changed. Dan Reeves was thinking about specific plays to run from around the twenty, where he figured the Broncos would start. He even told Elway that if Denver got decent field position, they'd run a flea-flicker or trick play. Clearly, those plans went out the window.

Also out the window went Reeves' belief that this drive wasn't necessarily crucial. Had the Broncos started around their own twenty and were unable to pick up more than a first down or two, they still could have punted back to Cleveland with three-plus minutes left, then let their defense try to stop the Browns around their own thirty. If successful, Denver could get the ball back in workable field position to try a last drive in the final two minutes. But now, if the Broncos couldn't move the ball, a punt from the end zone would probably give the Browns the football in Denver territory, possibly already in field-goal range. Then, even if Cleveland didn't add the back-breaking score, after a punt, the Broncos would be almost right back where they started—pinned deep with three less minutes to work with.

In other words, this was it.

"If someone had offered a set of circumstances short of a guaranteed win," Ernie Accorsi would say, "that's what you'd ask for."

The Broncos huddled in the end zone, admittedly terrified. Though the crowd was set back from the field at that end of the park, the Broncos felt surrounded, buried in a din of decibels. "I just waited for guys to run into me," Denver left tackle Dave Studdard would later say of the forthcoming plays. "I could not hear." Even veteran players who never admitted defeat until the final gun sounded were preparing themselves for the offseason. And with good reason. Things had worked out perfectly for the Browns. Now, Denver would have to literally drive the length of a torn-up field on a cold day toward the most rambunctious group of fans in the NFL.

But Broncos' guard Keith Bishop saw it differently. Seeing the looks of shock and awe on his teammates' faces, he grunted, "Hey, we got these fuckers right where we want them."

The other players turned to him, exasperated for a moment, then several burst out laughing. Whether he intended to or not, Bishop had broken the tension and loosened up a team that stood on the gallows with a noose around its neck.

The Browns weren't planning on loosening the rope either. The decision was made immediately not to switch their defensive philosophy for this final drive. They had held the Broncos in check all day. Ten of their thirteen points came off turnovers when they only had to drive a fraction of the field. Their touchdown had been the result of a fluke defensive miscommunication. Denver had managed just 21 total yards on its last two possessions. And most importantly, Elway had been contained. As he called the play in the huddle, he'd completed fourteen of twenty-six passes for 116 yards. Aside from his 34-yard scramble, he'd rushed for a mere two yards. As a team, Denver had gained just 216 total yards.

The Browns' defense just had to do what it had been doing. And coordinator Dave Adolph thought he could end the game on first down. Expecting a pass, he sent an extra lineman (Dave Puzzuoli) in and called for a blitz, hoping to get to Elway in the end zone. If nothing else, it proved the Browns wouldn't be using a "prevent" defense.

But the Broncos had the perfect play called. Rather than take a long drop-back into the end zone and looking upfield, giving the line time to crash toward him, Elway took four steps back, then fired a screen pass to Sammy Winder to his left. With no outside linebacker there to cover him, a wide-open Winder caught it at the four yard line and tumbled out to the seven before Hanford Dixon came up to tackle him in bounds after a five-yard pickup. It wasn't a major gain, but it was a key play. Now Elway at least had some room to work with. It brought up second-and-five from the Broncos' seven.

Proving that the Broncos weren't desperate yet, the next call was a conservative right sweep to Winder, who broke off a block by tackle Ken Lanier before Reggie Camp brought him down at the ten. The Broncos, who had now had the football for just over a minute, called their first time out. It was now third-and-two, and Reeves was one play away from seeing how desperate he really was.

If the Broncos couldn't convert the first down, he would have to choose between punting from his end zone and going for it on fourth down inside his own fifteen. The Browns knew this could be the play of the game. If nothing else, a stop would force Denver to take its second time out to think about it—a large price for what would almost certainly be a gain of minimal yardage on fourth down. Though it would sound ridiculous later, the entire game hinged on the Broncos converting a third-and-two from their own ten.

The playcall was "20-fold-influence," a simple draw to Winder up the middle. The key was center Billy Bryan, who had to push Bob Golic to Bryan's left to open up just enough space for Winder. And for the second time in three plays, the Broncos benefited from a minor stroke of good fortune. First, though Denver only needed two yards, the Browns expected pass and lined up in their usual 3-4 alignment rather than a short-yardage stack with extra linemen. Also, Golic was lined up slightly to his right, making Bryan's mission that much easier. After snapping the ball, Bryan did his part and pushed Golic far enough out of the way for Winder to cross the line of scrimmage. But reacting quickly were Camp, Ray Ellis, and Mike Johnson, who combined to stuff Winder near the twelve—right at the marker. The officials called out the chains to measure. Winder had the first down by the length of the football, and the Broncos were able to postpone their doomsday decision. Four minutes and eleven seconds remained.

On first down from the twelve, the Broncos again surprised both the Browns and millions of fans by calling for another handoff to Winder. Carl Hairston took out left tackle Dave Studdard and cleared a path for linebacker Anthony Griggs to crush Winder after three yards. The clock was now under four minutes, and the Broncos still had 85 yards to go.

On second-and-seven, the playcall was the same as the first play of the drive, though this time Steve Sewell was the intended target coming out of the backfield. Seeing him covered, Elway then looked to Gerald Willhite, running the same swing pattern Winder had on play one, and saw him open. But now at the fifteen rather than the two, Elway wasn't willing to settle for a short dump-off that would eat up clock and probably wouldn't pick up a first down. Instead, he stepped forward to avoid Sam Clancy bearing down to his left and scrambled forward across the fifteen, then the twenty. He dove out to the twenty-six yard line before getting hit, picking up Denver's second first down of the drive. While good news for the Broncos, matters were still dire. By the time Elway took the next snap, 2:26 remained. In just over three minutes of possession, Denver had marched a mere 24 yards. Though they weren't dawdling, they weren't picking up yardage in big chunks like they needed to. That was about to change.

The call on first-and-ten from the twenty-six was "Fire Pass 94," a variation of the previous play, only run to the opposite side. Sewell was again the intended target, and after an Elway playfake to Willhite momentarily froze the Cleveland linebackers, Sewell was able to sneak behind them and between the Browns' safeties over the middle. Elway spotted him and fired the first downfield pass of the drive. Sewell leapt up and snagged the football in stride, then was popped by Chris Rockins at the Denver forty-eight for a 22-yard gain and another first down.

The Cleveland Stadium crowd, which had been maintaining jet-engine sound level throughout the drive, suddenly hushed. They weren't silenced, just subdued. They now realized the Browns' forthcoming trip to the Super Bowl would not come quite so easily. The Broncos had dug out of their field-position hell and now had just half a field to cover and plenty of time to do it. The clock was no longer the Browns' ally. They'd have to do it themselves.

The Broncos hurried up to the line for first down. Elway took the snap and looked for his two primary targets, Clarence Kay and Gerald Willhite. Both were covered. So Elway, with plenty of time to throw, fired a toss for wideout Steve Watson running a curl pattern on the right side. Watson caught it at the Cleveland forty and was tackled there by Frank Minnifield after a 12-yard gain and yet another Denver first down.

And with it, the clock stopped for the two-minute warning.

Nervousness was spreading in the Cleveland Stadium stands. Just minutes after bearing witness to the Browns' rewriting of civic history, fans were beginning to wonder if they hadn't been through this before. How could a guy who had been labeled average and had really looked average most of the game suddenly start doing the things he was doing? The Browns weren't doing things any differently than they had the entire game. It was just that now they weren't working.

The scales of justice balanced a bit on the next play, first down from the forty. Not seeing anyone open, Elway fired a long toss down the right sideline for a streaking Mark Jackson, even though Jackson was covered. Ray Ellis was actually closest to catching the ball, which landed five yards ahead of him and two yards out of bounds. What Elway hadn't seen was a wide-open Clarence Kay standing alone to his left, with no Browns within 15 yards of him. This time, the Browns had caught a break, and it brought up second-and-ten.

Kay was the intended target this time, but Ray Ellis blanketed him in the flat. Elway saw this and stepped forward to avoid a blitzing Clay Matthews to his left. It was like stepping into a bear trap. He crashed into Dave Puzzuoli, but stayed on his feet as Puzzuoli hit the ground. But rather than allowing the elusive Elway to escape and make something of the play, Puzzuoli grabbed on to Elway's foot and wouldn't let go. Elway stumbled and hit the ground at the Cleveland forty-eight for an eight-yard loss. The tittering crowd roared, confident once again, as the Broncos called their second time out with 1:47 to play.

The momentum had swung.

The Browns were now two plays away from the Super Bowl. Nine yards or less on third down, eight yards or less on fourth down, and the Browns could then book their flight to Pasadena. The city of Cleveland's sports fans had not been this close to its dreams in twenty-two years.

Denver was two-of-thirteen for the day on third-down conversions. They had faced third-down-and-double-digit-yardage three times and failed to convert on any of them. During the timeout, Dan Reeves emphasized to John Elway that they didn't need to shoot for all 18 yards on third down. Just get about ten then worry about the rest on fourth down. Play the percentages. It was good advice, but Elway ignored it. He would go for it all.

As the Broncos marched up to the line of scrimmage, the Stadium throng again raised its noise level. This was the play of the game. If the Browns could just force an incomplete pass, it would force Denver into an almost impossible fourth-and-eighteen scenario. "*A trip to Pasadena,*" Jim Mueller told his radio audience, "*could boil down to this play.*" And for one brief second, it appeared the Browns would receive something even better than an incomplete pass.

Elway lined up in the shotgun and was using silent hand and foot signals to combat the crowd. Steve Watson was lined up beside him to his left, Willhite to his right. Elway wanted Watson to go into motion and snap the ball as soon as he started. But the heralded quarterback from Stanford then made the biggest mistake of the day. He lifted his right leg to signal to center Billy Bryan to snap the football when ready. Then he pointed to Watson, instructing him to start his motion. Watson made an "L," cutting in front of Elway running toward his right. The instructions had been backward. Elway meant to start Watson in motion then signal for the snap. Since Bryan already had the go-ahead to snap the football, he wasn't concerned with where Watson was. Bryan snapped the football just as Watson began his motion.

The ball glanced off Watson's tail and spiraled toward the ground on an angle. If it hit the ground and took any kind of bounce, the play was over. Elway would have to turn his attention to simply recovering the ball rather than going downfield with it. Assuming he even did recover, he would have been immediately tagged for a seven- or eight-yard loss, which would have set up an insurmountable fourth-and-twenty-five-plus situation.

For one instant, this drive was over. All the football had to do was hit the ground.

But Elway, whose baseball prowess had earned him Major-League interest, reached down and grabbed the football with his left hand as it spiraled toward the ground. In a flash, he was once again fully upright and backpedaling into the pocket. What could have been a season-ending mistake instead only created a one-beat delay.

Once again, the Browns were not taking a passive philosophy on third down. They were playing the Broncos man-on-man with two safeties deep and four linemen rushing. Elway's first look on "Release 66" was to tight end Orson Mobley, who was running an out-pattern that would have picked up the safe ten yards Reeves was looking for. But Elway wasn't interested in playing it safe. His second read was to rookie wide receiver Mark Jackson, who was running a deep crossing route on the left side more to clear out the defense in the middle of the field than to get open. Hanford Dixon was on Jackson, but allowed the rookie to get inside on him right off the snap. It was the only room Jackson needed. He motored upfield and before Felix Wright could react from his safety spot, Elway rifled a pass toward him. Jackson caught it at the Cleveland twenty-eight and was dragged down by Wright after a 20-yard gain and the biggest first down in Broncos' history.

The crowd once again hushed. The Browns had let two perfect opportunities go by the wayside on this drive. The Broncos now needed to go just 28 yards in ninety seconds. For the first time, fear crept into the hearts of the Cleveland Stadium faithful.

Around this time, NBC and NFL officials began to reconsider their location. They'd moved their equipment to the entrance of the Cleveland locker room for the presentation of the Lamar Hunt Trophy, given annually to the AFC champion. As the Broncos drew closer to the end zone, the entourage started to pack up.

Elway and company rushed up the line and snapped the football, and then Elway tossed it out of bounds to stop the clock with 1:19 left. It would be second-and-ten.

Meanwhile, high above the field, Denver offensive coordinator Mike Shanahan called for a screen pass to Steve Sewell that could take advantage of what he thought was a weakness in the Cleveland man defense. It worked like a charm. Elway looped a toss for Sewell on the left side. Sewell caught it at the thirty-five and followed his blockers through a minefield of Browns' defenders. Chip Banks dove but missed the tackle at the twenty-five, and Sewell continued upfield along the sideline. He had a chance to go out of bounds just inside the twenty, but wanted to make sure he got the first down. He cut back inside and dove out to the fourteen, giving the Broncos a fresh set of downs, though the clock was still ticking, now under a minute.

Elway took the snap and spotted the 6'4" Watson streaking toward the end zone while covered by the 5'9" Frank Minnifield. Deciding those seven inches were worth a quick shot, Elway lobbed a pass down the right sideline toward Watson, who leapt up across the goal line, caught the ball, but landed with both feet out of bounds. Minnifield had negated the height advantage and prevented the touchdown. Forty-nine seconds remained for second-and-ten from the Browns' fourteen.

Hoping to cross up the Cleveland defense, Reeves called for a quarterback draw. In the shotgun, Elway took the snap, but noticed immediately the Browns had clogged up the middle of the field. In the same moment, he noticed Chip Banks follow Gerald Willhite on an out-pattern to the right side, clearing an alley. Improvising as only a great athlete can, he meandered to his right until he had some blockers creating daylight. He pointed for right tackle Ken Lanier to take out Mike Johnson and angled toward the sideline inside the ten. Though Lanier didn't throw a clean block on Johnson, he ran enough interference to allow Elway to creep a few yards farther. He slid out of bounds at the five for a nine-yard gain. It brought up the third third-down of the drive with forty-two seconds left.

With one time out remaining Denver could afford to run, but Elway was hot, and everyone in the stadium knew it. In fact, the collective noise level of the fans had seemed to get proportionally lower as the Broncos got closer and closer to the end zone. Rather than being the cacophonous motley crew it had earned the reputation of, the denizens of the Dog Pound stood almost silent, as if waiting for a lethal injection. Radio broadcaster Jim Mueller even encouraged the fans to get into it, pointing out that this was no time to sit back in apprehension. To have any hope of victory, the Browns needed their fans to get back into it now.

But all that history they'd buried after Brennan's touchdown was back up and walking around in their heads. Wasn't this almost exactly how the Browns had seen their season end the year before—to a red-hot quarterback carving through their defense like Leinegen's ants? Hadn't the Indians just had their best season in decades, yet still finished eleven games out of first? Didn't the Cavaliers still stink? And wasn't this the same end zone where Brian Sipe was intercepted on Red Right 88? As the Broncos lined up for third down, many Browns' fans in the stands and in their homes either didn't look or knew they needn't.

Again from the shotgun, Elway's primary target would be Willhite on a short out into the end zone. But as he took the snap, he quickly noticed that Willhite was blanketed by Anthony Griggs. Willhite tried to lose Griggs when his pattern crossed with wide receiver Vance Johnson, but Clay Matthews came out of the cluster on Willhite, nullifying him as an option.

So for the second time in six plays, Elway focused on a rookie wide receiver who couldn't hang on to a pass in training camp five months earlier. Just as was the case on third-and-eighteen, Mark Jackson's primary purpose was to clear a lane for another receiver. He'd gone in motion toward the left side, and as the ball was snapped, encountered cornerback Mark Harper right off the line. Jackson made a quick move inside and, just like he'd done to Hanford Dixon five plays earlier, gained an angle on Harper. Just as Jackson broke free, however, so did Chip Banks, blitzing from the right side. Elway sensed the oncoming defender and reared back to throw what he would eventually admit was the hardest-thrown pass of his career.

The ball rocketed over the line of scrimmage as if shot out of a cannon. It slid over the outstretched arm of Carl Hairston and into the end zone, angling down toward the ground. Either Jackson would catch it or no one would. Jackson hit the turf, crushing God knows how many Milk Bones in the process, and gathered the football into his stomach. He appeared to bobble the football at first, much like a drop he suffered in the second quarter on a key third-down pass, but then regained control as he rolled over on his back, throwing his legs up in the air.

He finished his summersault at the exact spot where Mike Davis had intercepted Brian Sipe six years and seven days before.

Jackson got up in a daze. Looking like he'd just had an adrenaline injection straight to his heart, he leapt awkwardly up into the air and let loose possibly the oddest-looking, most melodramatic spike in NFL history—yet a well-deserved one.

After Red Right 88, the analogy was made that the Stadium sounded like someone had just unplugged a stereo on full-blast. After Jackson's touchdown, it was more like turning off a hair dryer. The crowd had already been subdued, expecting the worst. And now the worst had happened. A collective groan sighed across the bleachers, and a large rubber ball flew from that direction, bouncing back up through the end zone—a sign of either fan rebellion or frustration.

Bare-footed Rich Karlis booted the deceivingly critical extra point through the uprights, literally right into the face of the Dog Pound, and with thirty-seven seconds remaining, it was time to start up the engines again. After fifteen plays and 98 yards, this was a whole new game. The Browns were no longer the long-suffering also-rans who were about to be anointed by destiny. Now they were a team that had just squandered a chance for victory and would have to overcome the barreling pendulum of momentum to clinch their first trip to the Super Bowl.

After Gerald McNeil was the victim of a funny bounce on the ensuing kickoff, just as Gene Lang had the kickoff before, he was held to a three-yard return to the Cleveland fifteen yard line. There Bernie Kosar, whose touchdown pass to Brian Brennan now seemed to have been nine months earlier, threw a safe four-yard pass to Herman Fontenot, then kneeled out the final twenty-one seconds to concede to overtime.

As a reminder of how kind she had been just minutes before, fate threw Cleveland one more bone—so to speak. On the sudden-death coin flip, the Broncos called heads, and it landed on tails. The Browns would receive as Kosar would try to match Elway's heroics with a drive of his own. "Even though they were dejected because of the drive that had just happened and a lot of guys were just stunned, a lot of the people remembered the Jets game," Bob Golic said. "In the Jets game, we held it together."

Gerald McNeil returned the kick 15 yards to the Cleveland thirty. On first down, Kosar dropped back to pass, but his two primary options were covered. Instead of forcing anything, he stumbled forward for a two-yard gain. The Browns came out in a four-receiver set on second-and-eight, and as a result, Ozzie Newsome stood wide open at the Cleveland forty. But Kosar couldn't see him. Instead, he threw to the right sideline, where Brian Brennan reeled in the pass for a six-yard gain. It brought up third-and-two at the Cleveland thirty-eight.

While the Browns' defensive playcalling on Denver's final drive of regulation would be questioned afterward, Cleveland's strange call on this offensive play should have been questioned as well. Though he'd seen some time as a blocker and had caught a pass earlier, still-rusty Earnest Byner certainly wasn't an option. And despite having a bulldozer of a fullback in Kevin Mack, who had rushed for 94 yards on the afternoon, or even sparingly used Curtis Dickey, who hadn't touched the ball all day, the Browns didn't use either. But they didn't intend to cross up the Broncos by passing. On third-and-two, the call was a misdirected sweep out of a four-receiver set to Herman Fontenot, who would start to the left of Kosar, then run to his right around the end.

It was a peculiar call in any circumstance, but especially considering the Browns had not needed a first down all season the way they needed one now. The percentage call would have been Mack up the middle. Lower percentage, yet still plausible, was anyone on the Browns' roster running straight ahead on either a draw or an offtackle play. But the call was a sweep to Fontenot, who had carried the ball three times on the day for three yards.

What happened next was only natural. By the time Fontenot received the football, the play was busted. Karl Mecklenberg bounced off a block attempt by Dan Fike to bring Fontenot down for a yard loss. The Browns would have to give the ball back to John Elway, less than ten minutes removed from the greatest possession in NFL postseason history.

The Broncos took over at their own twenty-five yard line. Sammy Winder sprinted up the middle for five yards on first down. Then Elway reached into his bag of tricks once again. On second down, he connected with a diving Orson Mobley on the right side at the Cleveland forty-eight after a 22-yard gain. To the horror and negative expectations of the Stadium crowd, the Broncos had picked up right where they'd left off and were now less than 20 yards away from field-goal range.

Denver went back to Winder from the forty-eight, and he was trapped for a two-yard loss on a sweep around left end. On second-and-twelve from midfield, the Broncos called for the same screen to Steve Sewell that had worked for 14 yards on the game-tying drive. But whatever weakness Mike Shanahan had spotted before had been corrected, because the play was blown from the get-go. Elway wandered to his left but eventually had to lob the football into a crowd to avoid an oncoming Carl Hairston. On its awkward, wobbling path, the football came less than two inches away from the hand of 6'7" Sam Clancy. Showing off the basketball moves that had made him a star at the University of Pittsburgh, Clancy leapt up into the air and came ever so close to getting a hand on the pass. Instead, the football fell incomplete at the feet of Sewell, who wasn't going anywhere had he caught it.

The Cleveland Stadium fans, now running on emotional fumes, rose up once again. It was third-and-twelve. A Browns' stop would give them back the ball, albeit in poor field position. On the other hand, it would at least give the Denver offense some time to cool off and perhaps a chance for Bernie and the boys to warm up.

And just as had been the case on second down, the Broncos' third-down attempt looked bad from the start. From the shotgun, Elway took the snap and couldn't find anyone open. He began to scramble to his left toward the sideline, stumbled, recovered, and looked up again. Avoiding Clancy, he started to move upfield along the sideline and had some daylight before him. Hanford Dixon, whose job was to cover Steve Watson downfield, looked up to see Elway start to run. This froze him for one second of indecision—stick with Watson or run up to stop Elway. Either choice had risks and rewards, and it could have gone either way. But that one moment of indecision was all Elway needed.

As Dixon slowed down, Watson broke deep away from him down the sideline. Elway spotted him and lobbed a pass downfield. Compounding the Browns' problems was Felix Wright slipping on his way to help Dixon. Watson caught it on the sideline at the Cleveland twenty-three and Wright knocked him out of bounds for a first down on a 27-yard gain, the Broncos' longest completion of the day.

Denver could feel it now. On the strength of two long Elway passes, they'd driven 42 yards into field-goal range. And the Broncos weren't about to risk a Red Right 88. After a Browns' time out, Sammy Winder plowed up the middle through the exhausted Cleveland defense for a five-yard gain to the eighteen. He picked up two more to the sixteen on second down, and then was stuffed for no gain on third, though he was essentially just centering the football for the oncoming field goal.

Onto the field marched Rich Karlis, a native of Salem, Ohio, who had grown up a Browns' fan. He had more than fifty family and friends in attendance, more than any individual Bronco, even linebacker Tom Jackson, who had grown up in Cleveland and was possibly playing his final NFL game. He would now have a chance to break Cleveland's heart in a way it had never been broken before.

The snap and hold were good. Karlis brought his bare right foot toward the ball and booted it, just past the outstretched hand of Frank Minnifield, trying desperately to match his heroics in the Metrodome back in late October. The kick was high and sailed left toward the uprights at the closed end of the Stadium. With each passing yard, it continued to meander left at a dramatic angle. As it crept inside the ten, it was running out of leeway before clearing the left goalpost. When it finally reached the yellow stick wavering in the constant Lake Erie breeze, it actually was above it. Unlike most field-goal attempts which are clearly good or clearly not good, there was a moment in which no one knew.

Broncos' tackle Dave Studdard was so certain it was a miss, he closed his eyes and turned his head. Rich Karlis and his holder, backup quarterback Gary Kubiak, stood frozen. Browns' safety Chris Rockins stood to their left, motioning with his left hand that the kick was wide left. Marty Schottenheimer's wife, Pat, watching the game from a loge right behind the goalposts, forever maintained the kick was no good. "Marty," she told him that night, "the ball was not inside the uprights."

A year later, *Plain Dealer* sports editor Gene Williams would recount his perspective from the field behind the end zone: "The crowd behind the goalposts started to cheer, figuring the Browns still had life. . . . The referees standing under the post looked at each other as if to say, 'Do you really want to spend another minute out here? What time does our plane leave, anyway?'"

Though it seemed to stretch on for much longer than it did, the moment finally ended. Both goal-line officials raised their arms, and the Denver Broncos were going to the Super Bowl.

After coming so close to their ultimate dream, the 1986 Cleveland Browns season was over.

Cleveland Stadium stood almost completely silent, except for the whoops and screams of the jubilant Denver Broncos piling atop one another at midfield. Bob Golic, who came mere inches away from blocking the kick after exploding through the Denver line, lay atop the torn-up turf in disbelief. "It was like my heart dropped out of my chest," he said. "I remember laying there in the mud and the dirt and couldn't believe it was over. This was the team I grew up with, and I was helping it get to the Super Bowl, and all of a sudden I'm laying in the mud, and they're celebrating. I don't think I've ever felt so down."

"When I looked up and saw the officials rule it was good, I can't explain the feeling," Hanford Dixon said afterward. "It was almost like I didn't want to play football anymore. I don't ever want that feeling again." Neither did the nearly 80,000 people in attendance, many of whom had seen this mind-numbing conclusion coming for nearly a half-hour. They stood in stunned, heartbroken silence.

Then the silence broke. As the Browns started to walk off the field, someone began clapping. Someone else joined. Soon, this wave of applause spread through the stands, and it grew louder and more emotional. "They were thanking us for being the best God-damned Browns team they'd ever had," Mike Baab said. "It was one of the coolest things I've ever seen in sports." Golic added, "I think that was the one moment that solidified my belief that they were the best, that they could be so appreciative of what we had done that season."

But the Broncos had won the day. And no one would soon forget how.

"It was like somebody was shooting you in the shoulder," Brian Brennan would say, "then in the right forearm, then in the left foot. It was like a slow death."

"Elway didn't just pull victory from the Browns' mouth," Rick Telander wrote in *Sports Illustrated.* "He ripped the thing from halfway down their throat."

Rather than seeing Bernie Kosar take his long-suffering hometown team to the Super Bowl, as apparently was his destiny, it was oft-criticized John Elway who had enjoyed what he would later call his "coming-out party." "John shut a lot of people up today," Steve Watson said. But neither quarterback had a spectacular day statistically. Elway completed twenty-two of thirty-eight passes for the game for 244 yards with a touchdown and an interception. On Denver's final two drives, he was eight for twelve for 128 yards and rushed for twenty more. "We shut him down the whole game," Sam Clancy said, "and then in the last minutes he showed what he was made of."

Immediately, the media sought to blame Marty Schottenheimer and Dave Adolph for using a "prevent" defense on the final drive of regulation. But that criticism was somewhat flawed. "We definitely did not change our defense," Schottenheimer said. "We were mixing our coverages just as we had through the entire game." In other words, the architecture was solid, the execution was not. "It's easy, looking back now and saying they should've taken some bigger risks," Elway said afterward. "But I don't think there's really a whole lot they could have done. They just stayed with what had been successful for them the whole game, and we finally got on a roll.

"When you're up seven and the other team has 98 yards to go, you don't get away from the things that have been successful for you. And they definitely weren't in a prevent defense."

Meanwhile Kosar completed eighteen of thirty-two passes for 259 yards with two touchdowns and two interceptions—not bad, but a far cry from the 489 yards he tallied the week before.

Which is exactly what Joe Collier had in mind as he designed the Denver defensive game plan. Rather than trying to get to Kosar via the blitz as many teams had tried and failed throughout 1986, Collier conceded the pass rush and often dropped seven or eight men into coverage to try to fool Kosar. "He was rattled because we had everybody covered," Denver linebacker Ricky Hunley said. "For him it was like knocking on a door and nobody's home."

A sentiment Cleveland fans were quite familiar with. Many fans stayed in their seats, too exhausted or heartbroken to go home. Tears flowed, though mostly in silence. The scene was much the same in the Cleveland locker room. "Now I know how the Jets felt last week," Bernie Kosar said. Yet there were no emotional out-bursts. Just stunned silence and disappointment. "Being mature sucks," Mike Baab admitted later. "I wanted so bad to throw my helmet and let it all out."

Even Rich Karlis, the man who had started those tears, admitted he felt bad for the people of Cleveland, who had waited so long for a championship. Marty Schottenheimer echoed that feeling.

"One of my biggest disappointments is for the fans of Cleveland," he said. "I can't say how proud I am to be a Clevelander. The support and the spirit of this town over the past few months has been unbelievable, and it has been a privilege to be a part of it. If anyone deserved a Super Bowl, our fans did."

Instead, for the twenty-first straight year, the Browns and their fans would watch somebody else play on football's greatest stage. Rather than facing off with the mighty New York Giants in what would have been a wonderful throwback to past days of NFL glory, the Browns watched the Broncos get buried by the Giants, 39-20. Adding insult to injury, Elway racked up solid stats but was held in check in the second half and wound up getting drilled in the end zone for a safety. Worse, in the second quarter Rich Karlis missed a field goal that was actually shorter than the one he'd beaten the Browns with.

For as heartbreaking as the loss was, the pain dulled over the next few weeks, and Browns' fans began to look at the big picture. The team was relatively young. It had an able and disciplined coach and a young quarterback with indescribable potential just about to enter his prime. They'd gone 12-4 despite having their second-most-important offensive player miss half the season. Their defense had recovered from a horrible start to reach the level of expectations of the previous two years. Virtually no one, even those outside of Cleveland, thought 1986 was a one-shot deal.

"I said it after we lost to Miami in the playoffs last year, and I'll say it again," Schottenheimer said that gray January afternoon. "This team will be back. I guar-antee it."

They would. And so would the Denver Broncos.

12 Strike Two

There didn't appear to be much reason for the Browns' front office to tinker with personnel following the storybook 1986 season.

That's why the trade of linebacker Chip Banks came as such a surprise.

On draft day 1987, Cleveland had shipped Banks and its first- and second-round picks to the Chargers in exchange for San Diego's first- and second-round picks. Instead of selecting twenty-fourth and fifty-third overall, the Browns would pick fifth and thirty-second.

Banks wasn't exactly stunned, but he was surprised. He had just completed his fourth Pro Bowl season with the Browns. After molding some of his defensive strategies to fit Banks' liking, Marty Schottenheimer had pulled him aside after the season and complimented him on the year he'd had and talked about looking forward to 1987. Banks had one more year on his current contract and the problems between the team and its best linebacker seemed to be in the past.

But the Browns were on a different wavelength. They had a master plan to make the team better, and losing Banks was part of it. Many players talked about how while Banks was a dynamic, occasionally dominant player on Sundays, he often wasn't giving his all in practice. And though no one admitted it publicly, the players and front office hadn't forgotten Banks' offseason tomfoolery the past two years that not only embarrassed the team but prevented it from becoming better. When asked if this was a case of addition by subtraction, Schottenheimer replied, "That's a gross oversimplification." But he didn't say it wasn't.

"I'm trying to look at this as a business decision on their part," Banks said. "It could be personal. I don't know. I'd like to think they were big enough men to let bygones be bygones. I guess I shouldn't be so totally surprised, but it's hard to accept after the moments we shared last year."

Showing diplomacy that would have made the Swiss proud, Schottenheimer kept his opinion to himself—for the most part. "Very simply," he said during a press conference, "the thing we can never lose sight of is in the National Football League we're involved in a team sport. Chip is a fine player, but he's in the history of the Cleveland Browns now. I prefer to look at the future."

When a reporter asked if Banks simply did not have the intensity to be a Schottenheimer player, the coach craftily replied, "It would be unfair of me to comment on that, but I have always felt you're a very perceptive individual."

The trade was contingent on one factor. Of two specific linebackers eligible for the draft the Browns had their eye on to replace Banks, at least one had to be available. One was Penn State's Shane Conlan, who was considered by many draft prognosticators to be the second-best linebacker in the draft, behind only neon-haired loudmouth Brian Bosworth from Oklahoma, who would wind up with the Seattle Seahawks through a variation of the supplemental draft. But the Browns' first choice was less-heralded Mike Junkin from Duke.

Just as the news of the Banks trade was starting to sink in for the crowd at Madison Square Garden that spring afternoon, NFL commissioner Pete Rozelle stood at the podium and announced the real surprise. With the fifth pick in the NFL draft, the Browns had taken Junkin. This completed what would become the Browns' most talked-about draft deal since they shipped away Paul Warfield for the right to draft Mike Phipps seventeen years before.

Despite the initial shock of football fans across the country, it wasn't as if Junkin had come out of nowhere. He'd been a second-team All-American selection at inside linebacker as a senior, and both of the league's primary scouting combines had projected him as a good prospect, certain to start at some point in the future. Most "experts" tagged Junkin as a second- or third-round pick, at best a late-first-round choice. Even Junkin was surprised when the Browns picked him fifth. "I expected to go high," he said, "but honestly not this high." No one, at least not publicly, had thought he was good enough to go in the top five. No one, that is, except the Browns, who ranked him as the third best overall player in the entire draft, behind only Miami quarterback Vinny Testaverde and Alabama linebacker Cornelius Bennett, who went one-two.

Chip Falivene, Ernie Accorsi, and company had fallen for Junkin the previous autumn when Don Anile, one of Falivene's most trusted scouts, saw him play. After the game, Anile called Falivene and said, "He plays like a mad dog in a meat market." It was a comment that tied the Browns and Junkin together for much longer than anyone would have guessed. The Browns had no doubt that not only would Junkin be able to replace Banks but that he would make the defense even better. "Junkin will fill a role which will put us over the hump," Schottenheimer said. "I can't recall a time when the coaching staff and personnel people were so unified on one player. That makes me happy."

The coach added that Junkin was one of the two best college linebackers he'd ever seen, with Lawrence Taylor the other, and that Junkin reminded him of Jack Lambert. Ambitious statements, to be sure, but the Browns' actions spoke louder than their words. Cleveland entered the draft wanting to grab a dominant pass rusher, the one primary weakness of an otherwise strong defense. To pick Junkin, the Browns had bypassed highly touted prospects such as Conlan, Washington defensive end Reggie Rogers, and Miami defensive tackle Jerome Brown. The Browns were confident they had their man.

Most fans seemed to understand trading Banks, and virtually none were up in arms over it. But to do it all just to get Junkin had them scratching their heads. Partly because he played at a low-profile football program in the low-profile, run-happy Atlantic Coast Conference, Junkin had received very little national attention. But there were several other reasons to question why the Browns had invested so much to take this gamble. For one, Junkin had played his entire college career at inside linebacker. He would now be expected to replace an All-Pro at *outside* linebacker. It wasn't unheard of for a player to switch the intricacies of his position from college to the pros, but this was a bit dramatic—and many felt more than a bit risky.

To the Browns' credit, they knew they couldn't simply rest on their 1986 laurels and expect victories to just come. "We cannot afford to stand pat," Schottenheimer said. "Look what happened in '81. When teams stand pat, they usually wind up going south."

Aside from the Junkin Juxtaposition, the Browns made a handful of other minor yet notable changes prior to the start of the 1987 season. With the departure of Tom Olivadotti to Miami, Bill Cowher became the Browns' secondary coach after spending two years turning Cleveland's special teams into the best in the business. To fill Cowher's shoes, Marty Schottenheimer turned to his younger brother, Kurt, who had coached linebackers for Lou Holtz at Notre Dame in 1986 and held the same position at Louisiana State the previous two seasons. Later, with their second-round pick from San Diego, they selected offensive lineman Gregg Rakoczy from Miami. Rakoczy wasn't expected to step right in and start, but he was versatile enough to back up every position on the line and would be groomed to take over in the near future as the Cleveland line began to age.

With Earnest Byner set to return as healthy as ever, the Browns released Curtis Dickey before camp began. But they bolstered their backfield by drafting fullback Tim Manoa from Penn State in the third round. Conversely, Matt Bahr's prognosis for returning by opening day was not good, so the Browns maneuvered up to select kicker Jeff Jaeger from Washington in the third round. Jaeger would be the Browns' kicker, at least until Bahr was able to beat him out. Longtime role players Harry Holt, Curtis Weathers, George Lilja, and Scott Nicolas were all released in camp to make room for younger or flat-out better players. The Browns filled some of the pass-rush void they couldn't satiate in the draft with a late August trade with St. Louis that landed defensive end Al "Bubba" Baker, a veteran who specialized in pressuring the quarterback.

As camp began, expectations from the media and fans were higher than ever. Anything short of a Super Bowl appearance would be considered a disappointment. By mid-summer, more than 50,000 season tickets had been sold, the most since the post–Kardiac Kids season of 1981. For the Browns' first preseason game against the lowly St. Louis Cardinals, 78,650 packed into Cleveland Stadium—the team's largest preseason home crowd in sixteen years. Despite the excitement, large storm clouds hung over the team and the sport as the season drew closer. Primarily, the players association's agreement with the league was set to expire August 31, and as the summer droned on, the two sides drew no closer to drawing up a new one. Another strike, just like the one that had shut down the game for fifty-seven days in 1982, appeared eminent.

Less troubling but equally frustrating for the Browns was the absence of Mike Junkin, who held out for sixteen vital days, missing twenty-three practices and a scrimmage. Finally, on August 10 he agreed to a four-year contract worth $1.8 million with a $735,000 signing bonus. When he finally hit the field, Junkin looked exactly like a rookie who was being asked to play a brand-new position after missing two weeks of practice: awkward. He did show promise with a few nice plays in the exhibition games, including a 21-yard interception return for a touchdown in the finale to beat the Packers in overtime. But even this was a case of good news/bad news: the only reason Junkin was able to make the play was because he had blown his coverage of the tight end and should never have been where the pass was thrown. Not surprisingly, Schottenheimer determined that Junkin would not start on opening day. The inside linebacker spot would go to veteran Anthony Griggs, who had played a nice role for the Browns in 1986, but who would also have to switch spots from the inside to the outside.

After Reggie Camp had an uninspired preseason, Schottenheimer turned to Sam Clancy to make his first NFL start at left end. Going into Week One, the Browns had to hope that no one would notice that the left side of their defense was still undergoing massive construction. Unfortunately, after twenty years of incompetence, the New Orleans Saints were no longer that stupid.

Regardless of what faith they subscribed to, the Browns had to have a bad feeling going into the Louisiana Superdome on September 13. The previous afternoon, Pope John Paul II held mass at the Superdome, and the entire bayou was aglow with his papal presence. Never mind that New Orleans was an up-and-coming team with a dedicated and disciplined coach. A day after the pope essentially blessed the playing field, the Browns would have to play a team called the Saints. Talk about trying to beat the house.

As expected, the Saints ran to the left side of the Cleveland defense at every opportunity and the strategy worked like a charm. Second-year tailback Reuben Mayes carved through the Browns for 147 yards on twenty-four carries, a clip of more than six yards per rush. Of those yards, 104 were to the Browns' left, where Chip Banks no longer was. The Cleveland pass rush was non-existent, sacking quarterback Bobby Hebert just once. But where the Browns were really outplayed was special teams. The Saints blocked a Jaeger field goal, and their kickoff and punt coverage were superb. Five times Saints' punter Brian Hansen pinned Cleveland inside its own twenty yard line, and the Browns never started a drive past the twenty.

Despite the Cleveland defense's sloppy play and the field-position hindrance, the Browns' offense fought admirably. Every time the Saints took a lead, the visitors responded. When Bernie Kosar, who would throw for 314 yards and connect with eight different receivers, scored on a three-yard scramble with 12:37 remaining, the game was tied at twenty-one and appeared headed for a memorable conclusion. It was. Facing miserable field position, Kosar was belted for two safeties in the final ten minutes, and the Saints held on for a 28-21 win. In contrast to the incredible expectations for the season, the Browns were 0-1 for the fifth straight year. Worse, Cleveland was looking up at the rest of its division rivals, who had all won on opening day.

The mood in the Cleveland locker room afterward was easy to decipher: wavering between disappointment and disgust. "I think every one of us is bleeped off with himself," linebacker Eddie Johnson said. "One loss does not make a season, but it damn sure contributes to it."

After an offseason of wondering who was going to rush the quarterback, the Browns were now wondering if teams would even *need* to throw the ball. New Orleans racked up 191 rushing yards against a tired Cleveland defense that looked no better than it had early in 1986. Considering they had a divisional game upcoming in Week Two with Pittsburgh coming to town and the players association's strike date looming the following Tuesday, the Browns had to solve their defensive crisis in a hurry. Otherwise they might dig themselves an insurmountable hole in what appeared would be a shortened season.

To turn things around, Marty Schottenheimer decided to borrow from the best. Early in the week, as the Browns' coaches put their game plan together, Schottenheimer and Dave Adolph decided to mix things up a bit defensively. While watching the Chicago Bears carve up the defending world-champion Giants on the season premiere of *Monday Night Football* they decided to take a page from the Chicago Bears' defensive scheme and occasionally mimic the mighty Bears' 4-6 alignment. In certain situations, when the Browns decided to switch out of their usual 3-4 set, they'd bring in a fourth lineman, a third cornerback, and creep a safety out of the secondary to become essentially a fifth linebacker.

In football terms, one week into the regular season, this was godless anarchy. And it worked like a charm.

The Browns' defense throttled Pittsburgh from opening kickoff to final gun on a sunny afternoon on the lakefront. After the Saints had made the Browns' run defense look silly the week before, the Steelers were limited to 58 rushing yards for the game and a harmless 29 total yards in the second half, three rushing. Consistently inconsistent Pittsburgh quarterback Mark Malone claimed afterward he hadn't been confused by the Browns' defensive tilt-a-whirl, but his statistics suggested otherwise. He completed just twelve of thirty-six passes, threw five interceptions, and was sacked three times. It was, without question, a good old-fashioned September stomping by the Browns' defense in a 34-10 victory. Browns' fans couldn't help but feel good. This was the Browns' team they expected to see in 1987. This was the team that was just thirty-seven seconds away from the Super Bowl eight months earlier.

However, those summer storm clouds still loomed on the horizon. Junkin had looked better but still not anywhere close to how a first-round draft pick should. While the defensive strategy shift had worked against one of the worst offenses in the NFL, no one knew how long the illusion would last, if at all against a potent offense. And worst of all, barring an eleventh-hour miracle of modern negotiating, the fans and players would most likely be parting ways for an unpredictable amount of time. Less than forty-eight hours after the Browns proved that they would in fact be for real in 1987, outside events would conspire to suggest that the 1987 season itself might not be on solid ground.

The NFL's second regular-season work stoppage was about to begin.

It was a surreal scene, something straight out of an episode of *The Twilight Zone*. On a sunny mid-October afternoon, as one football team practiced, another paraded past it toward the locker room. The practice stopped as players and coaches watched a long line of familiar faces march through. For most of the players currently in pads on the practice field, this gauntlet represented the end of their short-lived football careers. For others, it signified the beginning of what would almost certainly be a long rebuilding process of broken friendships and strained professional opinions of one another.

But for one and all, the parade meant one thing for certain: the players' twenty-four-day strike had ended—and thus so did one of the wackiest, most controversial, and memorable months in the history of professional sports.

As midnight neared on the evening of Monday, September 21, 1987, football fans knew what was on the horizon. As the New England Patriots and New York Jets toiled through the night in the final game of the second week of the season, the clock ticked toward the beginning of the NFL's second work stoppage in five years. A game that began with every player on each team's roster running out to midfield to exchange a symbolic mass handshake ended with a 43-24 Jets' win that marked the final NFL game before the players' deadline for a strike.

Hopes for an eleventh-hour agreement had passed when there was no half-time announcement from Gene Upshaw, leader of the players' association. The basic agreement between the NFL and its players had expired three weeks earlier, and despite a summer filled with negotiations and a swarm of scrambled meetings through September, no compromise could be reached. So when the final gun sounded in the Patriots-Jets game, the players were officially on strike.

The primary sticking point in negotiations was free agency, a virtually non-existent possibility in the NFL that the players' association wanted to see adopted much as it had been in Major League Baseball. Under the NFL's current free-agency system, players whose contracts had expired could entertain offers from other teams, but his original club had the right to match any offer he received. But since the price for a new team signing any free agent was high—draft picks, at which level dependent on his tenure and value to his original team—there was little market to begin with. Over the previous ten years, just one NFL player had changed teams via this system. The NFLPA wanted to open up unrestricted free agency to any player who had been in the league four years. The league was only willing to "liberalize" its current policy.

Ironically, rumors spread through the grapevine that most players didn't really care about free agency. Most felt it was something only the upper echelon of players would truly benefit from, but even Bernie Kosar, the Browns' marquee player, said it wasn't a deal-breaking issue with him. He was happy where he was and had no intention of seeing if the grass was greener elsewhere. More important to Kosar (who would lose $50,000 per game during the strike) was standing with his teammates. "I promise you," Art Modell told a reporter at the strike's outset, "there are at least thirty-five to forty players on the Browns that if I told them they were a free agent, they'd pass out from fright. They don't want it."

As it turned out, Modell had hit the nail on the head. "I think the players felt a little bit misled," Bob Golic said. "The Browns as a team listed the top ten demands that we had. And at the time, free agency, what the union was saying was the biggest thing was like No. 8 on our list.

"When we called Upshaw and told him we needed to talk because things may not have been as we thought they were, he flew into town and basically read us the riot act. You feel all of a sudden like you're not being part of it."

Other, less glamorous issues were also on the table, such as adopting a league drug policy, changing roster sizes, and fine-tuning the league's pension system. But while free agency sparked debate across the country, it still wasn't considered by many to be a major issue. In 1982, when the players struck for fifty-seven days and wiped out seven games of the regular season, the debate was over how to slice up the pie of revenue between the league and its players—a much simpler and, frankly, more pertinent issue. Incredibly, as the 1987 strike wore on, the majority of fans actually sided with the owners, a hallmark sign of a lost cause for the strikers.

"That strike [in 1982] was real bad blood," Mike Baab said. "The strike in '87 was different. There was no solidarity at all. . . . The feel was very different. Lots of guys were making a lot more money. They did not want to strike. We weren't as together at all. Guys felt real funky. None of us really wanted to strike. We felt forced to strike. In '82, everybody wanted to strike."

Learning a lesson from almost two months without fielding a product five years before, the owners added a wrinkle to the negotiations. If the players wanted to strike, that was fine, the owners agreed late that summer. The season would go on. As soon as the teams signed enough non-union players to put a team on the field, the schedule would resume as planned. So as the strike drew closer, members of the Browns' front office not only were working to improve the team they had but also to put together a contingency team for when the players walked out the door.

Needless to say, the idea of their jobs being taken by "scabs" dramatically upset the Browns' players, as evidenced by a scene outside team headquarters on day two of the strike. Several Browns picketed outside the team's practice facility at Baldwin-Wallace College, many wearing signs. Though the actual marching was more of a display for the media than an actual method of protest, the strikers did attempt to get their point across. They received mixed reactions from drivers passing by, but spent much of their time signing autographs and posing for pictures with fans. The driver of a lawn-care service truck stopped by and offered work to any of the players needing money. After a talk with Mike Pagel, the team's new player rep after Curtis Weathers was cut in the preseason, drivers of UPS and Fed Ex trucks with deliveries for the front office turned back, deciding not to cross the picket. Steelworkers and other union jobholders came out to march with the players, empathizing with the players' cries against management.

"All the unions were telling us they'd help us any way they could," Golic said. "They were offering office space or copiers or telephones or whatever we needed to handle the business of the strike. Then we got a call from the ironworkers. We were expecting another offer for offices or whatever. They say, 'Listen, we hear they're having scabs coming in. If you'd like us to, for that first game, we'll take our people and surround the Stadium and we won't let people in.' We were like, 'Y'know what, can we call you back on that one?'"

Meanwhile, inside the building, the Browns' brass scrambled to put a new team together. The first player they signed was quarterback Jeff Christensen, a 1983 draft choice of Cincinnati who had bounced around the league in the last four years, never throwing a pass in a regular-season game. Christensen, who had been with the team in training camp in 1986 before being cut, had left his wife and child in suburban Chicago when the possibility of the strike became evident two weeks earlier and was working as a bartender in the Flats waiting for it to happen. He was a guy who was never going to be a starting quarterback in the NFL. In five years of trying, he couldn't catch on with a team, even as a backup. Now he was hoping when given a chance to shine during the strike, he might force people to take notice and might be able to extend his otherwise forsaken career once the strike was over. He didn't see his plan as harmful to others. "I'm not out to cause controversy," he said. "I'm not out to cost anyone a job. But if I was a player, and I chose to strike, I don't know if I would get mad at somebody else for feeding his family."

Unfortunately, the striking players felt differently. When Christensen unexpectedly (and perhaps unwisely) dropped by team headquarters that Wednesday, he was met with resistance on the way out. Mike Pagel had said from the outset that the players would not resort to violence or would not threaten any replacements. Christensen wasn't attacked, nor technically was he threatened. But he certainly was intimidated. As his car pulled up to the line, Browns' safety Ray Ellis placed a garbage bag full of pizza boxes and napkins on Christensen's hood, then argued with the Browns' new quarterback. The exchange went on for several minutes before Ellis barked, "If I ever get a shot at you, I'm going to take it." It matched the animosity shown by an anonymous Cleveland player, who told the *Plain Dealer* that if he came up against a scab player on the field when the dispute was over, he would "see to it that his kneecaps end up in Peoria and his knees in Baton Rouge."

Actually, things were much more hostile elsewhere. In Houston, a bus carrying replacement players into the team facility was egged. In Washington, a similar bus had its windows broken. And in Kansas City, a pair of striking players showed up on the picket line with shotguns (mercifully unloaded) intimating what they'd do if they spotted any scabs. "It's a special kind of strike," retorted John Hynes, a replacement tackle for the Los Angeles Raiders. "It's not like a blue-collar job where you would be taking food off someone's table. If they've got to eat, they can sell their Porsches." Adopting that attitude, more than eighty union players crossed the line to rejoin their team and earn their regular paychecks by playing in the replacement games. At first, none were Browns, who thus far were following Marty Schottenheimer's only advice to them entering the conflict: "Whatever you do, do it together."

Emotions were high. With teams still trying to fill replacement rosters, the league canceled Week Three games, but would be back up and running for Week Four. Not only would the league lose money from this decision but Cleveland fans would miss a shot at one of the most-anticipated rematches in team history. When Week Three went by the wayside, so did the Browns' Monday-night showdown with the now-hated Denver Broncos at Cleveland Stadium. The Browns would have to wait for their shot at redemption.

As Week Four rapidly approached, the NFL stood steadfastly by its plan to carry on. It would be forced to refund much of the money the television networks had forked out to broadcast these games, which were now at a much lower quality and less appealing to the average viewer. Teams would also take a bath in lost ticket sales, not only in seats not sold but on those they refunded to fans who'd already purchased them. Accordingly, for the Browns' first replacement game against the Patriots in New England on October 4, a mere 14,830 showed up. Most fans weren't exactly on the same wavelength as the players, and seemingly no one felt truly sorry for the owners. "If this strike thing keeps up much longer," Bill Livingston wrote in the *Plain Dealer,* "the poor NFL might have to recap the tires on its limousines."

Amidst this mess, the Browns indeed fielded a team—if you could call it that. Despite his limited resume, Jeff Christensen was actually one of the veterans of the group. There were lots of USFL castoffs who previously couldn't land a spot in the NFL and loads of low draft picks who couldn't make it out of their first training camp.

There was defensive end Darryl Sims, Pittsburgh's top draft pick in 1985, but who had been cut in the 1987 camp. There was nose tackle Mike Rusinek and safety Brian Dudley from Canada, kickers Brian Franco and Dale Walters (neither of whom had ever put a foot to a ball in an NFL game), and 6'5", 340-pound man-beast of a tackle Keith Bosley, who, despite his enormity, had also never played a down in the NFL. "They don't know his time in the forty because he doesn't run that far," NBC's Don Criqui quipped during a telecast. Major Everett, a solid special-teams player for Cleveland in 1986, was the team's only running back to speak of until Larry Mason finally decided to join the team forty-eight hours before the Patriots game. Mason, a USFL castoff with no NFL experience, had initially declined to play, but was eventually talked into it. Rather than watching names like Cody Risien, Webster Slaughter, and Clay Matthews lead the Browns, fans would be subjected to watching Blake Wingle, Perry Kemp, and Cliff Hannemann take their places.

While just their presence made several of the real Browns' blood boil, they knew they had a vested interest in what the "Tans"—so-called by the flustered Cleveland media—did on the field. "There's no way I can personally cheer on a bunch of scabs," Pagel said. "On the other hand, if the game counts it would be nice if they'd win." The players found themselves in a frustrating catch twenty-two. If the scabs win, your negotiating stance weakens but your team is in much better shape when you return. If they lose, your owner might press for a quick resolution, but your playoff hopes might already be dashed.

That was the good news/bad news scenario that the real Browns felt when they were watching their Week Four replacements slosh and flounder through the first half on a cold, rainy afternoon in Foxboro, Massachusetts. With many fans back in Cleveland tuning in simply to see just how bad replacement football could be, they got their answer right away. Despite the Patriots having five regular players cross the line to play, both teams looked miserable. There were fumbles, bad punt snaps, botched extra points, and lots of penalties. The Patriots cashed in on the early Cleveland miscues to snare a 10-0 halftime lead. It didn't look like these Browns would be able to score ten points the rest of the year, let alone in thirty minutes.

But in the second half, the discipline and patience the Browns' coaching staff had instilled all week began to pay off. Behind the strong running of Larry Mason, Cleveland began to dominate both the line of scrimmage and time of possession. Mason would finish the day with 133 yards on thirty-two carries, becoming only the second Cleveland player to ever carry the football that often in one game.

The other was Jim Brown. Though the Browns were using only a quarter of their usual offensive and defensive playcalls, they dominated the second half. Mason rushed for two touchdowns and sparked a dominant Cleveland running attack that out-gained New England, 217 to 31. On the other side of the ball, the Browns' defense was equally brutal, limiting the Pats to just three first downs and 35 total yards in the second half. The Tans rolled to a 20-10 victory. Never one to worry about the categorical overstatement, Art Modell said afterward, "I'm as proud of this team as I've been with any of my Browns' teams."

While the Cleveland replacements ran roughshod over the New England replacements, the real Browns were participating in a team workout organized by backup quarterback Gary Danielson. Though the practice drew more than 4,000 fans, it was fairly light and disorganized, which was fine with Danielson. He'd only come up with the idea after hearing union chief Gene Upshaw encourage players to disrupt the replacement games that afternoon. Danielson publicly disagreed with the suggestion and raised questions as to whether Upshaw really knew what he was doing.

Though the players abandoned the picket lines the following week, realizing it was doing little but attracting fans and a media circus, the team appeared to still be standing together in unity. But with more and more players from other teams crossing the line to play for their respective teams and earn their paychecks, most figured it was just a matter of time before one of the Browns broke ranks. As it turned out, it was the oldest member of the team. Defensive end Carl Hairston crossed the line the Wednesday after the win over the Patriots, four days before the Browns were to host the Houston Oilers in what was, for better or worse, a key divisional game.

"This was my decision and mine alone," Hairston said. "It's just something I had to do for my family. This is my twelfth year. I didn't feel I could sit out the year because next year holds no promises for me. I had to think about myself and my family." Though several of his teammates despised his decision, Hairston remained highly respected. He hadn't been afraid to express his beliefs and didn't get sneaky about revealing his intentions. He announced his decision to the players at a team meeting on Tuesday night.

Even with Hairston in the lineup the following Sunday, the Browns were no better than the week before. In an even sloppier display of football, Cleveland and Houston traded mistakes on the mud-soaked Cleveland Stadium turf before 38,927—the smallest Browns' home crowd in nine years, yet the second-largest crowd in the NFL that weekend. The teams combined for twelve punts, five fumbles, five interceptions, and a whopping sixteen penalties. The Browns' running game, which had been so colossal the week before, was non-existent. Cleveland managed just 50 yards as a team, and Larry Mason was limited to five yards on four carries. That left the burden to Jeff Christensen and the passing game, which hadn't looked good in victory the week before. With an extra week to prepare, it looked even worse. Christensen was sacked four times, including a game-clinching safety, and threw three interceptions. Fed up with Christensen's performance near game's end, witty Stadium fans consulted their programs and began chanting for backup Homer Jones, whoever he was.

With the heavens opening and a downpour ensuing as the clock ticked to zero, the Oilers sealed a 15-10 victory. The Tans had now dropped the Browns back to .500 at 2-2 with another key AFC Central contest set for the following week in Cincinnati. Clevelanders with hopes of seeing their team contend for the Super Bowl began to get nervous. In Houston, Oiler fans may have been hoping the strike would never end. With two victories from its B-team, 3-1 Houston was off to its best start since 1979 and stood alone atop the division. The AFC Central, along with the entire football world, had been turned upside down.

Seeming to understand the seriousness of the Browns' situation, Marty Schottenheimer began whistling a different tune the following day. Perhaps realizing a loss to the replacement Bengals could cripple the Browns' division title hopes, Schottenheimer amended his previous advice to the team to stick together. He told the media that each player needs to make a choice for himself, to determine for himself whether it was in his best interests to strike or return to the team. Art Modell followed up the comment with repeated invitations for any player to return to the team. With more players crossing the line around the league and no end in sight to the strike, the Browns' unity began to strain.

Players did nothing but argue for more than three hours at a team meeting Tuesday night. Reporters noted that it seemed the team had split into three factions: the hard-liners, determined to follow Gene Upshaw's lead; the moderates, who simply wanted to stay with the majority; and those who believed the strike was a lost cause. It was evident, particularly after third-party members Cody Risien and Brian Brennan stormed out of the meeting fifteen minutes before the conclusion, that several more players were poised to return for the Cincinnati game. "Anyone who goes in is a pretty boy," nose tackle Dave Puzzuoli said that night, "only thinking of himself."

Despite that sentiment, the floodgates opened on Wednesday. Eight Browns, plus seven more from the injured-reserve list, returned to practice in time to make the league cut-off date for players wishing to play in Week Six games. As expected, Risien led the charge, followed by Sam Clancy, Jeff Gossett, and Jeff Jaeger. Brennan and Rickey Bolden arrived soon after, but the real surprises came that afternoon, when Gary Danielson and Ozzie Newsome both rejoined the team. "I did what I thought was best for me, for the Cleveland Browns, and for the future of both," Danielson said, echoing the sentiments of his seven other comrades.

Needless to say, the day's activities evoked a strong reaction. "You're seeing a changing of the guard today," an upset Frank Minnifield said. "The guys who crossed today are not our leaders. We can't depend on them when we need them most. We need to elect new captains on this team." It was a comment that ruffled a few feathers and, in some cases, was more offensive than the players crossing the line in the first place. "Some of the guys have been very negative toward them," Bernie Kosar said of the line-crossers. "I have a lot of respect for those guys. I don't hold anything against them. They showed a lot of character, and they stood up for what they believe in. Those guys have been under extreme pressure."

More than just a shot to the striking players' stance, the exodus, which was taking place around the league, indicated that the battle was over. By the end of the day, a total of 228 players had crossed the line. "The owners got us beat," Clancy admitted as he returned. October 14 was to the NFL's second players' strike what D-Day was to World War II. It was now just a matter of time. But was it a good day or a bad day for the 1987 Cleveland Browns? "I'm really not sure," Marty Schottenheimer said, perversely.

Early Thursday afternoon, Gene Upshaw finally got the message. He ordered the players to return to work, even though they would not be eligible to play in that weekend's games, nor would they be paid for them, since the deadline was Wednesday. So as the replacement Browns, plus nine regulars, practiced Thursday afternoon, they paused to watch the remainder of the original Browns walk, defeated but still unified, toward their locker room. By the following day, the right nameplates had been returned to the right lockers and jersey numbers would soon be reunited with their rightful owners. After nearly four weeks and nothing accomplished, the strike was over.

Gene Upshaw and the union had been trounced. There would be no immediate change in the league's free agency policy, or on any of the other issues on the table. And worse yet, reports swirled that some owners may have actually *made* money during the strike. While attendance and television revenue were clearly down, the owners also did not have to fork out large weekly salaries to the players. Despite threats to the contrary, the networks had televised each replacement game. There was enough public curiosity to actually warrant attendance, and television ratings went up rather than down over the course of the three weeks. It wasn't ideal, but the league had weathered the storm.

Amidst the celebration of the end of a dark chapter, the Browns still had one more replacement game to play, though now there was little reason for concern. Cleveland had nine regulars at key spots such as quarterback, receiver, offensive line, tight end, and kicker while the Bengals had just two. Cincinnati owner Paul Brown complained that his squad was going into an uneven fight, that now that the strike was over, the games should be legitimate and fair. But the league stuck to its guns, sending the Bengals into a certain slaughter.

And was it ever. With experienced Gary Danielson replacing Jeff Christensen, who would never throw another pass in the NFL, the Browns obliterated Cincinnati on a crisp, sunny, autumn afternoon at Riverfront Stadium. Danielson was the catalyst, completing twenty-five of thirty-one passes for 281 yards and four touchdowns. The veteran quarterback hit Brian Brennan ten times for 139 yards. It was Danielson's first start since he'd directed the Browns to the crucial win over the Giants in the Meadowlands twenty-two months before, and unbeknownst to him at the time, it was also the last victory of his career.

With the Cleveland offense rolling up 410 total yards, the Browns' defense limited Cincinnati to a mere 95 yards of total offense. Cleveland ran twice as many plays, had twenty-nine first downs to the Bengals' six, and dominated time of possession by twenty-five minutes. At one point, the game's one-sided-ness was so bad, Doug Dieken told his radio audience, "You don't want to rout the Bengals to the point it might cost Wyche his job."

Sam Wyche kept his job, but his team was utterly dismantled, 34-0. The replacement Browns completed their stint by winning two of their three games, improving the club to 3-2 overall. The victory tied the Browns for first with Houston, who had lost in New England to the Patriots and newly acquired quarterback Doug Flutie.

The real Browns were now back, and ten games remained. Their record was the same as the year before at this stage. The pieces were still in place for a Super Bowl run. But while their place in the league standings had been salvaged, fans could only wonder if the rift between teammates could be mended. The players would now have to start over, reunite as one, and play the remaining two months of the season together if they hoped to achieve their ultimate goal for 1987.

"I don't know what's going to happen," Carl Hairston said in the Riverfront locker room. "I'm hoping it gets back to normal, but I really don't know. It's going to be one of those wait-and-see things."

After leaving Youngstown and going on to win a national championship at the University of Miami, Bernie Kosar, Cleveland's prodigal son, cashed in his success for the opportunity to come home and play for his beloved Browns. Photo courtesy of Diamond Images.

Brian Brennan, a small but reliable wide receiver, was a Richie Cunningham in a world of cocky, arrogant Fonzies. Photo courtesy of Diamond Images.

Haunted by the specter of the most infamous turnover in NFL history, Earnest Byner represented the heart and soul of the Browns in two separate tours of duty in Cleveland. Photo courtesy of Diamond Images.

The gangly but dangerous Webster Slaughter arrived just in time to help propel Cleveland's passing attack into the upper echelon of the NFL. Photo courtesy of Diamond Images.

Better known as "The Baabarian," center Mike Baab anchored the Cleveland front line—and the offense as a whole—for five seasons. Consequently, the Browns' ill-advised trading of Baab in 1988 was the first domino to tip toward the franchise's ultimate downfall. Photo courtesy of Diamond Images.

Linebacker Mike Johnson parlayed his strict upbringing in a military family into a quiet but highly effective career with the Browns. Photo courtesy of Diamond Images.

Cornerback Frank Minnifield, the Browns' first of many steals from the doomed United States Football League, helped turn the Cleveland defense into a group of bloodthirsty hellhounds. Photo courtesy of Diamond Images.

Clay Matthews, perhaps the most valuable defensive player in Browns' history, was a rock at linebacker for sixteen seasons in Cleveland—and in back-to-back games in 1989 was involved in two of the most memorable plays in the annals of the franchise. Photo courtesy of Diamond Images.

Shown here in his early days with the team, Ozzie Newsome—"The Wizard of Oz"—became the finest tight end in team history and reserved himself a spot in the Hall of Fame. Photo courtesy of Diamond Images.

Outspoken cornerback Hanford Dixon was the man who created a monster and began a new era of Cleveland Browns' football by simply barking at his teammates during a preseason practice. Photo courtesy of Diamond Images.

Bob Golic (number 79), Cleveland native and nose tackle, traveled a winding road from the wrestling mats at St. Joseph's High School to anchoring the defensive line of the team he grew up rooting for. Photo courtesy of Diamond Images.

Soft-spoken Kevin Mack became one of the finest running backs in Browns' history—and then nearly threw it all away when he became entangled in the world of drugs. Photo courtesy of Diamond Images.

Though he looked more like an accountant than a football coach, Marty Schottenheimer was the right man at the right time for the Cleveland Browns, bringing organization and discipline to a talented but generally unrefined team. Photo courtesy of Diamond Images.

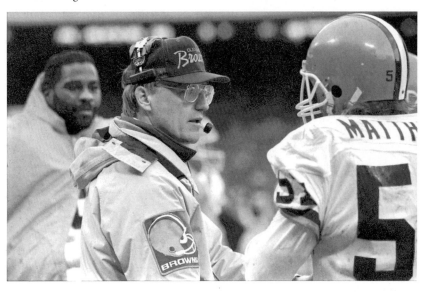

13 Game On

In sports, team chemistry is usually hard to recognize and even harder to define. Some even question whether it's a necessary ingredient to a championship team. So when the Browns—the real Browns—returned to practice after the four-week debacle of the strike, fans and team personnel alike were curious to see if the team would be able to regain the closeness it had in the previous few seasons. Would hard feelings remain, and if so, would this affect the team on the field?

By the end of the first practice after the reunion, they seemed to get their answer. On a rainy afternoon, as the session wound to its conclusion, Hanford Dixon, who had been critical of teammates who'd crossed the line, began playfully singing the theme song to *Gilligan's Island*. Many of the other players soon joined in and within moments, the practice field was echoing with the musical tale of a tiny ship's crew lost at sea. It may not have been a dramatic moment, but it served a purpose and symbolized the professionalism and focus of a determined group of individuals.

"Things were a little uptight," Ozzie Newsome said of that first practice, "but after ten minutes things started working back to normal. Most of the tension was gone by this time. It was business like usual. Just get yourself ready to play." Marty Schottenheimer set the tone right off the bat by telling his players, "The past three weeks are forgotten. It's over. I'm not going to talk about it, and I don't want any of you dwelling on it."

The players, upset and angry as they might have been, realized that carrying grudges would do them and the team no good. "For us to be a successful team this year, animosity must be over as soon as possible," Bob Golic said. "I know it will take longer with some than others." "You don't forget," Eddie Johnson added. "But you forgive and go on from there."

For the Browns, the next step was a Monday-night clash with the struggling Los Angeles Rams. John Robinson's squad was thought to be a Super Bowl contender in the preseason, but thanks to three losses by their replacement squad, the Rams had fallen to 1-4. Worse, their star running back, Eric Dickerson, was pouting and wanted either a bigger contract or to be traded. Many expected his on-field performance would be affected. In fact, Dickerson would not start at tailback. Instead, the job would be handed to a familiar face to Cleveland fans: Charles White, the Browns' first-round draft pick in 1980 who had spent five disappointing seasons with the team while dealing with a ravaging drug problem.

An early Felix Wright interception set up a field goal, and the Browns made the lead 10-0 early in the second quarter when Kevin Mack exploded up the middle and broke four tackles on the way to a 16-yard touchdown run. Moments later, things got even better when Jim Everett was again intercepted by Felix Wright, this time at the Los Angeles forty yard line, and the Browns' safety ran untouched into the end zone for a 17-0 Cleveland lead. The Browns were looking dominant on national television, and the hometown fans were going nuts. So much so that the field officials asked the Browns to make an announcement over the public address system asking fans in the Dog Pound to stop throwing bones onto the field. Browns' officials declined the request, fearing it would only escalate the problem.

With the Cleveland defense shutting down Dickerson, the lead swelled to 30-7 early in the third quarter on a long Kosar-to-Brian Brennan touchdown pass, and the Browns coasted to a 30-17 win. The Browns were now 4-2 and undoubtedly united once again.

Cleveland's November 1 match at San Diego had been circled on one man's calendar for nearly six months. Though he wouldn't say so publicly, this was the day Chip Banks was going to show the Browns and the entire football world how foolish Cleveland had been to trade him the previous spring.

The Chargers had welcomed Banks with open arms, and though the change in scenery may not have dramatically improved his on-field performance, he seemed happier than he'd ever been in Cleveland. Ironically, thanks to three wins from their replacement team, the Chargers were 5-1 and sitting pretty in the AFC West. Some conjectured the Browns' trip west might be a preview of a potential playoff game, not to mention Super Bowl XXII—which would be played at San Diego's Jack Murphy Stadium in January. This was a contest swirling with intrigue long before kickoff.

Once the game began, the deck continued to be stacked against the Browns. On the second play of the game, Bernie Kosar was intercepted—by Chip Banks, who promptly returned the pick 20 yards to the Cleveland fifteen. One play later, running back Lionel James raced through the Browns' defense for a 7-0 Chargers' lead. Right off the bat, it appeared this wasn't going to be the Browns' day.

Things only got worse. Penalties wiped out a pair of thrilling plays that could have broken the game open: Gerald McNeil had a 92-yard punt return for a touchdown called back in the second quarter, and later a Kosar-to-Webster Slaughter 50-yard scoring pass was nullified due to an illegal-pick infraction. While attempting to block Chip Banks, left tackle Rickey Bolden went down with a fracture and dislocation of his right ankle and would miss not only the remainder of the game but also the rest of the season. And perhaps most ironic of all, while

Banks was playing like, perhaps, a mad dog in a meat market (later adding a fumble recovery to his early interception), the man the Browns had tapped to replace him suffered his own season-ending injury. Mike Junkin tore ligaments and suffered a dislocation of his left wrist. He continued to play through the pain, but the seriousness of the injury wasn't discovered for another week. Junkin, after amassing all of six tackles in four games in 1987, would have to wait until 1988 to try to meet the lofty expectations the team and the city had for him.

Despite a naval fleet of adversity against them, the Browns hung tough. They rallied and took a 24-14 lead into the fourth quarter. But veteran San Diego quarterback Dan Fouts rallied his team to tie the contest and send it to overtime. An ill-advised Kosar pass on Cleveland's first possession was intercepted, setting up the winning Charger field goal. It was a game the Browns had in their back pocket in the fourth quarter, but also a game they easily should have put away long before that. Worse, it was the kind of game a Super Bowl–caliber team would have won. Instead, the Browns found themselves at 4-3, a game behind Houston in the AFC Central, and the chances of playing in Jack Murphy Stadium again in ninety days looked bleak.

The good news for the Browns and their fans after an incredibly disheartening defeat out west was that the team would now return home to play the NFL's worst team: the hapless Atlanta Falcons. In the middle of its fourth straight losing season, Marion Campbell's 2-5 club came to Cleveland on an overcast afternoon on the lakefront. A crowd of better than 71,000 piled into the Stadium hoping to see their beloved team get back on track. However, the faithful met some resistance at the gates. Hoping to avoid debris-throwing incidents that had caused headaches in the Monday-night game against the Rams, Stadium officials searched for and confiscated any dog biscuits they found on fans at entrances. Field officials also asked Hanford Dixon to refrain from riling up the crowd. He went along, at least until their backs were turned.

Despite the efforts to curb their enthusiasm, the team and their fans could not be denied. Considering the Browns, thirteen-point favorites, were already upset and had some frustration to take out after their heartbreaker in San Diego, what transpired was only natural. Sparked by a 54-yard Bernie Kosar-to-Webster Slaughter touchdown pass, Cleveland sprinted to a 14-3 lead at halftime and coasted to an easy 38-3 victory. The individual highlight was Earnest Byner's three-touchdown performance. Byner was denied a fourth touchdown when he fumbled at the Atlanta two with the game out of reach. "I've got a bad habit carrying with my left hand," confessed Byner, whose fumble was forgotten in the glow of his three scores.

The Falcons proved to be the perfect elixir for a frustrated football team, which was now 5-3 and locked in a three-way tie with Houston and Pittsburgh for first in the AFC Central.

The Browns would receive a much steeper challenge the following week when the rapidly improving Buffalo Bills came to town. The team had strengthened dramatically the previous year by bringing in quarterback Jim Kelly, but since the Browns had last seen them, the Bills had now an almost entirely new defense, which appeared would soon become one of the best in the NFL.

Accordingly, on an unseasonably mild, sun-splashed November afternoon on the lake, the Browns rose up to the challenge. After Buffalo safety Mark Kelso returned a Kevin Mack fumble 56 yards for a touchdown and a 7-3 lead late in the first quarter, Cleveland took over. Behind a red-hot Kosar, the Browns sprinted to a twenty-point fourth-quarter lead and held on for a 27-21 win.

For the second straight week, the Browns had passed their test with flying colors. The defense had held the explosive Kelly in check until the final two minutes. Offensively, the Browns racked up 421 total yards behind an exquisite performance by Bernie Kosar, who out-dueled his former college teammate with twenty-four completions in thirty-four attempts for 346 yards.

It was as sweet-tasting a victory as the Browns had enjoyed all season, and it came at a perfect time. With a 23-3 stomping of the Steelers in Pittsburgh, the Oilers remained tied with the Browns in first place with identical 6-3 records. And the following week, the division leaders would clash for sole possession of first place in the Astrodome. With the strike now a memory and the Browns grabbing three victories in their first four games back, Marty Schottenheimer proclaimed the team was now back to where it was before the walkout in September. The team's Super Bowl journey was back on course.

There was, however, some turbulence ahead.

As the 1980s wore on, it became more and more clear that the Houston Oilers were having the kind of decade the Cleveland Browns had endured in the 1970s.

After being considered the second-best team in the NFL throughout the later years of the Pittsburgh Steelers' magnificent four–Super Bowl run from 1974 through 1979, the Oilers had fallen on hard times after firing head coach Bum Phillips after the 1980 season. Houston suddenly went from being one of the league's best to one of the worst, seemingly overnight. A 7-9 mark in 1981 began a string of six consecutive losing seasons, including a pitiful 16-57 combined record from 1982 through 1986. The Oilers hadn't made the playoffs in seven years, hadn't won a postseason contest in eight, and still had never won a Central Division title. Rumors swirled early in the 1987 season that the Oilers might be moving to Jacksonville, but not surprisingly, few in Houston really seemed to care.

But as the 1987 season wore on, something strange began to happen. The Oilers actually started to look and play like a winning football team. With the help of a pair of victories by its replacement team in Denver and Cleveland (places the real Oilers almost certainly wouldn't have won) Houston found itself at 5-2 after the regulars returned, all alone in first place in the AFC Central. Entering

Week Eleven, the Oilers stood at 6-3, tied with the Browns for first place. And on November 22, Cleveland would come calling.

It had been seven years since the Houston Astrodome had hosted an Oilers' game with so much importance. A Houston victory would put the upstarts in prime position to win the division, as it would complete an unprecedented sweep over the two-time defending champs. The replacement Oilers' 15-10 victory in Cleveland a month earlier was looming bigger and bigger as November wore on, since it could give Houston the edge in any tie-breaking situation. "They beat our scabs," Hanford Dixon said. "It's totally different this time. They've got to see the boys." But unless the boys could come up with a win in the Astrodome, where they almost always seemed to struggle, they would have to make up two games on the Oilers to win their third straight crown.

And for the first time in years, the Browns would face an Oiler team that was not only laden with talent but believed in itself. Under head coach Jerry Glanville, Houston had adopted a slightly arrogant team philosophy. They were energetic, cocky, and outspoken. With quarterback Warren Moon finally starting to look like the playcaller the Oilers envisioned when they forked over a Brinks truck to lure him from Canada three years earlier, the Houston offense had become one of the most potent in the league. Offensive coordinator June Jones had constructed an attack nicknamed the "Red Gun," which dusted off a handful of quirky back-of-the-playbook nuggets such as direct center snaps to halfback Mike Rozier, the shotgun formation on first down, and the quarterback option. The Oilers planned to exhaust their playbook and come right after the Browns' defense, especially their secondary. Wide receiver Ernest Givins in particular spoke about how Houston would come out firing at the Dogs. Gary Danielson heard Givins' comments and made sure to mention them to the defense. Soon after, the Cleveland defensive backs, never ones to shy away from a challenge or verbal slight, joined hands and began chanting, "Death to Givins."

It set the stage for the first legitimate grudge match in the AFC Central since the division was the powerhouse of the NFL in 1980. That year, the Browns had marched into Houston, forced five turnovers, and marched out with a 17-14 victory that turned out to be the difference in clinching the division crown. Now, seven years later, they found themselves in almost an identical position.

On the game's very first series the Oilers proved their talk of an aggressive game plan wasn't just rhetoric. With a standing-room-only crowd of 51,161 ready to tear the roof off the Astrodome, on first down from the Houston eight yard line, the call was a flea-flicker pass in which Warren Moon handed off to Mike Rozier, who then tossed the football back to Moon. Moon then threw long for wide receiver Curtis Duncan, but the pass was underthrown and fell incomplete. It was a harbinger of things to come.

Houston drove to the Cleveland twenty-two and was poised to draw first blood before the Oilers' goofy playbook blew up in their face. They called for

Givins on a reverse end-around, but he was drilled by Browns' linebacker Lucius Sanford for a 13-yard loss. Then a play later, Rozier took the snap from center and started up the middle, hoping to surprise the Browns. But Dave Puzzuoli buried him for a four-yard loss, and the promising drive was over. And so, as it happened, were the Oilers' hopes for victory. "They came out thinking they'd be aggressive and challenge our defense," said Cleveland safety Al Gross. "I don't think they had a Plan B."

"It was like they said, 'We know how strong you are,'" Dixon said. "'We can't beat you doing the things we had done to beat everybody else.'"

The Browns marched right down the field on their first possession and took a lead on a one-yard touchdown run by Earnest Byner. Houston's second possession was even less substantial than its first. On first down, Warren Moon was drilled by Carl Hairston and lost the football. Al Baker recovered at the Houston nine yard line, and the turnover resulted in a Jeff Jaeger field goal and a 9-0 Cleveland lead. When the Oilers got the ball back, Frank Minnifield intercepted a Moon pass, setting up another Jaeger field goal and a 12-0 advantage early in the second quarter. In their biggest game in seven years, the Oilers had yet to show up, while the Browns were as hot as a Texas July.

The trend continued when the Oilers coughed up the football a third time late in the second quarter, a Rozier fumble recovered by Clay Matthews. This miscue led to a five-yard touchdown run by Kevin Mack and a 19-0 Browns' advantage with 2:33 left before the intermission. The Browns added another score on a long Kosar-to-Webster Slaughter pass with four seconds left in the half. By the time Byner broke free for a 17-yard touchdown run on the Browns' first possession of the third quarter to make the margin thirty-three points, the largest Astrodome crowd in five years had dwindled to the size of an amateur rodeo.

After an essentially meaningless second half came to a close, the Browns had scored a resounding 40-7 victory. "I really don't want to say too much about the Oilers," a jubilant Hanford Dixon said afterward, "so I'll just let the score speak for itself."

And the score, along with the final statistics, spoke volumes. The Browns racked up 457 yards of total offense and held Houston to 247. They dominated time of possession, holding the football for nearly forty-three minutes, while the defense forced six turnovers. Warren Moon was absolutely miserable, completing just five of twenty-three passes, and dropped to 0-7 lifetime against the Browns. Meanwhile Kosar was once again dominant at fifteen of twenty-six for 257 yards, and improved to 5-0 against Houston. Kevin Mack rushed for 114 yards, the Browns' first 100-yard rushing game of the season, and the team racked up better than 200 yards rushing for the first time since the Byner-Mack-Break-Your-Back days of 1985.

"We wanted to go out and set the tempo from the first minute of the game," Gerald McNeil said. "We had a mission to accomplish. We wanted to finish everything we started. We did that. We are the two-time champions of the division. We just wanted to make sure everyone knows that the Cleveland Browns are for real."

By sunset, anyone who doubted the Browns belonged in the upper echelon of the NFL had little evidence to back up his thinking.

"Talk about a whipping," Ray Yannucci wrote. "This was downright obscene what the Browns did to the supposedly big boys on the block." Accordingly, Ozzie Newsome likened the beating to the days of his youth growing up in Alabama. When a new kid comes into your neighborhood with an attitude, the first order of business is to show them they don't belong there.

Echoing that sentiment, Frank Minnifield silenced Ernest Givins in dramatic fashion. Primarily covering fellow former Louisville Cardinal Givins, Minnifield picked off three Oiler passes, the first Brown to do so since Hanford Dixon in a win over Pittsburgh in 1982. In the locker room afterward, Minnifield said the magnitude of the beating could be traced back to Givins' statements about coming after the Cleveland defense. "I put all of this on Givins' shoulders," he said, "because everything Givins said is what our defense reacted to."

With the win over the Oilers, the Browns could somewhat relax in the division race. At 7-3, they led Houston and Pittsburgh by a game and had wiped out the Oilers' tie-breaking advantage. Tough games lay ahead for Cleveland, but Houston and Pittsburgh would both have an even tougher slate over the final five weeks. The Browns were back in the driver's seat, thanks to a carbon copy of their thumping of the Bengals at Riverfront to clinch the division the previous December.

For as well as the Browns had played and as much as they deserved to be confident, there would be a price to pay for such resounding success. "I tell you what, I don't want to sound too cocky about our team," Dixon said, "but we have a helluva team. And we're starting to put everything together in all phases of the game."

Little did Dixon know that things were about to fall apart all over again.

The week after the Browns buried the Oilers, the local and national media began heaping praise upon them—more than any Cleveland team had seen in decades. Many, including the Browns themselves, declared Cleveland to be the finest team in the AFC, a Super Bowl favorite. "We're at a point now where we walk onto that field and, in our minds, the game is won," Reggie Langhorne said. "Then, we just go to work. There's a nonchalant way of being cocky, and we've learned it." The following Sunday, they would get a chance to prove themselves even further.

Three days after Thanksgiving, the Browns would travel west to face the 8-2 San Francisco 49ers on a Sunday night, marking the first time a Browns game would be broadcast on the cable network ESPN, in its first season of televising NFL games. A Cleveland victory would solidify the club's status as one of the finest in the league, and support San Francisco coach Bill Walsh's statements earlier in the week. He told the Cleveland press in a conference call he felt the Browns were the best team in the NFL, and that his team would have to play its finest game of the season to win. Though Walsh's comments may have had a psychological angle to them, many others looked at the game as a possible Super Bowl preview. Both clubs were led by top-notch quarterbacks, and both were galvanized by strong defenses. With the AFC wide open and the defending champion Giants in a downslide, the Browns and 49ers were as likely as anyone to meet in San Diego on January 31.

But on this November night, San Francisco proved the Browns still had a long way to go before they started thinking about the Super Bowl. The 49ers were simply too much for the Browns offensively and defensively in a 38-24 win.

Though the blow was tough psychologically for the Browns, no real damage had been done. They were now 7-4 and, thanks to losses by Pittsburgh and Houston earlier in the day, still hung on to sole possession of first place in the Central Division. Yes, they'd been beaten soundly, but to a team that was now 9-2 and would not lose another regular-season game on its way to the NFC West title and the NFL's best record. Things could have been far worse.

Seven days later, they got there.

Though the Browns would return home, where they'd yet to lose in 1987 with their regular squad, they apparently had left their hearts and self-confidence in San Francisco.

Their Week Thirteen match with the Indianapolis Colts was important, but nowhere near as glamorous as the Browns' previous three games, two of which they'd shown up for and one of which they'd tanked. Add to that the Colts were a rebuilding team coming off a 3-13 season, and the recipe for a letdown was in place. True, under new head coach Ron Meyer, Indianapolis had turned things around. The Colts stood at 6-5 and were right in the mix in the AFC East, and thanks to a blockbuster October trade, had acquired the services of star running back Eric Dickerson. Clearly, this squad was a far better one than the Browns had manhandled in the Hoosier Dome the year before, but the Browns would find that out a bit too late.

Going into the first weekend of December, even the Cleveland coaching staff seemed to take an exhausted attitude toward the Colt game. Despite four consecutive impressive performances by the offense, Lindy Infante and Marty Schottenheimer concocted an oddly conservative game plan, of which Bernie Kosar later said, "a high-school quarterback would have been embarrassed to run." With this attitude, the Browns backed in to that Sunday's game, and not surprisingly, played poorly.

The offense not only didn't score in the first half but it managed only five first downs. While the defense played well, it made its share of mistakes, and thanks to three Dean Biassucci field goals in the second quarter, the Colts led at the half 9-0. It appeared the Browns got a wakeup call late in the third quarter when

Herman Fontenot broke through to block a Rohn Stark punt that Tim Manoa recovered at the Indianapolis thirty-six yard line. The Browns cashed in moments later when Kosar hit Brian Brennan for a 19-yard touchdown pass to cut the margin to 9-7.

Early in the final period, the Browns finally started to put it together. They marched from their own thirty to the Colt five, thanks to two impressive receptions by Earnest Byner. But after the second catch, Byner took the handoff on first and goal, was hit at the line, and as he was falling backward, fumbled the football. Safety Mike Prior recovered for the Colts at the four with 11:51 remaining. "Just before the play I was thinking about protecting the ball," Byner said later. "I had both arms around it. I don't know how it came out." Though plenty of time remained, Byner's fumble cost the Browns their final scoring opportunity.

The Cleveland defense forced three Indianapolis punts in the final eight-and-a-half minutes, but all three times, the Browns' offense failed to cross midfield. When the final gun sounded, the Browns left the field scratching their heads, having lost back-to-back games for the first time in more than two years. Two weeks earlier, they were being considered one of the best teams in the NFL. Now, they found themselves locked in a three-way tie for first place in their own division after the six worst quarters of non-strike football Cleveland fans had seen in the past three seasons. "If the Browns were knocking on the door of the penthouse two weeks ago," Ray Yannucci wrote, "Sunday they started up the sidewalk to the outhouse."

The Browns' lethargy seemed to trace back to its ambiguous game plan. "They were more scared of losing than being concerned with beating us," said Colts' linebacker Barry Krauss. "It's a damn shame with all the talent on this team it isn't taken advantage of," said a frustrated Reggie Langhorne. Reflecting that sentiment, Kosar showered, changed, and was out of the locker room quicker than ever before in an attempt to avoid the media.

The running game also struggled, epitomized by Byner's 19 yards on six carries. But more notable was his fumble that cost the Browns a chance to score the winning points in the fourth quarter. To his credit, he stood tall and blamed no one but himself when surrounded by the media afterward. "I'm hurtin', really hurtin'," he said. "I feel I let the team down." His stance led *Plain Dealer* columnist Bill Livingston to conclude, "You would not impugn the character of the man, only the clasp of the ball." It was Byner's third fumble inside the opponents' five-yard line in five games. Up to now, his heroics had overshadowed his propensity for turnovers. But for the first time, Byner's mistake outweighed his success. "From hero to goat in a couple of seconds," he said as he left the locker room that evening, having no idea the harbinger that statement would mark.

Now the Browns had some serious work ahead of them. Their Super Bowl aspirations had been dialed back to focusing simply on out-muscling the Oilers and Steelers for the division title. Three games remained. They'd return home to face Cincinnati then hit the road to face the Raiders in Los Angeles, where the Browns had not won in twenty-nine years. Cleveland would then close the season against the Steelers at Three Rivers Stadium, where they held a lifetime record of 1-16. All the hopes and dreams of the entire 1987 season would be determined within twenty-one fateful December days.

"Right now, frankly, these guys look like mad dogs in a flea market," Livingston wrote. "In the final three games of this confusing and inconsistent season, we will see what the heart of the Browns, Kosar, and what their soul, the Dogs, are all about."

Indeed they would.

14 Three for Three

That week, Art Modell challenged the "real" Browns to step up now that the chips were truly down—which they always seemed to be for Cleveland around this time of year. "I've been here eight years," Marty Schottenheimer said. "And we've never done anything easy around here."

Also looking for answers was Earnest Byner, who had special films cut together so he could try to figure out why he'd been fumbling so much lately. "I want to look at it so I can visualize the best way I should run with the ball," he said. "Most of the time, I have had two hands on the ball. It's just something that happens." Byner had now fumbled five times in 1987.

Before they could turn their thoughts to jockeying for postseason position, first the Browns would have to avoid a second straight embarrassing loss, for which all the ingredients were on the table.

The Cincinnati Bengals would come to Cleveland for a December 13 showdown, eager to avenge the Browns' 34-0 slaughter of the replacement Bengals in October. Though Cincinnati was having a down year, the Browns knew it was still a dangerous team, and if the Browns couldn't improve from their apathetic performance against Indianapolis the week before, they could lose to anyone in the NFL.

No one could quite put his finger on exactly what had happened to the 1987 Cincinnati Bengals. Picked by many to either challenge the Browns or unseat them for the division crown, Cincinnati had slowly fallen apart after a promising 10-6 finish in 1986, coming up just short of a playoff berth. Injuries had played a role in 1987, as had some unavoidable bad luck. But the primary factor most pointed to as the reason for the Bengals' downfall was head coach Sam Wyche.

Wyche had always been outspoken and colorful, which was fine when his team was winning. When it wasn't, he was a distraction, and his sideshows usually detracted from his molding the Bengals into a playoff team. Despite having what many felt was the most talented roster in the Central Division, Wyche was unable to put it all together. The Bengals lost three key division games in 1986 that could have made it a very different season. In 1987, Wyche made some truly peculiar decisions that only got stranger as the year wore on.

It all started in Week Two. After a narrow win in Indianapolis to open the season, the Bengals were poised to start the season 2-0, leading the San Francisco 49ers 26-20 with just six seconds remaining at Riverfront. Cincinnati had the ball at its own thirty, facing fourth down. Rather than either punting or designing an elaborate clock-killing play, Wyche called for a simple handoff to running back James Brooks. The 49ers crashed through the line almost simultaneously with the snap of the ball and collared Brooks for a five-yard loss. Two seconds remained, and the 49ers would take over at the Cincinnati twenty-five with one shot at the end zone to win the game. With that one snap, quarterback Joe Montana hit a ridiculously open Jerry Rice (single covered by a rookie cornerback, incidentally) in the end zone, and Ray Wershing's extra point with no time showing gave the 49ers a somewhat hilarious 27-26 victory. The Bengals had lost a game they'd had in their back pocket and had no one to blame but themselves—and Wyche.

That defeat set the tone for the remainder of the 1987 season. The replacement Bengals lost two of three games, and when the real ones returned, things got no better. Trailing the Steelers by three in the waning moments in Pittsburgh, Wyche opted for one more play rather than attempting a game-tying field goal. Quarterback Boomer Esiason was sacked, time expired, and the Bengals had lost again. "Well, looks like Wicky-Wacky screwed up another one," Steelers' running backs coach Dick Hoak said after the game. "He's got the best material in the division, and he still can't win." They would have been fighting words—if only they weren't true. "The best thing any team that plays the Bengals has going for it is Sam Wyche," Pete Franklin wrote, adding that Browns' fans should start a petition drive to keep Wyche on as Cincinnati's coach. "Why, Sam Wyche is the best thing to happen to Cleveland football since Bernie Kosar," wrote Bob Kravitz in the *Plain Dealer*.

The following week they blew a fifteen-point lead in the final six minutes and lost at home to Houston. In November, the Bengals were poised to kick a go-ahead field goal with less than two minutes to play in New York, but the kick was blocked and returned for the game-winning touchdown for the Jets. "You can say one thing for Wyche and his team," Franklin added. "They have found creative ways to lose close games and keep the opposing fans entertained." Along the way, their downfall had opened up the Central Division. Rather than it being a two-horse race for the title between Cleveland and Cincinnati as it had been in 1986, the slightly-better-than-mediocre Steelers and Oilers were both in the hunt for the crown as December rolled into its second week.

Though Bengals' owner Paul Brown pledged not to fire a coach in the middle of the season, most figured Wyche would be canned shortly after. With his club standing at 4-8 going into its rematch with the Browns, a winning record was out of reach. The only way Wyche could keep his job, some conjectured, was to finish the season strong and/or beat the Browns.

After an awkward first quarter that ended with Cincinnati holding a 3-0 lead, Cleveland's A-game finally returned. In what would become a record-breaking second quarter, the Browns took two weeks of frustration out on the punching-bag Bengals. First, Bernie Kosar hit Webster Slaughter with a looping 22-yard pass down the left sideline into the Dog Pound to take their first lead since the first half in San Francisco. Two more touchdowns followed, both by Kevin Mack. The Browns led, 21-3, as the half drew near, but the still-explosive Bengals' offense put together an impressive drive seemingly destined to cut into the lead. But Clay Matthews intercepted Boomer Esiason at the Cleveland four yard line, returned it 36 yards, then lateraled to Carl Hairston, who lumbered another 40 yards. The Browns added another touchdown moments later to make the halftime margin 28-3 and set a new team record for points scored in the second quarter.

The Bengals made things slightly interesting in the second half, but every time they challenged, the Browns answered. The Browns put the icing on a 38-24 victory with fifty-two seconds remaining by adding a 27-yard field goal by Matt Bahr. Fed up with his inconsistent kicking game, on Friday Schottenheimer had made two dramatic changes. Bahr, finally healthy after ripping up his knee thirteen months earlier, was activated, and Jeff Jaeger was placed on the inactive list. George Winslow, heir apparent to Jeff Gossett, was waived and replaced by Lee Johnson, signed as a free agent after three years in Houston. Ironically, Johnson had just lost his job with the Oilers to Gossett, whom the Browns' divisional rivals had signed shortly after his Cleveland release. In a case of beauty being in the eye of the beholder, the Browns and Oilers had each released their punter, only to have the other pick him up. While Gossett and the Oilers lost in New Orleans, Johnson and the Browns remained in a tie for first with Pittsburgh.

Thus, technically, the Browns' Week Fifteen match with the Raiders in Los Angeles was meaningless. With their win over Cincinnati the week before, combined with the Oilers' loss to the Saints, the Browns could win the Central Division simply by defeating the Steelers in the season finale. A loss to the Raiders could only factor into whether or not the Browns got to play at home in the divisional playoffs.

But the Browns knew better. They knew a win would clinch a Wild Card spot, but even more importantly, they knew losing in Los Angeles could be disastrous. They saw how their last defeat on the West Coast had disheartened them and translated into a second straight loss a week later. And after an up-and-down month, the Browns knew they needed to build some momentum if they hoped to do anything in the playoffs. This was crunch time, and every game was critical.

Not only would Cleveland have to contend with the rough-and-tumble Raiders but also with recent history. They'd lost eight straight to the Raiders and hadn't won a game in Los Angeles in twenty-nine years. For the third time in 1987, the Browns would have to jet across the continent for a West Coast game, of which they'd lost six of their last seven and held an all-time record of just 12-21. The only good news was that the Raiders were mired in a sub-par season and stood at just 5-8 going in, plus they would be without the services of dazzling first-year fullback Bo Jackson, out with an injured ankle.

For the first time in recent memory, the Browns played on the West Coast much like they did in the rest of the country: well. They roared to a 17-3 lead on two Byner touchdowns. Los Angeles was poised to narrow the margin on its first possession of the third quarter, but Browns' linebacker Mike Johnson stripped the football from running back Marcus Allen and safety Chris Rockins recovered at the Cleveland seven, halting the drive. It was the kind of play the Browns were beginning to expect from Johnson, who had quietly become one of the leaders of a very strong defense.

Johnson, the son of an Air Force master sergeant, had been acquired in the critical 1984 supplemental draft, when the Browns selected him with their own pick of the first round after snagging Kevin Mack with Chicago's selection. He had been an Academic All-American at Virginia Tech before joining the Baltimore Stars in the USFL in 1984. He played two years there then was released just before the league folded in August of 1986. The Browns quickly signed him and by the end of the season, he was a regular on-field contributor at inside linebacker. He won a starting job early in 1987 and would lead the team in tackles the next three years. The fall of the USFL and the Browns' foresight had once again paid dividends.

Following the fumble Johnson caused, the offense embarked on a thirteen-play, 93-yard drive and stretched the lead to 24-3. Just as had been the case the week before, the Browns had secured a comfortable lead, and then made the big plays necessary to hold it down the stretch. After the Raiders cut the lead to 24-10 on an interception return for a touchdown by defensive back Stacy Toran a minute into the fourth quarter, they scored again with 1:51 left to make it 24-17 in the final two minutes. But a clutch 21-yard run by Earnest Byner on third-and-seven twenty seconds later clinched the Browns' first win over the Raiders in fourteen years.

And now, after fourteen games, one strike, a handful of personnel crises, and seemingly countless ups and downs, it all boiled down to the finale. In one afternoon, the Browns could accomplish their initial mission of the 1987 season.

The day after Christmas is not typically one marked on many people's calendars. Schoolchildren are still on vacation. Many hit the malls for post-holiday sales. Others just laze around the house, basking in the glow of having survived another Yuletide season.

But on December 26, 1987, the Cleveland Browns and Pittsburgh Steelers would wage a war. The 8-6 Steelers were out of the running for the division title, but with a win could still make the playoffs as a Wild Card team in one of 128 different playoff scenarios heading into the final weekend of the season. In fact, one possibility had the Browns returning to Pittsburgh for the AFC Wild Card Game the following week.

For the Browns, their quest was much simpler: win this game and capture their third straight Central Division title. Even if they lost, they could still take the crown with a Houston loss to Cincinnati the following afternoon in the Astrodome. But the Browns had come too far and been through too much to pin their hopes on Sam Wyche's bungling Bengals, who had blown a 24-3 lead to the Saints at Riverfront in a 41-24 loss the previous week.

"I don't want to hear about if we do this or if we do that," Eddie Johnson said. "The *only* thing that's significant is we go to Pittsburgh and kick their butts, which we're capable of doing. Forget everything else. The only thing that should be on our minds is beating Pittsburgh's butt."

Meanwhile, the Browns' front office was quietly trying to recapture the recipe that led to the Browns' breaking the sixteen-year-old Three Rivers Stadium Jinx the year before. Art Modell constructed the exact same seating arrangement in his loge. Ernie Accorsi wore the same socks. Fourteen months earlier, while leaving for the airport to travel to Pittsburgh, radio broadcaster Doug Dieken found a black cat in his garage. This time, he pledged to pet the same cat before departing for Pennsylvania.

From the get-go, even with everything at stake, it was clear this was going to be a typical Browns-Steelers game: close, violent, and ugly. Several fights would break out on the field, and the teams would combine for fourteen penalties, eleven by Pittsburgh. It was "football by grindstone and gut-check," Bill Livingston would write.

The Browns took a 3-0 lead into the second quarter, then built on it when Kosar hit tight end Derek Tennell for a touchdown from two yards out early in the period. But the margin remained 9-0 when rookie Pittsburgh cornerback Rod Woodson broke through to block Matt Bahr's extra point. Just when it looked like a blowout seemed eminent, Pittsburgh defensive coordinator Tony Dungy pulled the rug out from beneath the Browns and switched to his own version of the Bear defense. It quashed the Cleveland running game and slowed the offense to a crawl for the remainder of the period. A goal-line interception by Eddie Johnson preserved the Browns' 9-3 lead at halftime.

The teams traded field goals in the third quarter and entered the fourth with the Browns up, 12-6. Two critical personal fouls on Pittsburgh cornerback Delton Hall kept a Browns' drive alive early in the final stanza, then Earnest Byner snuck around right end and slid into the end zone from the two, giving the Browns a 19-6 lead with just under ten minutes remaining. When Hanford Dixon intercepted Mark Malone at midfield on Pittsburgh's next offensive play, it appeared the game was just about wrapped up. But it was as if the Browns realized nothing else had come easy in 1987, so why should the division title?

Two plays later, Pittsburgh cornerback Cornell Gowdy intercepted Kosar and returned it 45 yards for a touchdown with 7:33 remaining. The primarily sardonic crowd of 56,394 sprang to life as the Steelers' playoff hopes and the possibility of starting a new Three Rivers Jinx looked realistic once again. One more defensive stop and/or turnover and touchdown and Pittsburgh's two-year postseason hiatus would end, all at the expense of their arch rivals.

There seemed to be too much time remaining for the Browns to simply kill the clock, especially with the way their running game had been struggling. But like a true championship team, Cleveland rose to another level when it needed it most. "In the past, our attitude might have been, 'Oh, no. Here we go again,'" Eddie Johnson said later. "Not today." Starting at its own twenty-three yard line, the offensive line shrugged off the effects of an otherwise frustrating afternoon and began opening holes for Byner and Mack. The gains weren't huge, but they kept the chains and the clock moving.

The Browns marched into Steelers' territory as the final minutes melted down. Thanks to a key tripping penalty that gave the Browns a first down inside the Steeler twenty-five with two minutes left, it appeared the visitors might be able to keep the home team from ever touching the ball again. After another third-down run that set up fourth-and-one at the Pittsburgh sixteen, with the Steelers out of time outs, the Browns didn't need to run another play. Bernie Kosar stood behind the line of scrimmage and raised his arms triumphantly into the air as the clock ticked down to zero. The Browns were AFC Central Division champions for the third straight year and had, without a doubt, laid the Three Rivers losing streak to rest. "Ding-dong," Doug Dieken told his radio audience, "the Jinx is definitely gone."

And it was all thanks to the greatest display of fourth-quarter clock management in team history. Not only had the Browns run out the final 7:27 but they'd only permitted the Steelers to run one offensive play in the fourth quarter, and that was Hanford Dixon's interception of Mark Malone. Behind a dominating performance by the offensive line, eleven of the twelve plays on the final drive were handoffs to Byner or Mack. "When we needed it, the line just crushed people," Byner said.

Meanwhile, the Cleveland defense did its best to crush the lethargic Pittsburgh offense. The Steelers managed just ten first downs and 221 total yards for the game—without having to face the anchor of the Browns' defensive line. By the end of the first quarter, Bob Golic knew he'd done something to his right arm but wouldn't admit to himself how serious the injury was until the pain became unbearable. He sat out the rest of the game with a broken radius bone in his right arm—the same injury Rickey Bolden had suffered at Three Rivers the previous season. As Golic answered questions from reporters after the game and talked about his injury, he did his best to fight back tears. Then, when it hit him that he would miss the playoffs, he was unable to curb his emotions. Bob Golic's 1987 season was over.

But for the rest of the team, it was just getting started. The playoffs now loomed ahead, and considering the almost Shakespearean drama the Browns had encountered there the previous two years, the city of Cleveland was once again prepared for a thunderous crescendo to cap a thrilling season.

"Hang on to your pulse rate, fans," wrote the *Plain Dealer*'s Lou Mio. "Here we go again."

Over the following week, many of the Browns strayed from the conventional wisdom of professional athletics. Finding themselves in the awkward, yet typical, position of being a division champ who wouldn't know whom they'd play in the divisional playoff until after the AFC Wild Card Game, many players gave their honest opinion when asked who they'd rather play.

Their options were either the Seattle Seahawks or the Indianapolis Colts. With the embarrassing 9-7 home defeat to upstart Indianapolis still fresh on their minds, some Browns weren't afraid to make their intentions clear. "Revenge!" the usually mild-mannered Brian Brennan shouted in the locker room when asked the question. "That's why I want to play the Colts again. No doubt about it. We should have scored more." Though some weren't as overt in expressing their opinion as Brennan, certainly the feeling that the Colts had gotten away with one pervaded the Cleveland locker room.

That Sunday afternoon, the Browns got their wish. The Oilers knocked off Seattle in overtime to earn a trip to face the Broncos, ensuring a Colts-Browns rematch in Cleveland on January 9, 1988. For as bad as the Browns had felt after losing the first meeting, the Colts had gone on to finish the season by capping one of the great turnarounds in NFL history. After losing the first thirteen games of the 1986 season, head coach Rod Dowhower was fired and assistant Ron Meyer was promoted to the position. Rather than subtly waltzing through the final three games to secure the top pick in the college draft and acquiring Heisman Trophy winner Vinny Testaverde, Meyer directed the Colts to victory in their final three games to set the tone for the following year. Indianapolis, aided by the blockbuster Eric Dickerson trade in October, went on to post a 9-6 mark in 1987 and win the mediocre AFC East. It would be the Colts' first playoff game in ten years, and they hadn't won a postseason tilt in sixteen. Ironically, their last victory was a 1971 divisional playoff in Cleveland, when the Colts buried the Browns, 20-3. But then they had been the Baltimore Colts. It would be the first playoff trip for the Colts since their move to Indianapolis following the 1983 season. Still, of the 234 media-credential requests for the game, 6 were from Baltimore outlets, which apparently still felt obligated to cover the old hometown team.

For the first time in twenty years, the Browns entered the postseason not only expecting to win but knowing that the success of their season would depend on what they would do in the next few weeks. The last two years, the Browns and their fans were almost satisfied with what the team had accomplished in the regular season, and any postseason achievements would be icing on the cake. But in 1987, the regular season had been nothing but a prelude for the playoffs.

Anything short of a Super Bowl appearance would be a major disappointment. A loss in the divisional playoff, particularly a second loss in five weeks to an inferior team, would be catastrophic.

As the Browns meandered off the field toward the locker room at the conclusion of the first half, things weren't quite catastrophic—at least not yet. As some mild boos trickled out of the stands directed at the home team, the best word to describe the mood at frosty Cleveland Stadium, where the game-time wind-chill factor was five degrees, was "precarious."

The Browns really hadn't played that badly. They were tied with the Colts, 14-14, but as they had in the first meeting, the Browns weren't able to pull away from a team they were clearly better than. Interestingly, the first-half frustrations were the converse of the headaches of the December 6 encounter. Instead of the Cleveland offense floundering and struggling, it was the Browns' defense that couldn't stop the Colts.

Eddie Johnson carried that sense of aggravation into the locker room at the half then allowed it to take over. Even before Marty Schottenheimer and the coaches could illustrate their adjustments for the second half, the man called Assassin ripped into his teammates with the vehemence of a cold-blooded killer, screaming and swearing. "I just got on everybody's butts and told them we couldn't play that way in the second half if we were going to win," Johnson said later. "I said I was tired of coming close and not getting the job done. I said there are no excuses. If you're good enough, you get the job done.

"When I talk, they shut the hell up and listen. They're smart guys."

Johnson had also made his presence and opinion known earlier in the week when he pulled Bernie Kosar aside. Apparently adopting the same play-not-to-lose philosophy that had enveloped the first meeting with Indianapolis, Schottenheimer and Lindy Infante were prepared to implement a simplified offensive game plan centered on not making mistakes rather than attacking the defense.

Kosar had expressed his concern over the plan and knew if the Browns went into the game with it, they'd once again be selling themselves short and would eventually find themselves in a dogfight. Johnson, captain of the defense just as Kosar was the leader of the offense, saw Kosar's frustration and agreed with his concerns. So rather than standing idly by, he convinced the Browns' quarterback to scrap the game plan and either call plays himself or allow Gary Danielson to send in his own signals. Though it may have qualified as defiance, Johnson was simply doing what he felt needed to be done, and the loss to the Colts justified his mission. He refused to be fooled into defeat twice and see Super Bowl dreams go down the drain. He convinced Kosar to do the same. Accordingly, in the first half, it was clear if the Browns were going to lose, they wouldn't go down in the same fashion they had in December.

Playing on the dark-green painted dirt of Cleveland Stadium ("The field is wearing more makeup than Tammy Faye Bakker," NBC's Ahmad Rashad quipped during the pre-game show), the Browns had taken the opening kickoff and marched 86 yards in fifteen plays, converting on four third downs along the way. The Browns took a 7-0 lead when Kosar hit Earnest Byner over the middle for a ten-yard touchdown pass. The crowd of 78,586 roared with joy and relief, as the Browns only took a few minutes to match all the offense they could muster in the teams' first meeting. But unlike the first game, when the Cleveland defense held Indianapolis in check all afternoon, the Colts responded with a long drive of their own. They marched 74 yards in ten plays and tied the game when Jack Trudeau hit tight end Pat Beach for a two-yard score.

Late in the second quarter, from the Indianapolis thirty-nine Kosar flung a deep pass for Reggie Langhorne, who made a diving catch at the Colts' five. As he rolled forward to the two, Langhorne realized he hadn't been touched by an Indianapolis defender. So he simply got back up, and as Robinson attempted to tackle him, fell forward into the end zone for a dazzling touchdown. But the Colts tied the score again with a touchdown just before the half. Fear and worry were once again prevalent at the old ballpark on Lake Erie.

After the Browns conservatively ran out the second-quarter clock, the home-town fans expressed their mild disapproval. This wasn't the way it was supposed to happen. The Browns were supposed to come out and show the world that the 9-7 loss five weeks earlier was a fluke, that Cleveland was a much better team than the Colts. Instead, though a different brand of game, it was essentially the same story. It appeared the Colts still had the Browns' number.

Worse yet, storm clouds were brewing over the potent Cleveland offense. After a few strong carries on the opening drive, Kevin Mack was forced to the side-line with a bad stomach flu, and guard Larry Williams was knocked out of the game with a badly sprained ankle. To account for Mack's departure, the Browns would slide Earnest Byner into the primary ballcarrier role at fullback and bring in Herman Fontenot to take Byner's spot as backfield blocker and receiver. Rookie lineman Gregg Rakoczy, who had seen virtually no game action all season aside from goal-line and short-yardage situations, was sent in to replace Williams in the biggest game of the year.

With two key players sidelined, the Colts taking the momentum into half-time, and the home crowd doubtful, all the ingredients for a disaster were on the counter.

Despite Eddie Johnson's locker-room tirade, the Browns' defense looked no better in the opening minutes of the third quarter. The Colts took over at their own fifteen and immediately began driving toward the Cleveland end zone. The

Browns' defense was constantly one step too slow, and mental mistakes began to take their toll. Indianapolis reached the Browns' twenty yard line and was poised to take the lead.

Desperate for a tide-turning play, Browns' defensive coordinator Dave Adolph decided it was time for something completely out of left field. For the next play, he called a blitz the Browns hadn't tried in a game all year. From the Bear defense, Adolph would send inside linebackers Mike and Eddie Johnson crashing into the line in the hopes it would force a Colts mistake. It worked like a charm.

Indianapolis was prepared for half of the blitz, as Eric Dickerson picked up Mike Johnson and blocked him. But Eddie Johnson smoked through the line untouched. "I don't blitz that much," he said later. "When I get a chance, my ears go back like a Doberman." And before Trudeau even had a chance to glance at the middle part of the field the Browns had left open on a gamble, Eddie Johnson was in his personal space. He tried to loft a pass downfield for Matt Bouza, but Johnson's outstretched arms impeded Trudeau's motion. The ball fluttered high into the air, and Bouza couldn't see it. Felix Wright did see it, however, and he fought around Bouza to intercept the pass at the fourteen, halting the drive and swinging the pendulum of momentum back into the Browns' favor. Trudeau himself said it best: "It was kind of like a nightmare."

Though there was still a quarter-and-a-half of football remaining, deep down both the Colts and Browns knew that the game was over. Less than a half-hour after demanding his teammates step up their game, Eddie Johnson did so himself and may have saved the Browns' 1987 season in the process.

The remainder of the game flowed like a Robert Frost poem for the Browns.

Kosar and company took the turnover and drove 86 yards for the go-ahead touchdown, a two-yard Earnest Byner run. The Cleveland defense, still basking in the glow of Wright's momentous interception, stuffed the Colts on three plays on the next possession, and the visitors punted back to the home team as the third quarter ended. Thanks to a long completion to Ozzie Newsome, the Browns extended the lead to 24-14 on a 23-yard Matt Bahr field goal three minutes into the final stanza.

The Colts were once again faced with a three-and-out and punted, and once again, the inspired Browns were not to be denied. With Byner taking handoffs and carving through the defense like he had regularly two years before, Cleveland marched back into scoring territory and made it 31-14 on a short Kosar-to-Brennan scoring pass with less than four minutes remaining.

After the Colts cut the lead to ten with a minute to play, the Browns added the final touch to what had become a very satisfying afternoon. On fourth-and-twenty from the Colts' thirty-one, backup quarterback Sean Salisbury's desperation toss was picked off by Frank Minnifield at the forty-eight yard line, and the Browns' cornerback wove downfield through a gauntlet of blue jerseys. He didn't stop until he'd dragged Salisbury the final five yards into the Dog Pound end zone for Cleveland's fifth touchdown of the day with thirty-nine seconds remaining.

"It was very rewarding to me that the touchdown came at that end of the field," Minnifield said. "Those fans mean an awful lot to us."

It made the final 38-21, and it was once again party-time in downtown Cleveland.

It was almost poetic how everything worked out in the second half for the Browns. All of the halftime worries they and their fans had turned into gold.

Gregg Rakoczy stepped right in, and the Browns' offensive line didn't miss a beat. He held off the Colts' talented defensive end Jon Hand and instantly earned the respect of his fellow linemen. With Rakoczy as the sparkplug up front, Earnest Byner made Kevin Mack's absence a moot point. Running as inspired as he ever had, Byner racked up 122 yards on twenty-three carries, his first 100-yard game since the playoff loss in Miami two years before. Byner, leading a Cleveland rushing attack that racked up 175 yards, had more than redeemed himself for the costly fumble in the teams' first meeting. "I think Earnest Byner would have had a big day today if he had been there by himself," Marty Schottenheimer said.

"I started thinking about being more aggressive after I lost that fumble in the first Colts game," he said. "It was tough to take. It probably was the lowest point in my career."

While Byner and Rakoczy had both played major roles, without Eddie Johnson's ferocious blitz early in the third quarter, the remainder of the game might have been quite different. "After that play, we totally dominated the second half," Johnson said.

The Browns had held Eric Dickerson in check for the third time in 1987, as the NFL's second-leading rusher managed just 50 yards on fifteen carries. Dave Puzzuoli, making his first start at nose tackle in place of the injured Bob Golic, set the tone on the Colts' first play from scrimmage, stuffing Dickerson for a loss of two. With Puzzuoli holding his own against Colts' All-Pro center Ray Donaldson in perhaps Puzzuoli's greatest performance of his career, the Browns were dominating on run defense. In all three of the Browns' 1987 meetings with Dickerson, they'd held him to under 100 yards. Dickerson himself was impressed. "They have the best defense in the NFL," he said. "It's the best defense I've played against in a few years."

As fans poured out into the streets of Cleveland to celebrate the Browns' first "easy" playoff victory in eighteen years, they soon began to turn their attention to the following afternoon's AFC Divisional Playoff in Denver.

If the Houston Oilers could upset the heavily favored Denver Broncos in Mile High Stadium, Jerry Glanville's club would come to Cleveland the following Sunday for the AFC Championship. But if Denver won, as many expected they would, the Browns would be trekking to the Rockies for a rematch of one of the most memorable conference title games in league history.

As much as fans wanted to enact some revenge on the hated Broncos for what they had done in Cleveland the previous January, they knew the benefits of home-field advantage. Of course, they also wanted the edge of playing a team the Browns had emasculated by thirty-three points on the road two months earlier.

But after two shocking upsets followed the Browns' win over the Colts (a stunning win by the Wild Card Vikings over the 13-2 San Francisco 49ers on Saturday, then a Washington win in Chicago in the early game Sunday), the playoffs returned to a sense of normality. The underdog Oilers were pounded in Denver, 34-10, as the Broncos secured home field for the conference championship the following week.

Three-hundred-seventy-one days after these two teams had fought a brutal and epic struggle, they would meet again, with the stakes exactly the same. The stage was set for the most memorable rematch in the history of the National Football League.

15 Breathless

The plane soared high above North America in total darkness. Any light signifying life through the winter night laid thousands of feet below. For a few brief hours, the passengers could feel like inhabitants of outer space, free from the disappointment they departed on Earth and the inevitable wave of heartbreak that awaited them upon their return. But in the interim, everyone on board the plane was happy for the intermission.

Friends and colleagues who had worked together for months sat together silently. Though there were dozens of people on the flight, each felt almost isolated, adrift with his thoughts as they passed silently through the heavens.

One man in particular sat alone. He stared out the window at the nothingness enveloping him and his fellow travelers, still in disbelief over what had transpired just hours before. This man had acted heroically. He'd done everything asked of him and more, performed at a level rarely reached by anyone in his profession. He'd poured his heart and very soul into battle and somehow wound up a villain.

When playwrights and poets craft tales of tragedy, they never are able to explain how their victims sift through their woe after the curtain falls. The audience is left to visualize for itself, though most probably don't. It's better to leave the tragedy on the stage rather than take it home with you, best to leave the suffering in the dimension of fiction and not have it intrude on your voyeuristic reality.

But this man's suffering would take place in a public forum long after the final act of the drama had concluded. In some ways, despite a gargantuan effort that likely would never be fully appreciated, he would simply remain the same character in the same tragedy until the end of time.

On one winter night in the mountains, his life had changed forever—and thousands of hearts and dreams had crashed along with it.

It was as good as anyone could have written it.

A year after waging one of the most memorable gridiron struggles in history, the Cleveland Browns and Denver Broncos would meet again, this time in

Denver. Both teams had endured rougher roads back to the championship and a highly anticipated regular-season rematch between the two in September was wiped out because of the players' strike. It was the stuff of movie sequels. The only question was Would the hero be the same?

For only the third time ever, the AFC Championship game would pit the same two teams against one another two straight years, though none of those previous rematches were following up a truly classic game. While all of those contests had been memorable for one reason or another, none had been bona fide classics, to be remembered in the annals of pro football forever. Though it was only a year old, most football fans were already acknowledging the 1986 AFC Championship Game in Cleveland as one of the finest contests ever played—maybe the best AFC title match ever. And as the Browns and Broncos prepared for their rematch at Mile High Stadium in mid-January 1988, players, coaches, and writers alike seemed to be expecting another football smorgasbord.

Meanwhile, the Cleveland Browns, a year after one of the most dire heartbreaks in team history, were anticipating revenge.

No one in Cleveland had forgotten the previous January, when the Denver Broncos had stolen away the Browns' first Super Bowl berth with a last-gasp drive and overtime culmination of victory. "I'm sure every weight the Browns' players lifted this year, they've thought about that game," Denver coach Dan Reeves said. No one denied it.

Nor did anyone contend that these were not the conference's two finest teams. Over the previous two years, the Browns and Broncos had compiled the best records in the AFC and had maneuvered back into a title-game rematch despite season-long challenges for both. Though they posted a 10-4-1 record on the year, the Broncos had spent much of the early season looking up at the fast-starting San Diego Chargers. But Denver surged as the Chargers folded, and after the Broncos won six of their final seven games, they'd captured the AFC West title for the second straight year. Then, they'd quickly slapped down the trash-talking Houston Oilers in the divisional playoff, taking advantage of early mistakes to coast to a comfortable lead.

John Elway was still the heart of the team, and many of his weapons were the same, with the rise of the "Three Amigos": wide receivers Vance Johnson, Ricky Nattiel, and Mark Jackson, who'd caught the game-tying touchdown pass in Cleveland the previous year. Johnson wouldn't play due to a groin injury suffered in the Houston game, but the Bronco offense was as potent as it had been in 1986, if not more so. The Denver defense had lost three starters to retirement after 1986, but Joe Collier still managed to maintain the Broncos' lofty standing among the league statistics.

Though both squads' records were actually slightly worse than the year before, both felt they were better. The Browns believed they entered the game with two primary advantages they hadn't had the year before: their new Bear defense as a wrinkle for Elway to deal with, and a healthy Earnest Byner.

Through much of December and early January, Browns' officials noted that the mania surrounding the team seemed to be a bit less frenzied than it had been the year before. The fans were as interested as ever, but the breaking point between interest and all-out insanity had been pushed up a bit after the accomplishments of 1986. The Browns knew that if they went far enough, the fans would go loony once again. And as they prepared to face the Broncos that week, Cleveland had indeed re-entered that wonderland.

At the Cleveland Museum of Natural History, a replica of a 150-million-year-old stegosaurus was fitted with a Browns' hat and gloves and pennants were stuck in his tail. Bridal-shop mannequins carried footballs and Browns' banners. Electronics stores rented out every big-screen TV in stock. The homicide units of the Cleveland and Denver police departments made a friendly wager on the contest, each betting a collection of baseball caps.

Browns Mania spilled over into the world of politics. A little-known Tennessee politician named Al Gore, jockeying for the Democratic Party's nomination for president that summer, was in town giving a speech that week wearing a Browns' button on his suit. But an even bigger Browns' endorsement came from the other end of the political spectrum. That Monday, after President Ronald Reagan gave a speech to the City Club of Cleveland at Stouffer Tower, he was handed a sweatshirt reading "Go Browns! Win One For the Gipper!" He held it up for photographs that were published coast-to-coast. The pictures didn't go over well in Colorado, a Republican-dominated state Reagan had carried in 1980 and 1984.

"There is no worse sin among Coloradans this week than to align yourself with those sleazy bone-hurling BrownDogs [sic] fans," wrote opinionated Buddy Martin in the *Denver Post*. "Better he should have admitted during the Iran-Contra hearings to peddling weapons off the back of a flatbed truck in Nicaragua."

Somewhat lost in the madness, late that week two historic occurrences in the world of sports set in motion a chain of events that would alter Browns' history forever. On Thursday, Green Bay Packers' (and former Browns') head coach Forrest Gregg resigned to take over the head coaching position at his alma mater of Southern Methodist University, which was in the midst of hard times following recent NCAA sanctions. The Packers were now looking for a new leader, and Lindy Infante was rumored to be one of the prime candidates.

The following day St. Louis Cardinals' owner William Bidwell announced his club would be moving to Phoenix, marking the NFL's first relocation since the Colts left Baltimore for Indianapolis in 1984. In making his decision, Bidwell had considered, but turned down offers from Jacksonville, Memphis, and Baltimore. Shortly after, the city of Baltimore was assured by the NFL that if it didn't

171

attempt to lure any existing franchises to move, the league would eventually expand to replace the Colts.

But getting passed over by the Cardinals began a long, frustrating journey for Baltimore, which would eventually become so desperate for professional football it would go back on its good-faith assurance to the NFL. No one in football-mad Cleveland could possibly imagine where Bidwell's announcement that Friday would eventually lead.

Though the Browns felt they were a better team than they'd been a year before, they knew this would be a much tougher challenge. Defeating the Broncos was one thing, beating them at Mile High Stadium was quite another. Since Dan Reeves became Denver's coach in 1981, the Broncos held a home record of 42-11. They hadn't lost a non-strike game at Mile High in 1987 and had looked all but unbeatable the previous week against Houston. Plus, the Browns had lost four straight games in Denver, not earning a victory there in fifteen years. Appropriately, the Broncos were favored by three points. Still, most Browns' fans were optimistic. The previous year, the Broncos had broken the Browns' hearts at home, this time it was Cleveland's turn to do the same.

Bob Golic, for one, was optimistic the Browns would win. Fitted with a prosthetic limb which stretched from his knuckles to his shoulder, he would sit out the Denver game but was already thinking past it. "I told Marty if we made the Super Bowl, I was playing," he said. "All we had to do was win, and they were going to put a pad on this thing, and I was going to look like a Transformer.

"I remember standing in the back of the meeting room in Denver hitting my hand against the wall, trying to see how much it hurt and to get used to the pain so I'd be ready to play."

Win or lose, Browns' fans were eager to rid themselves of the memory of the 1986 AFC Championship. "That's all I've heard about since last year," said Terry Akers, president of the Browns Backers of Colorado. "I'm hoping for a replay of last year except I don't want The Drive at the end of it. I don't want to hear any more about The Drive."

As it turned out, Akers' wish came true to some extent. The rematch would rob The Drive of some of its historical significance.

"From Mile High Stadium in Denver, Colorado, it's the rematch the Browns have long awaited," Nev Chandler said, painting the picture for his radio audience with his trademark snap-crackle rhythm prior to kickoff. *"They've been waiting an entire year to get revenge against the Denver Broncos for losing the AFC Championship last year in Cleveland. Now the time is here. The Browns against the Broncos for the right to go to the Super Bowl."*

It was a picture-perfect day for football. The temperature hovered around forty degrees, and sun splashed through Mile High Stadium. Yet despite the ideal conditions, even before kickoff, there were omens this wasn't to be the Browns' day. In what may have been a psychological attack, highlights of the 1986 AFC title game played on the Mile High scoreboard as the teams warmed up. And prior to kickoff, Buffalo's Shane Conlan, the linebacker the Browns had passed over in the draft nine months earlier to select Mike Junkin, was presented with the NFL Rookie of the Year Award. The bad karma carried over onto the field.

On the opening kickoff, Gerald McNeil was smothered at the Cleveland twelve yard line, and the capacity crowd roared, shaking the NBC cameras. The noise level grew stronger on first down when Bernie Kosar couldn't find any receivers, tried to scramble away, and was caught by defensive end Simon Fletcher for an eight-yard loss. After Earnest Byner sprinted for seven yards up the middle on second-and-eighteen, Kosar backpedaled and slung a pass for Webster Slaughter cutting open over the middle. Slaughter had the ball in his hands, but it slipped out, bounced off his knee, and was intercepted by Broncos' defensive end Freddie Gilbert at the eighteen. The Mile High crowd nearly exploded as John Elway and the Denver offense took the field with little real estate in front of them. The Browns had made the first mistake of the day. Three plays later, Elway hit Ricky Nattiel for a touchdown.

With the crowd still humming, the Browns stayed calm and turned to the ground game on their second possession. On third-and-one at the Denver forty-five, Kevin Mack took a handoff and exploded through a hole on the left side of the line to pick up the first down, but as he fought for extra yardage, he was tied up by Broncos' safety Tony Lilly. Lilly got his hands underneath the football and wrested it from Mack's clutches, sending it bouncing ahead of him. Denver free safety Steve Wilson recovered at the Denver forty yard line, and the Bronco faithful again went bonkers. Just as the Oilers had the week before, the Browns had committed two early turnovers and appeared to be digging themselves a deep hole.

Their troubles deepened a play later, when fullback Gene Lang slid through a hole on the left side and scampered 42 yards downfield to the Cleveland eleven. Not only was the Browns' offense shooting itself in the foot but the Dog Defense was clearly not in sync. After a critical holding penalty on Frank Minnifield gave Denver a first down at the two, Steve Sewell scored on a reverse to make it 14-0 eleven minutes into the game.

The Browns had spotted the favored Broncos two turnovers which had turned into two touchdowns. This was no way to win a championship game—particularly in a stadium where the Broncos had won at home more than any other NFL team over the previous four years. Still, as the Browns' offense took the field for its third possession, Bernie Kosar and company knew they had only stopped themselves. They'd proved they could move the football and simply had to hang onto it to turn the game around. They proceeded to do just that, driving inside the Denver ten and getting on the board with a Matt Bahr field goal. But along the way, Mike Baab was lost for the remainder of the game with a twisted knee. Gregg Rakoczy, starting for injured left guard Larry Williams, slid to center, and Williams hobbled in off the sideline to replace Rakoczy.

The Denver offense picked up right where it had left off. Combining short runs by Sammy Winder and tosses from Elway, the Broncos methodically drove down the field. Lang put the exclamation point on the drive with a one-yard scoring plunge, giving Denver a seemingly insurmountable 21-3 lead. The Browns were getting blown out of the Rocky Mountains, and worse, they were primarily doing it to themselves.

Things only got more frustrating. Kosar was sacked by Rulon Jones on third-and-seven from the Cleveland twenty-three, and the Browns were forced to punt. Quickly, Denver marched back into Browns' territory, but the Cleveland defense stiffened, forcing three straight Elway incompletions from the thirty-three yard line. The bleeding slowed somewhat when Rich Karlis missed a 50-yard field goal attempt wide left. Finally, something had gone the Browns' way.

And with the first half waning, the visitors were desperate to do something positive before the intermission. They maneuvered to the Denver forty-three, but then once again became their own worst enemy. After a Kosar pass for Webster Slaughter fell incomplete on the next play, a frustrated Slaughter took a swing at Denver's Tony Lilly. It resulted in a personal foul, and on second-and-twenty-five, Brian Brennan fumbled after snagging a pass from Kosar at midfield. Steve Wilson recovered his second fumble of the day, this one caused by a backup safety named Jeremiah Castille, who'd stripped the ball from Brennan.

"This has really been Murphy's Law time for the Browns," a distraught Nev Chandler told his radio audience. *"Everything that can go wrong has gone wrong and will go wrong. And the Browns have greased the skids with plenty of mistakes on their own behalf."*

But there were more to come. After a Denver punt, a hurried Cleveland drive ended with Bahr missing a field goal. It remained 21-3 as the teams returned to the locker rooms.

It had been the biggest nightmare of a half in Cleveland postseason history. Ironically, though, the dream-like afternoon was just beginning.

In the locker room, the Browns looked at one another, stunned at what had happened on the field. They just couldn't figure it out. They were prepared. They were focused. They'd had a good week of practice and were clearly motivated. They felt they were a Super Bowl-caliber team but looked like a bunch of players going through the first day of practice. "We were anxious to play," Carl Hairston would say later. "Maybe we were too anxious. Maybe we tried too hard to make things happen."

As it happened, the Broncos needn't have even tried. Good things just landed in their laps. The Browns had turned the ball over three times and consequently, gift-wrapped fourteen points. The teams' total yardages were comparable, with the Broncos accumulating 160 and the Browns 148. But, untimely mental mistakes had buried the Browns in the first half.

Still, despite the huge deficit in the toughest stadium to win in the NFL, the Browns knew they weren't done yet. Lindy Infante, though he had every reason to be frustrated and desperate, maintained total control. He told his offense they were going to play in the second half like the score was 14-7. The Browns weren't going to use the two-minute offense; they weren't going to change their game plan. They were going to stick with the same philosophies that had made them one of the league's best offenses in 1987. They were going to be patient and wait for their talent to surface.

On the other side of the ball, Marty Schottenheimer pulled his defensive captains aside prior to the second-half kickoff. He told them not to worry about playing spectacularly, but rather asked them to just clear their minds and play just like practice. The theme of the halftime speeches was clear: we're too good to get desperate, and conversely, too good to get beaten so badly. Breaks would start to go their way, and then it would be up to the Browns to get back into the game.

But before the Cleveland offense could get a chance to cut into the Denver lead, the Browns' defense would have to get the football back for them before John Elway could make the hole deeper. The Browns did just that when a desperate third-down pass was picked off by Felix Wright and returned to the Denver thirty-five yard line. Finally, the Browns had caught a break. Bernie Kosar and the offense took the field not only sharper than in the first half but determined to eliminate the foolish mistakes which had dug such a deep hole.

Kevin Mack blasted for 13 yards on first down, then on second-and-six a play later, Bernie Kosar barked out an audible at the line of scrimmage. Driving toward the closed, loud end of Mile High Stadium, only half of the offense heard the audible. Luckily, Reggie Langhorne was part of that half. Bernie Kosar took the snap and even before he could lift his arm to throw, Rulon Jones crashed through the line straight for him. Kosar hung in there the extra second and launched an arching pass up over Jones' outstretched arms. Langhorne caught it streaking through the end zone for an 18-yard touchdown pass. With Matt Bahr's extra point, the margin was now 21-10, and the Browns were showing signs of life.

Things looked even better when a penalty turned a third-and-one situation for Denver into third-and-ten at its own twenty. Elway took the snap and could find no one open. He began scrambling, collided with guard Stefan Humphries, bounced off him and rolled to his right. He fired a pass along the sideline for Mark Jackson, who had lost Mark Harper on a pattern across the middle. Jackson caught the ball at the twenty-five, and Harper closed in on him to make the tackle that would have forced fourth down. But Jackson slipped through Harper's grasp and started upfield. Felix Wright then charged over to Jackson and made contact at the thirty, but again Jackson escaped with a stutter step. When Wright hit the ground, there was nothing between Jackson and the goal line. He sprinted down the sideline, with each step bringing Denver's dreams of a second straight

Super Bowl berth into focus. Ray Ellis sprinted after Jackson and finally caught up to him at the Cleveland five yard line, but on the tackle, Jackson fell into the end zone, completing an 80-yard touchdown pass, the longest in NFL postseason history.

Wright's interception and Langhorne's touchdown were wiped out. Five minutes into the third quarter, the Browns were right back where they had started the second half. Rich Karlis' extra point made it 28-10, and reality began to sink in for many Browns' followers.

"And that may be the one that turns the lights out on the Browns for the remainder of the afternoon," a downtrodden Nev Chandler said to his audience. *"They have a lot of work to do and a long way to climb here just outside of the Rockies."*

For all intents and purposes, the Browns had every reason to give up. Clearly, this was not their day. They'd turned the ball over on their first two possessions and trailed 14-0 before they even looked up. Then, just when it seemed they might be gathering some momentum, Elway made another athletic play, and the AFC's best defense suffered two sloppy mistakes that allowed a five-yard pass to become an eighty-yard score. Add to that the psychological disadvantage of having lost to the Broncos in Cleveland on this same stage a year ago, and many television viewers (including many Browns' fans) were flipping off their televisions, muttering under their breath about how the Browns never showed up in the big game.

Those who did turn away would miss one of the most thrilling second halves in the history of football.

Once again, the Cleveland offense took over possession of the football trailing by eighteen, yet they knew they were not being outplayed. The Browns had moved the ball all day and had finally punched it into the end zone on their previous possession. They just needed to keep doing what they'd been doing. And that's exactly what they did.

On third-and-four, Bernie Kosar hit Earnest Byner for 11 yards and a first down. On the following play, Langhorne pulled in his second reception, this one a 30-yard gain to the Denver thirty-three. And on the next snap, Kosar took a glance over the middle, found no one, and began scrambling to his right. Seeing Byner streaking toward the right sideline, Kosar stopped and looped a finesse pass over the oncoming Denver defense, and Byner reeled it in at the eighteen yard line. Angling toward the end zone, Byner sprinted toward paydirt, and following a key block by Mack, crossed the front corner of the end zone before collapsing into the sideline.

"Byner sneaks across the goal line, and the Browns are alive and kicking in Denver!" exclaimed a much more cheerful Nev Chandler.

The margin was 28-17. And despite uncountable reasons to the contrary, the Browns had wrestled control of the game's momentum from the Broncos. Their enthusiasm grew stronger on the next series as the Cleveland defense finally stopped the Denver offense. Mike Horan punted back to the Browns, and Gerald McNeil returned the kick to the Bronco forty-two. What just minutes before had appeared to be a blowout was suddenly a very competitive game.

And once again, the Browns wasted no time. Kosar hit Webster Slaughter for 16 yards, then after another eight-yard pass to Mack to the Bronco four, Earnest Byner exploded up the middle and into the end zone to make it 28-24 with 3:39 remaining in the third quarter. In twelve offensive plays, the Browns had marched 152 yards and scored twenty-one points. Mile High Stadium was as quiet as it had been all day.

The noise level spiked a bit over the next few minutes as the Broncos put together their fifth scoring drive of the day. Thanks to a 22-yard pass to Mark Jackson, who was having a career afternoon, the Broncos marched into Cleveland territory, where Rich Karlis booted a 38-yard field goal to push the deficit back to a touchdown at 31-24.

After Gerald McNeil was brought down at the Cleveland fourteen yard line on the ensuing kickoff, the third quarter ended. With dusk just beginning to fall and the Rocky Mountains silhouetted against a pink sky soft as dreams, one of the most thrilling games in the history of professional football would now be determined in a fourth quarter for the ages.

The Browns had fought nearly all the way back from two insurmountable deficits, but still did not have control of the football game. They had started the game the exact same way the Houston Oilers had the Sunday before at Mile High Stadium. After falling behind early, the Oilers had packed it in and lost in a rout. The Browns had done the opposite. Yet they still needed one more touchdown to complete the comeback.

Facing a critical third-and-five from the Cleveland nineteen, the Browns once again found themselves at the crossroads of momentum. Failure here would give Denver back the football near midfield with an opportunity to take a two-score lead with less than ten minutes to play. Kosar dropped back knowing the entire 1987 season may hinge on his next pass. And accordingly, he threw to the man who had come through so many times already that afternoon.

Kosar looped a pass over the middle, just over the outstretched arms of linebacker Rich Dennison and over Ernest Byner's shoulder at midfield. He caught the pass in stride and sprinted up the field with one man to beat. After scampering into Denver territory, Byner tried to cut back to avoid safety Tony Lilly but couldn't and was dragged down at the Bronco twenty-eight yard line after a 53-yard pass—perhaps the Browns' biggest play of the season.

On third-and-two from the twenty, the call was again to Mack, who this time exploded through the middle and bounced off a pair of defenders, stumbling forward and straining to the five for a 15-yard gain. The Browns were poised to score again. But after Byner was stopped for no gain and a second-down pass for Herman Fontenot fell incomplete, it brought up yet another third down. And for the third time on the drive, the Browns converted. Kosar took a four-step drop as Webster Slaughter froze cornerback Jeremiah Castille at the line of scrimmage, then, before Castille could close the gap between them, Slaughter darted to his right as Kosar whipped a sinking pass toward him. Slaughter caught it on the slant sliding into the ground in the end zone—almost identical to the area and fashion in which Mark Jackson had caught the game-tying touchdown pass in Cleveland 371 days earlier. Matt Bahr's extra point tied the game at thirty-one.

"In the mile-high atmosphere, we're a little bit short of breath," Nev Chandler said. "The Browns have battled back into an even-steven football game."

Ten minutes and forty-five seconds remained, and the Browns and Broncos were right back where they started from. The AFC championship was back on the table.

"We've got one going now," Doug Dieken declared.

Riding the wave of momentum, the Browns forced a Denver punt and took over at their own thirty-two. For the first time since the initial possession of the game, the Browns had the football with a chance to take the lead. Mile High Stadium hushed as thousands of Bronco fans began to get truly nervous for the first time all day. The Browns picked up a first down near midfield but were forced to punt shortly after, and the Broncos took over at their own twenty-three. Five minutes and fourteen seconds remained—exactly twenty seconds fewer than were on the clock when the Broncos took the field at their own two-yard line a year earlier in Cleveland. It was one final shot at redemption for the Browns' defense.

But on first down, John Elway showed he still had the upper hand. He hit Ricky Nattiel for 26 yards to the Browns' forty-nine, and the Mile High crowd once again got excited. After a three-yard run by Winder and an Elway incompletion, the Broncos were faced with a key third down of their own. But once more, Denver was up to the challenge. Elway hit Nattiel again on a crossing pattern to the left side for 26 more yards to the Cleveland twenty yard line and a first down. The crowd grew even more active.

On the next play, Elway again dropped back to pass, and Sammy Winder hung back behind the Denver offensive line, then snuck past the Browns' front line as it crashed through. Elway tossed a screen to Winder, who scampered around and through the scattered Cleveland defense and into the end zone for the go-ahead touchdown. The Mile High crowd exploded, reaching noise levels not heard since the 21-3 moments of the second quarter.

As the Broncos celebrated in the end zone, several of the more conscientious players began to worry. Four minutes and one second remained. The Browns' offense had been all but unstoppable in the second half. Now, with the game on the line, would the Denver defense be able to stop red-hot Bernie Kosar?

Rich Karlis' extra point made it 38-31. On the ensuing kickoff, with the crowd roaring like waves crashing upon the ocean shore, Gerald McNeil raced from the Cleveland seven to the twenty-four, where he was tackled. The stage was set for the most incredible finish to any AFC Championship Game.

As Bernie Kosar and the Browns' offense jogged out onto the field, dusk had begun to yield to dark. The sky, an electric blue under a crisp winter sun at kickoff, had melted into a palette of subtle purples and pinks. It was an appropriately dramatic backdrop.

Had anyone tried to write a script, they never would have been able to put a finer point on the 1987 AFC Championship than this. A year after John Elway drove his team the length of the field in the final minutes to tie the championship game and send it to overtime on the opponent's field, Bernie Kosar would now have the exact same opportunity under an almost unbelievable crescendo of drama.

Three minutes and fifty-three seconds remained. The Browns needed to drive 76 yards to wipe out all the memories of one drive and replace them with another. More than 73,000 fans at Mile High were on their feet and holding their breath, and millions across the nation were glued to their television sets. Once again, the hearts of Cleveland were in the Browns' hands.

"It's time for the comeback kid from the comeback town to put it all together again," Doug Dieken said.

Yet with all eyes on Kosar, the Browns crossed up everyone. On first down, Kosar handed off to Earnest Byner, who streaked like lightning through a gaping hole on the left side of the line and sprinted to the Browns' forty-one yard line for a 17-yard gain. Instantly, the Broncos' defense was on its heels. In one play it was made clear that Denver would not just have to stop Bernie Kosar to reach the Super Bowl, but Earnest Byner as well.

Byner was harnessed for a two-yard gain on the next play, but on second-and-eight, Kosar hit another old reliable, Brian Brennan, on the left side for a 13-yard gain to the Denver forty-four and a first down. With the clock ticking down to the two-minute warning, the Browns were up-tempo but not hurried. They gathered again for the next snap, which Kosar took and dropped back. Finding no one open, he began to scramble to his left, where he slung a pass for Brennan, which he caught at the Denver thirty-two and scampered forward to the Bronco twenty-four—a 20-yard gain and another first down.

" . . . And the Browns stage a monumental march," Nev Chandler reported, his voice humming with excitement.

The clock stopped for the two-minute warning. The pulse of the entire sports world was racing. The epic, sweeping drama of the 1987 AFC Championship would fittingly come down to the very final moments.

Before the Browns could get off the fifth play of the drive, Denver left end Andre Townsend jumped offside, moving Cleveland to the nineteen. The playcall on first-and-five was "13 Trap." Dan Fike pulled from right guard and cleared a space for Earnest Byner, who took the handoff. Byner blasted through the hole for six yards to the Denver thirteen for another first down—the fourth of the series. The Bronco defense was running out of real estate to defend.

On the next snap, Kosar tried to cover the rest. He dropped back and slung a pass over the middle for Byner breaking open in the end zone. The pass was a bit too hot for Byner, bouncing off his hands in the back of the end zone, though had he caught it he would have been out of bounds. But for one brief moment, Browns' fans' hearts surged into their throats as the tying touchdown nearly played out before their eyes.

It brought up second-and-ten from the Bronco thirteen with 1:15 to play. Kosar again dropped back and fired a pass for Reggie Langhorne inside the five which fell incomplete, but again Denver was penalized. Linebacker Karl Mecklenberg was flagged for being offside, and the Browns took the penalty, setting up second-and-five from the eight with 1:12 remaining.

For the second time in four snaps, the playcall was "13 Trap."

"*Bernie Kosar up under center Gregg Rakoczy . . .*" Nev Chandler described to his radio audience.

Kosar took the snap, and again Dan Fike swung over to the left side to clear a path for his halfback, pummeling Rulon Jones.

"*. . . handoff to Byner on a draw . . .*"

Byner took the handoff and immediately shifted direction, angling toward the gap created by Fike. As Byner cleared the line of scrimmage, he and every Browns' fan watching was thinking touchdown.

"*. . . inside the five . . .*"

Almost as if in slow motion, Byner began to prepare to be hit by safety Tony Lilly, the only man standing squarely between him and the goal line. But upfield to Byner's left, something was happening.

Webster Slaughter had begun the play as the far receiver on the left side, with Jeremiah Castille lined up on him, preparing to bump Slaughter off the line. Slaughter's mission on the play was simple. If Castille was playing him bump-and-run, he was to cut outside and take Castille with him to the corner of the end zone, safely out of Byner's path. If Castille played off of Slaughter, giving him the time and vision to see the play was a draw and not a pass, Slaughter was supposed to block Castille.

Brian Brennan, lined up just to the right of Slaughter, had the same instructions. With safety Dennis Smith playing up on him, Brennan ran his route into the end zone, taking Smith with him and out of harm's way. Half of Byner's path to the outside was now clear.

But a second before Bernie Kosar took the snap Castille remembered the last time the Browns were in this position. He remembered getting burned by Slaughter on a quick slant at the five-yard line and was worried the Browns would try the same play again. So at the last possible moment, he took two steps back off Slaughter on the line, giving himself a larger margin for error if Slaughter cut quickly, plus a better angle on what was happening in the pocket.

"... *to the four* ..."

Having backed off, Castille could now see it wasn't a pass. He saw Byner plow through the hole in the Denver line toward the end zone. Castille abandoned Slaughter and angled toward Byner. His path was clear because Slaughter cut inside on his pass route and missed the block on Castille. Had Slaughter made contact, Castille never would have reached Byner in time.

With each step Byner took, Nev Chandler's voice now rose in almost poetic crescendo.

"... *to the three* ..."

Byner was prepared to plow into Lilly at the goal line and fall forward for the game-tying touchdown. Lilly was all that stood between the Browns and over-time. In that instant, both Byner and Browns' fans watching at home on television knew he was going to score.

Neither the fans nor Byner ever saw Jeremiah Castille.

Castille was arriving too late to make the tackle, and he knew it. And after seeing Byner mow through Bronco defenders all afternoon, Castille knew his only chance to disrupt Byner's path was to try to strip the football. As Byner cruised to within six feet of the end zone, Castille made contact and a swiping motion.

"... *TO THE TWO, TO THE ONE* ..."

In the next half-second, Browns' fans began to rejoice. Byner bounced off Castille and began to fall forward. To millions of fans watching on television, for one split second, it appeared as though Byner had scored. At countless parties and bars around Northeast Ohio, fans roared with joy. For one divine moment, the Browns had tied the game and were headed to overtime with momentum, destined for their first Super Bowl appearance.

But almost before fans could completely raise their arms in celebration, they knew something didn't look right. As Byner landed, he had sort of twisted at an odd angle and was facing backward. In that instant, they knew something was wrong.

So did Nev Chandler. After following Byner's path to the one, he paused, re-flecting that momentary mass confusion. Then he realized what happened and completed the playcall as his voice sunk from its previous level of enthusiasm.

"... *HE* ... *fumbles the football and the Broncos have it—I believe.*"

Doug Dieken added, almost in a whisper, "*Oh my goodness.*"

"*Let's wait and see when they unstack.*" Chandler continued.

Byner had traveled the last two yards of his journey without the football. Cas-tille had knocked it out back at the two. When Byner hit the ground on one knee, his other leg sprawled out in front of him as he turned back to see the pileup at the three-yard line.

Art Modell wasn't sure exactly what had happened. Due to a quirk of architecture, from the visitor's owner's box at Mile High Stadium, the view to the north end zone was partially blocked by three windows from the box next to it. Looking through the windows, the image was distorted, almost abstract, just a whirl of colors and motion. But even through the looking glass, Modell knew something wasn't right.

"*Huge pileup at the three yard line, and the Broncos have it,*" Chandler said, with the roaring of the relieved Mile High crowd in the background.

"*Earnest Byner has played his heart out,*" Dieken added. "*To have that happen—unbelievable.*"

After a long, breathless moment of silence, Nev Chandler summed up what was in the heart of every Browns' fan.

"*It just doesn't seem fair.*"

After he turned back to see the pileup, Earnest Byner slowly collapsed to the ground and didn't bother to see the official signal. He lay on his left hip on the goal line, resting on his elbow, head down. It was the classic image of the agony of defeat.

Slowly, he peeled himself off the ground and began walking, slowly, back to the Browns' bench with his teammates. As the NBC cameras found him, then began showing a slow-motion replay of his fumble for the first of what would become thousands of times, Browns' fans began to remember Byner's history.

They remembered how he'd always had trouble holding onto the football. They recalled him saying he'd never learned how to hold the ball correctly growing up and would often fall back into bad habits. They remembered a cold Sunday afternoon six weeks earlier when he fumbled at the five yard line, costing the Browns a chance to beat the Colts. And those with even better memories recalled numerous other fumbles in 1987, several inside the opponent's five yard line.

Now, Earnest Byner's one weakness had cost him and his team a chance at a championship.

He found a spot on the sideline, set his helmet down and sat on it. As if surrounded by a cloud, Byner sat alone. "I can't even describe the depth of the pain that was in his eyes," Mike Johnson would say later.

As the Browns' offense returned to the sideline in disbelief, the defense took the field hoping for some kind of miracle. One minute, five seconds remained, and the Bronco offense lined up for first down at the two with one mission: Don't do anything stupid to lose the game.

Elway plowed forward for two yards, and the Browns called their second time out with 1:01 left. The Browns jumped offside on second down, moving Denver out to the nine, where Elway again muscled straight ahead for two yards. The Browns called their final time out with fifty-two seconds left to play.

During this final pause, Bernie Kosar came over to Earnest Byner. He squatted down next to him and hung his left arm around Byner's neck. It was the final vision of disappointment that caused the Browns' fans still watching to feel their hearts crumble into a million pieces.

Elway ran around left end for a yard on third down, and though it wasn't enough for a first down, it kept the clock running. Out of time outs, the Browns were now helpless to stop the clock. Denver ran it down as far as it could, finally calling time out with a mere thirteen seconds to play.

Mike Horan was called on, but not to punt. He took the snap, which hit the ground before reaching him, and ran out of the end zone for a safety, avoiding the possibility of a blocked kick for a touchdown. Now leading 38-33, the Broncos would free-kick from their own twenty with eight seconds left. The Cleveland offense would get to take the field one more time.

Horan's free kick drifted to the Browns' twenty-three, where Gerald McNeil fair-caught it. Facing the hopeless task of having to go 77 yards in eight seconds with no time outs, the Browns did all they could. Bernie Kosar whipped a desperation pass high into the Denver night sky down the right sideline, hoping for the miracle of miracles. The ball was tipped at the Denver forty, and Brian Brennan made a diving catch on the sideline at the forty-one, landing at the feet of Broncos' coach Dan Reeves. But officials ruled Brennan had been out of bounds.

The clock had hit zero. The Browns' 1987 season was over.

For the third straight year, the Browns sat exhausted in their own locker room, unable to fully comprehend that their season was over despite a Herculean effort. But this one was by far the worst.

"We wanted this one so bad, so bad," Eddie Johnson said. "When you lose at this point, everything you've accomplished is insignificant. This one hurts more than last year because our level of expectation was higher this year. And when something like this happens, it's sad."

All the work and planning the Browns had done in 1987 was now over. They had overcome the pressure of lofty expectations and survived the tumultuous player's strike. They'd successfully switched defensive philosophies and improvised when their top draft pick turned out to be a bust. They'd withheld energized runs at the division title by hungry Houston and Pittsburgh teams and had honed their offense and defense into two of the NFL's very best. And finally they'd maneuvered through the divisional playoffs to set up the rematch they'd only dreamed of getting. But in the end, it was all for naught. For the twenty-second straight year, the Browns would not be playing in the Super Bowl.

"Not many people get a second chance in life," Ozzie Newsome said. "We did, and we didn't win. That makes this loss twice as frustrating as last year."

"This is a sad day for Cleveland," Bernie Kosar said. "Words cannot describe the way I'm feeling right now."

Nor could words truly capture the way Kosar and the Browns' offense had played in the second half. The statistics were simply amazing. In two quarters,

Kosar had completed fifteen of twenty-two passes for 246 yards and three touchdowns, winding up with 356 passing yards on the day. The Browns rolled up 316 yards of offense in the second half alone, 464 for the game. As it was, the teams combined for 878 total yards and seventy-one points, the second-most ever scored in an AFC Championship.

"There was no stopping Bernie," Elway confessed. "We just had to do what we could to outscore him."

"I don't know what it was," Kosar said, "I just got hot."

Getting just as hot and playing just as vital a role in the second half was Earnest Byner, though many forgot all he'd accomplished when his final carry ended in disaster.

Byner wound up with fifteen rushes for 67 yards and caught seven passes for 120—187 yards of offense, more than any other player in the game. It was his biggest game since the Browns' playoff loss in Miami two years earlier, again proving that when the season was on the line, Byner would be there. Fans could only wonder what might have happened in the 1986 AFC Championship had Byner been healthy.

"Byner symbolizes that great fighting spirit," Pete Franklin would write. "He is the guy who refuses to give up, who keeps battling the opponent, who never gives up."

And members of the Cleveland media and Browns' coaches and players alike agreed that it was ridiculous to blame the loss on Byner. "I told him our football team would not have been in position to win if not for Earnest Byner," Marty Schottenheimer said. "If not for Earnest Byner and his heroics, we would not have been looking at the kind of football game we looked at today."

"If it had been anybody in the world but Earnest, we would have killed him," Mike Baab said. "But without Earnest, we never would have gotten there. Earnest was that kind of person. He was a team leader, and we all knew Earnest came straight from the heart."

To be sure, had the Browns not completely self-destructed in the first half, they never would have needed a last-gasp drive in the first place. "Without those turnovers the Broncos are not in the game," Byner said. "It's not even close."

"I've never seen a luckier team in my life," Brennan added. "We outplayed them. Take away our three turnovers, and they're not even in the game. Even though we've lost to them two years in a row, I feel we're the better football team."

"The fact of the matter is, we had no business even having a chance to win at the end," Schottenheimer said. "We had done enough things wrong early in the game that the only reason we had a chance was because of the character of this team."

Yet naturally, Byner was swarmed by the media, questioning what he had done and how he felt about being the guy who many people felt had single-handedly lost the game. Under the weight of the most media scrutiny any professional athlete had faced for an on-field incident since Bill Buckner of the Boston Red Sox, who watched a harmless ground ball roll through his legs and secure defeat in the 1986 World Series, Byner stood tall.

"I left everything I had on the football field today," he said, adding that he thought he actually felt worse after the fumble that blew a chance to win the Indianapolis game. "I gave it my all. We just came up a little bit short. Overall, I thought I played an excellent game.

"What am I supposed to do? I'm being a man about it. I left everything I had on that field today. I won't be a baby about it. I'm not going to stand up here and cry and feel sorry for myself and my teammates. All I can do is work harder and try to get here again."

Byner seemed to typify not only the Browns but the city of Cleveland. He was a good-hearted, hard-working man plagued by bad luck of biblical proportion. To Marty Schottenheimer, Byner's heroics were at the heart of an incredible display of loyalty and pride that he would never forget.

"I've been involved with a lot of teams and a lot of players in my years in this game," he said with a quivering voice at the post-game press conference, "but I've never been more proud of a group of men than I am today of that group, the Cleveland Browns."

It only seemed appropriate that even a few hours after the game was over, the Browns' adventures were not yet complete.

"We'd gotten on the airplane, started down the runway, and all of a sudden we hear this bang," Schottenheimer remembered. The plane's engine light had come on due to an oil leak, and the Browns de-boarded and sat around the terminal, drinking beers and commiserating together for four-and-a-half hours while the problem was fixed. "There were a number of players who came up and said, 'Coach, I'm not getting on that airplane,'" Schottenheimer said. "'I'm going to take a bus home.' They were scared. It was kind of a fitting conclusion." Expected to return to Cleveland at 1 a.m., the team wouldn't touch down until 4:30.

And when they did, nearly a thousand fans were waiting for them, enduring the long wait and rain showers. They cheered the players and held up signs. One in particular seemed to sum up the attitude expressed toward Byner and the Browns: "No Apologies Needed." Cleveland still loved these Browns and saw a little bit of themselves in those orange helmets, particularly on a night like this. "What we did in the second half, I think, exemplified our city," Ozzie Newsome said. "A city with character and the ability to come back."

Echoing that sentiment, Byner would receive dozens of encouraging telegrams and "enough flowers to fill a hospital ward," Browns' director of public relations Kevin Byrne said.

Despite the forgiving, resilient attitude displayed at Hopkins Airport that morning, there were many Browns' fans that had come to a depressing conclusion.

"After seeing their team fall so close two years in a row, there probably are a lot of Browns' fans today who are starting to believe that time will never come," Ray Yannucci wrote in *Browns News/Illustrated,* "that perhaps some teams, their beloved Browns being one, are destined *not* to attain the ultimate."

While the team was still relatively young and was expected to only get better, realistic fans had to be concerned that the Browns' window of opportunity in the late 1980s was now beginning to close. They'd played in two AFC title games and were poised to win both, only to come up shy. It was hard enough to reach that level, let alone play well enough to win at it. Two golden opportunities had gone for naught. Just earning a third, while still very possible, would be even harder.

"The Browns, as they are currently composed, may have already come as close to the Super Bowl as they are ever going to get," Bill Livingston wrote in the *Plain Dealer* that Monday.

As it turned out, he was right.

The 1987 AFC Championship had contained all the elements of great literature. It had history and a compelling back story. It had rich subplots. It had rising action and a heartstopping climax. It had a twist near the end. The overall theme concerned one of its principal characters earning a shot at redemption. And it ended with the heartbreak of a hero.

As the team plane soared through the winter night, Earnest Byner weighed all of this on his mind. He replayed the key moments of the game over and over. He thought of how he'd stood steadfast in the locker room, refusing to give the voyeuristic public what it really wanted: a front-row seat of a professional athlete's emotional breakdown.

But sitting alone on the plane, Byner's shield finally caved in. He began to cry, shedding the tears of the greatest disappointment of his professional life. Contrary to what Byner had said in the locker room, they were not tears of weakness or self-pity. They were tears of despair, of disappointment, of heartbreak. They were the tears of a man who felt he had let himself and his fellow warriors down.

As the plane glided across the continent, neither Byner nor his teammates could possibly know that the Cleveland Browns' dark, haunting path toward professional sports' ultimate disappointment was about to begin.

16 By Their Wits

Though to many fans and to much of the national media it appeared as though the 1988 Cleveland Browns bore little difference to the two teams which had preceded them, beneath the surface the 1988 Browns were going to be a very different team indeed.

The first major change occurred just a few weeks after the 1987 season ended. Lindy Infante left the team to become head coach of the Green Bay Packers. The first question posed to Marty Schottenheimer concerned whether the Browns would go shopping for a new offensive coordinator or simply promote from within the organization. As it turned out, Schottenheimer had a different plan. When Infante was being considered for the Packer job, Schottenheimer told reporters that whether or not his offensive coordinator returned for 1988, the Browns would not be changing their offense. So when Infante left, Schottenheimer decided against bringing in a new offensive coordinator, who would likely want to bring in his own system.

So who would call the plays in 1988? Simple, Schottenheimer explained; he would.

Though it may have sounded a bit peculiar for a lifelong student of defense and special teams to take over one of the league's most potent offenses at the drop of a hat, Schottenheimer had support. "Marty is a very bright student of the game," Art Modell said. "I don't have the slightest qualms about him taking over the offense." Even Infante added, "Marty spent time with the offense and knows it well. I don't see any problem."

To help take some of the load off Schottenheimer's shoulders, the Browns hired Marc Trestman to serve as quarterbacks coach, a role also handled by Infante. Trestman had held the same position with Tampa Bay in 1987 and had worked with heralded rookie Vinny Testaverde. Previously, he had been Minnesota running backs coach for two years and had been one of the factors the Vikings had used in the spring of 1985 to lure Bernie Kosar into entering the college draft and playing in Minnesota. Kosar and Trestman had worked together at the University of Miami when the Hurricanes had won the national title in 1983.

■ 187

In fact, it had been Trestman who had recommended to Miami head coach Howard Schnellenberger that Kosar start over Testaverde that year.

With the offense going through a managerial transition, the Browns focused on rebuilding their aging defense in the college draft. And by its completion, even the most doubtful and cynical of Cleveland's media were praising the 1988 draft as one of the best in team history.

Rather than simply resting on their laurels, knowing they'd had one of the best defenses in the league in 1987, the Browns were cognizant of the age factor creeping up on many of the key members of the unit. So rather than waiting until the older players were through, the team decided to start retooling for the future immediately.

With their first-round pick, the Browns selected linebacker Clifford Charlton out of Florida, and many were surprised Charlton had even survived as long as he did. Projected as the sixteenth or seventeenth pick, Charlton had drawn national attention as a junior at Florida in 1986, racking up 121 tackles and eleven sacks. The 6'3", 240-pound outside linebacker with running-back speed was expected to follow in the footsteps of previous great Gator linebackers Wilbur Marshall and Alonzo Johnson. Charlton expected to give the Browns the dominant pass-rushing threat they'd been searching for for years, and with him in the lineup it would allow the team to move Mike Junkin back to inside linebacker, where he had excelled in college.

If the selection of Charlton wasn't enough to highlight the Browns' emphasis on reloading on defense, they spent their next four picks on the same side of the ball, marking the first time in franchise history the team had used its first five draft picks on defense. The most notable came in the second round, when Cleveland snatched up Michael Dean Perry, a small but successful defensive lineman from Clemson.

Perry, better known for being the little brother of William "Refrigerator" Perry than a darned good football player in his own right, had been projected as a late first-round, early second-round pick. The Browns had even considered selecting Perry in the first round had Charlton not been available. They were shocked when Perry was still there when they came up again at pick No. 50. But at 6'0", 280 pounds, many NFL teams shied away from Perry, feeling he just didn't have the size to be a major factor. In that regard, many scouts thought Perry would make a better nose tackle than defensive end. But the Browns had taken note of Perry's quickness and weren't about to let it go to waste. "He's an extremely quick player—as quick as any player I've seen," Marty Schottenheimer said. "William is probably stronger, but Michael Dean is quicker."

Michael Dean Perry had been the 1987 Atlantic Coast Conference Defensive Player of the Year and had broken the conference's all-time sack record held by his older brother, who had also attended Clemson. But it was William, not Michael Dean, most football fans thought of when they heard the name "Perry," something that would dog the "Mini-Fridge," as some began calling him, for much of his career.

"I hope I don't go through my NFL career being known as William's little brother," Michael Dean said shortly after the draft. "I hope I can establish my identity as I did at Clemson. And hopefully they'll forget I'm his brother, but I doubt it."

Altogether, seven of Cleveland's ten draft picks were on defense. With most of the offensive weapons just entering their prime and the defense apparently about to undergo a serious upgrade, it was easy to see why the Browns were being praised. "If the Browns had this draft last year," Doug Dieken said, "they would have gone to the Super Bowl last season."

Not surprisingly, following the success of 1987 and the draft of 1988, many were not only picking but expecting the Browns to go to Super Bowl XXIII in Miami the following January. Las Vegas had the Browns at 4-1 odds to win the Super Bowl, the best in the league. *Sports Illustrated* not only said Cleveland would beat San Francisco in the Super Bowl but put Bernie Kosar on the cover of its football preview issue with a lengthy feature article inside. Despite back-to-back colossal January heartbreaks, Clevelanders were going bonkers over the Browns. The team had sold more than 51,000 season tickets, the second most in their history, trailing only the 1981 season. In that spirit, better than 78,000 packed into Cleveland Stadium for the Browns' first *exhibition* game. "Folks, people don't act this way for just any team," Ray Yannucci wrote in *Browns News/ Illustrated.* "People act this way when they envision monumental success for their team."

Not only was Kosar receiving substantial national attention but he was close to achieving something on the homefront no Cleveland athlete had ever done before. Entering the fourth year of his five-year contract, he was negotiating a lifetime contract with the Browns, ensuring he'd spend the rest of his career with his hometown team. "It's just a matter of time before it happens," said Kosar's agent/dentist John Geletka. "One thing's for sure—Bernie wants to spend his entire career in Cleveland." Art Modell agreed. According to Kosar, Modell wanted to reward him "for what I've done the last three years, for giving the city a breath of life."

As training camp began, the Browns were enjoying a golden era of popularity. Needless to say, it didn't last.

As camp progressed, the Browns' brass realized exactly what the old saying about the best-laid plans of mice and men meant.

The anchor of their new-age defense, Clifford Charlton, was consistently outplayed at outside linebacker by the surprise of 1987, David Grayson, who would eventually win the starting job. It was one of the only cases of an old face staying put in the face of new competition. Old standbys defensive end Reggie Camp, nose tackle Dave Puzzuoli, and safeties Al Gross, Ray Ellis, and Chris Rockins were all released.

But perhaps the most frustrating of all for many members of the defensive unit was Eddie Johnson constantly taking a back seat to Mike Junkin. Many felt Johnson, who got fewer opportunities than Junkin at inside linebacker, was still outplaying the so-called Mad Dog. Facing competition in training camp was nothing new for Johnson, but the team's constant doubting of his abilities was beginning to wear on him. "I'd love to come to camp once," the seven-year veteran said, "and have the coaches say, 'Eddie, it's your position, let someone take it from you,' instead of saying the job is open, and the best in the preseason will prevail." Junkin, admittedly improved, eventually won the job and would start the season at inside linebacker. And just when it appeared the Browns would trade Johnson as camp ended, they instead dealt veteran linebacker Anthony Griggs, who had filled in admirably the previous two years.

But perhaps the most surprising transaction in a camp full of fireworks was the final move the Browns made before the season began. In what had become a bitter battle for the starting center position between incumbent Mike Baab and second-year man Gregg Rakoczy, the Browns had deemed Rakoczy the starter. When Schottenheimer informed Baab, he told his coach he couldn't accept a backup role. Respecting his player's wishes, Schottenheimer and the Browns traded Baab to the New England Patriots for a fifth-round draft choice in 1989.

It was a tough pill to swallow for Baab, who had epitomized the toughness of the Cleveland offensive line for the previous five years. He had made sixty-two consecutive starts despite undergoing three knee surgeries. In the middle of camp, he'd made strong comments about Rakoczy in a *Plain Dealer* article: "Me and (Rakoczy) in a major challenge? Give me a break. It was a stiffer challenge when George Lilja was here. Gregg's still young. George was a good veteran player." Though Baab may have had a point, the comment embarrassed Rakoczy, and combined with offensive line coach Howard Mudd's subtle comment, "If it ain't broke, don't fix it," added some fire to an already spicy battle.

Needless to say, when the team finally began preparing for the first game of the season, a September 4 contest in Kansas City, it closed the books on one of the wildest training camps in team history. But perhaps it was a little too wild for a team that had been inches away from a Super Bowl berth each of the previous two seasons. "As close as we came last year, I expected some tinkering, maybe," Cody Risien said. "But an overhaul? Wow. This is something."

It was perhaps the most tumultuous training camp in Cleveland Browns' history. And appropriately, set the tone for perhaps the most tumultuous regular season.

You'd mention the *Sports Illustrated* cover jinx and people would just laugh. No such thing, they'd argue, contending that the rash of bad fortune that seemed to accompany a surprisingly high number of individuals who appeared on the popular magazine's cover shortly after they did was mere coincidence. Sixteen minutes into the 1988 season, that jinx was no laughing matter in Cleveland.

As Bernie Kosar dropped back for a third-down pass fifty-six seconds in to the second quarter, Kansas City strong safety Lloyd Burruss came crashing through the Cleveland line to Kosar's right. Burruss slammed into Kosar with the ball slung back ready for release. It wasn't the contact that made the play memorable, but rather how Burruss hit Kosar. With his arm in the most vulnerable position of the throwing motion, Kosar's elbow was stretched back when Burruss' helmet hit it, causing a slight tear of fibers in the ligaments.

Kosar was up immediately as the Browns' punt team took the field, and it didn't appear he was hurt badly. At first, even Kosar thought the injury was just a bruise. But after receiving medical attention on the sideline, it was deemed best for the franchise quarterback to take the rest of the day off. Not even two quarters old, the Browns' 1988 season was off to a shaky start. "To go two-and-a-half years like he did," Gary Danielson said, "sooner or later it had to happen."

Danielson now took over the reins of the offense, playing in his first "real" game since his heroic performance against the New York Giants three years before. But with the combination of adapting to a new playcaller and losing its field general, the Cleveland offense couldn't get going. And making matters worse, as the game wore on, more Browns—key Browns—dropped like flies. Kevin Mack left the game with a sprained neck. Mike Johnson injured his shoulder but managed to stay in the game, as did Bob Golic, who pulled an abdominal muscle. Frank Minnifield was forced out with a pulled groin, and Gerald McNeil hurt his nose and thigh. Over the course of the game, five Cleveland Pro Bowlers were on the sideline due to injury.

In what would become a war of attrition, the Chiefs persevered. When Danielson directed the Browns into field-goal range midway through the second quarter, Matt Bahr's kick was blocked by Burruss, who was becoming a thorn in the Browns' side. A few plays later, Kansas City took a 3-0 lead on a field goal of its own. The Browns tied the contest by halftime, and the score remained 3-3 deep into the fourth quarter. With just over six minutes left, Danielson began a slow but effective march downfield that resulted in the game-winning field goal with thirty seconds showing. The Browns escaped with an admirable, yet expensive 6-3 victory.

Danielson had done as well as could be expected in relief, but the question around Cleveland Monday morning was clear: When would Bernie be back? After further examination, doctors determined Kosar would miss anywhere from four-to-eight weeks—a good prognosis since the ligaments were only slightly, not completely torn. And the Browns were still in good shape at quarterback with Danielson and Mike Pagel behind him, both of whom could start for many NFL teams. Marty Schottenheimer even made a point to mention the vital roles former backup quarterbacks like Earl Morrall and Don Strock had played for their respective teams. Most Browns' fans concurred there was no reason to panic.

For as much as the Browns tried to downplay the loss of Kosar, most fans were convinced the team would be a very different one with capable yet aging Gary Danielson at the helm. The good news was that the Browns would return home in Week Two to host the New York Jets, who were far removed from the 1986 version that had nearly upset the Browns in the playoffs. Even with Kosar out and the team banged up, the Browns were nine-and-a-half-point favorites in what most felt would still be a gimmee game.

But for the Cleveland offense, Week Two was eerily similar to Week One. The Browns could move the ball with Danielson at the helm but couldn't score. The Cleveland defense once again hung tough, and the Browns only trailed 6-3 at the half. But things would take a dramatic turn in the third quarter.

That's when bad luck hit a Browns' quarterback for the second straight week. Midway through the quarter, after back-to-back sacks on a corner blitz, Danielson broke his left ankle—the same ankle he'd shattered two years earlier. He stayed in the game for one more possession then realized he could go no further. After a medical examination, doctors determined Danielson would be out at least eight weeks. "Maybe it's time to call in an exorcist," Ray Yannucci wrote.

Enter Mike Pagel, who had been with the Browns for two full seasons but had only thrown three passes in a regular-season game. It was yet another strange twist in Pagel's winding NFL career, which had begun with the Baltimore Colts when they selected him in the fourth round of the 1982 draft. Pagel had excelled in a pro-style offense at Arizona State, where he earned honorable mention All-American honors as a senior after initially backing up future Pittsburgh quarterback Mark Malone. Interestingly, picking Pagel had been more of an afterthought for the Colts, who had mortgaged the future on the selection of Ohio State quarterback Art Schlichter in the first round. At best, Pagel was expected to be a backup.

But to the surprise of many, Pagel beat out Schlichter for the starting job that fall, and wound up being the starter for the next four seasons on some bad Colts' teams. After a typical rookie season of ups and downs for Pagel in 1982 (which included getting knocked unconscious in his first NFL game), Baltimore decided it wanted more from the position, and drafted John Elway the following spring. But when Elway refused to play for the Colts, they wound up trading him to Denver. And Pagel remained the starter.

After a similar season in 1983, Pagel stayed with the Colts as they abandoned Baltimore for Indianapolis in 1984, though he only fared slightly better there as the Colts posted a seventh straight losing record. After another mediocre 1985 campaign in which Indy finished 5-11, the Colts decided to go another way. They drafted Jack Trudeau from Illinois and traded for longtime Dallas backup Gary Hogeboom, making Pagel expendable. They shipped him to the Browns for a ninth-round draft choice in 1986, giving the Browns an experienced, if not great, backup quarterback. Mike Pagel came to the Browns with a 15-31-1 record as an NFL starter, having thrown for 7,400 yards and thirty-nine touchdowns with forty-seven interceptions in four years with the Colts.

Now, after Kosar and Danielson had gone down with serious injuries, he would be counted on to direct the 1988 favorite to win the Super Bowl. "I'm not looking just to keep the team together, I'm looking to go out and win," Pagel said later that week. "Who knows how long Bernie and Gary will be out?"

But for the remainder of that afternoon, Pagel couldn't do either. The Jets stretched their lead to 9-3 entering the fourth quarter then blew the game open. Blitzing off the bus trying to take advantage of Danielson's—and now Pagel's—new role, New York's defensive game plan worked like a charm. The Browns were held to a woeful 27 rushing yards (their lowest total in seventeen years) and 218 yards of offense. Meanwhile the defense finally wore down in the fourth quarter—both by the persistent Jets and by the losses of Frank Minnifield and Hanford Dixon to injuries. New York made it 16-3 four minutes into the final quarter on a Roger Vick one-yard scoring plunge, then Vick added another touchdown four minutes after that to put the game away at 23-3.

What was left of the Cleveland Stadium crowd booed its team, which had now failed to score a touchdown in its first two games. And consequently, with the offense struggling and the Jets maintaining possession for nearly thirty-eight minutes of the game, the Cleveland defense looked average by game's end. "This is not the way the Cleveland Browns play football," Bob Golic said afterward.

With fourteen weeks to go, the Browns already looked like a beaten team. Talk of a championship hushed. The fans' focus turned to simply surviving until Kosar could return. "The Super Bowl juggernaut appears temporarily grounded," Bob Kravitz wrote in the *Plain Dealer*. "Who could have imagined? How do you explain this curse that consistently plagues teams from this vicinity?"

The franchise quarterback was hurt, as were several other veterans, and the backups looked vulnerable. The team's confidence level had reached a new low, and the schedule hadn't even gotten tough yet.

The 1988 season had become a living nightmare. And there were still fourteen weeks to go.

The Browns would now pin their hopes on their third-string quarterback, who would enter a must-win game at home on *Monday Night Football* against his former team. Mike Pagel would get his first NFL start since 1985 against the team he last started for: the Indianapolis Colts, who were making their first primetime appearance in ten years.

While the Browns had confidence in Pagel, they were now out of quarterbacks. When Kosar was placed in the disabled list, the team re-signed Steve Slayden, a twelfth-round draft choice of the Browns that spring who had been released in training camp. The idea of Slayden under center terrified fans and the front office equally, but Pagel wasn't worried. "You've got to say the odds are in my favor of staying healthy," he said. "I've seen the number-one quarterback get hurt. I've seen the number-two quarterback get hurt. Three in a row? C'mon, the odds have to be with me." Still, the team's brain trust knew they needed someone with more experience backing up Pagel.

Within minutes after Gary Danielson left the Jets game, Ernie Accorsi was on the phone trying to locate Don Strock, the longtime Miami backup who had retired when he couldn't agree with the Dolphins on a new contract in the off-season. At 12:30 A.M. that Monday, he agreed to a one-year contract reportedly worth $480,000—a large sum of money for a stop-gap player, particularly considering Pagel was only making $300,000 in 1988. Strock flew from Miami to Cleveland Monday night to sign the contract and would spend the following Monday night in streetclothes, still trying to absorb the Browns' offense. Luckily, neither Strock nor Slayden were needed.

Easing the severed nerves of Browns' fans everywhere, Mike Pagel played well and showed he could not only win but beat a playoff-caliber team. Using a low-risk passing attack, Pagel hit on twenty-three of thirty-eight passes for 255 yards as the Cleveland offense finally put together the type of game expected of it, leading the way to a 23-17 victory. Mike Pagel had proven he could win. Instead of just worrying about buying time until Bernie Kosar could return, the Browns and their fans started to get optimistic. With a win in Cincinnati in Week Four, they could be tied for first place and would be in great shape entering the middle portion of the schedule.

But the Browns had used up their good-fortune allotment for September against the Colts. At Riverfront Stadium six days later, they ran into a dramatically different Bengal team than the one they'd seen the previous December. Though everyone in the universe figured wacky Sam Wyche would be canned after single-handedly blowing several games en route to a 4-11 record in 1987, Paul Brown decided to give Wyche one more chance in 1988. And rather than choking or making ridiculous decisions in the final moments, the Bengals had won their first three games in the fourth quarter, all by seven points or less. Boomer Esiason and the passing game looked more like the potent attack it'd been in 1986, and the defense, while far from dominant, was also improved. The Bengals, considered by many to be a mass head case, were playing with swagger.

And the Browns did what they could to give the Bengals a massive boost of confidence early on a sunny September afternoon on the Ohio River. On the game's fourth play, Kevin Mack took a handoff and tried to break outside. But when he ran into a pack of Cincinnati defenders, he dropped the football. Bengal cornerback Lewis Billups scooped up the fumble and raced 26 yards for a touchdown, giving the home team an early lead and setting the tone for a frustrating 24-17 Browns' loss.

After a one-week respite, the Browns were back to being worried sick. They were 2-2, but were now two games back of the high-flying Bengals and a game behind 3-1 Houston. Worse, the Browns now had to travel to Pittsburgh in Week Five, where a loss to their arch-rivals would put them all alone in last place.

Dark storm clouds were brewing over the 1988 Browns, though the rain had yet to fall.

17 Plan D

In order to prevent the season from tumbling into a tailspin, the Browns would now have to win at Three Rivers Stadium. Just three years earlier, that task would have seemed almost impossible, but by 1988, winning in Pittsburgh was no big deal.

Plus, it was the perfect time to be playing Pittsburgh. After posting their first back-to-back losing seasons in fifteen years in 1985 and 1986, the Steelers looked worse than ever in 1988, losing three of their first four games. Still, the Browns' offense was a question mark and not only would enter its fourth straight game without Bernie Kosar but also would go to battle without Kevin Mack, who had injured his groin. As it happened, the Browns' beleaguered offense would get a reprieve. On a cool, overcast afternoon in Pittsburgh, the defense finally stepped up and paved the way.

Things looked shaky early. The Cleveland offense couldn't get going against the NFL's worst defense and trailed 9-7 at the half. Mike Pagel was decent, but couldn't connect on a big play. Luckily, the Browns' defense did. Eddie Johnson came up with a big interception to turn the tide and set up the go-ahead points, and rookie safety Brian Washington clinched a 23-9 victory with a 75-yard interception return for a touchdown.

The 3-2 Browns had survived another test, but they still stood two games back of Cincinnati, who buried the Raiders in Los Angeles.

By the time the Seahawks came to town October 9, many Browns' fans had made their peace with Mike Pagel. He was after all, a third-string quarterback who by the law of averages never should have played a down all season. In three starts since Gary Danielson had gone down, Pagel had been decent. He hadn't single-handedly won a game, but he hadn't clearly lost one, either.

With Kosar on the mend, the Browns would likely only need Pagel for two more starts. If Pagel could engineer a split, or even two wins, the Browns would be in good shape when Kosar returned. And things started off the right way against Seattle. On their first possession, Pagel and the Browns marched 69 yards and took a 7-0 lead. Things looked even better when Cleveland forced a Seattle punt, but Gerald McNeil fumbled the kick, and the Seahawks recovered at the Browns' twenty-four yard line. Five plays later, the game was tied. The tone had been set.

The Browns picked up where they'd left off on their next possession, again driving down the field. When the drive stalled, Matt Bahr was called on to attempt a chip-shot 25-yard field goal. Pagel, as he had been ever since punter Lee Johnson had been cut two weeks earlier, was the holder. The kick was blocked by Seattle defensive end Jeff Bryant and scooped up by Seattle's Paul Moyer, a former teammate of Pagel's at Arizona State. Moyer was off to the races down the sideline, apparently destined for a touchdown. As it turned out, the touchdown would have hurt the Browns less in the long run. Pagel sprinted after Moyer on an angle and caught up to him at the Cleveland twenty. He dove and knocked Moyer out of bounds after a 62-yard return, saving the touchdown. But his shoulder felt funny when he got up. As it turned out, it was separated, and he would have to leave the game.

Enter ancient Don Strock, who jogged onto the field a few minutes later to become the Browns' fourth quarterback of the season. For the remainder of the game, he would have to direct an offense he'd been a part of for less than a month. The Browns' inexplicable 1988 curse continued, and the hopes for their Super Bowl season now rested with a thirty-eight-year old career backup.

Many Browns' fans remembered, after Kosar went down, Schottenheimer had made an analogy for the unprecedented success of backup quarterbacks on winning teams and mentioned Strock as a prime example. That's exactly what he'd been in fourteen seasons in Miami, going to three Super Bowls with the Dolphins, who had selected him in the fifth round of the 1973 draft. He'd appeared in 163 games, but started only twenty. He had never thrown more than 135 passes in a season, yet had earned a league-wide reputation as one of the finest backup quarterbacks in the game and for backing up some of the best quarterbacks ever to play. He began his career spelling Earl Morrall, then Bob Griese, then David Woodley, and finally Dan Marino. Strock's most memorable performance came in relief, in a divisional playoff game against San Diego in January 1982, when he took over for an ineffective Woodley and brought the Dolphins all the way back from a 24-0 second-quarter deficit. Miami wound up losing in overtime, 41-38, but Strock was magnificent, throwing for 397 yards and four touchdowns. Yet the following year, he was back on the sideline, and the year after that, the Dolphins invested the future on a young hurler from Pittsburgh named Marino.

He became almost a mascot with the Dolphins over the next four years, rarely getting into a game in place of one of the NFL's top playcallers. He would throw just fifty-eight passes from 1984 through 1987. Strock was even willing to return to the clipboard-and-sun-visor duty for 1988, but couldn't work out a new contract with the Dolphins and never attended training camp. When the Browns literally lured him off a Miami golf course in mid-September, he arrived in Cleveland not having played football in nearly nine months. At the end of his first week of practice, his shoulders ached—not from throwing, but from the irritation caused by his shoulder pads, which he hadn't put on for almost a year.

In Strock's first year, 1974, Bernie Kosar turned eleven years old. Steve Slayden, who would now be the Browns' backup quarterback, was seven. Strock was now seven weeks away from his thirty-eighth birthday. He was like a dispatch from another time, as if the Browns had opened a time capsule and would now try to win with what was inside.

Adding to the insanity was the way in which the Browns would send in plays to their new quarterback. Not having had enough time to memorize the entire playbook, Strock had fifty-five plays written out on a sheet of paper by Schottenheimer's secretary and taped to his forearm. A player would run into the huddle from the sideline and give Strock a number. He would then match the number with the corresponding play on his "cheat sheet," and call the play in the huddle.

All things considered, and there were plenty, Strock wasn't terrible in his first appearance in a Cleveland uniform. He fumbled near midfield with just over a minute to play in the first half, and it led to another Seahawk field goal and a 13-7 halftime deficit. While Strock and the Browns' offense proved capable of moving the ball, they just couldn't put points on the board. A late Cleveland field goal after a long drive cut the margin to 16-10, but even with time running out, the Browns' coaching staff didn't see the need to be in a hurry. In the days to follow, Schottenheimer's abilities as an offensive coordinator began to be seriously questioned for the first time. "By year's end, it will be time to re-evaluate Schottenheimer as head coach/offensive coordinator," Bob Kravitz wrote in Monday's *Plain Dealer*. "Two jobs, one man. It might be too much to ask." It would not be the last time this issue would be raised.

After the field goal, the Seahawks successfully ran out the final two minutes and escaped Cleveland with a victory. The Browns now stood at 3-3, their worst record after six games in four years, and were three games back of the still-undefeated Cincinnati Bengals.

"While it might not be time to write them off altogether," Kravitz wrote, "it might be a good idea to sharpen your number-two pencil or check the ink level in your Bic."

Worse, the Browns and their fans had to wonder how, if they couldn't beat the mediocre Seattle Seahawks, they would be able to take on Buddy Ryan's up-and-coming Philadelphia Eagles the following week. And they'd have to do it with Strock, since Bernie Kosar was still another week away from returning to action. Thus, a thirty-seven-year-old, gray-haired quarterback who had been enjoying his retirement five weeks before would be making his first start in nearly five years.

The Eagles entered the contest right about where the Browns had been two years before. They were young, full of potential, yet still needed to prove themselves. Clearly, this was not a team the Browns wanted to mess with in their hobbled state.

The primary problem the Browns had suffered from to this point, most fans and pundits believed, wasn't so much the number of injuries they'd endured but the fact that no one phase of the team had stepped up when the other was struggling. With the offense now on its fourth starting quarterback, the Browns couldn't count on outscoring the Eagles in a shootout. Victory would rest in the lap of the defense. And there it would be claimed.

The Cleveland defense, ranked No. 1 in the AFC and No. 2 in the entire league, embarked on one of the most dominating defensive performances in club history that sunny October afternoon on the lakefront, clobbering up-and-coming quarterback Randall Cunningham and the Eagle offense. The fleet-footed Philly playcaller was brought down nine times for sacks, and Philly only managed 119 total yards for the game. With a pair of second-half touchdown passes from Strock, the Browns coasted to a 19-3 triumph. The plainspoken Buddy Ryan put it best: "It was an ol' fashioned butt-kickin'," he said.

More good news filtered in from Massachusetts when the Bengals finally lost their first game, a 27-21 decision to the Patriots. The 4-3 Browns were back to within two games of first place.

But continuing the year-long trend, any good news had to be set against some bad news. With just over six minutes remaining in the fourth quarter, Webster Slaughter broke his left forearm when it snapped against an opponent's helmet. Slaughter, in becoming the sixth Browns' starter to miss at least one game to injury, would be out the next eight-to-ten weeks.

Certainly, there was a palpable sense of dread as the Browns would now likely have to get through the remainder of the regular season without their top receiver. However, through the rain clouds, a powerful beam of light cracked through. Not only were the Browns back in the race after an impressive win over a playoff-bound opponent but their chances for returning to the top of the division were about to grow dramatically stronger.

Number nineteen was ready to return to the huddle.

Whatever the rest of the sports world felt about Cleveland Browns' fans, it certainly couldn't deny their ability to put their enthusiasm to music. The week after their team's mid-October victory over the Philadelphia Eagles, a new song blitzed the radio airwaves. Sung to the tune of the Angels' 1963 hit "My Boyfriend's Back," the song "Bernie's Back" expressed the joy most Browns' fans were feeling about having their beloved quarterback back in the huddle. It became official that Wednesday when Kosar took over the first-team offense in practice and was soon activated back to the roster. Ironically, he took the spot vacated by Webster Slaughter, who would have surgery that week to replace what were actually two separate breaks in his right arm.

Even without his top receiver, Kosar's return came just in time. After the win over the Eagles, the Browns were 4-3 and two games back of the Cincinnati Bengals, who would host the Houston Oilers the following Sunday in a key AFC Central battle. Meanwhile, later that afternoon, the Browns would take the field in Phoenix to battle the resurgent Cardinals, who also stood at 4-3. Still, with Kosar back at the controls, anything short of victory would be a colossal disappointment.

He could have asked for a slightly more accommodating location for his triumphant return. It was October 23, but temperatures reached 115 degrees on the field at appropriately named Sun Devil Stadium. Yet despite not playing in nearly two months, Kosar came out just as hot as the scorching Arizona sun.

With the Phoenix pass rush gunning for him on nearly every play, Cleveland's matinee idol rose to the occasion, dicing the Cardinals for twenty completions in the first half for a whopping 224 yards and a pair of touchdowns. The first was one of the wackiest plays of the Marty Schottenheimer era: a tackle-eligible toss to Rickey Bolden. The second came on a diving catch by Reggie Langhorne for a 29-yard scoring pass midway through the second quarter. The Cardinals rallied to take a 21-20 lead early in the fourth quarter, but a third Kosar touchdown pass and a game-clinching safety gave the Browns a satisfying 29-21 victory. They improved to 5-3, still two games back of Cincinnati, which had throttled the Oilers at rainy Riverfront earlier in the afternoon.

For the first time since the 1988 season began, the Browns' future looked as bright as the Phoenix horizon. Bernie *was* back and showed no ill effects from seven weeks off. He threw for 314 yards and three touchdowns against an aggressive defense, and he had done it without his top receiver and top running back (Kevin Mack left the game with a pinched nerve in his neck on the first play). But those setbacks seemed less damaging now that The Franchise had returned.

"With Bernie in there," Schottenheimer said, "we have the ability to run our entire offense; to use all of the weapons available to our offense."

Even Art Modell was glowing about Kosar's return: "He's one of the best competitors the Browns will ever have. He's as fine a performer at quarterback as there is today. He can become awesome before his career is over."

With Kosar back and the defense finally clicking, the Browns were in perfect position to enter the biggest game of the season and the biggest game in the history of their rivalry with the Cincinnati Bengals.

Through the first eighteen years of the Browns-Bengals series, the teams had managed to pretty well avoid matching one another's competitive ebbs and flows. When the Bengals surged in the early and mid-1970s, the Browns floundered. When Sam Rutigliano injected new life into the franchise in the late 1970s and early 1980s, the Bengals collapsed. While the Browns mobilized in the mid-eighties, the Bengals were talented, but inconsistent. Consequently, very few Cleveland-

Cincinnati games provided excitement outside of the state. Even less had major playoff or division-title implications.

Such was not the case on October 30, 1988. On the eve of Halloween, the Browns and Bengals would square off for the first time with both considered to be in the upper echelon of the NFL. Football fans across the nation sat up and took notice. It was the game of the weekend, the hottest ticket in the league. More than 250 media representatives requested credentials. NBC sent its No. 1 broadcast team of Dick Enberg and Merlin Olsen. Even Spuds McKenzie, Budweiser's promotional pit-bull mascot, was in town for the game. The 7-1 Bengals would face the 5-3 Browns in as hostile an environment as there was in professional sports. It was the stuff NFL dreams were made of. The showdown "was the topic most discussed in every bar and pub from the Ohio River to Lake Erie," Jim Mueller wrote in *Browns News/Illustrated.*

While the Browns, with a healthy Kosar, appeared to be back on track, the real story surrounding the game was the resurgent Bengals. After finishing 4-11 and nearly getting booted out of town the year before, Sam Wyche had turned the tables with essentially the same cast of characters. He'd dialed down some of his "Wicky-Wacky" decisions but still managed to be innovative. But what had brought even more attention to the Cincy offense over the first eight weeks of the season was Wyche's selective use of the huddle. Rather than just using the traditional gathering of the offense after each play, the Bengals employed a variety of huddles. There was the sideline huddle, typically used after a change of possession, when the players would gather around Wyche on the sideline, get the play, then run up to the line of scrimmage. There was the no-huddle, and in between, the "sugar" huddle, so named since it was short and sweet. Esiason and the offense would linger three yards behind the line of scrimmage and quickly relay the play call down the line.

While all this was elaborate and entertaining, it was in place for two reasons. First, to try to prevent defenses from making mass substitutions in between plays and therefore set up matchup advantages for the offense. And second, to draw five-yard twelve-men-on-the-field penalties when a defense got caught in the middle of a substitution. Most NFL coaches rolled their eyes at the Bengals, seeing the huddles as short-term trickery and, in the long run, not worth the elaborate efforts. "They try to trap you with the wrong guys on the field or to trick you," Hanford Dixon said, "instead of playing football the way it's supposed to be played." The *Plain Dealer's* Bill Livingston said it was as if Wyche wanted to "play his panty raid against your Chinese fire drill." But it was something for defenses to be wary of and prepare for.

If Wyche's trick-or-treat offense was effective on this sun-drenched Halloween Sunday on Lake Erie, the Browns would have to surrender any hopes of capturing their fourth straight division title. If they dropped to 5-4, it would be time to start playing for a Wild Card spot—and even that wouldn't be easy with

Cleveland's upcoming schedule. But with a win, the Browns would improve to 6-3 and pull to within one game of the Bengals with seven games to play. And now they had Kosar.

Ironically, with so much attention on both offenses, it was the Cincinnati defense that landed the first blow, when defensive back Ray Horton intercepted Kosar on the first series of the game. The Browns endured and grabbed a 3-0 lead on their next possession. A fourth-down stop of Bengals' rookie fullback Ickey Woods deep in Cleveland territory gave the hometown team further momentum, but it shifted three plays later when Kosar was picked off again, this time by Cincy safety David Fulcher, who backed up his talk by rumbling 16 yards for the go-ahead touchdown. The capacity crowd of 79,147 was silenced.

Like in any big game, however, another punch was forthcoming. Special-teams captain Herman Fontenot received the ensuing kickoff at his own six yard line and rifled through the Bengals' coverage and across midfield as the home crowd sprung back to life. He cut back across the field and was eventually dragged down by Bengals' kicker and former Brown Lee Johnson at the Bengals' ten after an 84-yard return. A play later, Manoa crashed into the end zone from the two, and the Browns had the lead back at 10-7 with just over two minutes remaining in the half. But the Bengals responded and closed the half with a game-tying field goal. For all the hype, the contest was living up to expectations.

After forcing Cincinnati to go three-and-out on its first possession of the second half, the Browns' offense once again got rolling, taking the lead back with a 40-yard Bahr field goal. The Browns then forced the Bengals to go three-and-out again on their ensuing possession. Yet it was the Cleveland special teams that were about to steal the show.

On fourth-and-eight from the Cincy twenty-three yard line, Frank Minnifield and Fontenot lined up side-by-side in the middle of the line of scrimmage to rush the Cincinnati punt. Fontenot crashed through and wove to his right to take out blocker Stanford Jennings, while Minnifield followed him with a clear path toward punter David Fulhage. Minnifield dove and blocked the punt. Fontenot recovered the football at the one and rolled into the end zone for the Browns' second touchdown and a 20-10 lead with six minutes to play in the third. The sell-out crowd went bonkers.

"That play seemed to crush them," Minnifield said. "Until then, they were having a pretty good day."

Still, Wyche's crew wasn't done just yet. The Bengals drove into Cleveland territory and pulled back to within a touchdown when Jim Breech booted a short field goal. As the third quarter neared its conclusion, the Browns' offense also had to rise to the occasion. It did, sparked by a 49-yard pass from Kosar to Clarence Weathers, who was having the finest day of his career. It led to another Bahr field goal and a 23-13 Cleveland lead that would be too much for the Bengals to overcome. Cincinnati did manage one more field goal, but the Browns then turned their attention to clock management and didn't relinquish possession until there were seven seconds remaining. The 1988 Browns were still alive, and had put the upstart Bengals (who reportedly had champagne on ice waiting for them in the locker room had they won) back in their place—at least for a week.

The Browns' defense certainly played like it was mature, shutting down both the Bengals' air and ground attacks and preventing the Cincinnati offense from scoring a touchdown for the first time since the 34-3 spanking the Browns had laid on the Bengals in December 1986. "I've been here nine years," Schottenheimer said, "and it's the finest defensive performance we've ever had."

Part of the reason for the Dogs' success was that they didn't fall into the Bengals' trap. After getting called early for twelve-men-on-the-field and scurrying players in and out between plays, the Browns had had enough. "Finally we just said to hell with it," Eddie Johnson said. "We just lined up in our [base] defense and played the way we are capable of playing, and we kicked their butts."

The Browns had every reason to feel good about themselves. They were tied with Houston for second place in the division. Schottenheimer even noted that this game, specifically the way it turned on a blocked punt, reminded him of the Minnesota game in 1986 that turned the season around.

"It was almost a must-game, and our team really rose to the occasion," Kosar said. "It showed a lot of character, and good teams show that at times like this."

18 The Coming Storm

After weathering a violent storm that at times never appeared would end, the Browns had somehow made it safely to port. Now they would have a chance to do some conquering and pillaging.

With a Monday-night win in Houston on November 7, the Browns could secure sole possession of second place and remain within a game of the front-running Bengals. The Oilers, meanwhile, had also persevered after Warren Moon went down for five weeks with a fractured shoulder blade. Houston was poised to become a better team than they'd been the year before.

They certainly were the better team that Monday night.

In a matter of a few hours, the Browns' three-game winning streak had been snapped, their hopes for rallying for their fourth straight division title were now all but lost, and the newfound optimism that had seemed boundless when Bernie Kosar returned two weeks earlier now seemed like a mirage. All were casualties of a 24-17 loss to the Oilers which Ray Yannucci described as the "kind of game that can tear at a man's soul."

Not only were the Browns beat but they were beat up. Kosar, who wound up with a few chipped teeth, would say he couldn't remember ever being pounded harder in a game than he was by Houston in what the Oilers were now calling the "House of Pain."

Ten minutes into the second half, after Houston blocked a Browns' punt (the fourth blocked kick Cleveland had allowed in 1988) and another long scoring drive, it was 21-3, and the Browns were playing scared. They clawed their way back into the contest, narrowing the margin to 24-17 before a bad center snap resulted in a game-clinching fumble recovery for Houston in the final minutes. At 6-4, now two games back of Cincinnati with six to play, the Browns would need a miracle to pull off the four-peat.

And in case Cleveland hadn't already noticed, miracles were in short supply in 1988.

In one of the "quirks" of the season's NFL schedule, Cleveland would now have to endure as difficult a travel week as possible. They left Houston early Tuesday morning to fly back to Cleveland, where they would stay for three days before getting back on a plane to head back across the continent to Denver, Colorado, where they would face the Broncos six days after getting pounded on *Monday Night Football*. After traveling more than 7,000 miles in seven days, what happened next was no real surprise.

Though the Broncos were also struggling, hovering around the .500 mark, they punished the Browns, 30-7. In almost an identical performance to their first-half suicide show in the AFC title game ten months earlier, the Browns committed four turnovers in the first thirty minutes and allowed the Broncos to score on all six of their first-half possessions. But unlike the championship game, this hole was far too deep, and these Browns were far too out-manned.

With their tenth straight defeat to the Broncos, the Browns became one of six AFC teams with a 6-5 record. It spoiled a golden opportunity for Cleveland to make up ground, since both Cincinnati and Houston lost. Instead, the Browns remained two back of the Bengals and a game behind Houston with just over a month left in the season. If the playoffs began after Week Eleven, Cleveland would not qualify. "It's an all-time low for this team in the Marty and Bernie era," Ozzie Newsome said afterward. "It's really going to take the entire team to come together to be able to handle the stretch drive the way we did the past couple of years," Kosar added.

But after watching their team get physically dominated in two straight critical games, Browns' fans didn't want to hear talk of a stretch drive. By all appearances, the 1988 Browns had instead begun a swan dive.

The good news: Next up was a home game with the hapless Pittsburgh Steelers, who had only gotten worse since the teams' first meeting in early October.

Though it was a perfect opportunity for the Browns to break out of their surprising doldrums, as it happened, they didn't even need to. On a dreary, cold, and rainy November Sunday, the Steelers did everything they could to serve what turned out to be a 27-7 victory to the Browns on a silver platter. An interception on the game's second play led to a field goal, and two special-teams miscues—a bad punt snap and a blocked punt—resulted in two Browns' touchdowns.

The victory improved the Browns to 7-5 and kept their quickly dimming playoff hopes alive. But Cleveland would have to play much better if it hoped to defeat the defending world champion Washington Redskins at RFK Stadium the following Sunday. A loss in D.C., always a tough place to win, would drop the Browns back to just a game over .500 with time running out in the 1988 season.

"When you are ready to administer last rites, they rise up and make your spirits soar," Kravitz wrote. "When you are ready to hail them as Super Bowl champions, they screw up and undermine your undying faith in them. They are as unpredictable as they are unfathomable.

"The truth, uncut and unexpurgated, about the Browns? Stay tuned. There will be much more madness before it's over."

On the Sunday after Thanksgiving, the Browns once again found themselves enduring a cold and depressing pre-winter rain. For many in the media, the weather conditions provided the perfect backdrop for what they were certain would be the final demise of the 1988 Browns. It seemed no one expected the Browns to win, even though the 6-6 Redskins looked much different than the team that had won the Super Bowl ten months before.

The Browns took a 3-0 lead to the half, then quarterback Mark Rypien led Washington on a 73-yard drive on their first possession of the third quarter and grabbed a 7-3 lead. With the soaked crowd buzzing, the Redskins then appeared to turn the lights out on the struggling Browns. Running back Mike Oliphant blocked Max Runager's punt on Cleveland's next possession, and the Redskins recovered at the Browns' nine yard line, setting up a field goal. The Browns responded, marching 76 yards in sixteen plays and taking nearly eleven minutes off the clock. They tied the game at ten on a one-yard Mack plunge with 9:41 remaining in the game. In less than ten minutes, one of these teams' playoff hopes would be rinsed away with the rain.

The Redskins then showed the poise that had earned them two Vince Lombardi trophies in the previous six seasons. Washington drove into Cleveland territory and took back the lead on a 40-yard Chip Lohmiller field goal with 6:27 left. The Browns' offense, which had been efficient if not effective, regained possession at its own twenty with the franchise's hopes of a fourth straight postseason appearance hanging in the balance.

With the rain still pounding atop their helmets, the Browns picked up two first downs before facing third-and-ten at their own forty-seven yard line with three minutes remaining. And as they'd done all day, the Redskins came after Kosar like wild animals smelling raw meat. As Kosar set to throw, linebacker Wilbur Marshall and defensive end Charles Mann were both within arm's reach of the Browns' quarterback, who had no time to reel back and throw a conventional pass. Instead, while still moving backward, he flipped the football forward and crashed to the ground with Marshall on top of him. Kosar's toss was based more on faith than logistics.

Brian Brennan reeled in the pass across midfield and sprinted for a 21-yard gain and a crucial first down at the Redskins' thirty-two. "That had to be luck," a disbelieving Marshall would say later. "No way should he have completed that. I was right on top of him." It certainly wasn't the first time in the past four years Browns' opponents were left scratching their heads after an unorthodox, yet ultimately successful throw from Bernie Kosar. But the Browns still weren't out of the woods yet.

Two plays after Brennan's catch, the Browns faced another third down at the two-minute warning, with five yards to go at the twenty-seven yard line. Failure here would force Cleveland to attempt a 45-yard field goal to tie the game and leave Washington nearly two minutes to try to win it.

By late November, Marty Schottenheimer had already taken a proverbial beating from the media and fans for his work as the Browns' offensive coordinator. Even when they weren't decimated by injury, the Browns had shown little imagination and even less of the element of surprise to opposing defenses all year. But on third-and-five, Schottenheimer cooked up his best playcall of the season. He called for a four-receiver set, since the Redskins were expecting pass. But rather than risking a sack or interception, Schottenheimer called for a handoff on a trap play to Earnest Byner. If it failed, it would have been the last straw for many Browns' followers, whose confidence in Schottenheimer was seriously wavering, and it would almost certainly set up Cleveland for defeat. But if it worked, it might just save the season.

As soon as the ball was snapped, even before Byner took the handoff, the Browns' offensive line cleared a path through one of the NFL's mightiest front walls, giving Byner had all the room he'd need. He crashed through the line and plowed through two diving tackle attempts as he sloshed through the mud toward the end zone. Holding onto the football with both hands, he crossed the goal line and his momentum carried him out of the end zone and into the padding separating the field from the stands. Byner, who had been labeled as a "garbage-time player" by Bill Livingston of the *Plain Dealer* the week before, then let out a primal scream of triumph—a victory cry he'd been waiting ten months to enjoy.

Technically, victory wasn't sealed until Mark Harper intercepted Rypien a few moments later, but as soon as he scored, the Browns and their fans knew that Byner's touchdown had clinched as satisfying a victory as the team had tasted all year. Kosar successfully kneeled out the final minute, and the Browns' playoff hopes had survived for another week with a gritty 17-13 win in the nation's capital.

It was only appropriate that the game-winning touchdown be scored by the team's grittiest player, a man who had had as rotten a 1988 as any NFL player. True, Kevin Mack had sparked the offense by rushing for 116 yards, but it was Byner who made the play when it mattered most. Ignoring almost a year of abject criticism, Byner had proven he was still the same player he'd been before the fumble that seemed to change everyone's perception of him.

"I can't let the negative things being said and written about me affect me," he said. "Nobody will run me out of town. There's no way to fight back except by making plays like the one I did today."

With Byner at the vanguard, the 8-5 Browns still had some fighting back to do as the calendar turned to what would become one of the most unpredictable and crucial months of Cleveland sports history.

For the second time in two weeks, the Browns' drive to the playoffs would be fortified by an apparent cupcake on the schedule: a home game with another of the

NFL's worst teams, the 2-11 Dallas Cowboys. By all appearances, it would be an easy day for the Browns on a sunshiny Sunday afternoon on the lakefront. But like most predictions for the 1988 Browns, this one would be proven utterly untrue.

The game would become an unexpectedly heated battle, but it wasn't because the Browns came out flat. The Cowboys simply answered every Browns' blow and took a 14-10 lead into the fourth quarter. The Browns rallied, surging to a 24-14 lead on a pair of Kosar touchdown passes, and hung on for a 24-21 victory. The result was still in doubt until a potential game-tying Dallas field goal in the final two minutes was wiped out on a penalty and the re-kick fell short.

While the Browns had improved to 9-5 with their third straight win and sixth victory in eight games, melancholy still permeated from the media and the fans. True, the Browns had won their last three games, but the teams they'd played had a combined record of 12-30, none with a winning record. Case in point: at one point, the Browns' special teams lined up for a Dallas punt with only nine players on the field. A mix-up such as this was embarrassing enough, but since it marked the fourth time in five games the Browns had lined up for a play with either less or more than the eleven players necessary, it was downright humiliating.

Still, there was more reason to be pleased than disappointed. Cleveland had kept its playoff hopes alive and those aspirations looked considerably brighter late that evening, when the Houston Oilers managed to blow a four-point lead in the final minute in their beloved House of Pain and lose to the hapless Pittsburgh Steelers, 37-34. It dropped the Oilers into a second-place tie with the Browns and opened the door for Cleveland to potentially host the Wild Card Game, something that looked like a pipe dream after the loss in Denver.

With a victory the following Monday night in Miami and another win in the regular-season finale against the Oilers, the Browns could clinch their fourth consecutive playoff berth. While neither game would be a "gimmee," both were very winnable. By all appearances the Browns had weathered the storm. The hard part of 1988, it seemed, was over.

In actuality, it was just about to begin.

Though the Browns' dreams of winning the division went by the wayside the previous Sunday, the Oilers' hopes stayed alive despite their embarrassing loss to Pittsburgh. Seven days later, Houston blasted Cincinnati in the Astrodome, 41-6, holding the Bengals' heralded offense to a harmless 226 total yards. The win improved the Oilers to 10-5, one game back of Cincy, and they could win the division if the Bengals fell at home to Washington the following Saturday and then the Oilers beat the Browns in Cleveland. Ironically, after beating the Bengals, Houston could secure a playoff berth if the Browns won on Monday night. A Browns' loss, however, would keep the Oilers from clinching until the following week.

There wasn't any reason to expect the Browns to have any trouble with the struggling Miami Dolphins. Don Shula's once proud Miami squad, much like fellow 1970s juggernauts Pittsburgh and Dallas, had deteriorated into a below-average team that depended solely on Dan Marino's right arm to win football games. The Browns, a team that needed a win to bolster its still-tenuous playoff positioning, should make quick work of Miami—or so the pundits believed.

Instead, this primetime showdown two weeks before Christmas turned into an offensive fireworks display, as neither defense could consistently stop the opposing offense. After Tim Manoa fumbled on the second play of the game, marking the seventh time in 1988 the Browns had turned the football over on their initial possession, and the Browns threw in their customary penalty for having twelve men on the field, Miami took the lead and held a 17-10 halftime advantage.

Things got worse for the Browns in the third quarter. With the Browns' pass rush tamed and the secondary unable to keep tabs on the Miami wideouts, Marino was having a field day. He extended the margin to fourteen points with another scoring pass four minutes into the third. Up to the challenge, Kosar marched his team 72 yards in thirteen plays and cut it to 24-17 with a two-yard touchdown scramble. Again, however, Marino topped it, and Miami led 31-17 with twelve minutes left. And things were about to get even worse.

A few plays after the touchdown, Kosar dropped back to pass and flicked a pass over the middle. Miami linebacker John Offerdahl came crashing through the line low and barreled into Kosar's knees. The Browns' lanky quarterback fell to the ground in obvious pain. He stood up and shook off attempts by the trainers to help him off the field, but instead hobbled to the sideline himself. As Kosar's left knee was examined, Don Strock jogged onto the field with 9:17 showing. He received a standing ovation from the crowd of 61,000-plus at Joe Robbie Stadium, which remembered all he'd done for the Miami Dolphins for the previous fourteen seasons. Even the Miami players might have been rooting for Strock a bit deep down. Marino, who was one of Strock's best friends, wouldn't allow anyone to move into Strock's old locker next to his own. Strock's nameplate still hung above it, serving as a reminder of how much he had meant to so many people within the organization, not to mention its franchise player.

But instead of reveling in a defining moment, Strock did what he could to disappoint all of those who were cheering for him. He took over at the Miami thirty-five and marched the Browns down to the Dolphin three yard line, where he looped a perfect touch pass into the arms of Langhorne in the corner of the end zone to cut the margin to 31-24 with 6:18 remaining. Now came the hard part: The Browns' defense had to keep Miami from scoring again.

And for just the third time all night, they were able to do so. Six plays after Langhorne's score, a Marino pass was tipped and picked off by Mr. Monday Night himself, Felix Wright, who returned it 26 yards to the Miami thirty-eight yard line with 3:29 left. It marked Wright's fifth career interception in Monday-night games. Aided by a critical 25-yard Strock pass to Brian Brennan on fourth-and-five, with just over a minute left, the Browns were at the Miami two. And there,

Strock went to Langhorne again, this time on a short out pattern at the goal line, and Langhorne reeled in the pass and sliced into the end zone for the game-tying touchdown. Fifty-nine seconds remained. The Browns, it appeared, had a date with overtime.

But fifty-nine seconds was more than enough time for Marino on one of the best nights of his career. In two plays, he moved the Dolphins to the Cleveland forty-seven yard line then lofted a long pass down the left sideline for former Brown Fred Banks. Banks, an eighth-round draft choice of Cleveland in 1985 who was then cut three weeks into the 1986 season, made a juggling catch and wasn't brought down until he reached the Browns' one yard line after a 46-yard gain. On the next play, Lorenzo Hampton crashed up the middle for the winning touchdown with thirty-four seconds left. It had taken Marino all of twenty-five seconds to carve through the Cleveland defense.

Strock had run out of miracles. The Browns had lost, 38-31, and their playoff hopes would all come down to the final game. A game they would play without Kosar, who, it was revealed after the game, had suffered a second-degree sprain of his left knee. For the seventh time in 1988, the Browns' franchise player would stand on the sideline in streetclothes and watch his team play without him. And Kosar, who had been sacked twenty-one times in his previous six games, wasn't happy about it. "I've been taking hits like this the last few weeks," he said afterward. "It was really inevitable. This was inevitable." Kosar wouldn't lay the blame directly on the offensive line, but there was an unmistakable tone to his comments that did not go unnoticed by the local media—or by his teammates, he would later discover.

The Browns could not blame the loss to Miami on Kosar's injury. Don Strock had played wonderfully in an almost impossible situation, coming off the bench to lead the Browns to two straight touchdowns and helping tie a game they had trailed almost the entire night. With all the chips down, Strock had completed seven of eleven passes for 70 yards and two scores.

For the first time all season, a loss could not be blamed on the ineptitude or inconsistency of the Cleveland offense. This one was the fault of Cleveland's suddenly beleaguered defense, which allowed a whopping 497 total yards, including 404 passing by Marino. The Browns' pass rush, which had appeared to come alive six weeks before, was now non-existent once more, and injuries had yet again crippled the unit.

Now the entire Browns' season would come down to four more quarters against the red-hot Houston Oilers, who wanted nothing more than to end Cleveland's run of success with a resounding victory in the regular-season finale. Frank Minnifield said it best from the solemn locker room at Joe Robbie Stadium: "Five weeks of training camp, four preseason games, fifteen regular-season games, and it all comes down to just sixty minutes of football."

19

The Old Man and the Snow

Five months earlier, as the 1988 Browns had gathered to begin training camp, no one would have expected the regular-season finale would mean so much and, in a way, so little. Even before the preseason began, the 1988 Browns had been deemed a team of destiny, bound by history and expectation to, at the very least, win the division it had dominated the past two years and coast back into the playoffs. Once there, the third time figured to be the charm, and the Cleveland Browns would finally win a Super Bowl berth.

Those predictions seemed almost laughable in the week leading up to the final game of the schedule. Whatever happened that Sunday, the Browns wouldn't be "coasting" anywhere. With a win over the Houston Oilers, they would clinch a Wild Card berth, the division-title drive already long since abandoned. In July, a Wild Card invitation to the playoffs would have seemed a pittance to the Browns and their followers, the way weaker teams would try to sneak in the back door of the postseason tournament only to fold when they got there. Now, this team was desperate for any kind of invitation to the playoffs it could muster. With a loss to the Oilers, the Browns would finish their season.

Not only had the Browns put themselves in a do-or-die situation with their loss to Miami, they'd also given the Oilers more to play for. Instead of clinching a berth of their own with a Cleveland win, Houston entered Week Sixteen needing either a win or help. Plus, the Browns would limp into this showdown at Cleveland Stadium without Bernie Kosar, Kevin Mack, or Hanford Dixon. The Oilers charged in on the strength of a five-touchdown victory over Cincinnati, ready to prove they were playing better than either division rival when the games mattered most.

True, the Browns would have the home-field advantage, and not counting the strike-replacement game in 1987, the Oilers hadn't won in Cleveland since 1981. But a victory just didn't appear to be in the cards. For one thing, did a team that allowed nearly 500 yards to a mediocre Dolphin squad really deserve to make the playoffs? For another, after the season the Browns had just endured, would a playoff berth be truly appropriate, especially compared to the previous two seasons? It depended on how you looked at it.

Take for example the pickle the Browns found themselves in when it became official Kosar couldn't play against Houston. Don Strock would start, and Mike Pagel was physically ready to return to the team as a backup, but he couldn't. The week before, hoping to get Webster Slaughter a few snaps to get back into the flow of things after recovering from his own injury, Marty Schottenheimer had used the team's final "free" roster move of the regular season. That meant that in order to activate Pagel, he would have to clear waivers first—and there was no way he would without another team picking him up. Instead, the Browns hurriedly re-signed (for the third time) Steve Slayden in outright desperation to back up Strock for the most important game of the year. Certainly Schottenheimer could not have foreseen Kosar getting hurt, but maybe, his critics contended, he should have. Based on his postgame comments in Miami, it seemed Kosar had.

The members of the offensive line took personally Kosar's sideways slap about his injury and spoke out about it. "I was standing right next to him in the locker room when he made the comment, and I couldn't believe it," one lineman told the *Akron Beacon Journal.* "It was like he was some god passing judgment. It really made us determined to win with Don Strock.

"I know a lot of people are questioning our ability because there aren't any No. 1 draft picks on our line, but we have been busting our butts for that guy. And then he goes and says something like that."

Kosar tried to clarify his comments, but things only got muddier. "My comment was not meant for the offensive line specifically," he said, which made some think he was pointing the finger at line coach Howard Mudd, who was also receiving his share of criticism for the four quarterback injuries. "There's frustration all over," said a source not with the team but close to the situation. "Bernie hasn't lost confidence in the line, but after a while, those hits get frustrating."

It seemed like ages had passed since Kosar had drawn praise from teammates and the media for buying each member of the offensive line a case of champagne the previous two Christmases. In 1988, the line "will be lucky to come away with a warm, half-empty can of Diet Coke," wrote Bob Kravitz. "These are the frustrations of a season that failed to deliver on the promise," he continued, "the frustrations of a team that knows deep down inside that it is nearly finished.

"Unhappy team. Unhappy season. And most assuredly, an unhappy ending."

Making all of this worse was that the bitter end would come against the arrogant, rebellious new pirates of the NFL, the Houston Oilers, coached by Jerry Glanville, the man in black. Glanville hadn't been taken very seriously over the previous two seasons, with his team still fluctuating between above-average and underachieving. But as 1988 wore on and the Oilers gradually improved, Glanville became more visible, more colorful, and more outspoken. At whichever visiting stadium he was coaching, Glanville would get attention simply by leaving tickets. He left two for Elvis Presley once, in New England for the Boston Strangler. Against the Bengals, he left tickets for Loni Anderson, television star of *WKRP in Cincinnati.*

But it wasn't all fun and games with Glanville. A feud that had begun with Chuck Noll the previous year continued as neither coach could look the other in the eye after their games. The spat had begun when Noll accused Glanville and the Oilers of playing dirty and trying to hurt opponents—an accusation that gained momentum around the league. At season's end, Houston would be the league's most penalized team, and Glanville would go so far as to say that he didn't think his team could win without committing at least ten infractions every Sunday. If not, they weren't being aggressive enough, he felt.

Still, many Clevelanders had no real opinion of Glanville prior to that week. But in one telephone press conference, he made sure he would be a topic around barstools and dinner tables for years to come. As far as anyone could tell, it started off as fun, Glanville just being Glanville. But by the time he was done, he sounded like a bad comedian. Worse, he sounded like a bad comedian taunting the crowd before which he was about to perform.

He was asked about the irony of having to root for the Browns to beat the Dolphins in order to clinch a playoff berth. "I never thought I would root for Cleveland," he responded, "except to root for them to have two sunny days in a year." Without a "But seriously, folks," Glanville continued about the Northeast Ohio climate. "The weather in Cleveland won't be that much of a factor. It's not like we're going there to live." He added, "The best thing for us is that after the game, we get to leave. We don't have to stay." These comments would have been "humorous" to any Cleveland steel worker regardless of where they were coming from, but since Glanville was born in the paradise of Detroit and grew up in Perrysburg, Ohio, their depth and wit were downright hilarious.

Still, Glanville wasn't done. When asked about the Oilers playing their first game of the season on grass, he countered, "Grass? That's not grass. That's painted dirt. . . . I'm not sure, but I'm told Modell is responsible for spending money to improve the facility. I sure haven't seen any. First thing I do when I go there is bring a hammer and a nail so I have some place to hang up my clothes."

So much for sneaking in under the radar. Glanville was declaring a war on Cleveland that he said he would be coming to town to win. Accustomed to such verbal slights about their city, the local media struck back, with Bob Kravitz, however down on the Browns he might have been, leading the charge. Glanville, he said, not only "looks like Barney Rubble" and "dresses like Johnny Cash's illegitimate brother," but he came from good old Houston, which "was nothing more than a rancid, impoverished cowtown everyone left when the wells went dry." Clevelanders may be colder, but they knew about loyalty. Kravitz continued: "In

Cleveland, 80,000 people show up to cheer their team—in cold, in snow, during plagues of locusts. . . . In Houston—your beloved Houston—you can't even find 51,000 fans to fill your temperature-controlled pleasure dome."

No one could say what kind of an effect Glanville's comments had on the team. But for sure, it fired up the city and took the Browns-Oilers rivalry to new heights. Instead of trodding out to the old ballpark to watch their team blandly draw the curtain on a disappointing season, Clevelanders were foaming at the mouth to fill up Cleveland Stadium and face this cartoon-shaped twerp and his band of thugs dressed in baby blue.

Someone should have mentioned something to Glanville about kicking a dog while he's down.

Some of the intrigue for Sunday's game, at least for the Houston Oilers, disappeared on Saturday afternoon. After entering the weekend still with the hopes of capturing the Central Division title, the Oilers' balloon deflated when the Bengals pulled out a 20-17 overtime win at Riverfront over the Washington Redskins. A Cincinnati loss and a Houston win in Cleveland would have given the Oilers the division. And it appeared, when Washington kicker Chip Lohmiller lined up for a chip-shot, 29-yard field goal with seven seconds left in a tie game, the Oilers would get to control their own destiny. Instead, Lohmiller missed the kick, the Bengals won in overtime, and Houston was crestfallen.

Glanville's crew got a pick-me-up with Saturday's second game, a New England loss in Denver. Had the Patriots won, they would have secured a Wild Card spot for themselves. Instead, with the loss, the Oilers clinched it. Still, there would be plenty to play for on Sunday. If Houston lost, it would return to Cleveland on Christmas Eve for the Wild Card Game. If the Oilers won, they would host the Indianapolis Colts on December 24. Considering Houston was 7-1 in the Astrodome and just 3-4 away entering Week Sixteen, there would be plenty of incentive for the Oilers to beat the Browns.

Adding a natural wrinkle to the contest, meteorologists were calling for snow flurries throughout Sunday's game. But the real question, one which even a qualified weatherman wouldn't have tried to tackle, was Which Browns' team would show up? The "Up" team that had persevered through so much adversity and had racked up impressive wins over contenders like Philadelphia, Washington, and Cincinnati; or the "Down" team, which had compounded the casualties with listless play and bonehead mistakes?

"Oh, the Up one," Bob Golic answered when asked the question on NBC's pre-game show. "I looked in the locker room, they're in there. The Down one stayed home." Then he paused, and with a small, almost humorless smile added, "I think."

Ridiculous as it may have seemed, the Browns were pretty comfortable sending Don Strock onto the field to win the most important game of the season on a cold, gray afternoon on the lakefront. Bernie Kosar was still the guy for the Browns, and despite innuendo from the front office to the contrary, it was unlikely Strock would even return to the NFL in 1989. But in a pinch, there weren't many guys in the league who could bring as much to the table as Don Strock. Not only had he started and won a critical game in mid-October while understanding barely half the Cleveland offense, he'd come off the bench and rallied the Browns from a fourteen-point deficit in the final nine minutes of a Monday-night game. He wasn't terribly athletic, but his fourteen years of experience made up for it. Bottom line, he may not have been a guy who could win a game for you, but he almost certainly wouldn't lose it.

That's what made the first quarter so hard to understand. The oldest, most experienced man on the field possibly playing the final game of his career suddenly looked like a raw rookie playing his first. On the game's third play, Strock's initial pass was intercepted by Houston corner Domingo Bryant at the Oiler forty yard line and returned to the Browns' thirty-eight. It was the eighth time in 1988 the Browns opened the game with a turnover on their first possession, and boos rang out of the Stadium stands. Houston parlayed the pick into a Tony Zendejas field goal. On his second series, Strock screwed up again. This time he was intercepted by cornerback Richard Johnson at the Oiler forty-one, further exacerbating the home crowd and halting a potential scoring drive. The Cleveland defense held and after a punt, the Browns took over at their own fifteen. Two plays later, Strock hit rock bottom.

On third-and-seven, he spotted Webster Slaughter coming open on a slant to the left side and launched a pass in that direction. But the toss was wildly off-target, and Slaughter actually had to stop and turn around to see it fall into the arms of Bryant at the thirty-eight yard line. Bryant motored up the sideline untouched and crossed the goal line to give the Oilers a 10-0 lead.

The Cleveland Stadium crowd (which numbered 74,610, marking the second-highest season home-attendance total in team history at 615,545) was stunned almost past the capacity to react. Dramatic heckling eventually cascaded out of the stands toward Strock, who trudged off the field looking like a guy who could not wait to retire. For a fleeting moment, the thought of inserting Steve Slayden crossed the minds of more than a few Clevelanders. But if things were bad under Strock, they'd be catastrophic if an unproven rookie who hadn't thrown an NFL pass entered the game. As NBC's Bob Trumpy told his television audience, "It's Don Strock, or it's the single wing."

Some felt the Browns may have cheated fate somewhat with their good fortune and depth at quarterback all season. Though none of the replacements were as good as Kosar, none had out and out blown a football game. Now, it appeared, Strock was doing just that. Only one of his first six passes had been caught by a teammate. Three others had been caught by the opponent. The Oilers were a hard enough team to beat without handing over the football, but almost impossible to knock off under these circumstances. And things would only get worse.

Strock managed to get through a series without an interception and drove the Browns to the Houston forty-one. But he was sacked on a key third down, and the Browns were forced to punt. Houston took over at its own ten yard line and converted a first down at the twenty before Warren Moon dropped back for a second-and-ten pass. Before he could release it, David Grayson bounded through the left side of the line and smashed into Moon at the fifteen, popping the football loose. Rookie lineman Michael Dean Perry scooped it up at the ten and rumbled into the end zone to bring the Stadium back to life in the opening moments of the second quarter.

But the Cleveland defense couldn't hang onto its newfound momentum. On their ensuing possession, the Oilers drove 55 yards and extended their lead to 13-7 on a Zendejas field goal. The Browns were still in it, but their chance to take control of the contest had passed. Houston added to their woes by forcing a punt then Warren Moon and company drove back down the field. Dodging snowballs thrown by the denizens of the Dog Pound, the Oilers marched into field-goal territory and made the margin nine points with another field goal.

With the disastrous first half dwindling toward its conclusion, Strock made a valiant attempt to redeem himself for his previous mistakes. Converting on a pair of key third downs, the Browns drove to the Houston six, where on third-and-goal with twenty-four seconds left, Strock dropped back to pass and began to cock his arm to throw. But before he could, the football slipped out of his hand, was picked up by Houston's Keith Bostic, and after a few moments of confusion and a replay review, it was correctly ruled a fumble, Houston's ball. It was Strock's fourth turnover of the half and kept momentum safely in Houston's corner.

As the clock hit zero and the teams began to clear the field at the intermission, the Stadium once again echoed with boos. The Browns had played so valiantly and fought through so much adversity all year. To go out in this fashion was staggering, not to mention unacceptable after the January rhapsodies of the past two years.

The Browns needed a spark. And Mother Nature was about to provide one.

As if giving the Oilers four turnovers in thirty minutes wasn't enough, the Browns would also have to kick off to start what appeared would be the final half of their season. And things looked no different. Moon directed his offense 74 yards, and right in the face of the Dog Pound, hit Haywood Jeffires for an eight-yard touchdown pass on third-and-goal.

It made the score 23-7. Nine minutes and three seconds remained in the third quarter. The odds of the Browns simply making a game of this thing and getting obliterated outright were about the same. Considering the man in charge of leading the comeback looked more like a golf pro moonlighting as a quarterback, the blowout possibility seemed eminent.

But any longtime football fan watching this game could recall the crowning achievement of Strock's career. In one of the most thrilling games in the history of the sport, he had led the Dolphins back from a 24-0 second-quarter deficit to tie and eventually take a lead over the San Diego Chargers in a divisional playoff game in January 1982. Of course, the Dolphins wound up losing that game in double overtime, but the comeback is what made the game particularly memorable. He'd done it before, now would have to do it again.

But while that game was played on a sultry evening in south Florida, this one was set on a frozen tundra beside Lake Erie. And as the Oilers moved toward the end zone for their latest score, the snow area weatherman had been calling for finally began to fall.

And with that, the backdrop was set for one of the most remarkable comebacks in Browns' history.

Perhaps one of the primary benefits of a fourteen-year career is the ability to forget the past and focus on the present. That's exactly what Strock did on the Browns' next possession. Ignoring the nightmarish first half, he completed five of seven passes on the drive, including a three-yard scoring swing pass to Earnest Byner. With snow falling harder and beginning to pile up on the field, the crowd roared with seemingly surprising confidence. This was Cleveland weather. It didn't matter what the snow did to the field conditions or how the wind affected the passing game. In a back-to-the-wall game, the Browns would have the elements on their side as the climax neared.

Now it was time for the on-and-off Cleveland defense to rise to the occasion. The Oilers were forced to punt for just the second time, then, from his own twenty-one, Strock instantly lofted a 32-yard pass for Slaughter, who was looking like he'd never missed a beat after sitting out two months. The march continued to the nine yard line, where Cleveland faced third-and-five. Strock fired a pass over the middle for Byner, but it bounced off his hands high into the air, signaling impending disaster for the home team. The football bounced off Houston linebacker Jason Grimsley's shoulderpad, then, before it could hit the ground, Herman Fontenot found himself in the right place at the right time. He snagged the pass and fell forward to the two to give the Browns a first down and more importantly, avoid total disaster.

It was, many felt later, perhaps the first time in 1988 the ball had bounced the Browns' way.

On the strength of their good fortune, the Browns wasted no time. On the next play, Byner took a handoff, swept around right end, and stretched into the end zone for a touchdown that made it 23-21 with just over thirteen minutes to play. Once again, the crowd, now enjoying the afternoon like kids let loose into the snow, went bonkers. The game, which at one point had appeared would be a total washout, was now the Browns' for the taking. And what followed was only natural.

After another defensive stop, red-hot Don Strock and company took over at their own eleven with 10:54 remaining and continued their clinic of how to run an improvised offense to perfection. With snow falling steadily and now blanketing the field, Strock hit Byner for eight yards, then Langhorne for thirteen and a first down a play later. A play after that, Strock looped a 27-yard toss to Langhorne down the right sideline, but moments later, Cleveland faced fourth-and-three at the Houston thirty-two. It was too far for a field-goal attempt in these conditions and too close to punt, so with just over seven minutes left, Schottenheimer opted to go for it. Strock once again hung tough and took a fierce hit, but rifled a pass to Langhorne on a post for seven yards and a critical first down at the Houston twenty-five. The Cleveland Stadium crowd roared through the snowfall, but not quite as loudly as it would a play later.

From the twenty-two, Strock made the playcall in the huddle, then pulled Webster Slaughter aside and told him to eschew the route he was supposed to run and to run a post pattern to the end zone instead. He did as the fourteen-year veteran instructed, and sure enough, after Strock looked off safety Jeff Donaldson, he pushed a pass into the waiting arms of Slaughter who, at the goal line, leapt into the end zone for one of the most satisfying touchdowns in Browns' history.

Fans all over Cleveland and beyond danced in front of their Christmas trees. Sure, 6:23 remained, but with the snow continuing to roll in off Lake Erie and the Oilers looking defeated by both the elements and the Browns, the outcome of this game was clear.

With the crowd rocking, the Oilers took over at their own twenty-eight yard line and picked up a first down at the thirty-nine, but the Cleveland fans didn't seem to panic. They weren't thinking about The Drive, nor were they considering the bad luck that had followed them like a shadow throughout 1988. For one afternoon, karma was on the Browns' side, and everybody knew it. So when Moon followed the conversion with three straight incomplete passes, the roar was more of jubilation than relief. The Oilers punted, the Browns took over at their own thirty-six, and Strock proved he had one more trick up his sleeve.

On third-and-seven with just under four minutes left, Strock hit Slaughter, who would rack up 136 receiving yards on the day, for a 19-yard pass and a very important first down. Two plays later, facing third-and-four, Earnest Byner took a handoff and plowed into the Houston line, kept driving after being hit, and wound up with a five-yard gain and another first down. The Oilers were forced to take their final time out.

The Browns finally did punt with twenty seconds left, but Houston could only run two plays before time expired. And when it did, many fans sprinted from their seats to line up at the ticket windows, where playoff tickets would go on sale the following morning. Cleveland had lived to fight another day in what NBC's Don Criqui and Bob Trumpy, as well as longtime Cleveland sports fans everywhere, agreed was one of the finest overall comebacks in Browns' history. But within the team comeback was as impressive an individual turnaround in the course of one game as there had ever been in Cleveland.

Don Strock had gone from an old man embarrassing himself to a fine wine aged to perfection. After three of his first six passes had been intercepted, he rebounded to complete twenty-five of forty-one passes on the day for 326 yards, 212 in the second half as he led his team back from a sixteen-point deficit created almost exclusively by his own mishaps. "This was a great game for the Cleveland Browns," Strock said, "and I'm glad I was part of it."

Not only had the Browns won a do-or-die game in dramatic fashion but they'd also given Jerry Glanville exactly what he didn't want: a chance to return to Cleveland six days later. Still, Glanville was actually humble afterward. Given the chance to blame the loss on the snow or the painted dirt he so loathed, he deflected it. "I can't blame the loss on bad footing, though, I blame Cleveland," he said. "They came out and won it."

Ernest Givins was a bit more blunt. "We're coming back to the rat hole," he said. "This is not what we wanted."

It was, however, exactly what the Browns wanted. All the controversy and tension of the previous week swirled away into the snow-swept winds. "Dissension is for newspapers," Schottenheimer snapped in the postgame press conference. "There is no dissension on this team. Do you think there was any evidence of dissension out there today?"

Still, almost as if a scar of the previous week, the members of the triumphant offensive line refused to talk to the media. To be sure, there were still problems lurking ahead for the Cleveland Browns.

But for the moment, that didn't matter. The Browns were headed to the playoffs for the fourth straight year, the first time in two decades they'd accomplished such a feat. And they would face these same Oilers, who would no doubt be less swaggering and more nervous for the Christmas Eve showdown.

This victory would turn out to be the defining moment for the 1988 team. And although no one knew it yet, also the last time Marty Schottenheimer would win a football game as head coach of the Cleveland Browns.

20 Silent Night

A little more than four years, three division titles, and a quartet of playoff berths after becoming head coach of the Cleveland Browns, Marty Schottenheimer was finally receiving some of the praise that had eluded him through much of the adverse 1988 season. "Yes, Marty deserved some of the criticism he's received this year, but you have to give him his due," Ray Yannucci wrote. "During a season of mass injuries and other adversity, he's been able to keep the team together."

That he had. And by weathering a tempest of injuries and adversity that would have crippled many if not most NFL teams, the Browns had come out on the other side with a 10-6 record, ironically just a half-game worse than their mark in 1987, when all smelled like roses in December. While there was much cause for celebration and congratulations that Christmas week, the Browns still were not out of the woods yet.

While oft-injured Kevin Mack and Hanford Dixon would both return to the lineup for the Christmas Eve rematch with the Oilers, Bernie Kosar would not. He gave it a go that Wednesday in practice, but his knee was simply too sore to play on.

Once again the Browns would turn to Don Strock to rescue the team, and after his second-half heroics in the finale, few doubted his capabilities to win the big game. Almost as an afterthought, just in case an emergency arose, the Browns used the "free" roster move granted for making the playoffs to activate Mike Pagel, back at full strength after missing eleven weeks with a separated shoulder.

Back in Texas, Jerry Glanville was whistling a completely different tune in the days after Houston's collapse. While most of the nation was bemoaning the Cleveland fans for their snowball-throwing antics, Glanville had nothing but nice things to say about his latest Cleveland Stadium interlude. "They had three nails and a hammer waiting for me," he said. "It was very cordial of them."

Glanville also spent much of the week before Browns-Oilers Two telling anyone who would listen that the Browns clearly had an advantage going in. His Oilers, he repeated, were a defeated team. "I'd say they probably have twice the emotional edge that we do," he said. "They're probably not even worried about us or are preparing for us because of that edge."

To be sure, not only were the Browns preparing for that Saturday's game but the front office was as well. Following an emphatic and official complaint to the league by Houston general manager Ladd Herzeg about the way his players and coaches were treated by the Cleveland fans, the NFL contacted the Browns to investigate the matter. Art Modell assured them that there would be extra police in place for the Wild Card Game.

And what a game it promised to be. With this being the third match of the season between the Browns and Oilers and second in six days, neither Schottenheimer nor Glanville expected to surprise each other. "They know what we're going to do and we know what they're going to do," Schottenheimer said. "It comes down to who does it best."

Ordinarily, a winter day in Cleveland in which thermometers read forty degrees Fahrenheit or above is a reason for levity. But on December 24, 1988, with the afternoon temperature hovering around forty-two degrees, the Browns and their fans were muttering under their breath.

Ideally, the weather would have been just like the week before: cold with a Currier and Ives snowscape to celebrate the holiday. Instead, the entire residue from Sunday's Snow Day had melted to create a damp and soggy field, accentuated by heavy rain showers and wind Friday. At one point, the forecast for Saturday's game was "football in a car wash," as NBC's Don Criqui would describe it, but the rain blew back out to Lake Erie by Saturday afternoon, instead setting a gray, overcast, almost melancholy backdrop. Much to the Oilers' delight, the game would be played without fear of projectile snowballs or ice clumps.

Still, Cleveland Stadium was rocking by kickoff. Dangling over the upper-deck railing on one side of the field was Jerry Glanville hung in effigy. On the other side hung, no doubt to Ernest Givins' delight, a dead rat. The denizens of the Dog Pound were ready for their fourth home playoff game in three years.

With the sellout crowd roaring, the Browns kicked off to the Oilers, who then did their best to imitate the Browns of the week before. On the second play, Warren Moon was picked off by his old nemesis from their days together in the Canadian Football League: Felix Wright. Wright returned the interception 12 yards to the Houston thirty-two, and just like that, the Browns were in business. The drive stalled at the Houston sixteen, and Matt Bahr was called upon and hit a 34-yard field goal to give the Browns a 3-0 lead five minutes into the contest. So far, so good.

But rather than melting in the face of adversity as they had the week before, this time the Oilers responded. Taking over at his own eight after a penalty on the ensuing kickoff, Warren Moon guided his offense nearly the length of the field on a seventeen-play drive. Aided by three third-down conversions, the Oilers took the lead when Moon hit Allen Pinkett on a short swing pass. Houston's scatback broke a Frank Minnifield tackle and raced into the end zone for a 14-yard scoring pass on the first play of the second quarter. The momentum had swung. And the Browns would regress back to their follies of the previous Sunday.

On first down from his own twenty following the kickoff, Strock mishandled the snap from Gregg Rakoczy. The ball bounded behind him and was recovered by Houston lineman Richard Byrd at the Browns' sixteen yard line. As if the turnover wasn't bad enough, in the scramble to recover the football, Strock had fallen awkwardly on his right wrist and sprained it. Like the oft-repeated refrain of an old song, the 1988 Browns had suffered yet another quarterback injury— their fifth in less than four months. Strock was done for the day.

Adding insult to injury, it took the Oilers just one play to add to their lead. Pinkett took a handoff from Moon, started to his right, then reversed field and scampered through a broken field to score on a 16-yard touchdown run. In fifteen seconds, the Oilers had gone from trailing by three to leading by eleven. And along the way, the Browns had lost their starting quarterback. Only in 1988 could such a turn of events have seemed not only possible but expected. For the fifth straight week, the Browns would have to play catch-up.

Enter Mike Pagel, less than twenty-four hours after being activated. He had actually been out of action so long that his memory and execution of the offense was a bit rusty. So taking a cue from Strock, Pagel had the plays taped to his forearm as a quick reference guide. The entire wacky season would now rest on his recently healed shoulder. As it happened, the injury may have actually helped his game. Instead of whipping the football toward receivers like a bullet, Pagel was using a softer touch on the tender shoulder. It was working like a charm as he drove the Browns into Houston territory on his first possession.

Unfortunately, as Pagel was heating up, so was the overall temperature of the teams, with multiple fights breaking out and both squads being penalized for personal fouls. Cleveland was forced to settle for a field goal to cut the margin to 14-6. More importantly, the tone for the remainder of the contest had been set, and it wasn't exactly going to be in tune with the Christmas spirit.

The Oilers were forced to punt on their next possession, and the fisticuffs started up again once the Browns came back out. Another Houston personal foul gave the Browns a first down at the Oiler thirty-six, and set up another Bahr field goal. It was now 14-9 with 3:19 left in the half. A potential Oiler scoring drive just before halftime was halted by another Wright interception, this one in the end zone, and the Browns went to the locker room down by five.

They would retake the field fifteen minutes later for one of the most bizarre second halves in the history of Cleveland football.

Hanging in there as best they could, on their first possession of the third quarter the Browns were poised to either cut into Houston's lead or take it away completely. The home team came out hot and wound up at the Oiler twenty-five. But after Kevin Mack was halted for a one-yard gain on second-and-four, the seams began showing.

On back-to-back plays, Earnest Byner was penalized: First for a personal foul for retaliating to what he thought was a cheap shot, then for unsportsmanlike conduct when he complained to an official. The Browns were forced to punt. Byner had single-handedly cost his team a chance to score.

The Cleveland defense hung tough, forcing a Houston punt. Then the Browns came face-to-face with one of the NFL's most controversial inventions.

On the next play, Pagel fired a pass deep down the left sideline that Webster Slaughter caught at the Houston eleven for what would have been a 25-yard gain. However, the officials said Slaughter didn't catch the ball with both feet in bounds and ruled the pass incomplete. Upon first glance of NBC's replay angle, the call was proved wrong, and play was stopped for the call to be reviewed by the replay official, George Sladky, high above the stadium. Despite every angle demonstrating that Slaughter had both feet in before going out, the call was upheld. Later, at his postgame press conference, Marty Schottenheimer said there was a league official in the replay booth who wasn't supposed to be there. When Sladky determined that Slaughter *did* have both feet in bounds, the official overruled him. Instead of first down at the eleven, it was second down at the thirty-six. Things would only get worse.

The drive stalled there and the Browns, once again out of field-goal range, punted to Houston. Max Runager pinned the Oilers back at their own ten, and after a two-yard run by Pinkett moved them to the twelve, Moon took the second-down snap, faked a handoff as he dropped back, and at the six, cocked his arm to fire a screen pass to Pinkett. The football hit Pinkett's shoulder and fell to the ground as Pinkett's motion relaxed, since he simply assumed the play was over. But Clay Matthews, who had crashed through the line toward Moon, noticed Pinkett was just inside the five at the four, meaning that Moon's pass had actually traveled backward. It had been a lateral. And since it was a lateral, not a forward pass, it was a live ball even after hitting the ground.

Matthews scooped up the football at the two, took two tentative steps into the end zone and raised his arms right in front of referee Jerry Seeman, who looked like a deer staring into headlights. For one long moment, he made no gesture and didn't blow his whistle. Then, with Matthews right in front of him, he snapped back to life, blowing his whistle, moving his arms back and forth in front of him to signal an incomplete pass. The official on-field call was that Moon had thrown a forward pass that became incomplete when it hit the ground. Just as the Slaughter catch a few minutes before, this play went up to the booth for review. And just as he had before, NBC's Bob Trumpy said this was a no-brainer. It was clearly a backward pass, and the Browns had recovered the fumble.

What happened next was quite possibly the most embarrassing postseason moment for any NFL officiating crew. After conversing with the replay official over the phone on the sideline, Seeman marched back onto the field, flipped on his microphone, and made history.

"It was determined that it was a backward pass and not a forward pass," he explained, and the Cleveland Stadium crowd began to cheer. After all, if it was determined to be a backward pass, it meant it was a live ball when Matthews recovered. The game was about to turn around, and the Browns were about to take control. But Seeman wasn't done yet.

"The covering official," he continued, "signaling incomplete, blew the whistle, so the ball is on the five yard line. It will be Houston's ball."

Before any of the Browns' backers could even muster up the strength to protest, a confused, stunned silence swept through the ballpark. *What did he just say?*

As the boos began to trickle down, they were joined by a tirade from Trumpy, who was downright furious in the NBC booth. "No!" he screamed. "That cannot happen! No! On a backward pass, the ball is live! The whistle cannot blow! The ball is live on a backward pass!"

Basically, Seeman confessed first of all that the covering official, in this case line judge Ray Dodez, had botched the call by blowing his whistle and signaling dead what should have been a live play. But interestingly, rather than standing by the call that was made, however erroneous it may have been, Seeman was going to split the difference between right and wrong. Yes, it was an incomplete pass, but rather than it being third-and-eight at the twelve, the Oilers would get it third-and-fifteen at the five yard line, where the pass hit the ground. Though in that tiny sense the call was beneficial to the Browns, the overall perversion of the rules only angered the Browns and their fans further.

Art Modell blew his top and paced around his owner's box like a caged tiger. Next door, Trumpy continued to berate Seeman and his crew. "That's as bungled a call as I've seen," he said. "They just got the shaft, I think, twice." Moments later, he added what every Cleveland fan in the stands and watching at home was already thinking: "How in the world can that call be made?"

"The proper mechanics on that play," Seeman would explain later, "is that the line judge determines whether the ball goes forward or backward. He determined the ball went forward. The ball hit the ground. He blew his whistle at that point."

In that sense, it was described simply as a blown judgment call. Those things happen. But three troubling elements remained. First, if it was simply a blown call, why not stand by it? Why officially second-guess yourself by ruling it a seven-yard loss? It was the first incomplete pass in NFL history that resulted in a loss of yardage. Second, even more frustrating was that replays showed Dodez did not even have his whistle in his mouth until *after* Matthews recovered the football. If Dodez didn't blow his whistle until then, the play wasn't officially dead until the ball was in Matthews' hands, wiping out their official ruling. Plus, if Dodez didn't blow his whistle immediately after the ball hit the ground, what did Seeman hear? Or perhaps more appropriately, why did he say he'd heard something that he hadn't? And third, if Seeman and Dodez both knew the whistle had blown and the play was dead, why did it have to go to instant replay at all? The replay official couldn't tell them when or even if the whistle blew. And that was the only issue at hand, Seeman claimed.

Something smelled bad in Cleveland.

In their best impression of the Warren Commission, Seeman and his crew had not only completely botched what would turn out to be the biggest play of the game but they then went back and tried to cover up the manner in which they screwed it up.

The overall level of frustration in Northeast Ohio then spiked on the next play when Warren Moon hit Drew Hill for 22 yards and a first down. The Browns would have to refocus and fast. With the third quarter quickly waning, another Houston score might be too difficult to overcome. Luckily for the heart conditions of Browns' fans everywhere, justice was about to be served.

On third-and-twelve from the Oiler twenty-five, Moon scrambled to avoid the Browns' pass rush and fired a pass upfield that was tipped and intercepted by Mark Harper at the forty yard line, then returned to the twenty-five. It might not have been as good as a fumble recovery inside the five, but it brought the Browns and their fans back to life.

And two plays later, after two negative rushing plays, Pagel dropped back and fired a pass for Slaughter on third-and-thirteen from the fourteen. Just as he had six days earlier, Slaughter caught the ball on the angle of a post pattern in the end zone for a touchdown that sent the Stadium into hysterics. With 2:36 remaining in the third, the Browns had come all the way back, and Matt Bahr's extra point made it 16-14, Cleveland. The game was once again theirs. *"And the Browns have overcome eight tons of adversity to take the lead,"* Nev Chandler told his radio audience.

Once again, the 1988 Browns had proven their mettle. And for the fourth straight year, the Browns' playoff fortunes would rest on the ability of their defense to hold onto the momentum. And for the fourth straight year, the Dogs would fail dazzlingly.

With the crowd rocking, perhaps basking in the glow of the holidays for the first time on the afternoon, the Oilers took over at their own twenty-four and played the Grinch to Cleveland's Who-Ville. In just over two minutes, the Oilers drove to the Browns' fourteen and momentum had swung back to Houston as the game entered the fourth quarter.

After Lorenzo White picked up three critical yards on third-and-one from the Browns' five, he finished the job on the next play, crashing into the end zone from two yards out. Almost as quickly as they'd lost it, the Oilers had taken back the lead at 21-16 with 12:25 to play in the game. The burden would now fall back to Mike Pagel and the Cleveland offense.

After an exchange of punts, Cleveland took over at its own forty-nine with 7:33 to play. The stage was set for the game-winning touchdown drive the Browns had been waiting for all season. Instead, it went like so many of their other drives in 1988.

Mack was stuffed for no gain. Rickey Bolden, starting in place of injured Larry Williams, was penalized for a false start. Gregg Rakoczy forgot the snap count, thus when his ten teammates took off, he was still crouched down holding the football. That was five more yards, now making it second-and-twenty. Pagel hit Clarence Weathers for nine yards, but on third-and-eleven, another pass intended for Weathers was tipped and intercepted by Houston cornerback Richard Johnson at the Houston thirty-six. The Browns had blown yet another opportunity. And second chances were getting harder to come by.

Once again, the fate of the season would hinge on the Cleveland defense's ability to stop the Oilers and, now with just over six minutes to play, stop them quickly. Instead, the opposite happened. Houston marched into Cleveland territory and Tony Zendejas connected on a 49-yard field goal just inside the two-minute warning to give the Oilers a comfortable two-score lead at 24-16. With the Browns out of time outs, the 1988 season was all but over.

Still, as they had all year, they continued to fight even though the odds were stacked against them. They quickly drove down the field, and Pagel hit Slaughter for another touchdown with thirty-one seconds left. All Houston had to do was fall on the onside kick. It took three tries, but after two kicks went out of bounds and the Browns touched the third too early, Houston was awarded the ball. Warren Moon knelt once to wind the clock down to zero, and that was that.

The Houston Oilers were headed to Buffalo to face the Bills in a divisional playoff on New Year's Day, and the Browns were headed into the dark months of the offseason, once again denied their goal. Though the Wild Card Game was wildly frustrating to them and their fans, Bob Trumpy for one noted the value of the contest to the average viewer.

"Both of these games between these two teams belong in a time capsule," he said. "They have absolutely played to the last ounce of their emotional ability." Trumpy went on to add that in the final two games of the 1988 season, the Browns had "shown as much character as any football team I have ever seen."

On the other hand, wrote Bob Kravitz, "guts were not enough. That, in fact, may well be the epitaph of the Cleveland Browns in this decade of the 1980s."

Despite just making the playoffs after a season with five quarterback injuries and a handful of others to key personnel, the more Browns' fans examined the loss to Houston, the uglier and more unacceptable it became.

The teams combined for a whopping twenty-two penalties, an NFL playoff record. Included in the string were seven personal-foul or unsportsmanlike-conduct fouls, four on the Oilers and three on the Browns. One unofficial count noted ten dead-ball scuffles in the first half and five in the second. "With all the poise of a street gang in a pickup game," Tony Grossi wrote in Sunday's *Plain Dealer*, "the Browns personal-fouled and false-started their way out of the play-offs yesterday."

Yet the Browns confessed all three of these disturbing counts favored the Oilers. "They threw us off," Reggie Langhorne said. "That's exactly what they were trying to do. The free safety would hit you in the back and then smile. I've never had to play a team that's so damn dirty." Earnest Byner agreed: "There was a lot of cheap-shotting going on. When a free safety hits you in the back on a pile . . . well, I'm not going to let that happen. It sort of got out of control."

Regardless of who started which fight and who got the benefit of which bad call, the Oilers were simply better than the banged-up Browns. Of that there was little debate. Without their top rusher, Mike Rozier, lost on the first play of the game with bruised ribs, the Oilers still managed to pick up 129 yards on the ground to the Browns' sixty-eight. Illustrating the Browns' running woes were Kevin Mack's abysmal 14 yards on twelve carries. Earnest Byner had played well, but his two penalties that wiped out a scoring opportunity were too much to overlook in what turned out to be a one-point game.

Mike Pagel had also played well. He completed seventeen of twenty-five passes for 179 yards in three quarters of work and brought the Browns back from a 14-3 deficit in what was probably the finest game of his career. But it would gain little, if any, notice. A season that began with an outright expectation of a Super Bowl championship had ended on a dreary Christmas Eve three games short of its expected climax.

To be sure, there was plenty of fixing needed for the Cleveland Browns, and everybody knew it. Some even called for dramatic changes, such as the removal of Marty Schottenheimer as coach. To any reasonable fan, this seemed ridiculous. Schottenheimer had proven, if nothing else, that he was a winner. When he became head coach, the Browns were an undisciplined team floundering along in a meaningless season. No one would have expected that same team to go on to four straight playoff appearances. And once that level of success was established in 1986, most accomplishments after that were more expected rather than celebrated, which fit Schottenheimer's personality and professional style of getting the job done with little fanfare.

"Maybe that's the problem some people have with Schottenheimer," Bob Kravitz wrote. "He's not ready with the clever quip, not willing to bare his soul and speak the unencumbered truth through the media."

"There is room for improvement," Jim Mueller wrote in *Browns News/Illustrated*, "but why the crusade to sharpen axes and start swinging? . . . Some changes might be necessary to affect that improvement. But they should be made after careful thought and study of the broad picture, not out of frustration and emotion."

Yet as they always seemed to in the cosmos of professional sports, frustration and emotion were about to govern the improvement process.

In the coming days, there were obvious hints that some big changes were coming down the pike. In an interview with the *Lake County News-Herald* following the Houston loss, Art Modell said, "one conclusion you can draw safely is the Cleveland Browns' organization will not preserve the status quo for 1989."

He felt the Browns had been "treading water" while both Cincinnati and Houston had zipped past them within the division. It was an observation made clear by midseason, but, Modell added, "I try not to disturb matters during the season. Now it's my ballgame. I'm going to run my ballgame. I'm the owner, coach, president, general manager, and trainer."

Which left Browns' fans wondering exactly what that meant. Would Modell clean house? Was Schottenheimer to be fired? How about his assistants? Would the Browns hire an offensive coordinator? Were the rumors true about canning Ernie Accorsi? Would some players take the fall?

The intrigue grew stronger when, at his final press conference of the season that Monday, Schottenheimer said not only was he satisfied with his job as offensive coordinator but that he didn't see any reason for widespread changes. "My feeling is we have a very good coaching staff," he said. "They did a good job. In light of the adversity we faced, it would not be in the best interests of our football team and its progress to make changes."

"That might be his personal perception," Modell said when told of the comments. "I might have a different one. That's the purpose of getting together."

Ten o'clock Tuesday morning in Modell's office, by all appearances, would be high noon within the Cleveland front office. "Here's hoping both can bend a little bit so the most important thing, the club itself, doesn't break," Jim Mueller wrote.

After three days filled with rumors and innuendo, ten o'clock Tuesday finally arrived. With Ernie Accorsi and executive vice president Jim Bailey also in attendance, Modell mapped out his plan to Schottenheimer for improving the Browns for 1989.

First, he listed a handful of assistant coaches he wanted replaced. Though it was never made official, the list was believed to include offensive line coach Howard Mudd, running backs coach Joe Pendry, and special teams coach Kurt Schottenheimer. Even defensive coordinator Dave Adolph's job was thought to be in trouble by Modell's cryptic yet accurate comment: "For four years now we've been unable to stop a team from moving on us."

Also, the assistants that would stay and Marty Schottenheimer himself would play a smaller role in the evaluation of college talent prior to the draft. Modell was frustrated with the way Schottenheimer and his coaches would overrule months of scouting work after one workout session just before the draft. That's how, he implied without naming names, the Browns wound up with first-round duds in Mike Junkin and Clifford Charlton.

But the most important demand Modell hammered home was also the most obvious: Schottenheimer would have to turn over the reins of the offense to a co-ordinator. The experiment of a lifelong defensive coach suddenly mapping out the offensive strategies and calling the plays had clearly not worked in 1988. Later, Modell said he would have been willing to extend Schottenheimer's contract as a compromise for the changes, but the topic never came up.

Schottenheimer, who a source close to the situation described as "smug" during the meeting, returned to his office at the Browns' practice facility at Berea. About an hour later, he called Modell to set up another meeting for just the two of them. Back at Modell's office, Schottenheimer drew his own line in the sand. "I just felt as I looked at it that it was time to move on," he would say. "I had pretty much made a decision that it was going to be in everybody's best interest if Marty Schottenheimer moved on."

"Marty, to his credit, was candid and frank, as he always has been with me, and said he could not accept those conditions," Modell would say. Later, two rumors formed a confluence that possibly explained each man's thinking at this point. It was believed Schottenheimer was ready to leave Cleveland to begin with and knew he could get a job somewhere else without having to endure the pride-bruising process of revamping his staff at someone else's whim. Schottenheimer wasn't stupid, and even before the playoff loss, knew that demands would be forthcoming.

"Every player thought he reacted strangely during and after the Houston game," one player said anonymously. "He didn't argue any of those bad calls. After the game, he talked about playing golf." Another player added, "Can't you see how calm and collected Marty is through all of this? He has got to have something lined up. . . . He wouldn't let that go so easily without having another job ready."

"I had no job at the time," Schottenheimer said. "Notwithstanding those who would have suggested otherwise, I had no job."

Modell, some felt, entered the meeting secretly anxious to lose Schottenheimer, and knew that the coach's stubbornness and pride would never permit him to accept the changes Modell was proposing. Either way, the showdown in Modell's office typified a mysterious communication breakdown that had grown more prevalent as 1988 went on. "Throughout the course of that season, we'd lost our ability to continue to function as we had in the past," Schottenheimer said. "It wasn't the same kind of relationship that we had. I'm not quite sure why."

So perhaps in some dark recess of each man's subconscious, the turn of events satisfied them. They reached a financial settlement on Schottenheimer's contract, which had one year remaining at $400,000, and parted "amicably" despite "irreconcilable differences," they both would say later.

"We agreed that it would be in everybody's interest that we part company in the friendliest fashion possible," Modell said, "which is exactly what we did."

And with that, the Marty Schottenheimer era came to a close. It didn't go unnoticed that it ended on December 27—exactly twenty-four years since the franchise's last world championship.

Though the writing had been on the wall, Schottenheimer's departure still took Cleveland by surprise. The local television stations interrupted their afternoon broadcasts to report the news. When Mike Pagel heard the news on the radio, he nearly drove his truck off the road. When Schottenheimer spoke to the team for the final time the day before, there had been no allusion that the coach might not return. He talked specifically about what the team needed to do to improve for 1989. "Nobody expected Marty to go," Bob Golic said. "We expected something just because of the rumors we heard. We thought maybe an assistant coach might go, or a change here or there. None of us felt it would be dramatic.

"It hit us pretty hard pretty quick. We sensed that things were starting to change."

To the casual observer, it didn't make sense. In four-and-a-half years, Schottenheimer had compiled an impressive 46-31 record. None of his five teams finished worse than .500 and he'd guided them to three straight division titles and four straight playoff appearances. He was a good coach directing a good football team in a good football city, so most fans could only shake their heads and wonder what happened and why. But in Cleveland, the answer was clear. "The problem was," Ray Yannucci wrote, "like his predecessor, Sam Rutigliano, (Schottenheimer) came close but no cigar, and also like Rutigliano, he got caught in the trap of becoming more than a head coach."

While both Schottenheimer and Modell felt the move was in everyone's best interest, it was still a somber day. "This is a situation that we are disappointed about—Art as well as myself," Schottenheimer said. "Nonetheless, I appreciate the opportunity he gave me to become a head coach. The only regret I have is, together, he and I were unable to reach the goals we had set. I know this, we did our best."

While all the issues the pair differed over were brought up and debated in the media, the smoking gun appeared to be Schottenheimer's refusal to hand over the offense to someone else. In all likelihood, had he agreed to do so, Modell would have backed off on some, perhaps all, of his other demands. And with the offensive coordinator position as the deal-breaker, to the fans and media alike, it became clear who was at fault. There was hardly anyone siding with Schottenheimer and even fewer who didn't think the Browns' offense had taken a dramatic step backward since he began running it.

In 1987, with Lindy Infante in charge of the offense, the Browns averaged more than twenty-seven points in each of the twelve non-strike contests. In 1988, the average dipped to nineteen—more than a full touchdown difference every Sunday. In 1987 they were ranked seventh in the NFL in total yardage, falling to eighteenth in 1988. The Browns had fallen from twentieth to twenty-fourth in rushing, sixth to ninth in passing, and a jaw-dropping third to nineteenth in scoring. To be sure, injuries affected the Browns' offense in 1988, but even when the team was relatively healthy, the offense never really got going. "I am not going to use the injuries as a means to say let us try again," Modell said. And that's not even mentioning the cavalcade of times the Browns had twelve or ten or even nine men on the field— a sure sign of a confused and ill-functioning offense. Even Modell admitted that had Infante still been with the Browns, the 1988 season would have gone completely different. Conversely, Modell added that even had the Browns somehow made it to the Super Bowl, he still would have insisted on bringing in an offensive coordinator for 1989.

To most, Schottenheimer's stance was completely unjustified.

"He feels he can function as a coordinator," Modell said. "I tried to explain to him that I think the organization, the team, needed his undivided attention in all phases of the game beside just the offense. After all, he was a brilliant defensive coordinator before I made him head coach."

"In our circumstance," Schottenheimer countered, "in this situation, I still believe that I did the right thing. I frankly thought we would go backwards by bringing in somebody new."

He was right about one thing. The Browns' offense had certainly gone backwards.

"As an offensive coordinator, Schottenheimer was offensive," Bill Livingston wrote. "That he could not or would not admit as much shows exactly how outsized the ego of the man had become."

It seemed inconsequential at the time. Most in attendance probably didn't even notice.

When Art Modell sat down at a table in a conference room at Cleveland Stadium to announce Schottenheimer's resignation, a large Browns' banner hastily taped to the wall behind him fell to the floor in a crumpled heap.

Following the events of December 27, 1988, the same was about to happen to the team that banner represented.

21

This Bud's for You

It didn't take long for rumors to swirl about who Marty Schottenheimer's replacement would be. Whoever it was, however, would accept one primary stipulation: Art Modell was in charge.

The new coach must "be able to work within the system and be a part of the kind of operation Art wants," Ernie Accorsi explained, meaning hard-headed, stubborn coaches used to getting their own way without question need not apply. Modell wanted someone with NFL experience, yet someone "fresh." At first, Modell hinted he would look for someone with an offensive background, but with a cavalcade of qualified defensive coordinators available, plus his desire to attempt to maintain the Browns' offensive philosophy, he quickly changed his mind.

Minnesota's Floyd Peters, Chicago's Vince Tobin, Fritz Shurmur of the Rams, and even a young New York Giants' assistant named Bill Belichick were all seriously considered. San Francisco's defensive coordinator, George Seifert, also popped up as a candidate a few days after the 49ers had triumphed over Cincinnati in Super Bowl XXIII. Seifert was even en route to Cleveland to meet with Modell when he was paged during a layover at the Dallas airport. 49ers' owner Eddie DeBartolo Jr. urged him to return to San Francisco, where he was informed head coach Bill Walsh had officially retired, and Seifert was to be offered the job.

For Modell, it had to be the right choice. With the team aging and the rest of the division improving, the Browns were at a critical nexus. What they did in the next year would likely define their path for the 1990s. Ray Yannucci noted, "not since he fired Paul Brown is there more pressure on Modell to make sure he makes the right choice."

When he fired Brown in 1963, Modell replaced him with Blanton Collier. After Schottenheimer left twenty-six years later, he would try to do the modern equivalent.

"It's almost eerie," Modell would say of the similarities between Collier and Bud Carson. "They have the same initials, are the same age when I hired them, both were failures as college coaches, both succeeded coaching legends and both wore hearing aids." True to form, when Carson first met the Cleveland media at a press conference announcing his hiring, he had to re-insert his hearing aid in order to hear a reporter's question.

Carson was far from being an old man, but at the age of fifty-seven, he had thought his chance to become an NFL head coach had long since passed. He had resigned himself to being a career assistant with some dynamite accomplishments under his belt. So when Modell and the Browns came calling, Carson took it very seriously. It would be his last chance to become a head coach.

Like Schottenheimer before him, he was born in Pennsylvania and grew up near Pittsburgh as Leon Carson. He played defensive back at the University of North Carolina from 1948 to 1952, then spent thirty months in the Marines. He began his coaching career in 1955 at Scottsdale High School near Pittsburgh, then two years later moved up to the collegiate level at his alma mater. He served as an assistant with the Tar Heels until 1964, spent one year at South Carolina, another year at Georgia Tech, then replaced legendary Bobby Ross as Yellow Jackets' head coach in 1967. In five seasons, Carson posted a 27-27 mark and led the Jackets to two bowls. Yet in retrospect, even he thought he had done a sub-par job. "I made all the mistakes I could make," he said. "I was no more ready to be a head coach than to fly." As it turned out, with his next job, he would soar to previously unheard-of heights.

In 1972, fourth-year coach Chuck Noll hired Carson to coach the secondary of the struggling Pittsburgh Steelers. "That was the start of a lifelong friendship from a guy who gave me a shot at the right time," Carson said. It was indeed the right time. The Steelers went 11-3 in 1972, won the AFC Central, and made the playoffs for the first time in twenty-five years. The following year, Carson was promoted to defensive coordinator and began to put together the most feared defense in the history of football. By the time he was through, he had created the "Steel Curtain" and won two Super Bowls.

He left in 1978 to join George Allen and the Los Angeles Rams as secondary coach—though he later would say leaving Pittsburgh probably cost him a chance at a head-coaching job. Allen was fired in the preseason and replaced by Ray Malavasi, and Carson was promoted to defensive coordinator. The following November, Carson's defense set an NFL record by holding the Seattle Seahawks to minus-26 yards of total offense. Two months later, Carson would face his old comrades, the Steelers, in Super Bowl XIV and gave them quite a match before falling.

In 1982, Carson moved on to Baltimore, and though the Colts suffered through an abysmal 0-8-1 strike-shortened season, Carson made an impression on then Baltimore general manager Ernie Accorsi. "His knowledge of the game vastly exceeded the talent we put on the field," Accorsi said. "His defensive schemes were always a few years ahead of his time." A year later, Carson served as Kansas City's defensive coordinator, but a personal conflict with Chiefs' head coach John Mackovic during the 1984 training camp resulted in Carson's resignation. He spent the rest of that season as an unpaid voluntary assistant breaking down defensive films for the University of Kansas.

In 1985, he resurfaced in New York as the Jets' defensive coordinator, took the remnants of the once-heralded "Sack Exchange" and rebuilt New York's defense into one of the NFL's finest. Behind a powerful front line, the Jets made the playoffs in 1985 and got off to a 10-1 start in 1986. But a five-game losing streak saw them back into the playoffs as a Wild Card, where they wound up facing the Browns in their historic divisional playoff. For fifty-six minutes, Carson's defense completely shut down the Browns' running game and consistently confused Bernie Kosar. But, as Clevelanders well remembered, Kosar redeemed himself in the final four minutes, pulling off one of the greatest comebacks in NFL history and ending the Jets' season.

Though the team hovered around .500 the next two years, New York's defense was consistently effective under Carson's regime. Modell, for one, recalled how an apparently undermanned Jets' team had thoroughly dominated the Browns in a 23-3 win in 1988. And so it happened that on January 26, 1989, over a bottle of white wine in an Italian restaurant in Greenwich, Connecticut, Carson became the eighth coach in Cleveland Browns' history, agreeing to a three-year contract. Around the same time, the seventh coach in Browns' history, Marty Schottenheimer, agreed to become the new head coach of the Kansas City Chiefs. The cynics believed both Schottenheimer and Modell had received their respective wishes.

Most interesting, however, was that the issue that most convinced Schottenheimer he had to leave Cleveland was not an issue in Kansas City. Joe Pendry, who had been the Browns' running backs coach, would follow Schottenheimer and serve as his offensive coordinator.

When Bernie Kosar heard that Bud Carson was his new coach, he was on a golf course in Florida. "I threw for over 400 yards against his defense," he reportedly told his playing companion. "Why are we hiring him?" While the specific sentiment may have been unique, the question was one of several swirling around Cleveland.

Certainly, Carson was neither unqualified nor an unknown. But many fans found it curious that Carson or any truly confident coach was willing to accept so many of the stipulations Art Modell had packaged with the job.

For starters, he would play essentially no role in the upcoming draft, with the reins instead being handed to Ernie Accorsi. Modell felt this was absolutely necessary to avoid the draft-day follies of the previous years. "One mistake we have made over the years was having coaches go out in April and at the last minute interviewing different players and coming back with a positive recommendation which is contrary to that of the scouts. . . . That has cost us heavily, particularly in the past two drafts. I don't want to repeat that."

Secondly, while Carson would be free to fill the majority of the coaching staff as he saw fit, at least one primary position was already taken care of. The ultimate

irony surrounding the joust with Schottenheimer over hiring an offensive coordinator was that Modell already had the candidate picked out.

As the 1988 season wore on, the owner explained, he noticed not only that
the offense wasn't as potent but that a few subtle changes had been made from
Lindy Infante's system, and those changes were not as suited to Bernie Kosar and
his style of play. "I've said it time and time again that I view Kosar as the franchise
quarterback for the Cleveland Browns, one we haven't seen since Otto Graham in
the 1950s," Modell said. "I consider him more important than the owner. You can
always get rid of me, but you can't find a quarterback of stature easily these days."
In 1988, Kosar had taken a back seat in the Browns' offense. Symbolizing this was
a shot on television of Schottenheimer admonishing Kosar for hanging around
the sideline conversations among Don Strock and the coaches during the win
over Houston in the regular-season finale. That was not the way you treated your
franchise player in Modell's view.

Enter Kosar's mentor from Miami, Marc Trestman, brought in for 1988 as
quarterbacks coach, then, according to some critics, outright ignored by Schottenheimer, Joe Pendry, and Howard Mudd over the course of the season. Though
he'd never served as an offensive coordinator before, Trestman was given the job
even before the Browns had settled on whom the head coach would be. Carson
thus accepted the position and Trestman as his offensive coordinator.

Trestman was just thirty-three at the time of his promotion. He had little playing experience—after serving as a backup quarterback for the University of Minnesota for three years, he was twice released in training camp by the Vikings in
1979 and 1980—before beginning his coaching career while attending law school
at Miami. As a volunteer assistant in 1981 and 1982, he spent a lot of time with a
pair of redshirt quarterbacks in Kosar and Vinny Testaverde. In 1983, Trestman
was named the Hurricanes' quarterbacks coach and, in Kosar's first year as the
starter, Miami won the national championship. The pair again worked together
in 1984, the final collegiate season for both, as it turned out. They'd been reunited
in 1988, and in 1989, would have total control over the Cleveland offense. Though
Trestman had never been an offensive coordinator, Modell was confident he was
only three or four years away from becoming a head coach in the NFL.

Trestman, wide receivers coach Richard Mann, and strength coach Dave Redding were the only assistants who would return. The majority of the previous
assistants followed Schottenheimer to Kansas City, including Bill Cowher, who
was rumored to be a candidate for the Browns' defensive coordinator.

While both the offense and defense would be directed by new coaches, they
were heading in opposite directions. Modell made perfectly clear that the offense
shouldn't change much at all, and Trestman agreed. The defense, on the other
hand, would undergo a dramatic philosophical twist. "I'm a defensive coach who
basically believes you attack on defense," Carson said at his introductory press
conference. "You don't sit back and wait. I think that day is over. I think today is

the day of more aggressive defensive football than you've seen in the last ten years, the (3-4) defenses, the bend-but-don't-break defenses. . . . I want to have an aggressive-type of defense that people like to play. I think anybody who plays in our defensive system loves to play in it because we turn people loose and allow them to do, hopefully, what they are most capable of doing."

In other words, for better or worse, the days of the "rubber-band" defense were over. The Browns would switch from the 3-4 base alignment to the 4-3, which would require a stronger and more aggressive defensive line than the Browns had ever had under Schottenheimer since the 3-4 switch in 1980.

Was this what the Browns' defense, which had always been strong but also seemed to melt at the critical moments of playoff games, really needed to put the team over the top? Would a change in philosophy counter the team's overall aging? Would the new draft syllabus finally result in some young, impact players? And ultimately, would Bud Carson match—if not exceed—Marty Schottenheimer's achievements? To Modell, there was no question.

"We are absolutely confident that Bud Carson is the right man to help us make the next step, which is to win the league championship," he said, "and hopefully more than that one.

"This is it for me," he added later. "I've conducted my last coaching search. I've waited a long time to win, and I think he's the man."

"I hope, first of all, that we do exactly what the Browns have done the last four years—go to the playoffs," Carson added. "That's the bottom line as far as I'm concerned because I know this organization expects that. I don't come in with any illusions about what's expected of me. You've been there, and you certainly want to go back. They didn't bring me here for there to be any slide backwards. The first order of business is to see that there isn't."

But there was. And it was already happening.

From the moment the 1988 season ended, Earnest Byner had a feeling his days in Cleveland were numbered. And when Schottenheimer left town, there was no doubt in his mind he too would be leaving Cleveland.

The year before, the coach had said Kosar and Byner were the two players he would never trade. But following The Fumble, then a quiet 1988 season that ended on the sour note of provoking two penalties that cost his team points in the playoff loss, and then Schottenheimer's departure, the writing on the wall was clear. The new regime wasn't likely going to appreciate Byner as much as the old. "He likes Byner because Earnest is an overachiever, and Marty was one himself," Modell said just after Schottenheimer quit.

Carson tried to keep his options open: "I'm sure there are a lot of people in this organization who are down on Byner, but this coaching staff isn't down on him." Perhaps not, but plenty of others were. Two days after Schottenheimer's resignation, Bill Livingston wrote a scathing analysis of Byner in the *Plain Dealer*.

He accused Schottenheimer of "making this temperamental player of average ability the focus of his offense." Further, he added, Byner was too emotional on the field, and it hurt him and his team. "Wherever he lands, I hope Schottenheimer will, like Frankenstein and the monster, want his little creation with him. Final memo to Marty: Take Earnest Byner. Please."

As it turned out, Schottenheimer didn't take Byner. Instead, the Browns finally found a taker on draft day in the Washington Redskins. After some hemming and hawing over the final details, it appeared the deal would fall through. But finally an agreement was hammered out.

Earnest Byner was traded straight up for running back Mike Oliphant, a 1988 third-round draft choice from Puget Sound University who was hindered by a groin pull through most of his rookie season with the Redskins and only carried the football eight times. For this, the Browns were sending Washington a twenty-six-year-old player in his prime who had rushed for more than 2,600 yards in just over four full seasons.

"I thought it was relatively small," Byner said after the trade, "but that's what the Browns wanted and that's what they got. I think the Redskins got in return someone much more seasoned and someone who has much more to offer a team than Oliphant."

After the trade was official, Ernie Accorsi was asked who would take over as the heart and soul of the team now that Byner was gone. "I don't know," he replied. "We've got a lot of souls out there." Yet later that summer, as training camp wore on, Washington offensive coach Joe Bugel noted that acquiring Earnest Byner was "the best trade the Redskins have made since I got here nine years ago."

By all rights, the Byner trade should have been huge news. But considering everything else the Browns had done that day, it was merely a sidebar.

"OK, I'll say it," Art Modell said at the completion of a jaw-dropping draft day. "The future is now. . . . A Super Bowl contender might have been born."

"On this day in April," Ray Yannucci would write, "the Browns went from playing the slot machines to playing the high-stakes, high-risk game of rolling the dice. And they want to hit the jackpot. Now."

With Ernie Accorsi running the show for the first time, the Browns wasted no time in being aggressive. They made four trades that day, including Byner to Washington and—much to the delight of his critics—Mike Junkin to the Chiefs for a fifth-round choice. Schottenheimer would take his "mad dog in a meat market" with him to Kansas City. "I'm not going to sit here and tell you we're proud that we took the fifth player in the draft (in 1987) and had to turn around and trade him for a fifth-round pick," Accorsi said. "He had a bad experience here, and it was a bad experience for us. Our coaches now really didn't feel he was going to have much of an opportunity to make the team, so we just had to get what we could out of it."

Then, with the Browns holding the twentieth pick in the first round, they realized they could not get the player they really wanted. So just before the New York Jets could snag him at number fourteen, the Browns sent their first-, second-, fifth-, and ninth-round picks to Denver for the thirteenth overall pick in the draft. With it, the Browns got their man: running back Eric Metcalf from the University of Texas.

But the Browns weren't done. As the second round unfolded, they saw an opportunity to get the number two man on their list. Accordingly, they shipped their third-round pick, the first-round choice the following year, and versatile Herman Fontenot to Lindy Infante and the Green Bay Packers to move up seventeen spots and take Auburn wide receiver Lawyer Tillman.

Though the price for both players had been high, the Browns were beside themselves with giddiness. To be sure, Modell's concern that the Browns didn't have enough playmakers had been addressed. Instantly, some began comparing Metcalf to Greg Pruitt, who had become a legend for the Browns in the 1970s. At 5'9", 182 pounds, Metcalf was of similar size to Pruitt, but may have been even quicker. Most believed he was already faster than his father Terry, who had gone to three Pro Bowls while with the St. Louis Cardinals in the mid-1970s. He not only had racked up nearly 5,700 all-purpose yards for the Longhorns in his career but also was a world-class long-jumper. In fact, Metcalf had originally wanted to attend Kosar's alma mater of Miami, but chose Texas because it had a better track program.

And as a result of his track prowess, Metcalf was about to introduce the Browns to a never-before-seen running style. "To be a better long-jumper, you definitely have to have body control," Metcalf said. "I think that has carried over to football. When I'm running the football, I can stop and cut without turning my body. I can control my body without thinking." In terms of athleticism and quickness, on paper at least, he was exactly what the Browns were looking for. "Eric Metcalf is like a time bomb ready to explode every time he touches the ball," draft analyst Mel Kiper Jr. noted.

Tillman held similar promise. At 6'4", some thought the Browns might try to turn him into a tight end, as they'd done with Ozzie Newsome a decade earlier. But with Tillman's potential at wide receiver, plus the residue left over from the last time the Browns had tried to fiddle around with the position of a high draft pick in Junkin, he would stay as a wideout.

So the Browns got the players they wanted. As satisfying as that was, was it worth what they gave up? "People will have strong opinions on the price we paid," Accorsi said. "Well, we paid a hell of a price for Bernie Kosar, too. You never pay too high a price for great players. We just better be right."

As that fateful summer of 1989 began, it appeared all the pieces of the new Browns were coming together. That is, after several of the old pieces had been replaced.

In the debut of the NFL's free-agency era, originally called "Plan B," each team was permitted to reserve thirty-seven of its players under contract and leave all others available to be signed by other teams. The bottom third of most NFL rosters was left off the list, as were several mid-level players making too much money to likely be attractive to other teams. As was the case with many teams, the Browns brought in several good players, but mostly just to replace the good players they lost under the system.

Punter Max Runager signed with Kansas City, so the Browns landed punter Bryan Wagner from Chicago. Sam Clancy left for Indianapolis, so to bolster the defensive line, the Browns reacquired Al Baker after a year in Minnesota and also added youngster Tom Gibson from New England. They lost long snapper Frank Winters and brought in Tom Baugh from the Chiefs to do the same thing. Offensive guard Larry Williams left, but the Browns bolstered their beleaguered line by signing guard Ted Banker from the Jets. Clarence Weathers expressed his unhappiness by departing for Indianapolis.

But by far the most heartbreaking transaction of Plan B for the Browns was the loss of Bob Golic, who signed with the Los Angeles Raiders. Even after Carson was hired and everyone knew the Browns were going to be switching to the 4-3, which eliminates the nose tackle, Golic was eager to return. "Unless something dramatic happens, like somebody offering me a million dollars, I'll be back at Lakeland in the summer," he said that winter. But as time wore on, it became clear to him that the Browns no longer needed his services.

"I thought I'd retire in a Browns' uniform," Golic said. "I loved playing for the Browns and I wish things would have worked out differently. The toughest part about this decision was thinking about the fans. I grew up here, and since I came back in 1982, everybody has been behind me."

Shortly after Schottenheimer's departure, things began to change. One day when Golic happened to stop by the Stadium offices, one of the team's VPs spotted him and pulled him aside. Glancing around to make sure no one saw them talking, the VP said, "If you have an opportunity to leave, you should take it."

"At the time, I thought to myself, 'Well that sucks,'" Golic said. "'He doesn't want me anymore.' But I realized very quickly after that he knew what was happening to the team. He was giving me a heads-up."

Sure enough, a few weeks later as Golic was about to walk out the door to attend a banquet with the Akron Browns Backers at which he was about to receive their Man of the Year Award, his phone rang. It was the Browns, saying they wouldn't be bringing Golic back for 1989. Golic hung up the phone and drove to Akron, knowing he'd have to talk about what a great organization the Browns were and how great it felt to be named the team's Man of the Year.

With the departure of Golic, the Browns' defense had lost its native son.

Meanwhile, neither Gary Danielson nor Don Strock returned, leaving the backup job to Mike Pagel. And the Browns locked up their native son on offense for the immediate future by signing Bernie Kosar to a six-year contract extension through the 1995 season. It was the final touch on Art Modell's plan (expressed subtly in the departure of Schottenheimer, the promotion of Trestman, and the hiring of Bud Carson) to keep Kosar in Cleveland for his entire career. Essentially, all that had been done in the months following the 1988 season was directed toward that purpose.

On June 27, Kevin Mack had what strength coach Dave Redding called a great workout at the Browns' training facility in Parma Heights. It was reflective of Mack's new attitude for the 1989 offseason. With Byner gone, Tim Manoa still a work in progress, and a pair of unproven youngsters in Eric Metcalf and Mike Oliphant as the only incoming weapons, Mack knew he would be asked to play a bigger role in the Cleveland offense that fall. Accordingly, he was working harder than ever in the offseason.

That's why his arrest for drug possession on June 28 was so surprising.

He was taken into custody by the Cleveland police just after 6 p.m. along with a man and a woman who were sitting in Mack's car at the corner of East Fifty-Fifth and Scovill. Mack, who police determined had cocaine in his system at the time, was at the wheel of the car, which had eleven bags of cocaine and a crack pipe in the back seat. He would be indicted on four drug charges: drug abuse, aggravated trafficking in cocaine, use of a motor vehicle for drug abuse, and possession of criminal tools. If convicted, Mack could serve a prison sentence of anywhere between six months and twenty years. And he had no idea if the NFL would let him play football ever again. Suddenly, contending for the Super Bowl was inconsequential. One of the Browns' best-known players was a drug addict.

"Regardless of what happens, we are going to try to make this as positive of a thing as we can, not turn it into a negative," Bud Carson said. "Hopefully, something good will come out of all this. It will perhaps wake some other people up and make us more alert to some of the things that can happen."

Yet previous incidents of this nature hadn't. The number of professional athletes who were known drug addicts had skyrocketed as the 1980s wore on. Former Browns' linebacker Chip Banks, for one, after he'd been traded to San Diego, had been arrested four times for marijuana and cocaine possession in just over two years. And the day before Mack's arrest marked the third anniversary of Don Rogers' death due to a cocaine overdose.

Mack, released on a $2,500 bond, spent the next month in a rehabilitation program at the Cleveland Clinic. He spoke to the media by reading a prepared statement on July 28. Barely raising his head and never making eye contact, Mack looked embarrassed and ashamed. His voice was low and somber as he read.

"As you all know, I'm not one of the most outgoing people for talking," he said. "I'm a little nervous now with all the eyes on me, but it's something I have to deal with. . . . Right now, I don't know if I have the right words to say how badly I feel about what I've done."

The tone of the message was remorse. The hope for redemption was evident, but not necessarily on the football field: "I've made a lot of mistakes in my life, but it's time for me to start taking responsibility for those mistakes and to try to change things. . . . I hope in the future that people can judge me for what I'm striving to be, not for what I've done in the past."

On August 30, Mack pled guilty to the charge of cocaine use, with sentencing possibly as harsh as eighteen months and a $2,500 fine—to come a month later. The next day, the NFL, treating Mack as a second-time offender because the justice system was involved, suspended Mack for four games—the final preseason contest and first three weeks of the regular season. His trial date was set for September. Thus, the Browns would enter training camp, and then the regular season after that, with their top running back standing trial. Even before the Browns' first practice had begun, with the arrival of a new coach, the departure of a handful of anchor players, and now a case study on the relationship between drugs and professional athletes about to begin in their front yard, the 1989 season was already one of the most tumultuous in team history.

Making matters more complicated was the Browns' commitment to travel to London with the Philadelphia Eagles for a week of training camp prior to the NFL's annual preseason game played at Wembley Stadium. While the trip did some good for the league from a public-relations standpoint, it did little good for the Browns in terms of preparation, especially with a new coaching staff and a handful of new players in the mix. The Browns, looking typically sluggish in the first exhibition game, lost to the Eagles, 17-13.

The headaches continued back in Cleveland, highlighted by both Metcalf and Tillman holding out, each missing all of training camp. But perhaps the most notable obstacle in the minefield of the 1989 camp was Bud Carson's unceremonious demotion of Hanford Dixon from cornerback to safety. Eyebrows were raised on the second day of camp when Carson, after being asked what was the difference between Dixon and Frank Minnifield, replied, "Minnifield's not over the hill." True, Dixon, entering his ninth season, was clearly on the down side of his career, but he was still a Pro Bowl cornerback and one of the team's clear-cut leaders. As camp wore on, Carson suggested moving Dixon to free safety and replacing him at corner with youngster Anthony Blaylock. Not only was Dixon not crazy about the move but Felix Wright, coming off a dazzling 1988 season at free safety, was suspicious as well. He would be moved to strong safety, a position he had never played with the Browns.

Yet after several weeks of watching Blaylock struggle, on the eve of the opener, Carson scrapped it all. He moved Dixon back to right corner, but kept Wright at strong safety, and Thane Gash stepped in at free safety. Blaylock just wasn't ready yet, he explained. Nor, some noted, was Carson ready to earn the respect of a veteran-laden team.

And through it all, the Browns looked progressively worse with each exhibition game. After a win in Detroit, Cleveland dropped its final three dress rehearsals to bottom-dwellers Pittsburgh, Phoenix, and Tampa Bay. The Browns finished the preseason with a 1-4 record, their worst mark in seventeen years. It wasn't just the results that were upsetting. In the five games, the Cleveland offense scored a measly two touchdowns, and while the new "attack" defense had flashes of brilliance, it had been inconsistent.

It didn't take long for the press to start looking for reasons for the malaise. "This team misses Earnest Byner and Herman Fontenot more than the front office expected when it gave away both in draft-day trades made to improve team speed," Tony Grossi wrote in the *Plain Dealer.* "They were leaders by example, overachievers whose passionate hustle inspired everyone. Stars looked up to those guys." Grossi added that the Byner trade in particular "is going to hurt the Browns, and even us long-time Byner critics admit that. Though he was vastly overrated, Byner is nonetheless missed."

The Browns limped out of the preseason already looking like a team well past its prime, flailing with desperation in attempts to hold onto the same level of success.

"All of it is shaping up like a giant blind date," Bob Kravitz noted.

Almost as a sidebar to the headaches of training camp, Art Modell called a press conference the first week of September to talk about the future of Cleveland Municipal Stadium. At the gathering on the Stadium infield, he proposed a dramatic plan to renovate the fifty-eight-year old ballpark, calling for an $90 million facelift over two or three years. He presented a model of what the "new" stadium would look like, and it was impressive. The infamous metal pillars would be completely removed from the Stadium's upper deck, and while the lower-deck posts would still be necessary, the seats would be rearranged in front of them, not behind, and moved closer to the field. The field itself would be lowered six feet and all the seats would be replaced. Additionally, there would be nearly twice as many restrooms, all of which would be modernized. Modell even suggested financial avenues for the funding, such as a sin tax on alcohol or cigarettes, or, he added, a lottery program similar to what was being used to finance a new sports complex in Baltimore.

It all seemed to make perfect sense. The only catch concerning the plan was that Modell needed his housemates, the Jacobs brothers and their Indians, to go along. At the time, the Jacobs were proposing their own tax-funded issue: a baseball-only park for the Tribe. Yet Modell said his plan would only work if the Indians were on board. If they weren't, however, Modell stated he would try to salvage as much of the plan as he could for the Browns.

Still, most felt the Indians would eventually back the proposal. "If the Jacobs Brothers see quickly their stadium plans are nothing more than a pipe dream, then they, if indeed they plan on keeping the Indians in Cleveland, should take a long, hard look at Modell's proposal," Ray Yannucci wrote, "and all the influential people in the area should put their heads together to come up with creative financing that will not burden the taxpayer.

"From the way things are going, the only stadium project that has any chance of flying is Modell's renovation of the Stadium."

If, however, the Indians somehow did get their own park, Modell added as an afterthought, he pledged he wouldn't threaten to move the Browns out of Cleveland.

No one really knew what to expect as the Browns entered their Week One clash with the Pittsburgh Steelers at Three Rivers Stadium. After a wobbly preseason, there was little optimism circulating through Cleveland. On the other hand, many fans figured, it was the hapless Steelers the Browns would open with. Even a sub-par performance should be enough to win. It was that thinking and the unwelcome anxiety orbiting the franchise out of training camp that made what happened that afternoon so interesting.

It all started innocently enough. Most of the first quarter passed with little incident. The Browns caught a break when Stephen Braggs downed a punt by newcomer Bryan Wagner at the Pittsburgh five yard line. Then, on the next play, Robert Banks, making his first Cleveland start on the defensive line, smashed into Steelers' rookie fullback Tim Worley, popping the ball loose. Clay Matthews scooped it up at the three and rolled into the end zone for the Browns' first touchdown of the 1989 season. The first score of the Bud Carson era was notched by the defense. It was 7-0, Browns. Worley's debut became even more nightmarish moments later when Mike Johnson stripped the football from him, and David Grayson recovered at the Pittsburgh twenty-four. Five plays later, Matt Bahr booted a 37-yard field goal, making it 10-0, Browns.

It took just twenty-two seconds for the Browns to score again. On Pittsburgh's next play from scrimmage, the call was a reverse to wideout Louis Lipps, who gained three yards before being stood up by Grayson at the twenty-eight yard line. Though it seemed Lipps' forward progress had been stopped, the whistle never blew. And in that extra second, Grayson tore the ball from Lipps' arms, spun around, and sprinted down the field. He crossed the goal line for the first touchdown of his NFL career on what was officially ruled a fumble return. It was now 17-0, Browns, and the beat went on.

The Steelers drove to their own forty on their next possession, but a desperate third-down bomb by Bubby Brister was picked off by Mark Harper in the end zone—Pittsburgh's fourth turnover in just over a quarter. And for the first time in 1989, the Cleveland offense was proactive, driving 79 yards for a field goal. It was 20-0, Browns, midway through the second quarter.

Just over a minute later, they regained possession after a Pittsburgh punt, and picked up where they left off, moving 70 yards on a drive capped by a three-yard

Tim Manoa scoring run—the first offensive touchdown of the season. It was now 27-0, Browns, still with more than three minutes to play in the first half. And when the two-minute warning arrived shortly after, the hometown crowd at Three Rivers let loose its loudest roar of the day.

The Browns weren't done scoring before the half. Thanks to a 42-yard punt return by Gerald McNeil, they added a 27-yard Matt Bahr field goal with thirty-nine seconds left before the intermission. It was now 30-0, Browns, and the Steelers were able to get to the locker room without allowing another score, but they were booed unmercifully as they came off the field.

Though the contest was clearly over, the Browns weren't done scoring. Just after the second-half kickoff, Tim Worley made it easy once again. Following his third fumble, this one caused by Mike Johnson and recovered by Banks at the Steeler fifteen yard line, the Browns cashed in on Manoa's second touchdown—this one from two yards out. It was 37-0, still with more than twenty-seven minutes to play in what was quickly becoming one of the most embarrassing moments in Pittsburgh sports history.

And it got even more humiliating when, on the Steelers' next possession, a Brister screen pass went through the hands of fullback Merril Hoge and into the waiting arms of David Grayson at the Pittsburgh fourteen. He motored into the end zone untouched to make it 44-0. With the return, Grayson became the first player in Browns' history to score on a fumble return and an interception return in the same game. Appropriately, he would be named the AFC Defensive Player of the Week.

Mercifully, the Steelers managed to keep the Browns off the scoreboard for the remainder of the third quarter. But they still had one more touchdown in them, coming with eleven minutes remaining when newcomer Mike Oliphant spun through a pair of tackles and reached the end zone for a 21-yard score. It made the final a record-breaking 51-0, the Browns' first non-replacement shutout in six years, the worst defeat in the history of Three Rivers Stadium, and the second-largest margin of victory in Browns' annals.

As rain fell down in sheets at the game's conclusion, Bud Carson knew better than to try to shake the hand of his former mentor. "What could I say?" Carson said. "I feel bad for him. He's a good friend, and we all have those kinds of days. Everything went our way and then it just snowballed. That doesn't happen very often, but it happened for us today." Noll and Carson nodded to one another as they made their way off the field.

The funny, or perhaps truly sad, part of the annihilation was that the Browns had not played all that well, and if they had, the score could have been even worse. The Steelers had all but handed them this game on a silver platter with eight turnovers, including five fumbles. "To be truthful, we had done a terrible job on stripping the ball," Carson said. "Until this game."

The Cleveland defense scored three touchdowns, while the offense cashed in turnovers for thirteen more points. Only seventeen of the fifty-one points origi-

244

nated from long drives by the Browns' offense, which had the football inside the Pittsburgh ten yard line four times in the first half and was only able to score one touchdown. Brister had been sacked seven times and threw three interceptions. The Steelers' offense managed just five first downs for the game. But the most amazing statistic of the day was Pittsburgh's total yardage: a mere 53, setting a new franchise record for both the Steelers' offense and Browns' defense.

All in all, it was a downright amazing start to Bud Carson's head-coaching career—against a team he had found his niche with thirty miles from his hometown, no less. And it all came after one of the most controversial training camps in Browns' history. Accordingly, the players tried to give Carson a game ball in the locker room after the game. Carson refused, instead giving one to each member of the team. It symbolized perhaps the biggest sigh of relief in recent Browns' history.

"He needed this more than I did," said Art Modell, who had spent eight hours with the coaches in meetings the previous Sunday trying to figure out what was wrong with the team. A meeting of the entire defense was called the following Monday, then a full team meeting on Tuesday. "It was a unifying thing," Ozzie Newsome said. "I think it set the foundation for this team."

The foundation looked mighty strong after the most one-sided opening day in Browns' history. Topping it off, the Bengals had lost in the fourth quarter to the Bears at Soldier Field, and the Oilers had been crushed in Minnesota. For one week at least, the Browns would be in first place entirely by themselves. "This was our day," Carson said. "This was a day when everything went our way. . . . I don't know if we'll ever have another day like we had today, so we'll take it.

"It was a great day for me. Whatever else has happened in my life, I feel thankful I was around long enough to enjoy this."

Reading in between the lines, many fans understood what Carson was really saying. But in case they didn't, Modell came right out and said it: "We're not *that* good."

In case they didn't believe it, the statement would become painfully clear in the near future.

In one of the quirks of the NFL schedule, in the Browns' Week Two home opener, Bud Carson would face another team he had spent a good portion of his career with: the New York Jets.

Yet it became clear early that Week Two would not be as easy as Week One had been. The Browns had clung to a 14-7 halftime lead thanks to yet another defensive touchdown on an interception return by Thane Gash. The Browns' offense finally got rolling in the second half, but the Jets hung close. A Bernie Kosar-to-Ozzie Newsome touchdown with eight minutes left turned out to be the backbreaker in a thrilling 38-24 Cleveland win. After the most productive back-to-back scoring performances by the Browns in twenty-one years, they were 2-0 for the first time since 1979.

With two convincing wins over former teams, things couldn't have looked much brighter for Bud Carson and the Browns. So far, the team's faults were being overruled by its big plays, and the new defensive philosophy was working like a charm.

But over the course of the next month, the big plays would be harder to find and those faults would become much more prevalent and impossible to ignore.

22 Reality

While the first two games of the season had been huge for Bud Carson and the Browns, their next two would be gargantuan. First they would take on the defending AFC champion Cincinnati Bengals in a Week Three Monday-night encounter then they would return home to face their nemesis, the Denver Broncos.

Even before the first game, the intensity—and perhaps the rivalry itself—shone through. Even before he'd taken the Cleveland job, Bud Carson had been a vocal opponent of allowing Sam Wyche and the Bengals to dictate a defense's substitution patterns with their heralded variety of no-huddle strategies. In 1989, the no-huddle was once again legal, and Carson fumed about it all week, no doubt to the delight of Wyche.

Wyche was at the center of further controversy prior to the game, accusing the Browns of spying on his team during the pre-game huddles by electronically accessing the material recorded by a camera and sound crew filming the Bengals. Wyche said his accusation was true because he and his coaches started saying funny things for the microphones and saw the Browns' coaches laughing with their headsets on across the field. "I guess when you're desperate you resort to whatever you have to do," Wyche said later. Ernie Accorsi categorically dismissed the accusation, saying the camera crew was filming for a local television station, and Wyche had known about it.

Ridiculous as the incident may have seemed, Wyche wasn't the only paranoid party that week. The previous Wednesday in practice, as Bernie Kosar walked up to take a snap with the first-team offense, he noticed an out-of-town television news crew filming the action. He pulled away from center and refused to play until the cameras had been turned off. The Browns-Bengals rivalry had entered a new dimension.

Unfortunately for the Browns, through the game's first half they still struggled with the elements that had plagued them against the Bengals the year before: no run game on offense and a defense in over its head. After two weeks of managing just enough of a rushing attack to be competitive, the Browns completely ignored the ground game, running just seven times for seven yards through the first three quarters. With Kevin Mack still serving his league suspension, rookie Eric Metcalf still learning the offense, plus the inconsistency of Tim Manoa, Keith Jones, and Mike Oliphant, offensive coordinator Marc Trestman simply decided to stick with what was working in the low-risk pass game.

Meanwhile, the Bengals' offense consistently moved up the field despite playing without fullback Ickey Woods, lost for the season the week before with a knee injury. Cincinnati took a 7-0 lead early in the second quarter on a short touchdown pass from Boomer Esiason to tight end Rodney Holman. But the Browns responded with a 78-yard drive solely on the arm of Kosar. On third-and-goal from the Bengal five, Kosar swung a screen pass for Metcalf. He caught it at the seven, made a cat-like cut sideways to evade a tackle attempt by Bengals' cornerback Lewis Billups, then without completely landing, bounced off the balls of his feet in the opposite direction to leave corner Eric Thomas with an armful of air. Metcalf then scooted along the sideline into the end zone, dropping jaws across the country after one of the most dazzling touchdowns in the history of *Monday Night Football*.

Unfortunately for the Browns, the Bengals' offense picked up right where it left off, marching back down the field and regaining the lead on another Esiason-to-Holman scoring strike. But Kosar and the Browns answered, tying the contest again on a six-yard touchdown toss to Manoa. The Browns were being outplayed, but went to the locker room with the score knotted at fourteen.

The seams began showing for the shaky Cleveland offense in the third quarter. The Browns went three-and-out on three straight possessions, amassing minus-17 total yards. Cincinnati took the lead back on their first series of the second half when Esiason looped a 19-yard touchdown pass over Clay Matthews to James Brooks. Things would have been even worse for Cleveland had it not been for the struggles of new Bengal kicker Jim Gallery, who missed a pair of field goals in the third quarter that could have stretched the lead to thirteen. For as poorly as they'd played, the Browns entered the final stanza still within striking distance at 21-14. What's more, Cleveland had two chances to tie the game in the fourth quarter, but twice failed to convert on fourth-and-short inside the Bengals' ten yard line.

It was a tough loss for the Browns, but not exactly a heartbreaking one, since they had been completely outplayed. Worse still, Carson was now publicly questioning the playcalling of his inherited offensive coordinator. "I have nothing to say except to say it looks like we had all the wrong calls," Carson said when asked about the final series, when the Browns threw three passes from the four, none of which went to the suddenly dangerous Metcalf.

The bright promise of the 2-0 start had now been darkened by some serious storm clouds. And with John Elway and the Broncos coming to town six days later, no one could say when the sun would shine again.

It was almost hard to believe it had been fifteen years since the Cleveland Browns had defeated the Denver Broncos. It wasn't as if Denver had been an NFL power in that time—far from it. Yet in each of the ten games since 1974, the Broncos always seemed to find a way to pull out a victory. "Weird things happen when we play them," Ozzie Newsome said that week.

The teams' October 1 showdown marked Denver's first trip to Cleveland since the now-legendary 1986 AFC Championship. The Monday-night revenge session was wiped out due to the 1987 strike, and the Browns had been spanked at Mile High in 1988. It would be the first time the denizens of the Dog Pound would have a chance to enact some revenge on the hated Broncos since the two playoff defeats. And as it happened, that intensity in the bleachers actually would play a major factor in the game.

From the get-go, something was very different from the Browns' side. Instead of playing Elway almost passively, hoping he would make a mistake, Bud Carson's attack defense was more vicious than ever, swarming Denver's Golden Boy from the opening snap, sacking him four times, and forcing him into what would become the worst game of his career. Late in the first quarter, a charging Michael Dean Perry knocked the football away from Elway, and it was recovered by defensive end Robert Banks at the Bronco fifteen yard line, to the delight of the capacity crowd of 78,637. A play later, the crowd ignited once again when Bernie Kosar looped a perfect scoring pass to a wide-open Webster Slaughter in the corner of the end zone.

Cleveland, wearing brown jerseys at home for the first time in six years, dominated play early but failed to build a lead. They took a 10-3 advantage to the half then stretched the lead to ten when Bahr hit a 48-yard field goal midway through the third. But Elway, still pressured by the slobbering Cleveland defense, pulled another rabbit out of his hat. He hit Vance Johnson for 68 yards to the Cleveland twelve to set up another field goal to make it 13-6 going into what would become one of the wildest fourth quarters in the history of Cleveland Stadium.

Early in the period, a Bryan Wagner punt pinned the Broncos back at their own four, right up against the bloodthirsty Dog Pound. The Pound was widely known for showering opponents with dog biscuits and the occasional snowball in wintertime. But as the Broncos huddled in the end zone, they were showered with a much wider and much more dangerous variety of debris. Yes, biscuits came flying, but so did raw eggs, one of which hit Denver lineman Keith Bishop in the eye. Then a double-A battery came flying from the bleachers, hitting veteran referee Tom Dooley in the head.

"I walked behind the huddle, and they continued to throw things," Dooley said. "After they were ready to play, they threw a rock about two-and-a-half inches in diameter, and they threw another egg which hit number 54 [Bishop], and they threw another egg which hit in the huddle as John was calling the play. They threw one more double-A battery, and I stopped it. I went to the other end."

With 12:31 to play, for just the second time in NFL history, an official had stopped play and forced the teams to switch ends of the field because he thought it was too dangerous to continue under the current conditions. It garnered little surprise to discover the other occasion occurred at Cleveland Stadium in front of the bleachers in a game against Houston in 1978. It was, along with the snowball-throwing at an unconscious cameraman the previous December, the absolute lowest the Dog Pound had ever sunk. "But while such behavior is inexcusable," Bill Livingston wrote, "it does show how frustrated people get around here at the sight of John Elway and his buck-toothed brilliance." Perhaps even worse than further tarnishing Cleveland's national image, now the Broncos would get to call their signals in the quieter end of the Stadium.

But when the drive stalled, Denver coach Dan Reeves requested the officials switch ends again but was denied. They would finish the game going the same direction. He believed there was a slightly stronger wind blowing toward the closed end of the field, the end the Browns were now driving toward, and didn't think they should be rewarded for their fans having thrown objects on the field. You never knew, he argued. The game could come down to a field goal.

"I don't agree with what Tom did," Reeves said later. "I never heard of such a rule. I thought we were going down there for one play and get it over with. . . . They let the fans dictate which end of the field you're allowed to play on. That's a joke."

The Browns halted Denver deep in its territory then parlayed the subsequent field position into a 42-yard field-goal attempt by Bahr, which he pulled wide, partially because the wind changed its direction. At the other end of the field, the kick likely would have been good. Reeves' argument weakened dramatically. "It's a matter of which horrendous end you want to kick from," Bahr said.

Denver took over at its own twenty-four yard line, and moments later, faced a first-and-twenty from its own forty-one. Again, Elway overcame the frustrations of what had become a long afternoon for another game-breaking play. This time he hit running back Steve Sewell, a vital component to The Drive three years earlier, for 53 yards to the Cleveland six. Three plays later, Elway hit his favorite target, Johnson, for a seven-yard touchdown pass that knotted the game at thirteen with 3:58 showing. Just like the Browns had done the previous Monday in Cincinnati, the Broncos were being outplayed but hanging in there.

On the following snap, they improved their chances dramatically. Kosar, who hadn't been intercepted in his previous 181 attempts, was picked off by Denver linebacker Marc Munford at the Cleveland forty-three yard line, and Munford returned it to the thirty-three with just over three minutes remaining. The game was in the Broncos' hands, thanks to what the media was prepared to start calling The Interception. And things only got worse for the Browns. Elway hit Johnson for 11 yards then fullback Jeff Alexander ripped upfield for 11 more yards to the Browns' eleven at the two-minute warning. Denver could now kill some clock and play for the go-ahead field goal to all but clinch its eleventh straight victory over the Browns.

Kosar paced back and forth on the sideline, praying for a shot at redemption. In 1986, it had been the Browns' defense. In 1987, it was Earnest Byner. Now, it appeared it would be Kosar who had cost the Browns a chance to defeat the Denver Broncos. Even though he'd been with the Jets at the time, Bud Carson later confessed he was thinking about those back-to-back AFC title-game defeats.

Running back Sammy Winder took a handoff for three yards to the Cleveland eight, and the Browns called a time out with 1:49 left. The Stadium was as quiet as it had been all day. The only real noise was coming from within the Browns' defensive huddle. "Somebody's gotta get it," Frank Minnifield barked to his teammates, several of whom grunted in agreement. As the Broncos broke their huddle and came to the line, Clay Matthews hollered out, "Strip the ball! Strip the ball!"

The second-down call was a pitch to Winder, who found no room to his left. Mike Johnson, who had dropped a sure interception for a touchdown when Denver was backed up against the Dog Pound, wrapped up Winder and started to bring him down. "He tried to pull away from me," Johnson said later, "and when he did that, I got my hand on the whole ball and started pulling it out, and it came out."

Most of the beaten crowd didn't see the football hit the ground. Many fans just saw a scramble of brown jerseys and rose to their feet in anticipation. The ball stood still on the ground for one long moment, anyone's for the taking. Then Minnifield, tumbling into the action, pulled the ball into his chest and "rolled up like a turtle," Johnson described. It was the Browns' football at their own sixteen with 1:42 left.

The reaction of the crowd wasn't so much jubilation or relief, but rather utter surprise. This kind of thing didn't happen to the Browns when playing the Broncos. To lose a fumble in this situation, sure. But to force and recover one, saving the team from almost certain defeat? No way. Not against these guys.

With the crowd going bonkers, the Browns had a decision to make: play it safe and shoot for overtime, or go for the win here and now. Kosar, his prayers answered, refused to play it safe. The Browns would pull out the stops and go to the hurry-up offense in the hopes of piecing together some sort of makeshift drive. While it was psychologically refreshing, it was a risky choice. For the second straight week, the Cleveland offense had been shaky, and a quick three-and-out here would simply give the Broncos one more chance to win the game in the final minute.

It looked like things might go that way when Kosar was sacked for a three-yard loss on first down. The crowd groaned and returned to its seats. Then Kosar hit Brian Brennan, who had been noticeably absent from the offense in the first three games, for seven yards. On a must-have third-and-six and the clock ticking down under a minute, Kosar went to Brennan again, this time for 13 yards and a first down to the Browns' thirty-three. Then Kosar rifled a short pass to Reggie Langhorne, who passed up a chance to run out of bounds and motored upfield for a gain of 14 to the forty-seven. After an intentional incompletion to stop the clock, an illegal-procedure penalty moved the Browns back to the forty-two for second-and-fifteen. Kosar came through yet again, hitting Slaughter for 19 yards to the

Denver thirty-nine, and the Browns called their final time out with twelve seconds remaining.

It was still too far for a realistic shot at a field goal. The Browns needed one more successful play, and they got it, thanks to a heads-up decision by Slaughter. On a play designed for him to run a deep route, he recognized the defensive alignment, and, as he'd done so many times in Lindy Infante's receiver-option offense, altered his route. Kosar fired a pass to him along the sideline, which he caught at the thirty and fell out of bounds with five seconds showing. It set up a long, but makeable 48-yard field goal attempt by Bahr, who still remembered all too well the 42-yard miss eight minutes earlier that had put his team in this predicament. He would kick toward the closed end of the Stadium, where a slight tailwind had gathered behind him.

But before Bahr could kick the ball, Mike Pagel had to get it down. After long-snapper Tom Baugh had been forced out of the game in the first quarter with a rib injury, center Gregg Rakoczy filled in for what would be his first appearance as an NFL long-snapper. He'd done the job on the previous four attempts, but this time, his snap was short and hit the ground a foot in front of Pagel. But just as the Browns had been lucky moments before when Winder's fumble stayed put on the grass just long enough for Minnifield to recover it, the ball bounced right up to Pagel, who quickly spun it around and placed it down for the oncoming Bahr. The veteran kicker connected and looked up, knowing the alignment was perfect. The only question was whether or not it had the distance.

It seemed like minutes went by as the spinning football arched closer to the goal post, the capacity crowd standing breathless, watching its path. Finally, it reached the crossbar and crept over it "by one or two coats of paint," Bahr would say later. After fifteen years and ten games, the Browns had finally defeated the Denver Broncos, 16-13.

Cleveland Stadium erupted. Fans leapt into one another's arms, and even those who had been throwing batteries and rocks forty-five minutes earlier cheered in jubilation. Fate had finally smiled on the Browns—or perhaps more appropriately, frowned on the Broncos in what Tony Grossi described as "a Hitchcock conclusion loaded with irony."

"We've had to live with The Drive and The Fumble, and it was nice we could get The Drive *and* The Fumble in one game," Bahr added. "I guess you could say we purged the ghost." Cody Risien agreed: "They say what goes around comes around. It finally did. We deserved it."

While the players certainly felt some measure of justice had been served, that paled in comparison to the satisfaction long-suffering Cleveland fans felt. "I'm happy for them as much as I am for this football team," Carson said. "It's been too long. I told the team it's time to erase all of that miserable history, and they did."

To be sure, it was a victory fraught with controversy. For instance, Tom Dooley's end-switch would be debated in the national media all the following week. But the Browns certainly deserved to win. For the first time, they'd utterly dominated John Elway, limiting him to six completions in nineteen attempts and just two rushing yards. Ironically, the immobile Kosar had out-rushed Elway on the strength of a 23-yard scramble in the fourth quarter. Thanks to Bud Carson's attacking defense, the Browns had finally solved the riddle that was John Elway.

And while the Cleveland offense, particularly the non-existent running game, left much to be desired for the second straight week, it was the Dog Pound that was responsible for the sour residue coming out of the victory. Art Modell pledged to double the Stadium security force and announced the installation of cameras to film the goings-on in the bleachers. Anyone caught throwing anything on the field would be summarily ejected. But some felt the measures still weren't enough. "What happened Sunday at the Stadium was an outrage," Bob Kravitz wrote, "a civic embarrassment that brought Cleveland right back to the days of burning rivers and ten-cent beer nights and flammable mayors."

Never one to back down from controversy, Sam Wyche promised that if anything was thrown at his players when the Bengals visited Cleveland on December 3, he would take his team off the field until either enough security was present to control the crowd or the bleachers were completely cleared out. "They need to be caged down there anyway," he added.

Not surprisingly, the Browns and their fans took a beating in the forum of public opinion the following week. But it didn't seem to matter. Wins over the Denver Broncos were few and far between, especially sweet ones such as this. And with the Browns at 3-1, their best start in ten years, and tied with Cincinnati for first place at the one-quarter mark, the problems in the stands and on the field once again seemed far, far away.

It took just two days for the Browns to come crashing back down to a hard, cold reality. That Tuesday, Cuyahoga County Common Pleas Judge Richard McMonagle sentenced Kevin Mack to six months in prison.

The ruling sent shock waves through the Browns' organization. Art Modell and the front office all assumed since Mack was a first-time offender that he would be punished accordingly, most likely meaning probation and a fine. Instead, Mack was hit hard by the law—perhaps unreasonably so in the opinion of many, especially considering former Brown Chip Banks hadn't spent a single day in prison following his four drug-related arrests over the previous two years.

In the days before, as his four-week league suspension neared its conclusion, the Browns had made room on the roster for Mack to be activated. "The guys still treat me as part of the team," Mack said. "They just look at it as just a matter of getting the suspension behind me and getting back out there on the field." He was still recovering from a knee injury that had required minor surgery during the suspension, but would be ready to play by the end of October. The Browns were targeting his return as the moment when the offense would finally start to play like it was supposed to.

Instead, Mack hobbled up to the defense table on crutches and found out he was going to prison. He would spend a few days in the Cuyahoga County Jail and would be transferred to the Ohio State Reformatory in Mansfield to begin his sentence. He would be eligible for shock parole after thirty days, but for an otherwise decent man who had never spent a day in prison in his life, thirty days seemed like an eternity.

Modell ordered the entire Browns' organization not to comment on the ruling, fearing any negative press might hinder Mack's chances for parole. But Modell made it clear the Browns would not abandon Mack even though it appeared he would not contribute to the team in 1989. "He deserves our support and will get our support," Modell said. "He's a good young man who made a mistake and is deserving of a second chance, and he will get that second chance."

While the Browns were mum on the subject, the Northeast Ohio media were all over McMonagle, who, many were quick to point out, was up for re-election in 1990. Many fans were irate as well, so much so that police were posted outside McMonagle's home after death threats were phoned in. Most were in agreement that Mack had gotten a raw deal. No one felt he should have received preferential treatment because he was a celebrity, but some feared he'd been treated harsher because of it. McMonagle, a Browns' season-ticket holder as it happened, disagreed. "I did not sentence him to jail because he was a celebrity," he said. "I sentenced him to jail because I was concerned about the man. . . . I know I'm going to get creamed for it, but I think I did what was best for him." As to the opinion of the fans and members of the media, he countered, "Tell them they don't know what I know." Within a matter of days, however, they found out.

The foundation for McMonagle's sentencing was based on a letter written by Dr. Gregory Collins of the Cleveland Clinic, who led the Browns' Inner Circle, to the Cuyahoga County Probation Department. Collins wrote that while this may have been Mack's first drug arrest, it was not his first foray into the world of substance abuse.

It was revealed Mack told authorities he'd used drugs on and off in college and two to three times per week while playing for the Los Angeles Express in the USFL. He had been convicted of drunk driving in South Carolina in 1984 and when the Browns acquired him through the supplemental draft that summer, he had a $400-a-week drug habit. Upon his arrival in Cleveland, after being enrolled in a rehabilitation program in St. Paul, Minnesota, Mack was placed in the Inner Circle. But in early 1986, he slipped back into the old habits and was put back in rehab.

For the next two-and-a-half years, there were no incidents. But late in 1988, as Mack battled a cavalcade of injuries that kept him off the field, the frustration led him to start drinking. And after good friend Earnest Byner was traded a few months later, the drinking increased. Looking for new friends, Collins wrote, Mack started hanging out at bars with his fellow players: "In my opinion, this surreptitious drinking weakened his resolve to remain abstinent from cocaine and, on the night before his arrest, it appears that he impulsively decided to obtain some cocaine for use."

In Collins' opinion, the combination of a difficult childhood and the sudden availability of money and drugs burdened Mack. His psychiatric assessment of Mack revealed "significant emotional problems, characterized by immaturity, resentments, self-pity stemming from early parent separation, and abject poverty. These early problems left him with deep self-doubt and impaired his ability to cope with stress."

On the surface, Mack had always been a quiet, shy man who never realized his own abilities because of a lack of confidence. But underneath, a cauldron had been bubbling, overflowing into drug addiction.

While the revelations certainly didn't do much for Mack's social standing, Modell's reputation was also impaired. That summer, after the *Plain Dealer* had reported Mack had a drug problem when in the USFL, Modell snapped back, "Anyone who says that Kevin Mack had a drug problem in the USFL is a liar." After Mack was sentenced, Modell stated that Mack had been clean since he came to the Browns in 1985 and that he would have known about any prior drug problems prior to Mack's joining the team. Modell was wrong on all counts. He clarified his position, saying the Browns didn't know he had a drug problem when they drafted him in 1984, but that they did know after he joined the team in 1985. Modell went on to explain that he didn't know which players were in the Inner Circle or which had relapsed on their rehabilitation unless it reached a point that the player was beyond saving.

After several days of controversy and debate, Mack was shuffled off to Mansfield, with the caveat that he would receive regular medical attention on his knee, without which his career might be affected. And the Browns were left to ponder over what to do for another month without a bona fide running back on offense. They entered the sweepstakes for disgruntled Dallas running back Herschel Walker, offering the Cowboys their number-one draft picks in 1991 and 1992 (1990's draft pick was already gone in the deal that landed Lawyer Tillman), their second-round picks in 1990 and 1991, plus a young defensive player, believed to be 1988 top pick Clifford Charlton. Walker eventually went to Minnesota in a blockbuster trade that gave Dallas enough draft picks to become one of the finest teams of the next decade. The Browns were also rumored to be interested in acquiring Oiler tailback Mike Rozier, but in the end, they would stick with what they had: backup fullback Tim Manoa, rookie Eric Metcalf, and a collection of unproven commodities in Barry Redden, Mike Oliphant, and Keith Jones.

While they tried and failed and the Browns' running game continued to flounder helplessly, Mack sat in a tiny jail cell, pondering what might have been—and what may never be again.

Ironically, with 141 rushing yards, it wasn't lack of a ground attack that cost the Browns a victory in Miami the following Sunday; it was crushing mistakes at critical moments.

The Cleveland defense once again rose to the occasion, managing Dan Marino, who hadn't been sacked in sixteen games. The Dolphin offense was held in check, but the Browns' offense, despite facing the lowest-ranked defense in the NFL, could muster few threats. Miami took a 10-0 lead in the second quarter after a pair of long drives, but the Browns cut the lead to seven on a 50-yard Matt Bahr field goal just before halftime. Cleveland tied it midway through the third after an 80-yard march capped by an eight-yard Metcalf scoring run.

With 1:08 remaining in the fourth, Felix Wright picked off Marino and returned it to the Dolphin thirty-seven. With one first down, the Browns could tiptoe into field-goal range then milk the clock to set up a hard-earned road victory. But a play later, Kosar tried to slip a pass to Eric Metcalf in the flat, and it was intercepted by Miami safety Louis Oliver, who returned it to the Dolphin forty-nine. As quickly as they had lost momentum, the home team recovered it, and now it was the Dolphins who were poised to win the game. Rookie kicker Pete Stoyanovich was called upon to attempt a 45-yard field goal with three seconds left, but missed it. The teams would go to sudden-death.

The Browns won the toss and crossed up Miami by switching to a no-huddle, hurry-up offense. They moved inside the Miami thirty and called on Bahr to win the game with a 44-yard field goal. Unlike the game-winner against Denver the week before, this time the snap and hold were both good, and Bahr later said the kick felt good as he connected with the ball. As it neared the goalpost, the Browns' sideline began trickling onto the field, celebrating what they thought was the game-winning kick. Instead, at the last moment, it hooked left, and the teams would play on.

Miami then caught a break when Stephen Braggs, filling in for an injured Frank Minnifield, was called for a questionable pass-interference penalty that gave the Dolphins a first down on what would have been a third-down incompletion. Two plays later, facing third-and-ten from the Browns' forty-seven yard line, Marino fired a laser shot to Freddie Banks, the former Brown, for 20 yards and a first down. For the second straight year, Banks made the Browns pay for letting him go. Moments later, Stoyanovich redeemed himself for the miss at the end of regulation by nailing a 35-yard field goal 6:28 into overtime. The Dolphins were victorious, 13-10. The Browns dropped to 3-2, and to make matters worse the Bengals won in Pittsburgh, improving to 4-1 and snagging sole possession of first place in the AFC Central.

More troubling than the loss was the realization that the Cleveland offense was AWOL for the third straight week. It was a problem that would have to be corrected quickly with the Bengals on a roll and the Oilers closing in after a slow start. "The talent is there, and everyone knows it is there," Marc Trestman said, "but we're not scoring touchdowns. There's no need to panic, but we just have to start doing it."

There was little doubt by most Browns' fans that things would get back to normal the following week when the Steelers came to town. After all, Cleveland had crushed Pittsburgh in the opener by fifty-one points at Three Rivers, and the Steelers hadn't won in Cleveland in eight years. This was a no-brainer. By sunset on October 15, the Browns would be 4-2 and, thanks to a stunning loss by the Bengals at home to Miami earlier in the afternoon, back in first place.

The only real suspense seemed to surround the Dog Pound. It would be the Browns' first home game since the battery incident, and Art Modell and the front office held their collective breath over how the fans would behave, particularly with a packed house of 78,840 fired up with hated rival Pittsburgh in town. As promised, security forces had been doubled, and surveillance cameras had been installed to monitor the Pound. Additionally, a flyer encouraging fans to behave themselves was passed out at the gates with a message from Bud Carson and Hanford Dixon, the man who had started the Dog craze five years before. Now he feared it had become like Frankenstein's Monster. "I never thought it would get to this point," Dixon said. "They've never been people with golden manners, but we could always control them. Now it's getting out of control. We want to emphasize that it's not everybody who sits in the Dog Pound. The majority are good people having a good time. There's only a few bad apples." To further attempt to thwart those bad apples, beer sales by roving vendors would stop after the first half.

As it turned out, the measures might not have been necessary. Cleveland Police later reported that it was one of the quietest games ever. That's because the Browns sucked the vigor and any rowdiness out of their fans by playing possibly their worst game in recent memory. But it wasn't as if the Steelers came out ready to play, either. The teams would combine for twenty penalties and fourteen punts and neither would collect 275 total yards of offense. Steeler quarterback Todd Blackledge, in for injured Bubby Brister, was atrocious, hitting on just nine of twenty-eight passes.

But the Browns were far worse. They turned the football over seven times, including four interceptions by Bernie Kosar, who suffered through the worst game of his NFL career. Kosar at one point missed on eleven straight pass attempts. On the day, he completed just fifteen of forty-one passes for 162 yards and, for the first time, was roundly booed by the hometown crowd. Things got so bad that a "Pagel! Pagel!" chant broke out in the fourth quarter, and Carson did talk to Trestman about the possibility of yanking Kosar.

Yet for as horrible as they had played, the Browns were in it all the way. Pittsburgh grabbed a 10-0 lead midway through the third quarter. The Cleveland offense continued to slosh through the second half before receiving a gift: a controversial pass-interference call on Steelers' cornerback Delton Hall on the Pittsburgh fourteen. Moments later, Metcalf dove into the end zone from the two to cut the margin to 10-7 with eight minutes left. Ridiculous as it seemed, with a defensive stop and one more scoring drive, the Browns could pull out a victory despite a downright putrid performance.

The Steelers took the intrigue out of the game's conclusion on the ensuing kickoff. Dwight Stone returned it 73 yards to the Cleveland twenty-five, taking the final burst of energy out of the Cleveland Stadium crowd. The Browns' defense fought but with their backs to the wall and were unable to stop the Steelers from tacking on the game-clinching score, a one-yard plunge by Warren Williams with 1:56 to play. The Steelers had stunned the Browns and their fans with a downright ugly 17-7 victory. Thirty-five days after their first meeting, there had been a sixty-one-point turnaround.

"I never would have imagined the Pittsburgh Steelers coming in here and dominating our offense the way they did," a flustered Webster Slaughter said. "We've got problems which have to be taken care of inside the team." Perhaps with a players-only meeting, one writer suggested? "It's past that point," Slaughter replied.

Kosar placed the blame solely on his shoulders. "I really feel like I let a lot of people down today," he said. "The fans, the front office, the coaching staff, and, worst of all, I feel like I let down the players. I'm very disappointed with myself and the way we let this game get away from us."

Now at 3-3 with three of the next four games against playoff teams, the Browns were also in a position to let the season slip away from them as well.

23 Gathering Clouds

Most concluded that Bernie Kosar's timing had never been worse than during that Sunday's encounter in Pittsburgh. But they reconsidered two days later when Kosar announced the release of a candy bar named in his honor and contingent upon his popularity to raise money to fight adult illiteracy. Actually, the timing of the announcement was mere happenstance and unfortunate to occur in the shadow of his worst professional game.

In between launching a gooey chocolate enterprise, Kosar spent the week working on fundamentals with Marc Trestman. Though as a precaution, Bud Carson had Mike Pagel take more snaps with the first-team offense. Clearly, if Kosar came out flat again, Carson wouldn't hesitate to yank The Franchise. Now at 3-3 with the toughest portion of the schedule yet to come, the Browns had little margin for error. Eight days after the debacle against Pittsburgh, the Browns would be on *Monday Night Football* hosting the perennially powerful Chicago Bears.

After a sluggish start, the Browns started to return to normal. They soared to a 17-0 lead in the third quarter, and then turned the lights out on Chicago with a record-breaking 97-yard touchdown pass from Kosar to Webster Slaughter. It was the highlight of what turned out to be a 27-7 victory. The Browns were back to life with a 4-3 record and, thanks to another collapse by the Bengals the previous afternoon, locked in a three-way tie for first with Cincinnati and the Oilers. "There comes a time when you've got to pick yourself up to be a contender," Kosar said, "and I think we did that tonight."

To be sure, Kosar had done his part. The difference was like night and day: twenty-two of twenty-nine for 282 yards with two touchdowns, and more importantly after throwing six interceptions in his previous two games, no pick-offs. But the hero of this balmy October evening was Slaughter, who reeled in eight receptions for 186 yards and the unforgettable 97-yard bomb. After spray-painting his shoes orange along with Eric Metcalf in the hopes of sparking a turnaround, Slaughter had done just that. And in the process, was named the NFL Player of the Week.

Yet six days later, on a sun-splashed Sunday afternoon at the Stadium, it appeared as if the Browns had slipped back into the doldrums. At halftime of their critical divisional showdown with Houston, the Browns were down 10-0 and were lucky it wasn't worse. The offense was back to its anemic ways, tallying 57 total yards in the first thirty minutes, including a mind-numbing nine on the ground. The Oilers, meanwhile, had rolled up 186 total yards, and had it not been for some untimely mistakes, could have been ahead by three touchdowns.

Still, Carson was relatively calm in the locker room. "I told the team at halftime that by all rights we should be out of this game, but we're not," he said later. "I said, 'We have nothing to lose. Let's throw everything we have at them. And basically, that's what we did."

Did they ever.

On their first possession of the second half, aided by an 18-yard run by Reggie Langhorne on a reverse, the Browns marched 71 yards and scored when Kosar meandered into the end zone from five yards out on an improvised quarterback scramble. After the Cleveland defense halted the Oilers, the Browns took over at their own twenty. Kosar got the call from Trestman, turned to his teammates in the huddle with a smile, clapped his hands, and said, "Have I got a play for you!"

After taking the snap, he handed the football off to Eric Metcalf, who sprinted forward, then turned and flipped the ball back to Kosar. He then fired a strike downfield to a wide-open Webster Slaughter, who ran untouched into the end zone for an 80-yard touchdown that gave the Browns a 14-10 lead with 5:11 left in the third quarter. The capacity crowd, which had booed the offense throughout the first half, was roaring.

But unlike the 1988 regular-season finale, when the Oilers folded up the tents, this time they responded. Warren Moon hit Curtis Duncan for 55 yards to the Cleveland one. From there running back Mike Rozier scored a moment later. With the third quarter waning, Houston had reclaimed the lead. But once again, the Browns would storm right back.

There was no flea-flicker this time, but the result was the same. On second-and-seventeen from his own twenty-three, Kosar dropped back and fired a frozen rope upfield that sliced between two Oiler defenders to Slaughter, who once again sprinted unchallenged into the end zone. The Browns were on top, 21-17, with the game's third touchdown in four minutes. After another defensive stop, Cleveland landed the knockout blow.

From the Cleveland thirty-nine, Kosar handed off to Metcalf, who handed off to Langhorne, who pitched back to Kosar, who then rifled a pass to Metcalf along the sideline for 25 yards. The crowd, delirious with joy and surprise, hadn't seen anything yet. A play later, Kosar brought another grin to the huddle. "Well, here's another one you're gonna love," he quipped. Metcalf took a handoff on a sweep around right end, then stopped and launched a perfect spiral to a wide-open Langhorne in the end zone—the Browns' fourth critical trick play of the day. *"It's science-fiction time at Cleveland Stadium!"* a jubilant Nev Chandler told his radio audience. Thirteen minutes remained, but the shell-shocked Oilers were done. And after the resurgent Browns' offense ran out the final nine minutes, Cleveland was victorious, 28-17, and they were tied with the Bengals for first at 5-3.

"They couldn't do nothing else, so they reached into their bag of tricks," Houston linebacker Robert Lyles noted. "Conventional football was sent hurtling back to the Dark Ages." And by unveiling the trickery at precisely the appropriate moments, the Browns had hurtled themselves back into contention, avoiding a loss that would have dropped them to 1-3 in the division with rematches with the Bengals and Oilers yet to come.

Yet as the wacky win came to a close a chorus of boos echoed through Cleveland Stadium. Astute observers had noted something had occurred that hadn't happened in more than ten years: Ozzie Newsome hadn't caught a pass.

Newsome had taken himself out of the game early in the third quarter after spraining an ankle. Though Carson himself later asked Newsome to go into the game and snag his token catch to extend his streak, the Wizard of Oz declined. He remembered 1986, when he tried to play through painful injuries and wound up having his worst season. Not wanting to hurt the team, Newsome stayed on the sideline. And his streak of consecutive games with a reception, which had begun October 21, 1979, ended at 150.

"I think this is the best way for it to happen," said Newsome, who had announced in the preseason he'd retire after the season. "I've always said and do believe that winning is more important than anything I can do personally. It came down to where I felt it was more important for me to be ready to play next week than to keep the streak alive.

"All good things must come to an end. I feel like I caught ten passes because we won."

Once their disappointment subsided, Browns' fans couldn't help but note the streak had ended in typical Newsome fashion: with pure class.

While Newsome's star faded, Slaughter's continued to shine. Though the league informed him he could no longer wear his spray-painted shoes, it didn't affect his performance. Bolstered by his two long touchdowns, he snagged four receptions for 184 yards. It was his third consecutive 100-yard game and capped a once-in-a-lifetime October in which he caught twenty-eight passes for 582 yards. Appropriately, he was named AFC Player of the Month.

All things considered, October had been kind to the Browns. But with November upcoming and three tough road trips on the horizon, there was still a long way to go.

As the critical third month of the football season began, the Browns got some very welcome news. After thirty-three days in prison, Kevin Mack was released on shock probation on November 6, though under strict guidelines from Judge McMonagle. Mack was placed on probation for two years, during the first of which he couldn't speak publicly about drugs or his drug-related problems. He was ordered to continue counseling through Alcoholics Anonymous and the Inner Circle and would be subject to frequent urine checks. "If you have one dirty urine," McMonagle warned, "I'll send you back to prison."

Mack had no fear of slipping. After losing twenty pounds in what had certainly been the most harrowing month of his life, he talked like a man who had learned his lesson. "The prison experience really scared me," Mack said. "It has been really tough, but I made it this far. I know I can do it."

After undergoing knee surgery a month earlier, plus not having even practiced in nearly twelve weeks, Mack was still a good three weeks away from playing condition. Considering his physical limitations, plus the psychological trauma he'd been through, some wondered whether Mack would even contribute at all this season. When asked point blank if he'd play again in 1989, Mack didn't hesitate to say yes.

Next up for the Browns was a deceivingly difficult game in Tampa. The Buccaneers were a typical 3-5, but had proven dangerous by winning three of their first five, including victories over perennial playoff contenders New Orleans and Chicago. True to form, Tampa Bay took its opening possession and marched 80 yards to take a 7-0 lead.

But on the Browns' initial series, the Eric Metcalf Show began, to the delight of thousands of Cleveland fans on hand celebrating the first-ever Browns Backers' reunion in Tampa that weekend. The Browns drove to the Tampa twenty-four yard line, where Bernie Kosar lobbed a swing pass to Metcalf along the left sideline. The scatback sliced and diced through a smorgasbord of Buccaneer defenders, not stopping until he spun into the end zone to tie the contest. It was the opening salvo in what would become a career afternoon.

The next fifteen minutes would serve as a microcosm of beleaguered Tampa quarterback Vinny Testaverde's shaky first three years in the NFL. Three interceptions led to twenty-one Cleveland points – including returns for scores by Felix Wright and Thane Gash – and gave the Browns a comfortable 28-7 advantage.

The remainder of the afternoon was a defensive coach's nightmare, with both offenses trading big plays. The Buccaneers cut it to 35-24 going into the fourth quarter before the Browns landed the knockout punch—thrown, appropriately, by Metcalf. In the opening minute of the final quarter, from the Bucs' forty-three, Metcalf took a handoff on a sweep around left end, faked a handoff to Reggie Langhorne then swept upfield along the sideline. When the defense began to surround him, he cut back like a gazelle on the Serengetti and ran diagonally until out of danger and angled his way into the end zone for yet another dazzling touchdown unlike any other Browns' fans had ever seen.

The final was 42-31 and the Browns escaped the Florida heat with a 6-3 record, and, after the Bengals lost to Bo Jackson and the Los Angeles Raiders later that afternoon, regained sole possession of first place.

The win had been sparked by the fatal combination of the Browns' attacking, touchdown-hungry defense and the uncanny broken-field running of Eric Metcalf. The rookie from Texas finished the day with 233 all-purpose yards: 52 receiving, 87 rushing, and 94 on kickoff returns. For one game at least, Metcalf had become the triple-threat weapon Ernie Accorsi had envisioned on draft day. And come what may, for the remainder of 1989 and beyond his exhibition in Tampa would serve as a sign for opposing defenses to be wary of his explosiveness.

As it happened, though Metcalf would still do some special things in the years to come, he was never again quite as good and as versatile as that magical November afternoon in Florida.

Next up was a headache-inducing trip to the Seattle Kingdome, where the Browns had lost five of seven games over the previous twelve years. But this time, the Browns emerged victorious in an otherwise bland 17-7 victory highlighted by another sterling defensive performance.

After their fourth straight win, the Browns stood at 7-3, a game in front of Houston and two up on the struggling Bengals. They were in the driver's seat for the division title, and some fans were already starting to talk about the possibility of locking up home-field advantage throughout the playoffs. October's sour stretch now seemed like years ago, and the Browns felt they were playing as soundly as they had at any point over the past five seasons.

And with everything running smoothly on all cylinders, Marty Schottenheimer would come back to town.

It was one of the most highly anticipated conference calls the members of the Cleveland media could remember. After more than four years of dealing with Marty Schottenheimer on a day-to-day basis, passionately praising and criticizing him through their respective forums, now he was just another opposing coach to whom they would fire off a round of questions about how he thought his team matched up with the Browns.

When Schottenheimer finally came on the speakerphone, he was unusually cheery, asking how everyone had been, almost as if he were an old friend who had moved away. But eventually he got down to the business at hand: denying that the upcoming Browns-Chiefs game had any truly special meaning for him or his seven former Cleveland assistants. Would it be his own personal Super Bowl, as Bud Carson had called the Browns' opener in Pittsburgh? "Not at all," Schottenheimer remarked. "You know me well enough."

Schottenheimer's former players certainly knew him well enough to see that what he'd done with the Chiefs was eerily reminiscent of what he started doing in Cleveland in 1985. The team wasn't a bona fide playoff contender yet, but it had shown the ability to compete with anyone. The Chiefs' strength was its running game, led by bruising fullback Christian Okoye, and a much-improved defense, which was ranked second in the league against the pass. While inconsistent, Kansas City was certainly dangerous.

Yet it wasn't exactly an emotional afternoon at Cleveland Stadium for Schottenheimer, though he expected it would be. He actually got lost in the bowels of the Stadium looking for the visitors' locker room, where he had infrequently visited previously. But as he wandered, he received several salutations from Stadium and Browns' employees, wishing him well and noting how nice it was to see him. Clearly, this was a man who had not been run out of town. On the other hand, Schottenheimer couldn't help but notice a cadre of Browns' fans behind the Kansas City bench prior to kickoff chanting "Marty sucks!" Schottenheimer turned to his sixteen-year-old son Brian and smiled. "Brian, listen," he said, "a year ago it was the other way around, so don't worry about it." Even aside from the former coach's homecoming, there would be plenty of emotion in a contest that would last more than four hours.

After a month of cruising along, the Browns were thrust back into the stagnation that plagued them in early October. They committed twelve penalties and turned the football over five times. They made inexcusable special-teams mistakes. The teams would combine for a record-tying twenty-three punts. And while the defense was once again powerful, holding Okoye to a harmless 40 yards on twenty-one carries, it was in over its head, particularly since the Chiefs' lone touchdown was scored courtesy of the Browns' offense. When Mike Oliphant coughed up a handoff from Kosar at the Cleveland three on the second play of the second half, Kansas City lineman Neil Smith recovered and rolled into the end zone for a 7-3 lead.

Still, behind their defense, the Browns hung tough and took a 10-7 lead on an Eric Metcalf touchdown plunge late in the third quarter. The game continued its staggering progression on a cold, gray November afternoon well into the fourth quarter, when a Metcalf fumble gave the Chiefs new life. Kansas City parlayed the miscue into the game-tying field goal with less than four minutes to play. After the Cleveland offense failed to ignite for a final drive, the Chiefs did, setting up with ten seconds left a 45-yard field goal attempt by Nick Lowery, one of the best kickers in NFL history. Lowery hooked it wide right, but the Browns' Mike Johnson was penalized for lining up offside and Lowery was given another chance. Incredibly, he missed again from 40 yards, this time wide left, and an ugly game plunged into what would be an even less attractive overtime session.

The Browns had new life and appeared ready to cash in on it after winning the coin toss and driving into Kansas City territory. But after taking a short screen pass to the Chiefs' thirty yard line, Oliphant did it again. He fumbled and Kansas City recovered, ending what would turn out to be the home team's final chance to win. The Chiefs, as it happened, would have one more.

With the sudden-death clock melting down toward zero, quarterback Steve DeBerg marched his weary offense into Cleveland territory to set up yet another chance to win the game for Nick Lowery, this time with a 47-yard boot with seventeen seconds left. But incredibly, Lowery, who had hit 78 percent of his field-goal attempts over the course of his career, missed badly, and the Browns and Chiefs lingered around the field looking at one another. Part of the shock was Lowery's miss. "I had never missed three straight kicks in my life," he would say later. But that was only the tip of the iceberg. The game was over, yet there was no victor. The result was a 10-10 tie, the Browns' first since 1973 and initial stalemate after the dawn of overtime in 1977.

Though they hadn't been defeated, the Browns looked and acted as if they had. "It was a tough game to lose," Bud Carson said at his press conference before quickly correcting himself. The good news was that technically, even though the Oilers won, the Browns still held sole possession of first place by a half-game. The bad news was that as they dragged their weary bones to the locker room after five exhausting periods, the clock was already ticking toward their next game. In less than ninety-one hours, they would suit up again in Detroit to face the Lions on Thanksgiving Day.

Still, most fans weren't worried. The Lions were, after all, 2-9, clearly one of the worst teams in the league, and had been decimated by injury. With the game just a short trip away in Pontiac, the Browns would have a strong contingent of support at what would otherwise be a phlegmatic Silverdome. That Tuesday, Bud Carson's wife Linda was being interviewed on a local radio station and remarked, "It's unthinkable that we won't win this game." So certain was she of victory, she would stay home and cook Thanksgiving dinner rather than attend.

The Browns apparently were thinking the same thing.

Despite facing the league's second-worst defense, the Cleveland offense was invisible for the second straight week, managing just ten points. And despite having seven starters out with injury, including starting quarterback Rodney Peete, the Lions looked like the better team all afternoon. Rookie running back Barry Sanders torched the Browns' defense for 145 yards—the first 100-yard performance against Cleveland all year. The Browns were once again self-destructive with ten penalties, two of which killed their final scoring threat in the fourth quarter. Aside from a 38-yard touchdown run by little-used Barry Redden late in the first half, the running game was atrocious.

Yet perhaps the most unnerving news came from Bernie Kosar. He had a decent game statistically, throwing for 296 yards, but said his right elbow, originally injured in Seattle ten days earlier then re-aggravated against the Chiefs, was still tender. There was no relation to the injury the year before for which he missed half the season, but many felt no matter how minor this was, it was affecting Kosar's game. It wasn't what Browns' fans wanted to hear taking a division race into December.

Add it all together and the Browns lost a very winnable game to the struggling Lions, 13-10. Though Cleveland caught a break the following Sunday when both

Houston and Cincinnati lost, a bad feeling slowly rippled through the team. The Browns would have ten days off to think about their embarrassing last two games before suiting up for a rematch with the also-slipping, 6-6 Cincinnati Bengals, who were one loss away from getting booted out of the title race.

"Now we have our backs to the wall," Bud Carson said after the loss in Detroit. "We can't back up anymore."

Yet as it turned out, they could.

There would be no reason to expect another sour performance December 3 when Cincinnati came to town, they assumed. After all, a win against Sam Wyche's bumbling Bengals, who had lost five of their last seven, would bring the AFC Central race down to Houston and Cleveland with three games to play.

What's more, the week before the game, Wyche was once again spouting off about the inadequacies of the Dog Pound. Calling the Dog Pound's conduct "a disgrace to their city," Wyche added, "Art Modell never said boo about it until the national attention began to bring some disgrace on his club. Let's just face it up to here. It's been condoned and really kind of supported by the Cleveland Browns' management over the past few years.

"Common sense has to jump in. So far, common sense has not been part of the credo of the Cleveland organization. It's been, 'Go for it, Dog Pound; throw everything you want.'"

With comments like these, one had to wonder if the showman Wyche was trying to get the Pound to stop or start throwing things.

Either way, the Browns certainly could not plead to lack of motivation. With their first-place standing on the line, plus a chance to shut up a mouthy arch-nemesis and enact revenge after a disheartening loss in Cincinnati in September, the Browns had every reason to play their hearts out.

Yet with a wind-chill factor of twenty below as the backdrop, they came out and looked worse than in either of their previous two disappointments. When the frozen dirt settled, the final was 21-0 Bengals, the first shutout of the Browns in five years and first in Cleveland in twelve.

Yet again, the Cleveland offense was putrid. Things got so bad that for the first time since his rookie year, Bernie Kosar (still nursing the sore elbow) was benched after three quarters in favor of Mike Pagel. It did little good. Nor did Carson's desperate decision to insert a still-unready Kevin Mack in the second half. Mack carried the football once and was pounded for a three-yard loss.

No one was questioning the Cleveland defense. It was Marc Trestman and the offense that was about to be run out of town after scoring a mere twenty points in three games. During that stretch, Kosar had gone fourteen straight quarters without throwing a touchdown pass. To no one's surprise, the running game was once again not a factor, though the Browns kept trying, perhaps resulting in their own undoing.

An already struggling offensive line got even more bad news when right guard Dan Fike went down with a ligament tear in his knee. He would miss the remainder of the season.

After three terrible weeks, the Browns had finally fallen out of first place and were looking up at Houston with the Bengals now just a half-game back and the resurgent Steelers closing in. Yet Cleveland still controlled its own destiny. With wins in its final three games, it could still win the division and make the playoffs. The Browns would look to the following Sunday in the Hoosier Dome in Indianapolis as the day everything would turn around.

Despite the fireworks that would come that late afternoon and evening, the most memorable moment for the Browns in Week Fourteen occurred in Cincinnati. As the Bengals battled the Seattle Seahawks in the second half of a close game, some fans at Riverfront Stadium began throwing snowballs at the Seahawks as they drove toward the Bengal end zone. It snapped Sam Wyche into action. He stormed over to a stadium employee with a microphone hooked into the public-address system and snatched it from him. Wyche then uttered the words that, for better or worse, would define his coaching career.

"Would the next person who sees anybody throw anything, point them out and get them out of here," he barked. "You don't live in Cleveland, you live in Cincinnati!"

The Riverfront crowd roared its approval. It mattered little that the snowball-throwing continued or that the Bengals managed to blow a ten-point lead and all but destroyed their division-title hopes by losing to the sub-.500 Seahawks. Wyche had once again scored points in his hometown by ripping on his upstate neighbors.

While his tactics gained much national attention, those who had followed Wyche's antics over the previous four years put the outburst in perspective. First, Wyche seemed to have ignored the fact that there had been no incidents of anything being thrown from the stands in the Browns' last five home games, including the week before when he all but implored the fans to fire away at his Bengals. Many wondered why Wyche kept bringing up the topic since it appeared to have been taken care of.

"Let me see if I have this straight," wrote *Plain Dealer* columnist Joe Dirck. "If a couple of nuts throw stuff in the Stadium, it's Cleveland's fault. But if a couple nuts throw stuff in Riverfront Stadium, why then it's . . . Cleveland's fault. Hmmm."

But even more conspicuous was Wyche's timing. With his Bengals faltering in the waning moments, he seemed to fall back on a tried-and-true method to take heat off his football team: make himself the story, not his team's underachieving play. Adding to this theory was Wyche's verbal attack of the officiating crew after a questionable call late in the contest. Wyche then barred reporters from the locker room after the game in violation of league rules. Altogether, it was classic

Wicky Wacky. And accordingly, Dirck encouraged Clevelanders not to take out their anger on the citizens of the Queen City. After all, he explained, "it's not their fault their football squad is in the hands of an unstable towel-snapper who leads the league in whining and always seems to be on the verge of a nervous break-down when his team goes in the tank."

Yet for all the tomfoolery taking place along the Ohio River, the Browns couldn't concern themselves with it. "I've pulled out all the stops this week," Bud Carson said. "I've told everyone else to, too. If we lose this one, we're done. This is it for us." And with the season hanging in the balance, they came out strong in Indianapolis, playing better than they had in the previous month. They surged to a 17-7 lead early in the third quarter when Keith Jones blocked a punt, and Lawyer Tillman recovered it in the end zone for a touchdown. They were then poised to salt the game away with just over five minutes remaining.

Leading 17-10, the Browns had driven to the Colts' ten yard line, where they faced third-and-goal. A field goal would force the struggling Indianapolis offense, which had lost starting quarterback Jack Trudeau to injury, to score twice in the waning moments. Rather than playing it safe, the playcall was a pass, which Bernie Kosar flung into the end zone in the face of a blitz, assuming he was throwing the football away. Instead, Brian Brennan had run the wrong route, taking two de-fenders with him right to where the ball was thrown. The Colts' Keith Taylor intercepted it and returned it 77 yards before Kosar tripped him up at the Cleve-land twenty-five. The Colts tied the game with just under two minutes remaining.

Despite being crushed by the kind of turn of events that had crippled the team over the previous month, the Browns didn't fold up the tents. They hurriedly drove to the Indy twenty-one and called on Matt Bahr for a chip-shot field goal to win the game with less than thirty seconds to play. The kick sailed left, over the upright, no good. The game would continue into sudden-death overtime, and so would the Browns' nightmares.

They once again appeared to have victory in their grasp on their second pos-session of overtime, when Gerald McNeil returned a punt 46 yards to the Colt forty-two. The Cleveland offense, untracked for the first time since Tampa Bay, marched to the seventeen and called on Bahr again for an even shorter field-goal attempt of 35 yards for the win. This one also hooked left, then bounced off the upright and fell away, no good. It seemed this was not the Browns' day.

Yet they continued to persevere. The defense held, and Kosar and company took over at midfield. However, when the Colts unleashed the same blitz package that had sabotaged the Browns late in the fourth quarter, Kosar made the same mistake. He hurled an ill-advised pass toward an unsuspecting Brennan over the middle. Brennan, simply clearing the Indianapolis zone for the other receivers, had no chance to catch the football, and it was picked off by Colts' safety Mike Prior at the forty-two yard line. Prior then sprinted upfield untouched and scored the game-winning touchdown, handing the Browns their most frustrating loss of the season. "After last Sunday," Ray Yannucci would write, "one gets the feeling this team is not supposed to win."

How else could you explain it? Bahr, who in his career had hit better than 83 percent of his field-goal-attempts within 40 yards, including his last twelve, missed two potential game-winners. Not surprisingly, Bahr called it the worst day of his career. The offense, under so much fire for the previous four weeks, exploded for 470 yards, but managed just seventeen points thanks to untimely mistakes and turnovers that included two fumbles inside the Indianapolis forty. Kosar threw for 353 yards, his best game of the year, yet tossed two inexcusable and uncharacteristic interceptions that cost his team the game. "We did all the things that losers do," a solemn Bud Carson said afterward.

More than bad luck, the Browns now appeared to have fires raging within the organization. Capping a week filled with criticism of Marc Trestman, former Washington general manager-turned-journalist Bobby Beathard reported on NBC's pre-game show that day that Bernie Kosar had been running the offense entirely on his own and that there would be major changes on the Browns' coaching staff for 1990. Adding fuel to the fire later that week was a rumor that Carson would take away the playcalling duties from Trestman and hand them to running backs coach George Sefcik. Then, a *Columbus Dispatch* story reported that Carson had called for a running play on the third-down interception that turned the tide in the fourth quarter and either Trestman or Kosar had overruled him and called for a pass. When asked about it later, Carson wouldn't deny it.

With controversy swirling, the Browns could only stand back and watch their 1989 season circle the drain. With Houston's win over Tampa Bay, the Oilers were a game-and-a-half ahead of Cleveland, which dropped to 7-6-1 and now hadn't won in four weeks. To stay alive, the Browns would have to beat the playoff-bound Minnesota Vikings in Week Fifteen and hope arch-nemesis Sam Wyche would come through by beating the Oilers in Cincinnati. If both happened, the AFC Central Division title would be decided in a regular-season finale showdown between the Oilers and Browns in the Astrodome.

The stage was set for an incredible finish.

24 Last Stand

There was nothing the Browns could do about the Oilers-Bengals game the following Sunday or their own matchup in Houston a week after. Their only choice was to focus on the Vikings, who themselves were one win away from clinching their first NFC Central championship in nine years. Though buoyed on offense by the midseason trade for star running back Herschel Walker, Minnesota's real strength was its defense, which entered Week Fifteen ranked first in the NFL and showcased the league's most ferocious pass rush. Instantly, there would be matchup problems for the Browns' banged-up offensive line. Right tackle Cody Risien had been playing hurt all year, continually putting off an inevitable knee surgery. Worse, Dan Fike was lost for the season, and in his place stepped little-used Tony Jones at right guard, signed as an undrafted free agent the year before.

The cold spell that had haunted Cleveland all month continued on Sunday, December 17, with the wind-chill factor at a ghoulish twenty-five below just two days after ten inches of snow had fallen on the city. Still, 70,777 braved the icy climate in the hopes that the Browns could salvage something out of what had somehow become a nightmarish season.

With the teams adjusting to the cold and the poor field conditions, there was little offense in the first half. A cavalcade of punts carried the game into the final moments of the second quarter, when Browns' running back Barry Redden fumbled and the Vikings recovered at the Cleveland thirty-six. The visitors cashed it in for a 44-yard field goal by Rich Karlis, playing his first game at Cleveland Stadium since he broke the Browns' hearts in the 1986 AFC Championship.

While the Browns and Vikings were locked in a polar war on the shores of Lake Erie, at the opposite end of the state, something bizarre was occurring in Cincinnati. By the time the Browns reached halftime, the Bengals led Houston 28-0, and things were just getting interesting. As welcome as that news was, if the Browns couldn't rally, the impending Oiler defeat would be meaningless to them.

And much to their chagrin, the second half began much the same way as the first, with an exchange of punts. But on the Browns' second possession, they finally caught a break. Minnesota was flagged for a 26-yard pass-interference penalty that gave Cleveland a first down at the Viking five yard line. On the next play, Kosar rolled out and finally ended his drought. He hit recently acquired tight end Ron Middleton in the end zone for a touchdown, giving the Browns a 7-3 lead and marking Kosar's first scoring pass in thirty-five days.

But just when it appeared the teams were destined for a single-digit outcome in single-digit weather, the texture of the game rapidly changed. After a punt, the Vikings began rolling into Cleveland territory, and Herschel Walker broke loose for a 26-yard touchdown run with a minute showing in the third quarter. Yet the Browns hardly broke a sweat. A play later, Kosar hit Reggie Langhorne crossing over the middle, and Langhorne scooted past Minnesota defenders that were slipping on the treacherous dirt-caked middle of the field and sprinted into the end zone for a lightning-like, 62-yard touchdown to close the third quarter. The Browns now led, 14-10, with fifteen minutes to play. And the Bengals now led the Oilers, 38-0.

Both defenses stepped back up for the fourth quarter. The Browns stuffed Minnesota on fourth-and-one at the Cleveland twenty-two with nine minutes left, but the Vikes forced the Browns to go three-and-out on two straight possessions. Finally, with veteran quarterback Tommy Kramer now at the controls in place of injured Wade Wilson, the Vikings once again took control. Using a short yet effective passing game, Kramer drove Minnesota to the Cleveland two yard line, where on fourth-and-goal with less than four minutes left, he lobbed a touchdown pass to tight end Steve Jordan to give the visitors a 17-14 lead. The entire season would now rest on the shoulders of the Browns' beleaguered and banged-up offense, which had already lost left guard Ted Banker with a rib injury earlier in the game and was about to lose Cody Risien on the ensuing drive. Rickey Bolden, just activated after missing most of the season due to injury, was thrust in at left guard, where he hadn't played all year. Tony Jones was shifted to right tackle and long-snapper Tom Baugh was inserted at right guard.

Yet the embattled Kosar wouldn't quit. Mixing effective passes with powerful runs by still-rusty Kevin Mack, the Browns reached the Minnesota fourteen with twenty-nine seconds left. For the third time in two weeks, they called on Matt Bahr to attempt a clutch field goal. With the Stadium crowd and thousands of other fans holding their breath at home, Bahr calmly pushed his 32-yard kick through the uprights to send the game to overtime. A frozen sigh of relief escaped from the more than 70,000 at the old ballpark on the lake.

The Browns won the coin toss, but were stuffed on their first drive as were the Vikings moments later. Taking over at his own twenty-one for the next series, Kosar dropped back behind his patchwork line and lofted a perfect pass down the sideline for Langhorne, who would finish the day with a career-best 140 yards receiving. He reeled in the pass for a 39-yard gain into Minnesota territory. Playing it safe from there, the Browns inched closer, and when they reached the Vikings' fourteen, Bud Carson called on the field-goal unit to end the game on third down.

Yet Browns' special teams coach Paul Lanham had an idea he lobbied to see executed. It was a play the Browns had worked on in practice all season but had never used in a game, though there had been discussion of using it in Indianapolis the week before. During the timeout prior to the play, he won Carson over, and as Bahr took the field, he was only one of a handful of people in the stadium who knew he wouldn't be kicking the ball. Holder Mike Pagel took the snap for what everyone thought would be a 32-yard field-goal attempt. Instead, as the Vikings burst desperately through the line, Pagel stood up, spun around, and lobbed a pass to linebacker Van Waiters, who had come off his block and turned upfield. Waiters caught the pass at the fifteen and waltzed into the end zone for a remarkable game-winning touchdown. He sprinted up the hill separating the bleachers from the stands and was engulfed by the Dog Pound in a massive celebration. The Browns had gritted out a frosty 23-17 overtime win against one of the NFL's best teams and had lived to fight another day.

And the victory wasn't the only thing that had fallen in the Browns' favor that afternoon. When the dust settled in Cincinnati, the Bengals had abused the Oilers to the tune of a 61-7 stomping. It became clear in the first half that it was Cincinnati's day, with the Bengals leading 31-0 at the intermission. But it was in the final thirty minutes that Wicky Wacky Wyche once again took center stage. Leading 45-0, he called for an onside kick. After putting his reserves in, he kept calling for long passes and used the same offensive game plan as the first team. Up 58-7 in the final seconds, he sent out his field-goal team. Wyche wanted to make a statement on the field. And naturally, when it was over, he made a few off it.

"They're just such an obnoxious team," he said of Jerry Glanville's Oilers. "We've sent them home with their tails between their legs, which is as it should be.... This is the dumbest football team, the most stupid, undisciplined team. It's just ridiculous.

"I don't like their team, and I don't like their people. I wish today was a five-quarter game."

While some wondered why Wyche would open himself up to future payback and ridicule, others noticed the continuation of a season-long trend. When the Bengals played Tampa Bay in late October, Wyche kept the full-court press on the Buccaneers to the tune of a 56-23 win. When they hosted Detroit three weeks later, the Bengals again racked up unnecessary points after the outcome had been decided in a 42-7 win. On both occasions, Wyche appeared to be trying to win two games at once. He knew his opponent was scheduled to play the Browns the following week, and perhaps a sound stomping would inspire and anger them to the point of pulling an upset over Cleveland. It didn't work with Tampa, but the Lions did manage to beat the Browns. Now Wyche, whose Bengals still had a chance to make the playoffs, was hoping the Oilers would come out with fire in their eye the following week and blast the Browns. If Houston won, then the Bengals were victorious in Minnesota Christmas night, Cincinnati would take the division title.

Of course, the wily Wyche didn't come right out and reveal his intentions. "I would hate to have to ride home on that plane and play the Cleveland Browns next week," he said. "Cleveland has no quit in them, no matter what. They are not that kind of people. I can't see that sorry team we played today doing any better next week than they did against us."

The Oilers would have plenty of reason to come out angry six days later. Conversely, the Browns were back from the dead. And the entire roller-coaster season would come down to an old-fashioned Saturday-night Texas shootout in the Houston Astrodome two days before Christmas.

"Get the smelling salt," Tony Grossi wrote. "The Browns are off the canvas with one more bloody round to go."

After enduring one of the cruelest and coldest Decembers in Cleveland history, the Browns received no respite upon their arrival in Texas. Houston was enduring record cold of its own, blanketed by snow for the first time in five years and belted by single-digit temperatures and a sharp wind-chill factor of nearly twenty below. Houston was brought to a standstill. Traffic crept along at a tortoise pace, hindered by nearly 200 weather-related accidents. As it happened, when the Browns arrived, the power was out in the Astrodome, so the team spent much of its Friday practice in the dark.

Luckily, the game would be played indoors, and both the Oilers and Browns knew that with a defeat, they would face the possibility of receiving criticism as harsh as the weather. "Never before in all my twenty years in the NFL have I been involved where one game meant the difference between a good season and a bad one," Ernie Accorsi said. True enough; a win would make 1989 quite a satisfying season for the Browns, winning the division after a year hiatus with a first-year coaching staff. A loss, on the other hand, would all but eliminate the team from the playoff picture with an unimpressive 8-7-1 record, wrapping up a season of underachievement. The Oilers were in a similar boat. This was supposed to be their year, and they'd been in the driver's seat to win the title two weeks before. But after getting emasculated in Cincinnati, to lose the division at home in the finale would be unacceptable. What happened in the previous fifteen weeks mattered little to either team. The 1989 season would be judged on what they did in the finale—just as had been the case one year earlier.

But the Browns were dealt a psychological blow when Neil Mullen, the man who had roamed the Browns' sideline at Cleveland Stadium dressed as Santa Claus for the previous few years, was not permitted to be on the field at the Astrodome for the game. A Cleveland television station made sure he had a seat, but fans could only wonder if that would count toward extending his streak: the Browns were 10-0 with Mullen on the field.

Even with St. Nick in the house, it would be anything but a silent night in Houston.

It was the largest crowd in Oiler history, and every fan made his presence felt from the get-go. Yet with the Astrodome rocking, the battle-fatigued Cleveland offense stayed calm. Bernie Kosar and his comrades, many of whom had once again spray-painted their shoes orange, took the opening kickoff and marched steadily down the field, taking a 3-0 lead on a short Matt Bahr field goal. Houston also came out hot on its first possession, with Warren Moon leading the way. But on third down from the Browns' twenty-eight, Moon threw an ill-advised pass that was intercepted at the one by Felix Wright, his old Canadian league nemesis, and the Browns took over. Two plays later, Kosar hit Eric Metcalf on a short pass over the middle, and the elusive rookie, making his first return to the state where he'd excelled in college, did his thing. He juked and cut through the Houston defense, angled along the sideline, and coasted into the end zone for a dazzling 68-yard touchdown that gave the Browns a 10-0 lead. The record crowd was stunned.

Things only got worse for the home team. After an exchange of punts, the Browns crossed midfield with two minutes to play in the half. From the Houston forty, Kosar, correctly reading a safety blitz, lofted a long pass for Slaughter on a fly pattern. Houston's Cris Dishman had perfect coverage, but Slaughter managed to trap the ball against his facemask as Dishman hit the ground, and the Browns' wiry wideout galloped into the end zone for another touchdown and a stunning 17-0 lead. The Astrodome echoed with boos as the largest crowd in Oilers' history turned against their home team. The Oilers salvaged themselves somewhat with a quick drive and field goal to cut the margin to 17-3 at the half, but the Houston faithful were in shock. Their team, which just two weeks before had all but sown up its first-ever Central Division crown, had now been outscored 78-10 in its last six quarters. The Browns were thirty minutes away from the playoffs. But naturally, things would not continue quite so easily.

Moon got the offense righted on its first possession of the third quarter, gliding 73 yards and making it 17-10 on a scoring pass to Drew Hill. The Browns' offense, which had looked so resourceful and poised in the first half, then reverted back to its late-November troubles. On their next three possessions, the Browns picked up just one first down and didn't cross midfield the entire period. As the fourth quarter began, Houston drove from its own one yard line to kick a field goal to make it 17-13. After another Cleveland punt, the Oilers began driving again for what appeared would be the back-breaking go-ahead score. They reached the Browns' fifteen with six minutes left. Then, with hopes for victory fading fast, one play epitomized the entire Browns' season.

On first down, Moon stood behind center in the shotgun barking out signals to his offense. But drowned in the waves of sound rocking the Astrodome, center Jay Pennison couldn't hear them. He snapped the ball toward Moon while his head was turned, and it sailed past him. Moon ran backward to recover it and fell on it at the thirty-five, only to have the football squirt loose again. At the thirty-three, Clay Matthews bent over and scooped up the football, and with that, thousands of Browns' fans sighed with relief. With the clock ticking down under five minutes, this turnover might just save the season. Even if the Browns' offense couldn't score, they could melt some precious time off the clock and limit Houston's chance to score again. After a dismal second half, Matthews had saved the day. Most fans were so swept with relief they weren't completely paying attention to what happened next.

Though Matthews had room to run in front of him, he stopped as soon as he had possession and spun around. He spotted Browns' lineman Chris Pike flanking him and, for reasons that may never be understood, flipped the football toward Pike. Though Pike was 6'7", Matthews' toss was well off the mark, floating over Pike and hitting the ground again, bouncing backward. Another pileup ensued at the Browns' twenty-eight, and it was there that Houston receiver Ernest Givins recovered, giving the Oilers not only possession but also a fresh set of downs following two changes of possession.

"What is Clay Matthews thinking of?!" Nev Chandler demanded on the radio, genuinely wanting to know. *"What is Clay Matthews thinking of?! The Browns had the football!"*

"Talk about a short circuit," Doug Dieken added.

"The Browns have to be shocked," Nev Chandler said, still in disbelief.

They were. So much so that their ill-conceived blitz on the following play was devoured by Warren Moon. He looped a precision pass for Drew Hill, who sprinted uncovered past Felix Wright and reeled in the toss for a touchdown and a 20-17 lead with 4:46 to play.

True, almost five minutes remained, but it didn't take much analysis to deduce two things. One, the 1989 Browns' season might very well be over. And two, if so, Clay Matthews was a dead man.

With the crowd now roaring louder than it had all night, the Cleveland offense looked scared on the ensuing possession. Under pressure, Kosar threw three straight incompletions, and the Browns punted with 4:13 left. The Oilers were now in the same position the Browns would have been had Matthews simply hung onto the football a minute earlier. With a couple first downs, Houston could clinch the division title and send the Browns whimpering back to Cleveland. But, crippled by a first-down holding penalty, the Oilers went backward. On third-and-eleven, Browns' corner Mark Harper crashed through to sack Moon and give the beleaguered visitors new life.

Two minutes and thirty seconds remained. The Browns would take over from their own forty-one yard line, realistically only needing 30 yards for a field-goal attempt. But considering how the team's previous four overtime games had gone in 1989, playing for the tie wasn't a comforting thought. Deep down, both the Browns and their fans knew that a touchdown was needed to secure victory—and this after two quarters of the offensive ineptitude that had characterized the previous month.

Kosar hit Slaughter for 11 then caught a break when Richard Johnson couldn't hang onto a potential interception. The Browns' beat-up quarterback then hit Langhorne for nine yards to the thirty-nine at the two-minute warning. On third-and-one, Kosar crashed forward for three yards. Then, with time running out and the Oilers expecting pass, the Browns switched gears. They would turn their hopes for the tumultuous season over to the only man on the team who had faced even more adversity.

Kevin Mack, who had carried the football just nine times all night and had been wheezing after his first full quarter of action in over a year, barreled through the line on first down and wasn't collared until he reached the Oiler twenty-four after a 12-yard gain. The Browns called their second time out, then were charged with their third when Lawyer Tillman was injured going for an incomplete pass on the next snap. One minute, twenty-five seconds remained. Kosar hit Lang-horne for nine, which set up the biggest third down of the season at the fifteen yard line. With the clock ticking down like the tapping foot of an executioner on the gallows, the call again was to Mack. And once again, he crashed through the line like a tank, rumbling over tacklers for 11 yards and a first down at the four.

The clock continued to run, and the Oilers were panicked. Once again, they anticipated pass, and once again, they were fooled. The play was as simple as football got: a handoff to Mack up the middle. He cracked into linebacker Robert Lyles at the four and bounced off. He then smashed into safety Bubba McDowell at the goal line and proved the stronger. Kevin Mack fell forward into the end zone for the go-ahead touchdown with thirty-nine seconds remaining. "He wanted that touchdown as bad as he's wanted anything in his life," Mike Johnson would say. The record crowd was silenced once and for all.

In the celebration that followed on the Cleveland sideline, it would have been easy to forget that just forty-eight days before, Mack had been sitting in a jail cell, wondering if he would ever play football again. He'd made the mistake of his life and had paid a dear price for it. Ashamed and scared, the days passed slowly—slower still as his team floundered without him. He'd persevered, returned to action, and though he played a small, almost insignificant role over the past month, he'd now scored one of the most important touchdowns in the history of the Cleveland Browns to signify one of the most important moments of his life.

The harried Oilers reached midfield with seven seconds left, where Warren Moon's final, desperate Hail Mary was caught, appropriately, by the guy who had followed him from Canada and continued to harass him on the football field: Felix Wright. Moon, despite establishing himself as one of the league's finest quarterbacks, despite going out of his way to point out why he didn't want to play in Cleveland when he came to the NFL six years earlier, dropped to 1-9 lifetime against the orange-clad warriors from Lake Erie.

The Cleveland Browns were the 1989 AFC Central Division champions. The regular season, after all its schizophrenic mood swings, finally had a happy ending.

Bud Carson had won two Super Bowls and had coached in another, but he didn't hesitate to call the 24-20 win the biggest of his career. Appropriately, the locker room festivities that followed felt like a big Christmas party.

"God bless us," Matt Bahr proclaimed in his best Tiny Tim impression, "every one!"

Kevin Mack, who kept the football, openly wept as Modell embraced and kissed him on the cheek. "It made up for some," he said of the touchdown heard 'round Cleveland, "but not all of it."

For the fourth time in five years, the Browns were division champions. And the little nagging details that hung over the victory like storm clouds over a parade didn't seem to matter: Warren Moon had carved up the attack defense for 414 yards. Eric Metcalf hadn't played in the second half with a toe injury. Despite the early fireworks and the classy final drive, the offense had still looked shaky. And of course, there was Clay Matthews.

"When Clay decided to lateral the football, I began to think it was not meant to be," Carson said. "I could have killed him. And I would have if we would have lost."

Carson would have had plenty of volunteers to help. Without the comeback, Matthews might well have never been able to set foot in Cleveland again. But Browns' fans seem to have forgotten that Matthews was a southern California guy. He was a Lakers' fan, a Magic Johnson fan, and it had been Showtime. He was a playmaker, and had done just that sort of thing before, most notably a lateral to Carl Hairston against the Bengals in 1987. But never had Matthews done anything so damaging or taken such an unnecessary risk at such an inopportune time.

"In retrospect," he said, "I guess it was a little silly."

Of course, had he not have done that and Mack's touchdown not have been necessary, it wouldn't have been quite as dramatic a finish to the 1989 season.

Perhaps appropriately, after the Browns arrived back in Cleveland at dawn on Christmas Eve, Matthews' 1973 Mercury Capri, which he had driven for his entire NFL career, wouldn't start. A teammate gave him a jump. The Browns, like Matthews' beat-up Capri, would keep on rolling.

25 One More Time

As the Browns caught their breath and enjoyed the week off that came with winning their division, they prepared to face a team that had been a shadowy reflection of itself in 1989. The Buffalo Bills, after going 12-4 and coming to within a game of the Super Bowl the year before, had begun the season with great promise, winning seven of their first ten games. Then, just like the Browns, they fell apart over the final six weeks of the season, losing four and barely securing the AFC East title in the face of some key injuries. But with quarterback Jim Kelly, running back Thurman Thomas, and wide receiver Andre Reed leading one of the league's most lethal up-and-coming offenses and defensive end Bruce Smith and linebacker Shane Conlan spearheading a formidable defense, defeating the Bills would prove no easy task in a divisional playoff at Cleveland Stadium on the first Saturday of the new decade.

Though the offensive line was still a shadow of its former self and Bernie Kosar was still nursing a myriad of injuries, the Browns felt good coming out of the bye week. Eric Metcalf's toe injury proved not to be serious, and he would play against the Bills. Kevin Mack, after proving his mettle in Houston, would become an even bigger factor as he continued to work his way into playing shape. And with the offense still capable of big plays, most assumed the 483 yards the attack defense had permitted in the Astrodome was simply an aberration. In the wide-open AFC, the Browns had as good a chance as anyone to reach Super Bowl XXIV.

And if this or any other playoff game in the Browns' immediate future came down to the final moments, Art Modell sang out a ringing endorsement of Bud Carson and his defense. "There's no question there's a world of difference defensively with this team and the team we had with the predecessor coaching staff," Modell said. "Like night and day. Forget the sacks and statistics. Stats are for losers. Just look at the team. It's not even close, our defense versus earlier years.

"We would have won the (Denver) game in '86, and I think we might have won the game in Denver the next year, too."

Then Modell, never afraid of the overstatement, went a step further. Referring to The Drive, he added: "This defense would never allow that. Never happen in a hundred years."

It seemed that it didn't matter how many times Modell made dramatic statements like this and was proven wrong. He simply continued making them. And by sundown on a gloomy January afternoon on the lakefront he would be biting his tongue once again.

One of the coldest Decembers in Cleveland history suddenly snapped in the first week of 1990. When the climate proved adequate, the Browns, who had flown to Dallas for a scheduled week of practice in good weather prior to the game, returned to Cleveland ahead of schedule. And as the Browns and Bills took the field, it was downright idyllic for the first week of January in northeast Ohio. The temperature hovered in the mid-thirties with virtually no wind. It was not what the fans and media from these two rust-belt towns had expected. It was supposed to be "Your mill workers against ours in a no-wrenches-barred brawl in the muck," as Bob Kravitz wrote.

While there would be no muck, the condition of the field would provide the only sore spot for the competition, so much so even the term "field" might have been debated. Stadium groundskeeper David Frey noted with a straight face that week that the field "has a lack of grass" and that it was "not perfectly flat." Bruce Smith put it differently: "This field should be banned from the league." Indeed, it would have been a perfect venue for sand volleyball. But it wasn't ideal for football, as both teams would discover.

The game would become one of the most memorable in recent Cleveland history. However, it got off to an unimpressive start. The Bills went three-and-out on their first possession, and an impressive opening drive by the Browns ended when Matt Bahr slipped on the sandy middle portion of the field and sliced a 46-yard field goal wide right. A play later, Kelly, buoyed by the fact the confused Browns had no defense called before the snap, hit Reed over the middle, and he sprinted through the sand for a 72-yard touchdown. A bad feeling starting to swell through the Stadium as the Browns had now given up nearly 600 yards of offense in their last five quarters.

The Cleveland offense, fueled by a handful of efficient Kosar completions, responded with a nice drive that ended in a Bahr field goal. And after a Buffalo punt, the home team picked up where it left off. Kosar and company marched to midfield, where on third-and-fourteen, Webster Slaughter sprinted past Buffalo corner Nate Odomes and Kosar lofted a picture-perfect, 52-yard scoring pass to him to give Cleveland its first lead at 10-7. But five plays later, the Bills took the advantage right back when Kelly, receiving ample protection, rolled to his right and hit veteran wideout James Lofton for a score from the Browns' thirty-three yard line. It was 14-10 midway through the second quarter, and the shoot-out was on.

After an exchange of punts, the Browns marched back into Buffalo territory and took the lead again when Kosar hit tight end Ron Middleton on a diving catch from the Buffalo four. The Bills drove into Cleveland territory, but the Browns snuffed out the threat and took a 17-14 lead to the locker room. The fireworks had just begun.

Unheralded backup corner Mark Harper intercepted Kelly on Buffalo's first possession of the second half, setting up another Kosar-to-Slaughter score, this one from 44 yards out. The Browns led, 24-14, and appeared poised to break the game open. Fullback Larry Kinnebrew fumbled on the Bills' next possession, and Felix Wright recovered at the Browns' twenty-five. But before the roar of the crowd could subside, Mack fumbled the football right back to the Bills. Five plays later, Kelly hit Thurman Thomas cutting past Clay Matthews over the middle for a six-yard touchdown pass to make it 24-21 with less than five minutes left in the third quarter. Suddenly, it was the Bills who had momentum. But not for long.

On the ensuing kickoff, Eric Metcalf, still not convinced of the durability of his injured toe, took off from the Cleveland ten. Behind perfect blocking, he wove through the league's best kickoff-coverage unit and sprinted down the sideline and into the end zone for a touchdown, pushing the Browns' margin back to ten. As the Browns took the lead into the fourth quarter, the crowd was rocking once again. The home team was fifteen minutes away from their third trip to the AFC title game in four years on the strength of the first kickoff return for a touchdown in Cleveland playoff history.

But, as they had done all day, the Bills refused to quit. Kelly and his comrades halted Cleveland's momentum and pulled back within one score on a short field goal by Scott Norwood. Not to be outdone, the Browns answered with another efficient drive resulting in a 47-yard Bahr field goal to make it 34-24 with 6:50 remaining. With one more defensive stop, the Browns would have victory in their grasp.

And it was at this point that Bud Carson and the Browns began embarrassing their owner, who had spoken so highly of them earlier in the week. Employing a bizarre "prevent" mode, the Browns focused solely on the Buffalo wideouts and left the short, middle portion of the field uncovered. The veteran Kelly took what the defense gave him and started hitting his running backs for short dump passes over the middle. On an eight-play drive, seven passes went to backs Thomas and Ronnie Harmon and covered the length of the 78-yard trek. Appropriately, Thomas capped the drive, catching a three-yard touchdown pass with 3:56 left.

But the home team caught a break thanks to the chewed-up turf. Just as had happened with Bahr in the first quarter, Norwood slipped on the point-after attempt and booted the football into his center's back. Cleveland now led by four, meaning a field goal on their final possession would do the Bills no good. But the Browns weren't out of the woods yet.

True to form, the Cleveland offense went three-and-out and gave the football back to Buffalo at its own twenty-six with 2:41 remaining. It was, in a way, the only appropriate way the game could end. This was ultimately why Bud Carson had been brought in, to succeed in situations like this. For four straight years, Marty Schottenheimer's defense had failed to stop the opposing offense with a playoff game on the line. This was where a tumultuous offseason would pay off in spades for Art Modell—or so he hoped.

Yet, with the Browns still entrenched in their conservative alignment, Kelly stuck to the same strategy that had motored his offense down the field so quickly minutes before. He hit Harmon twice for 16 yards to the Buffalo forty-two yard line before the Browns finally dug in at the two-minute warning. They forced three straight incompletions, bringing up fourth-and-ten with 1:36 to play. With one more stop, the Browns would escape. Instead, Kelly hit dependable Don Beebe for 17 yards and a first down at the Browns' forty-one. The uneasy feeling that had swept through the Stadium almost exactly three years earlier when John Elway was at the controls in almost the identical situation, once again circulated through Pandemonium Palace. "I've got to admit," Hanford Dixon said later, "during those final plays, The Drive crossed my mind."

Three plays later, the Bills once again were faced with a do-or-die fourth-down, this time with a yard for the first with fifty-two seconds showing. And once more, Kelly came through, hitting Reed for nine yards to the Browns' twenty-three and spiking the football to stop the clock with thirty-four seconds remaining. "Vietnam must have been like this," Al Baker said later. The Bills only needed 23 more yards.

On third-and-ten a play later, Kelly went back to Thomas again, this time for 12 yards and a first down at the Browns' eleven. After another Kelly spike, the confused and tired Browns called their final time out with fourteen seconds left. Modell sat brooding in his private box.

Kelly dropped back to pass again and saw victory flash before his eyes. Harmon, who had played such an instrumental role on Buffalo's last two drives, broke wide open on an out-pattern in the back corner of the end zone. Kelly lofted a pass toward him and Harmon leapt up and stretched out his arms to catch it, only to watch the football bounce off his palms and fall helplessly out of bounds, incomplete. It wasn't an easy catch, but certainly a makeable one, one that playoff teams usually pull off. Instead, with Browns' fans across the country feeling their hearts pounding in their chests, Kelly dropped back to pass again on third down with nine seconds left.

He tried to go back to the receiver-out-of-the-backfield well one final time. He saw Thurman Thomas, who'd already caught thirteen passes for a whopping 150 yards on the day, sprint over the middle at the goal line and fired a pass toward him, much as he'd done on Buffalo's third touchdown. On the earlier touchdown pass, Clay Matthews was trailing Thomas, unable to catch up. This time, he did. Kelly's pass floated into Matthews arms at the one. And as he admittedly should have done two weeks earlier, the veteran linebacker collapsed to the ground to end the play. The Browns had survived, 34-30, in one of the most exciting postseason games in Cleveland history, one that saw the teams combine for 778 total yards and forty-two first downs.

"It was one of those crazy, wild football games you get in about once every three years," Bud Carson said afterward. Matthews seconded the notion, but added, "It was a fun game to watch, but not necessarily to play in."

Particularly not for the Browns' revamped defense, which wasn't supposed to allow a game-winning touchdown drive like that at any point in the next century. Instead, Carson's crew permitted a paltry 453 yards of offense by Buffalo, including 405 via Kelly's arm in a career-best performance. As Art Modell suggested, perhaps stats were for losers. Yet the statistics had nothing to do with the defense permitting two lengthy drives in the final four minutes that could have—perhaps even *should* have—cost the Browns the game. "We stayed in that dumb-ass 4-4 (zone)," Carson said. "We got caught with a poor plan." Indeed, Carson not only added that it was the worst defensive performance he'd ever seen but also admitted that the Browns had been out-coached by Marv Levy and the Bills' staff.

Deserved or not, the Cleveland Browns were victorious and would play in the AFC Championship for the third time in four years. The following afternoon, their opponent was confirmed. The Pittsburgh Steelers, fresh off an upset victory in the Wild Card Game in Houston (which cost Jerry Glanville his job), grabbed an early 10-0 lead at Mile High Stadium, momentarily setting Browns' fans' hearts in motion. With a Pittsburgh win, the Browns would host the Steelers the following week for the AFC Championship. Instead, the hosts rallied and held off Pittsburgh in the final minutes to clinch a 24-23 victory.

Once again, to no one's surprise, the Cleveland Browns and Denver Broncos would clash for a trip to the Super Bowl.

Over the previous four seasons, Cleveland and Denver had posted the conference's best overall records. More than that, they just seemed to be on the same wavelength. When the Browns and Bernie Kosar rose to power in 1986, so did Denver, sparked by the maturation of John Elway. The trend continued for both in 1987. Then when the Browns slipped in 1988, so did Denver, falling to 8-8 and missing the playoffs. Both endured coaching-staff shakeups for 1989 and started fast, with Denver coasting to a 10-2 mark in late November. But like the Browns, the Broncos folded late, losing three of their last four, though they still hung on for the AFC West title. While Kosar's performance had been questioned all year, so had Elway's, as he endured a respectable, but not impressive season for the first time since his rookie year. The Browns and Broncos were like heat-seeking missiles, always pointed at one another.

Yet while the rivalry became one of the league's fiercest after the 1986 and 1987 title games, as the week wore on before Browns-Broncos Part Three, the hype and attention seemed somewhat stale.

If Denver won, it would be three-for-three in playoff games against Cleveland. Truly good rivalries had to be two-way roads. Yes, the Browns had defeated

Denver three months earlier, and Clevelanders clung to that fact to keep their hopes aloft. The Browns' defense had been dominating that day and had handled John Elway for the first time. The attack defense had its flaws, as Warren Moon and Jim Kelly had demonstrated, but perhaps this was the best way to combat the slippery Elway. "Enough about The Drive and The Fumble," Bill Livingston wrote in that Sunday's *Plain Dealer*. "Enough nonsense about past being prelude. Today really is another day."

That it was. And it would not be a good one for Cleveland or the Browns.

The PD headline the following day said it all: "OH NO, NOT AGAIN!"

Indeed, for the third straight time, the Browns had come up short against the Broncos in the playoffs. The only difference was that this time they never really had a chance. The final was 37-21, Denver, and some were quick to label this one "The Blowout."

For Browns' fans, the game played out like a superfluous sequel in an over-hyped movie series. It had elements of what had made the first two installments memorable, but in the end, was simply poorly conceived, not well-executed, and downright ugly.

All three descriptions fit the Cleveland offense, whose leader was literally being held together with a rubber band. Bernie Kosar, already hindered by an elbow injury which some felt might be jeopardizing his career, was still recovering from a staph infection in his right shoulder suffered in the Minnesota victory. To top it off, he added a hip pointer and a sprained right middle finger to his list of injuries against Buffalo. The hurt finger was particularly troublesome because it affected his throwing motion. To counter the problem, Browns' trainer Bill Tessendorf resorted to an unorthodox medical approach. He rigged together a makeshift splint with a rubber band stretching from Kosar's wrist to relieve pressure on the finger. Like nearly everything else the Browns tried that day, it didn't work.

They caught a huge break in the opening moments. A red-hot Elway drove Denver to the Browns' one, but on third-and-goal, an ill-advised quarterback option resulted in a fumble recovered by the Browns. On the next snap, Kevin Mack broke outside for a 20-yard gain, and for one brief moment, Browns' fans encountered that giddy sense that things might be different this time. It didn't take long to vanish.

It was clear something was wrong with Kosar. His throws had a tendency to sail, and he later admitted he was purposely aiming lower than normal to account for the plethora of injuries that led to his poor passes. But the handicapping attempts went awry. Cleveland's second series ended when a Kosar pass for Webster Slaughter sailed well off target and was picked off by Denver safety Dennis Smith. It led to a field goal, and the Browns' offensive woes continued. All but abandoning Mack and playing as if constantly trailing by twenty points, the Browns' game plan hitched their wagon to Kosar's beat-up arm. Accordingly, after Mack's opening run, the Browns would execute twenty consecutive plays without picking up a first down, which they finally did midway through the second quarter. Yet for as hopeless as the Browns' offense was, the defense kept them in the game, containing Elway with a smorgasbord of blitzes and stunts. When the Browns crossed midfield with just over seven minutes left in the half, they actually had a chance to take the lead despite being outplayed. However, the drive stalled, and three plays later, Elway scrambled away from the Browns' pass rush and rifled a bullet pass upfield for Michael Young, who broke free when Frank Minnifield fell down in coverage. Young caught it and scampered into the end zone to complete a 70-yard score. The Browns could muster no real threat for the remainder of the half, and Denver took a 10-0 lead to the locker room.

Most Cleveland fans felt they'd been here before. The Browns' first-half performance was remarkably similar to the AFC Championship two years before. Yet there was hope. For one, while Elway wasn't playing poorly, he wasn't dominating the game. But the brightest beam of hope may have stemmed from history. In the 1987 title game, the Browns were nearly buried, trailing 21-3 going into the second half. This time, despite an anemic offense and a weary defense hanging on by a thread, the deficit was a mere ten points. The 1987 Browns had stormed out of the locker room and played perhaps the finest thirty minutes of offensive football in team history. The 1989 team emulated that as best they could.

Kosar, after abandoning the rubber-band splint, turned to a no-huddle offense to start the third period, and it worked like a charm. Demonstrating rhythm and momentum for the first time all day, Cleveland motored down the field and got on the board when Kosar hit Brian Brennan for a 28-yard touchdown—Brennan's first in almost two years. The Browns were back in it, and with the offense re-ignited, it would be up to the defense to keep thwarting Elway. Yet on third-and-three from the Bronco twenty-seven, the shining jewel of the Denver franchise did it again. He spotted Young deep, this time for 53 yards and a first down at the Cleveland twenty. It seemed symbolic that on this long pass, Young had burned Hanford Dixon, meaning both Browns' corners who had anchored the defense for much of the decade had now each been badly beaten for a tide-turning pass. Two plays later, Elway hit tight end Orson Mobley for another score to put the lead back to ten. Denver extended the lead to 24-7 after a Cleveland punt and another long drive capped by a Sammy Winder touchdown run. Just over four minutes remained in the third quarter, and the Browns once again appeared dead in the water. But Bernie Kosar had one final charge left in him.

He drove his hometown team 72 yards in six quick plays and carved into the lead when he hit the man who had once upon a time been his most reliable receiver: Brian Brennan. The veteran reeled in a ten-yard pass for a touchdown, diving out across the end zone and curling up to keep the ball from hitting the ground. It was 24-14, and the visitors still had a pulse. It got even stronger a play later when Al Baker stripped the football from Denver fullback Melvin Bratton, and Felix Wright scooped it up at the Bronco twenty-seven yard line and motored to the one. A play later, Tim Manoa punched it in to cut the lead to 24-21 with a second left in the third quarter. Like they had two years before, the Browns had battled back and made a football game out of a rout. It appeared the stage was set for yet another classic Browns-Broncos finish.

But before sportswriters could begin to speculate which way fate would twist in the final moments this time around, John Elway provided the answer. It appeared the Browns would get the ball back with a chance to take the lead when they stopped the Broncos on third-and-fifteen, but Cleveland was flagged for jumping offside. On the subsequent third-and-ten, Elway again appeared in trouble, rolling to his left against heavy pressure. But he stopped and flicked a pass across his body over the middle for Vance Johnson, who hung on for a 21-yard gain and a first down. To no one's surprise, a play later, the Broncos scored on another well-placed Elway pass to Winder.

There was still plenty of time remaining, but any hope the Browns had of one more comeback all but perished when a third-down Kosar pass floated off target and was picked off by Darren Carrington at the Browns' forty. Elway, after a 12-yard scramble on third-and-four moments later, parlayed the turnover into a field goal. Cleveland's last attempt to make a game of it ended when another Kosar pass took off and was picked off by old nemesis Dennis Smith. Moments later, Denver put the game out of reach with a 37-yard field goal at the two-minute warning.

It only seemed appropriate that the Browns' final offensive possession of 1989 ended the way it did. Sandwiched around a Mack fumble he managed to recover, Kosar was sacked twice, including on the final play of the season with twenty-eight seconds left. The Broncos had defeated the Browns again, and no quotation marks or capital letters would be necessary this time. Kosar put it simply enough: "It wasn't meant to be."

John Elway had already enjoyed a prosperous career before January 14, 1990, but even he admitted this was his finest performance. "One guy can't win a game by himself," Michael Young said, "but he came pretty close." He threw for 385 yards, and Denver racked up 497 yards of total offense—nearly twice as much as Cleveland. "God," Al Baker muttered at one point in the locker room, "I hate John Elway."

The battered Kosar, meanwhile, had finally reached his breaking point. He suffered through one of the worst performances of his career, hitting on just nineteen of forty-four passes for 210 yards and three interceptions. "I tried to make things happen out there," he said. "But they just didn't happen."

It was an appropriate finish to a bizarre season.

Bud Carson did his best to find the silver lining, for both the Denver loss and the schizophrenic 1989 campaign.

"Everyone said we were finished," he said. "We got back up and came back. We didn't do it today, but I still think our ballclub made a hell of a run at it with a lot of tired players."

The feeling following the third AFC title-game loss was remarkably different than the first two. In 1986 and 1987, the disappointment was greater, since those teams were better and had each held a trip to the Super Bowl in their hands in the final minutes. And while there was a sense of urgency then, by the dawn of 1990, many felt that window of opportunity was already closed.

"Obviously we need to make some changes," Art Modell said. "We're going to look at our personnel across the organization and make whatever changes we need to make."

Any confidence in the forthcoming changes was shaken in the aftermath of Modell's most recent change. Bud Carson's defense, tapped to take the Browns to the Super Bowl, had been annihilated in the three most important games of the year, making it almost inexplicable that the Browns had managed to win two of them. In Cleveland's final three games, it had permitted almost 500 yards and nearly thirty points per contest. In contrast to Modell's overconfident statement of support the week before, intelligent fans knew that Marty Schottenheimer's defense never would have allowed such numbers—not in a hundred years.

"It obviously needed a transfusion at one time or another," Carson said of his beaten defense. "We just didn't have anyone to transfuse it."

In retrospect, the question around Cleveland the following week was how in the world did this team make it so far? And further, was the front office asking the same question? "This organization must not allow itself to think because they're so close, the next step to the Big One is a short one," Ray Yannucci wrote. "This team might not need a new transmission, exhaust system and engine, but it needs more than just a new tailpipe, headlight, and hood ornament."

Those upgrades, whether minor or major, would not come in 1990, nor after that. The Browns' gradual slide, which had begun two years earlier, was about to become a freefall, and that freefall would eventually turn into the darkest moment in the history of Cleveland athletics.

The fun-loving Dog Days of the late 1980s were over, and neither the Browns nor Cleveland would ever be the same.

Epilogue
Fall of the Canine Empire

Rapid regression, be it in business, politics or professional sports, can often be traced back to one similar theme: the parties involved don't realize they're slipping until it's too late. And by then, usually the only course of action is to simply start over rather than try to fix what's wrong. This is precisely what happened to the Cleveland Browns in 1990, but the problem was compounded when the repair process was ill-conceived and counterproductive in itself.

After five years of week-in, week-out competitive football that saw each season end with the Browns competing in the playoffs, on paper the franchise appeared as strong as ever. In reality, it wasn't. Its mistakes from the previous decade would catch up with the Browns in the early 1990s, as the team sloshed through four straight losing seasons, each of them more dismal than any moment of the late 1980s-era.

Yet no one saw that coming as the 1990 season drew near. As expected, the Browns made some changes in the offseason, most notably firing embattled offensive coordinator Marc Trestman and replacing him with veteran Jim Shofner, who had directed the Browns' offense during the Kardiac Kids era a decade before. For better or worse, the front office finally closed the book on Lindy Infante's offense, which had been unsuccessfully re-adapted twice. Shofner, while certainly respected, represented the fifth offensive coordinator in Bernie Kosar's six-year career. Kosar joked in the preseason that he shouldn't admit he enjoyed working with Shofner, because when he made statements like that, his coach usually disappeared.

While quite a fuss was made over Trestman's departure and Shofner's return, what was somewhat overlooked was what the Browns' *didn't* do in the offseason. Like Kosar's right arm, the Cleveland offensive line was in tatters at the conclusion of the 1989 season. Both starting guards, Dan Fike and Ted Banker, would miss almost all of 1990 with injuries suffered late in 1989. After eleven surgeries in eleven years, veteran right tackle Cody Risien finally decided to call it a career. Then, to everyone's surprise, two weeks later Rickey Bolden did the same, opting to pursue a career in the ministry even though he was only twenty-eight years old and was the leading candidate to replace Risien. It left Paul Farren and Gregg Rakoczy as the only 1989 starters returning.

While Bolden's retirement came out of the blue, the Browns entered the off-season knowing Banker and Fike would miss much of 1990 and that Risien wouldn't return. Yet, amazingly, they did almost nothing to bolster the unit, failing to select offensive lineman with a single one of their eleven draft picks.

What they did do was rectify an old wrong. Through Plan B free agency, the Browns re-signed Mike Baab, eager to return to Cleveland after two years with the Patriots. Symbolically, though Baab was entering the twilight of his career and Rakoczy was only into his fourth season, Baab was automatically returned to center and Rakoczy moved to guard, where he began the year as a backup. Thus, when the season began, the Browns' offensive line consisted of inexperienced Kevin Robbins, Ralph Tamm, and Ben Jefferson at the guard spots. The line, weak as it had been in 1989, was downgraded further in 1990. What followed was only natural.

The line was not the only area of significant change. The team parted with a handful of veteran players who had helped guide the Browns to so much of their late-1980s success. After the Browns signed aging free-agent corner Raymond Clayborn, Hanford Dixon took the hint and departed for San Francisco. He didn't make the team and called it a career that summer. Carl Hairston was waived and signed with Phoenix. Matt Bahr was released partially because of a nagging back injury. Gerald McNeil signed with Houston. Clifford Charlton, two years after being selected in the first round of the draft, was released. Even veterans who stayed didn't participate in camp. Frank Minnifield, Felix Wright, Clay Matthews, Mike Johnson, and Paul Farren were all involved in contract squabbles and held out. Minnifield, whom the team tried to trade to Atlanta for All-Pro offensive lineman Bill Fralic, missed the first four games of the regular season, then sued the Browns and the NFL for anti-trust violations. The only good news for Browns' fans that summer was the change of heart of Ozzie Newsome, who announced he would return for one final year.

Things started off bad and got worse. After a second straight 1-4 preseason, the Browns managed to defeat Pittsburgh in a horrendously played game on opening day. Bernie Kosar was sacked a career-high seven times, and the Cleveland offense amassed an embarrassing 158 total yards. They had no such good fortune after similar play the following two weeks, both losses to sub-.500 teams. But it became crystal clear something was dramatically wrong in Week Four, when the Browns were crushed by Marty Schottenheimer's Chiefs in Kansas City, 34-0. Cleveland was now 1-3 and rumors swirled that Bud Carson was contemplating quitting. Tony Grossi of the *Plain Dealer* reported that Art Modell had spoken with Jim Shofner about finishing the season as head coach if Carson was fired. Modell denied the story as well as the possibility of firing Carson in the middle of the season—much as he had done six years before with Sam Rutigliano. Grossi was suspended by the paper for three days, but maintained the story was accurate.

The one bright spot of 1990 occurred the following Monday night. The Browns rallied from a nine-point fourth-quarter deficit to defeat the Denver Broncos at Mile High Stadium on a last-second field goal by new kicker Jerry Kauric. It was Cleveland's first win at Mile High in sixteen years and provided some small measure of justice for past Bronco indignities. At 2-3, the Browns and their fans had hope again. It didn't last long.

They lost their next eight games, their starting quarterback, and their head coach. After the first three disheartening losses, Carson was looking for any kind of spark for a team that was dead in the water. On November 4, he pulled the trigger, opting to start Mike Pagel over a struggling Bernie Kosar. In a rematch of the previous year's divisional playoff with Buffalo, the Bills took their pound of flesh with a decisive 42-0 victory. The loss, combined with the benching of the franchise quarterback, represented the final straw for Modell. The next day Bud Carson was fired, and, as Grossi had suggested a month before, Jim Shofner took over the reins. Kosar once again became the starter.

Carson had been the Browns' coach for a mere twenty-seven games. He had accepted all the stipulations the Browns' front office had handed to him, went along with the coaches, players, and offensive philosophies thrust in his lap. He agreed to play little or no role in the draft and any other offseason moves. And for it all, he was booted out the door twenty-one months after Modell proclaimed he'd hired his last coach. Always one to be frank and forthright with the media, Carson spoke candidly with the press.

"Coaching here is a tough job," he said. "Your hands are somewhat tied. A coach of the Browns doesn't have much power." When asked if he had any regrets, he replied, "I'd have done everything differently."

It began a week-long public chess match between Carson and Modell. The former coach was set to be paid the remainder of his three-year contract totaling nearly $1 million, but a clause in the contract said he'd forfeit the money if he publicly criticized the team. He came very close to activating that clause. He said after the AFC Championship loss, he was told by a member of Modell's inner circle that "None of the assistant coaches are worth a damn, and we're not quite sure how *you* did."

"They just tied a ring around my neck," Carson said at one point, "and I could never get it off. I was coaching left-handed all the time."

Ultimately, Carson admitted it was a mistake to let a team dictate all the conditions the way the Browns had with him. It should have been *his* team, but instead it belonged to Modell's brain trust: VPs Jim Bailey and Ernie Accorsi, pro personnel director Mike Lombardi, son David Modell, and PR director Kevin Byrne. "The team was being run by Lombardi, not so much by Carson," Mike Baab said. "I remember on cut days, the coaches would say, 'Who's here?' because they had no input on who was going to be cut or kept. It was a very wild situation."

As it happened, Modell's entire inner circle, the ones who were actually in charge, retained their jobs. Though they did reveal some remorse and regret. "He didn't fail alone," Accorsi said of Carson. "We failed as an organization." Even Modell second-guessed himself, admitting perhaps he should have originally broadened his search beyond defensive coaches and perhaps given Carson more power. Given the same opportunity again, Modell would err in the opposite direction.

Fans and players alike felt Carson had gotten a raw deal. Of 17,000 callers into a local television poll, two-thirds thought Carson shouldn't have been fired. Be that as it may, it was up to Shofner to bring the ship to port amidst stormy seas. And things got no better. The Browns dropped their first four under Shofner, including a humiliating 58-14 spanking in Houston in which they trailed 45-7 at the half. While eking out an ugly win over Jerry Glanville's Atlanta Falcons in Week Fifteen, their final victory of the year, Kosar was lost for the final two games after injuring his thumb. With Pagel at the controls a week later, the Browns hit rock bottom in Pittsburgh. In a 35-0 loss, the Browns tied an NFL record with eight lost fumbles. The season ended with a surprisingly gritty performance on a rainy day in Cincinnati, though it resulted in a 21-14 setback that gave the Bengals the division title. When the dust settled, the Browns had finished 3-13, the worst record in team history. "It was a bad football team," Baab said. "In a million ways, it was a bad football team."

While the inadequate line set the tone for a miserable season on offense, the defense, which had been the catalyst for so much of the Browns' success in the late 1980s, shockingly fell apart. When Carson was fired, Cleveland had allowed 235 points in its first nine games after permitting just 254 in all of 1989. The 1990 Browns would wind up setting a team record by allowing 462 points—an average of nearly twenty-nine per Sunday. It was an aging defense that never had a dominant pass rusher to begin with, had lost its edge in the secondary, and was beginning to slip at linebacker.

It was made clear from the day Carson was fired that Jim Shofner was not the long-term solution as head coach. He moved up to the front office after the hellish season concluded, and Modell began searching for a coach once again. It led him to a young defensive assistant in New York who had just won the Super Bowl.

So how did the Browns fall so far so quickly?

Many variables factored in, but the most important and most telling was the team's fantastic failures in the college draft over the previous decade.

In 1978, the Browns struck gold in the first round of the draft, snagging both Ozzie Newsome and Clay Matthews within hours of each other. Over their next twelve drafts, the Browns would acquire just three players in the first round who would have a significant long-term impact on the team: Hanford Dixon (1981), Chip Banks (1982), and Eric Metcalf (1989). Don Rogers (1984) may have turned out to be another successful pick, but died before getting a chance to prove it. In the other nine drafts, the Browns either had no pick or did not choose wisely, opting for first-round failures such as running back Charles White (1980), and linebackers Mike Junkin (1987) and Clifford Charlton (1988). Perhaps the best example of the Browns' draft-day miscues came in 1979 when they traded their first-round pick to San Diego and took wide receiver Willis Adams with the Chargers' first selection, only to watch Adams have seven disappointing seasons. With the Browns' pick, San Diego selected Kellen Winslow, who would become arguably the greatest tight end in the history of football. (Interestingly, a quarter-century later, the Browns did the opposite to draft Kellen Winslow Jr., trading up a spot in the 2004 first round and drawing some criticism for giving away too much.)

But it wasn't just a first-round jinx. Of the twenty second- and third-round picks the Browns made from 1979 through 1990, only nine (cornerback Lawrence Johnson, Reggie Camp, Chris Rockins, Webster Slaughter, Gregg Rakoczy, Tim Manoa, Michael Dean Perry, running back Leroy Hoard, and defensive end Anthony Pleasant) would prove even marginally worthwhile. Altogether, in rounds one through three of the draft from 1979 through 1990, the Browns "hit" on just twelve of twenty-eight tries, to say nothing of the high-round picks that were traded away for little dividends. The Browns' rapid decline originated here. Ultimately, a team that doesn't draft well doesn't succeed in the long term.

So how were the Browns able to stay competitive despite their draft-day woes? For as poorly as they generally selected their early-round picks, the front office, led by Ernie Accorsi and personnel director Chip Falivene, pulled off some shrewd moves. Their most cunning was their use of the 1984 supplemental draft, which landed them the rights to USFLers Kevin Mack, Mike Johnson, and Gerald McNeil. Also, the Browns were able to wrest Frank Minnifield away from the USFL and Felix Wright from the Canadian Football League. And of course, there was the legendary 1985 supplemental draft, in which the Browns craftily maneuvered to acquire Bernie Kosar. These six players alone formed much of the core of the team through the late 1980s, and not one was acquired via the college draft or trades. The timely collapse of the United States Football League made all the difference.

The bulk of the remaining talent core came via draft-day serendipity. The Browns deserve some credit for landing so many important players in the late rounds of the draft, but this was as much luck as talent. Who could have foreseen Earnest Byner playing the role he did when he was drafted in the tenth round, or seventh-round pick Reggie Langhorne becoming one of the league's most respected receivers? Brian Brennan (fourth round), Mike Baab (fifth round), Eddie Johnson (seventh round), Cody Risien (seventh round), and Paul Farren (twelfth round) were all afterthought draft picks who became a part of the foundation and overcame the odds simply to make the team. That leaves Bob Golic (waivers) and Carl Hairston (trade) as the remaining core members acquired outside of the college draft.

While the Browns' front office was rightly criticized for its draft misses in the 1980s, its ability to collect talent through other means was both resourceful and commendable. However, these methods were simply shortcuts, temporarily canceling out draft-day failures. Eventually the Browns ran out of shortcuts.

On February 5, 1991, Bill Belichick was named the eighth head coach in Browns' history.

On November 6, 1995, Art Modell officially announced he was moving the Browns to Baltimore.

What happened in between will never forgotten by any Cleveland fan who endured it.

In many ways, Belichick was simply a younger version of Bud Carson. He'd been a natural candidate by way of the success he'd enjoyed as the defensive coordinator of the New York Giants from 1983 through 1990, helping the team win two Super Bowls. At age thirty-eight, Belichick became the youngest coach in the NFL, though not only had he never played the game at a major college or professional level, but he had never been a head coach at any level. Once again, Modell proclaimed he'd hired his last coach, and over the next two years, he subtly gave Belichick more power than any Cleveland coach since Paul Brown three decades before. After Belichick's first season, Ernie Accorsi stepped down, and much of his responsibility in terms of personnel decisions went to the young coach. As if making up for giving Carson no voice at all, Modell had granted Belichick enough power to make a dictator blush.

And the new coach wielded his power and ran the team in a tyrannical fashion. In some ways, his no-nonsense style was similar to that of Marty Schottenheimer. But the players who played under both could see obvious differences. "Marty was a nice man," Mike Baab said. "I liked Marty. We didn't like Bill. Bill was mean. Bill hated us. That was the difference. Marty loved us. We were his players. Marty used to cry on Wednesdays before the Pittsburgh game because he cared so much, and he liked us so much, and he wanted to win. Bill would cuss us out. It was a completely different way of looking at your players."

Sweeping together the remnants of the veterans left after the horrific 1990 season, Belichick went 6-10 in his first year, making the Browns competitive in nearly every game—a welcome development after 1990. Dramatic changes took place before 1992, as the Browns parted ways with all three of their valuable veteran receivers who had played such major roles in the late 1980s: Webster Slaughter, Reggie Langhorne, and Brian Brennan. Though all three had some respectable seasons left in them, Belichick and the Browns hardly batted an eye, instead turning to underachieving wideout Michael Jackson and always-injured Lawyer Tillman. And in continuing a trend from the previous administration, Belichick and company did little to bolster the still-struggling offensive line, thus the conservative defensive coach's desire to run a ball-control offense never materialized. By 1992, Mike Baab, Paul Farren, and Gregg Rakoczy were all gone, replaced by mediocre John Rienstra, overrated Ed King (another busted second-round pick who played just two years at guard), and past-his-prime Jay Hil-genberg.

Despite losing Kosar to injury twice, the Browns managed to compile a 7-9 record in 1992. This was a team held together by its defense, whose consistency and tendency to create turnovers almost balanced the often-ignored offense. Year Three of the Belichick Era brought high expectations—yet also marked the be-ginning of the final stanza of the Browns' tenure in Cleveland.

The team started hot, winning its first three, but along the way Belichick made it clear he'd had enough of Bernie Kosar. He benched Kosar in mid-October in favor of his old Hurricane teammate, Vinny Testaverde, a free-agent pickup the previous offseason. When Testaverde was lost to a separated shoulder a week later, it appeared Kosar would step in to finish the season. But Belichick and Modell had a different plan. Halfway across the continent, Marty Schottenheimer could smell trouble. He reportedly called Kosar and warned him to watch his step—he had a feeling the front office was setting him up.

In Kosar's next start, the Browns were handled by their old nemesis, the Den-ver Broncos, dropping Cleveland to 5-3 at the season's midpoint, though they were still in first place. Knowing Testaverde would be out another month and in-experienced Todd Philcox was the team's only other quarterback, Belichick boldly brandished all the power Modell had given him. On November 8, 1993, barely a month after signing his quarterback to a contract extension through the 1999 season, Modell called Kosar into his office to inform him he was being released.

It sent shockwaves across northern Ohio. The front page of the *Plain Dealer* was dedicated entirely to Kosar, under a Pearl Harbor-sized headline reading "Sacked!" Modell and Belichick both vehemently defended the decision and pub-licly criticized Kosar. They claimed Kosar's skills had deteriorated to the point he could no longer help the team. While it was certainly true Kosar wasn't the same quarterback in 1993 he'd been in 1987, it was utterly ludicrous to argue that Todd Philcox was a better quarterback than Kosar. Yet that's precisely what Belichick was saying. Worse still, Modell blamed injuries as the main reason for Kosar's de-terioration—this from the man who refused to put a decent line in front of him and a coach who had abandoned Kosar's three favorite receivers.

"I think it started in 1988 when Lloyd Burress hit his elbow in Kansas City," Modell said. "Since then, he has taken so much punishment—more than any quarterback I've ever known in this league."

And yet he never did anything to stop that punishment. When asked that very question, the reply was classic Modell: "I'm not going to get into who's at fault."

In an appropriate way to close out his career in Cleveland, Kosar, who received 500 phone calls of support that day, took the high road. "I'm not going to lower my standards to some of the things that have been said to rationalize the deci-sion," he said. It was obvious to insiders that Belichick had had enough of Kosar's back talk and the fact that many players respected the quarterback far more than the coach.

So a third-year coach who had won eighteen football games in his career released the most popular athlete in the history of Cleveland sports. In his eight years with the Browns, Kosar wound up second to Brian Sipe on the all-time franchise list for attempts, completions, and yardage, and third in touchdown passes. At 81.6, he notched the team's second-best career quarterback rating. Yet Belichick felt he was expendable.

Even the players smelled a rat. Kevin Mack, himself in his final year with the Browns, refused to speak to the media on the subject, though he looked obviously distraught. Most players were upset with the move, but wouldn't talk about it, fearing they'd be the next to go. Even Testaverde, who would suddenly be the Browns' No. 1 quarterback upon his return, admitted he didn't think Kosar's skills had diminished.

"He's our chief," offensive lineman Tony Jones said of Kosar. "You know what happens to the Indians when they take away the chief—they fold."

And that's exactly what the Browns did. The following Sunday in Seattle, Philcox fumbled on the first play, and it was returned for a touchdown. The Browns lost that game and would finish the year dropping seven of their final nine. More notable than the happenings on the field were the activities off it. When Kosar was signed by Dallas immediately after his release, fans began wearing Cowboy jerseys to Cleveland Stadium and donning homemade Bernie Kosar masks. They booed the team mercilessly, and on one occasion, as Belichick was interviewed in the bowels of the Stadium, the passionate chant of "Bill must go!" from the stands could be heard in the conference room.

The 1993 season ended fittingly. Kosar came off the bench to lead Dallas to a key division win over Phoenix when Troy Aikman was hurt. The Cowboys won the NFC East and then the conference title. Belichick and the Browns, out of the playoffs for the fourth straight year, watched as Kosar took the final snap in Super Bowl XXVIII, a Dallas victory over Buffalo. After nine years in Cleveland without a title, Kosar finally got his ring after just three months with another team. He would close his career in 1997 after serving three more years as Dan Marino's backup in his college town of Miami.

With Testaverde at the controls in 1994, the Browns turned things around for an 11-5 record and a Wild Card berth. But relatively few in Cleveland really seemed to care. After the Browns had clinched their first playoff spot in five years, it took them almost an entire week to sell out the game—this in a football-mad town that had a history of selling out playoff games in two or three hours. Many fans who hadn't stopped following the team when Kosar was released still wanted to root for the Browns, but couldn't stand Belichick or Modell. And it was this attitude that paved the way toward Baltimore getting professional football once again.

Technically, the decision to move the Browns was entirely Art Modell's. Bill Belichick, who was fired by Modell in between the last season in Cleveland and first in Baltimore, had no agenda to drive the team from Cleveland. But he'd played the second-most important role in this drama all the same. Modell's primary complaint against the city of Cleveland was that civic officials would not cooperate with him in trying to either refurbish the old stadium or build a new one with public money. A major reason for city officials' hesitancy to aggressively pursue such a solution had to do with the team's general unpopularity in the early and mid-1990s. You can't expect Cuyahoga County voters to foot the bill for a tax proposal to build a state-of-the-art facility for an owner they didn't trust and a coach they despised. The team was bland, monotonous, and disorganized throughout Belichick's tenure, which was forgivable. But releasing Bernie Kosar, who could have played anywhere else for more money out of college and might well have had a more fruitful career elsewhere, was irreconcilable. Kosar represented the heart and soul of Cleveland, and Belichick and Modell had driven him out of town without an ounce of respect or dignity. And now they wanted the taxpayers they had insulted to build them a new stadium?

So no effort was organized, no campaign launched until it was too late. Modell, despite vows to the contrary, got fed up and signed a secret deal on board a parked private jet late one October night in 1995.

Modell had originally made his fortune as a New York advertising man, yet his ultimate downfall in professional sports was caused not by anything that happened on the field but rather by bad public relations. More so than Modell's decision to move the team, it was this that was unforgivable. He claimed he had no choice. But the reason he had no choice was because of his own mistakes.

And it was Cleveland that paid the price for his ineptitude. Modell got his new stadium and was treated like a folk hero in Baltimore. Contrary to popular belief in Cleveland, Modell was not a criminal driven to do evil things. What he was was a poor businessman whose ego obliterated his common sense.

In the end, everything worked out for all parties. Cleveland got a new version of the Browns that would play in a brand-new stadium under respectable ownership. Modell, meanwhile, cashed out, and in so doing, actually became what he'd always sounded like: a living contradiction.

All that remains is the bitterness of the Browns' fans. Passionate and justified as it might be, one day that too will subside. But now, Clevelanders still remember all too well that in 1996, 1997, and 1998, just ten years after the most thrilling period in Cleveland sports history, there was no Browns' football. All Cleveland fans had on Sunday afternoons were memories of the good old days, most recently, the fun they'd enjoyed from 1985 through 1989.

So when did it all start? Modell's press conference on a sunshiny November afternoon in Baltimore was the end of the story, but when did the first domino fall?

To be sure, there were obvious benchmark moments along the way: Kosar's release, the hiring of Belichick, and Marty Schottenheimer's departure, to name the most obvious.

But the day it all began was quite pedestrian by comparison. No one, not even those involved, could have possibly foreseen that this move was the one that would start the wheels in motion toward the Browns' eventual departure from Cleveland.

It was August 29, 1988—the day the Browns traded away center Mike Baab.

Certainly, Baab did not go down as one of the greatest players in Browns' history, and even in 1988 he was not a bona fide star. He never played in a Pro Bowl and was probably better known for his role as "The Baabarian" than he was for his on-field efforts. The Browns, impressed by the potential of young Gregg Rakoczy, wanted to get the most out of what they felt was a promising second-round draft pick. So a week before the season started, they traded away a six-year veteran and one of the team's most popular players and handed his job over to a twenty-four-year-old prospect who had never made a professional start at center in his life.

"Marty brought me in in mini-camp," Baab explained, "and said, 'Mike, if you're ever not a starter, would you consider sitting on the bench?' And I said, 'No, Marty, I'll go crazy. I'll walk off the team.' I was young and stupid and cocky and in what I considered to be the peak of my career. I wasn't going to sit on the bench, particularly behind Gregg. It's no insult to Gregg. At that time, I didn't even consider Gregg to be competition for me. The day they traded me, I told Marty he would be sorry. And Marty was a big enough man to admit four years later that it was the biggest mistake he'd ever made in coaching."

In Rakoczy's first start, Kosar was lost for eight weeks to an injury, and the tone was set for the 1988 season.

"This was one of the moments where you began to dismantle that camaraderie and connection," Bob Golic said of the trade. "I don't think one guy would single-handedly destroy what was happening there, but it certainly signaled to us that there were some changes coming."

This is not to blame Rakoczy. He was a young player thrown into a difficult situation that he wasn't prepared for—probably a situation no young player could have excelled in. Even if Baab wasn't a dominant center and the Browns' offensive line wasn't exactly powerful, both were potent and had been very effective over the previous three seasons. And as the center, Baab was the heart of the line, its "quarterback," recognizing the opposing defenses and calling out the blocking schemes as only a veteran could working alongside other veterans he'd played with for years. Baab was the glue that held the line together.

"I don't want to blow my own horn, but that was my offensive line," he said. "I ran that offense. I'm the one that stood in the huddle and told everybody to shut up and get their eyes on the quarterback. I was the communicator between Bernie and the players. You don't want your quarterback bitching at the players . . . He

◄

would come to me and say, 'Can you go talk to so-and-so and say this-and-this.' And I'd go talk to them.

"When they took me out, they took out more than just an average center. I wasn't the world's greatest player, but I was OK. I was the glue. I say that with all humility, but I was the glue. When you take the glue out of an offensive line, it goes to pieces."

And it did—almost instantly.

In November 1988, when the Browns' offensive problems that would follow the team into the next decade were just beginning to manifest, Bob Kravitz traced the troubles back to Baab's trade. "It was as if all the good feelings, all the momentum that had built through the offseason and preseason had been summarily deflated. *Pop!* went the Browns. Something was lost. Bad feelings pervaded the place. The anger was palpable.

"It is impossible to quantify, perhaps even a reach, to suggest that today's problems, particularly on the offensive line, go all the way back to an isolated day in the preseason. But it's a gut feeling, a sense I've had since that strange day . . . Something happened that day, something that set the Browns back further than they had ever imagined."

Without Baab, the line struggled. And when the line struggled, not only did the Browns lose four quarterbacks to injury, but the running game never materialized, nor did the lofty expectations for the 1988 season. Schottenheimer was not cut out to be calling the plays, but it's very possible he would have done much better with the same offensive line Lindy Infante worked with and consequently, with the first- or even second-string players who wouldn't have been hurt had the line remained in tact.

Consider this possibility for 1988: the Browns keep Baab, the line stays strong, Kosar stays healthy. The Browns' offense is more successful, and even if the team doesn't win the division, it plays better overall, and there's no demand or expectation for major changes. Thus, Marty Schottenheimer is not given an ultimatum and either continues to call the plays or eventually relinquishes that role but not the handful of others he was being asked to hand over after 1988. Schottenheimer remains the Browns' coach in 1989 and likely into 1990.

Would the team have slipped to 3-13 and utterly fallen apart under his tutelage? As Art Modell once said, never in a hundred years. And if Schottenheimer remained the Browns' coach into 1991, Bill Belichick would have been hired by someone else and thus wouldn't have had the chance to drive a wedge between Cleveland and the Browns. And were the Browns simply playing as well and run as efficiently as Schottenheimer's Chiefs were in the early and mid-1990s, would city officials have been as hesitant to suggest helping the Browns out by publicly funding a new stadium? Absolutely not. And in that decision laid the Browns' move to Baltimore. Had Schottenheimer stayed for any additional period of time, it never would have happened.

Which isn't to say Schottenheimer would have stayed with the Browns indefinitely. But consider this as well: had Schottenheimer chosen to leave or even been forced out in the early or mid-1990s, a likely candidate to replace him would have been Bill Cowher. Had Schottenheimer stayed with the Browns, Cowher would have eventually been named defensive coordinator. And by the early-1990s, after serving as coordinator in Kansas City, Cowher was a solid head-coaching candidate. When Schottenheimer left, Cowher could have been strongly considered to be promoted from within, and it could have been the Browns, not the Steelers (who hired Cowher as head coach to replace Chuck Noll in 1992), who went on a run of success throughout the remainder of the decade and beyond. Would this have ultimately happened? There's no way to know. But it's reasonable to assume had the Browns been as popular in Cleveland as either Kansas City or Pittsburgh were under Schottenheimer and Cowher respectively in the first half of the 1990s, they never would have moved.

If you play out the remainder of the original hypothetical, Modell, who likely still would have been burdened by financial troubles brought on by a decade of sloppy front-office decisions and the money pit that was Cleveland Stadium, could have eventually sold the team to his good friend Al Lerner, turning the team over just as he eventually did in Baltimore. And the Browns, under Lerner's leadership, eventually would have begun playing in a brand-new stadium—the same result as in the aftermath of the Browns' move, only without a three-year gap of no football followed by two years of mind-numbing expansion football.

But this theory only holds up if you accept that the Browns were better off with Marty Schottenheimer than Bud Carson or Bill Belichick. Believe it or not, some would be hesitant to admit this.

Much has been made in the two decades since Schottenheimer left Cleveland about the coach's inability to reach the Super Bowl despite having superior teams. But for a moment, focus on the latter part of that sentiment. After leaving Cleveland, Schottenheimer did the same thing he'd done with the Browns: revitalize a struggling franchise. When he took over in Kansas City in 1989, the Chiefs had made the playoffs just once in the previous nineteen years since joining the NFL. When he stepped down in 1998, Kansas City had made the postseason seven times in ten seasons, winning the franchise's first three AFC West titles and twice notching the conference's best record.

True, Schottenheimer was just 3-7 in playoff games with the Chiefs. But in his ten years as their coach, he posted a record of 104-65-1, a winning percentage of .612. Over that same time period, the Browns went 48-63-1, a winning percentage of .429. Only a fool would argue the Browns were better off without Marty Schottenheimer.

If Schottenheimer had stayed, the Browns never would have traded Earnest Byner, at least not for unknown and ultimately useless Mike Oliphant (who missed the entire 1990 season to injury then appeared in just four games in his final NFL season in 1991). If the Baab trade began the dominoes falling toward the Browns' move, the Byner deal signaled the death of a solid Cleveland running game—a trend which has continued into the twenty-first century. While Byner only led the Browns in rushing one season, he was clearly the catalyst to the team's strong running attack from 1984 through 1988. In Byner's first five years in Cleveland, a Browns' running back rushed for a hundred yards or more in nineteen games. It would happen just once in the five years after Byner was traded, then three more times in the two seasons after he returned to Cleveland in 1994. He, along with Kosar, was the heart and soul of the Browns' offense and represented the fighting, if not flawed, spirit of the entire team and city.

"I would say of all the players I've ever coached," Schottenheimer said, "I don't know that I've ever enjoyed watching the development of a player as much as I did the development of Earnest. . . . He always will be one of my favorite people in this world. I don't know that there's ever been a guy that got more out of his ability than Earnest Byner."

And yet Byner, like Schottenheimer, was never really appreciated, either before or after his departure. He went on to a dazzling career in Washington, twice rushing for better than 1,000 yards in a season and propelling the Redskins to three playoff berths and a Super Bowl title in 1991. Reflecting the Cleveland Indians' infamous trades of and then for beloved outfielder Rocky Colavito in 1960 and 1965, Byner did return to the Browns as a veteran leader closing out a nice career in 1994 and was a major factor in helping the team reach the playoffs. He remained a leader through the tumultuous 1995 season, and appropriately, single-handedly carried the Browns to victory in their final game at Cleveland Stadium. Used sparingly all season, Byner exploded for 121 yards on thirty-one carries in a 26-10 win over the Bengals. He moved with the team to Baltimore, where he closed out his career in 1997 with 8,261 rushing yards and fifty-six touchdowns.

Yet for many, none of it will ever replace the memory of his turnover one evening in the Rocky Mountains. Many forgot that Byner had built his career as an overachiever and beat the odds to become possibly "the best tenth-round pick in the history of this league," as Schottenheimer once said.

Like the Browns teams of the 1980s, Byner's heroics and incredible spirit and effort were unjustly overshadowed by a horrible mistake at a dramatic moment.

All things considered, the era of 1985–89 was a satisfying one for the Cleveland Browns. They won four division titles and made the postseason five straight times—only the second time in team history that had happened. Only one itch remained unscratched.

Talented as they were, well-coached as they were for much of this period, the Browns could never figure out a way to beat the Denver Broncos. Even aside from the three conference-title-game losses, John Elway had the Browns' number. He faced Cleveland twelve times in his career, winning ten, and often was the difference in the game. It wasn't just against any single coach. He beat Bill Beli-chick four times, Marty Schottenheimer three times, Sam Rutigliano twice, and Bud Carson once. As it happened, Carson was the only one of the four to beat Elway, and he did it twice.

Still, the Broncos weren't exactly the Steelers or Bengals in terms of a natural rival. They were always ridiculed when they came to Cleveland, but it would be an overstatement to say they were hated. More accurately, they were disrespect-fully respected. What chewed at Cleveland fans more than losing three playoff games to Denver was the way the Broncos went out and humiliated themselves progressively worse in the Super Bowl. They lost to the Giants 39-20, Redskins 42-10, and 49ers 55-10. The Browns and their fans knew that they would never have been dominated like that in any of the three contests.

Instead, the Broncos became to the Browns what the New York Yankees once were to the Boston Red Sox: they had Cleveland's number. From 1975 through 2005, the Browns and Broncos played nineteen times. Though Denver was rarely clearly superior to Cleveland, the Broncos won an astounding seventeen of those games—ten with Elway, seven without. In that time period, the Browns lost more games to Denver than any other team outside their own division.

Had they faced any other team in any of those three AFC title games, it's very likely the Browns would have won at least one, if not all three, and gone on to the Super Bowl. And it's also quite likely that had the Browns played in all three of those Super Bowls, they would have won at least one. And if that had happened, these Browns' teams would hold an altogether different place in NFL history.

But that's not what happened. Every time the Cleveland Browns came close to achieving their dreams, up popped John Elway and the Denver Broncos. Every good story needs a villain, and the Browns of the late 1980s always had one.

Make no mistake; the five teams that closed out the 1980s were not the best in Cleveland Browns' history.

There's no comparison between these teams and those of the early 1950s, which won sixty-two of their first seventy-nine NFL games and took three league titles along the way. Even the Browns of the late 1960s may have been better, posting a 59-23-2 record from 1964 through 1969 and capturing the franchise's fourth crown in 1964. From 1985 through 1989, the Browns went 49-29-1, a victory clip of .620.

These latter Browns' teams had to deal with several factors the teams of before did not, such as free agency, parity, escalating salaries, and much less player/team loyalty. But that's not what makes the teams of the late 1980s the most memo-rable in Browns' history. Put simply, altogether they were the most entertaining consecutive athletic squads the city of Cleveland has ever seen.

In general, the Browns of the 1950s mowed down their opposition. And yes, while three of the six NFL Championship games they played in were decided by seven points or less, this was before the marriage of football and television. When the Browns played for the title in Los Angeles in 1951 and 1955 as well as in Detroit in 1953, was the entire city gathered around its collective television set back in Cleveland? More appropriately, how big was it when the Browns hosted the title game? Less than thirty thousand attended the classic championship with the Rams in 1950. Only fifty thousand showed up for what should have been a much-anticipated clash between the neighboring Browns and Lions in 1952 and even less (43,827) moseyed through the turnstiles in 1954, when Cleveland avenged back-to-back title-game losses to Detroit.

The Browns of the 1950s were good, yes. But popular, at least by any modern standard? Not nearly as popular as the Browns of the late 1980s.

The teams of the late 1960s, meanwhile, had both the big crowds that would become the franchise's trademark and the television audience that would prove to be the game's fossil fuel. But while successful, they lacked dramatic panache. When they won a title in 1964, it was in a washout, as they also triumphed in playoff games in 1968 (eleven points) and 1969 (twenty-four points). And they lost postseason games in similar fashion, falling by eleven points to Green Bay in 1965, by thirty-eight to Dallas in 1967, by thirty-four to Baltimore in 1968, and by twenty to Minnesota in 1969. These teams had their fair share of exciting, memorable games in between, but nothing like their descendents twenty years later.

Veering across the sports medium, the basketball Cavaliers only once came close to a run of comparable success, making the National Basketball Association playoffs seven times in eight years in the late 1980s and early 1990s. But Cleveland has never been a passionate basketball town, and with the Cavs' usual postseason failures combined with the monotony of an eighty-two-game season, it was hard to live and die with them.

The Indians, the old timers on the block, never had a run of notable year-in, year-out success until the 1990s. The teams of the 1950s were solid, but aside from a memorable 1954 season, the Tribe was best known for finishing second to the Yankees. After Jacobs Field opened in 1994, the Indians reached the postseason for the first time in forty-one years, and the city fell head over heels in love. The Tribe would go to two World Series over the next three years and reach the playoffs six times in seven years. The frenzy for the Indians during this time period is the only comparable phenomenon Cleveland has to the late 1980s Browns. Yet even this seems like something of a subset of those Sundays in the Pound. Ultimately, by the 1990s, Cleveland was more a blue-collar football town than a white-collar baseball town. It's also worth noting that the Indians' rise to power coincided perfectly with the Browns' departure. Had the Browns been around and been successful at the same time, would the Indians have been quite as popular? And the Indians also benefited from playing in a very different Cleveland in the 1990s—all thanks to the Browns of the previous decade.

"The city used to be referred to as the mistake by the lake, that you'd strike a match and set the lake on fire," Schottenheimer said. "They really began to get some measure of self-esteem, albeit vicariously through a football team."

"Go back and look at what happened to Cleveland as a city," Mike Baab said. "When I got to Cleveland in '82, that was a miserable rust-belt hole. It was awful. When I left, it was a vibrant, growing, exploding town with optimism. We had a lot to do with that. It's silly that a football team does that, but we did."

Along the way, they forged friendships that would endure well beyond the gridiron. Every Thursday night during this run was "Camaraderie Night." Ten or fifteen players would gather at a bar in Berea and simply shoot the breeze. "It wasn't about going out and partying," Bob Golic said. "It wasn't about chasing women. It was about sitting there with your buddies and having a beer and just talking. It was so important to a lot of us to be there and to hang with the guys. I think that was part of the stuff that kept us together."

"There was a terrific chemistry on those football teams," Schottenheimer said. "I have this sense that they really cared about one another, and I believe that's the cornerstone you have to have to be successful, not only in a football organization, but in any organization. You have to have people who are driven by the fact they don't want to let their teammate down. We had great, great character guys on those teams.

"In the final analysis, that's always what winning becomes. It becomes about people, not players. The whole objective is to try to build a football team, and you can't do that without quality people."

With a cast of those quality people, the Browns of the late 1980s became a soap opera almost every week. Rarely dominant, hardly ever dominated, they were in nearly every game and were usually entertaining for sixty full minutes. Fans, either watching at home or in the stands, remembered where they were when Bernie Kosar hit Webster Slaughter to beat the Steelers in overtime. They could recall who was with them when they watched the Browns rally from ten points down in four minutes to beat the Jets in double overtime. They would never forget their reaction when John Elway drove 98 yards or Earnest Byner fumbled. For better or worse, these memories highlighted moments of people's lives.

For five years, Cleveland lived and died with the Browns every week as never before—and loved every minute of it. "The team was bound to the city, and the fans appreciated that," Golic said. "I don't know if it's unique, but it's the coolest thing I've ever been involved in."

Those fans created their own phenomenon, transforming what once upon a time were nothing more than cheap seats into a destination, an on-field presence capable of winning games. Nothing reflected the incredible nature of this creation more than the inclusion of a new Dog Pound specifically designed and updated for Cleveland Browns Stadium in 1999. And all of it was sparked by a charismatic young man from Mississippi who simply tried to spice up a boring practice—by barking.

For the first time in memory, the city adored a professional athlete who was one of their own, a hometown kid who had gone off to fame and potential fortune but was willing to trade it in to come home, to be with the people he'd grown up with. After decades of strife with only the occasional lightning flash of excitement, this young man embodied all that the city had been missing, athletically or otherwise. Unlike most other sports figures, he was worth their adoration. He was hard-working, smart, and talented. But most of all, to these fans, he was one of them. Without him or what he represented, none of the success that followed would have been possible.

Here, too, a man who once appeared set for a career in real estate revitalized a downtrodden town with his meticulous organization and attention to detail. A wizard from Muscle Shoals, Alabama, reinvented the position he played. A personable lineman with an affection for comic books became a cult hero. A shy kid from a broken home in the foothills of North Carolina discovered himself and the loyalty of those around him. A fiery linebacker nicknamed "Assassin" refused to be replaced and persevered with zeal to become one of the franchise's most beloved players. A local wrestler used the skills he learned as a high school athlete to revitalize his career and become a stalwart for his hometown team.

In Cleveland, these men, these teams are still revered. Elsewhere, they are remembered solely for two capital-letter losses on national television. While it would be inappropriate to downplay the significance of those games, it's heartbreaking to see a five-year adventure swept under the headline of those losses like dust under a rug.

"I don't care," Mike Baab said. "We don't care. That's as close as we ever got. Who's come that close since? We believed we were going to win and the fans believed we were going to win. Have the fans, since that point, believed that their Browns teams were going to win? No . . . I haven't seen anything even remotely like that. The fans believed like we believed. The whole town believed."

The rest of the world be damned. Clevelanders know the double-overtime win over the Jets was a far better-played and more exciting contest than The Drive. They know the Browns had utterly outplayed the Broncos when it counted the following year. They're quick to point out Don Strock's finest game wasn't on a sultry evening in Miami but on a snowswept afternoon in Cleveland.

All of it is part of this city's lore. Even after a decade of adversity and bitterness, its citizens are still enamored with its football team, though they'd have every reason to forsake it. Abandoning this team, giving in to cynicism, are not options. They remember what a good football team in a great football town can be. They recall the Browns of the late 1980s and because of those memories their commitment to the future, when all that was once good will be again, remains strong.

In the meantime, they stand steadfast, as loyal as an old dog.

Bibliographic Essay

Now that I've done this a few times, I can say with certainty it's much easier to write about history when you've witnessed it. Unlike with *Kardiac Kids*, my previous Brown's book, for which I essentially pieced together a story I'd heard but didn't see for myself, *Sundays in the Pound* is as much a diary of my youth as it is a story of the 1980s Cleveland Browns. The structure, outline, and emphasis of certain topics and subplots were formulated principally from my own memories and experiences from following those teams.

That being said, my memory wasn't *that* good. Several sources were indispensable, two in particular. First, there were the countless editions of the *Plain Dealer*, which has always provided top-notch coverage of the Browns. And second, perhaps my inspiration for writing about the Browns to begin with, was *Browns News/Illustrated*, a weekly publication orchestrated by Ray Yannucci from 1981 to 2001. Thanks primarily to my father saving most of the back issues, I was able to put together an almost complete run, a collection of nearly five hundred issues. The game stories and player features proved to be the best club in my bag as I took the course for this project.

I also spent a good deal of time researching at both the Columbus Metropolitan Library and the Ohio Historical Society Archives/Library. But research originally began in the fall of 1998 in the bowels of the Vernon R. Alden Library on the campus of my alma mater, Ohio University.

The following is a list of books that came in very handy:

Brenner, Richard J. *John Elway Bernie Kosar*. New York: Lynx Books, 1988.

Knight, Jonathan. *Kardiac Kids: The Story of the 1980 Cleveland Browns*. Kent, Ohio: Kent State University Press, 2003.

Martin, Russell. *The Color Orange: A Super Bowl Season with the Denver Broncos*. New York: Henry Holt, 1987.

Morgan, Jon. *Glory for Sale: Fans, Dollars, and the New NFL*. Baltimore, Md.: Bancroft, 1997.

Neft, David S., Richard M. Cohen, and Rick Korch. *The Football Encyclopedia: The Complete History of Professional Football from 1892 to the Present*. New York: St. Martin's, 1994.

Rutigliano, Sam. *Pressure.* Nashville, Tenn.: Oliver-Nelson Books, 1988.

Silverman, Matthew, ed. *Total Browns: The Official Encyclopedia of the Cleveland Browns.* New York: Total Sports, 1999.

Strock, Don. *Behind the Lines: A Veteran Quarterback's Look inside the NFL.* New York: Pharos Books, 1991.

Total Football II: The Official Encyclopedia of the National Football League. New York: HarperCollins, 1999.

A handful of magazine articles also proved valuable:

Greene, Jerry. "The Miami Connection." *GameDay,* Oct. 18, 1987.

Grossi, Tony. "Bernie Kosar: Ready to Lead in '86?" *Ohio Football,* 1986.

———. "Brian Brennan." *Ohio Football,* 1987.

———. "Browns' Boy Wonder." *GameDay,* Sept. 25, 1988.

———. "Football's Wizard of Oz." *Street & Smith's Pro Football,* 1988.

Jackson, Mark. "The Game I'll Never Forget." *Football Digest,* July 1992.

Knisley, Michael. "First-and-98!" *1987 NFL Team Book.*

Looney, Douglas S. "There's a Love Feast on Lake Erie." *Sports Illustrated,* Aug. 26, 1985.

Reilly, Rick. "High and Mighty." *Sports Illustrated,* Jan. 25, 1988.

Swift, E. M. "Reprieve for the Browns." *Sports Illustrated,* Jan. 12, 1987.

Telander, Rick. "Brainy Brown." *Sports Illustrated,* Aug. 29, 1988.

———. "Getting There the Hard Way." *Sports Illustrated,* Jan. 19, 1987.

———. "Just Out of Reach." *Sports Illustrated,* Jan. 15, 1990.

Underwood, John. "No Team Was Ever Higher." *Sports Illustrated,* Jan. 9, 1984.

Williams, Gene. "Worshipping Bernie." *Plain Dealer Magazine,* July 31, 1988.

Zimmerman, Paul. "Back to the Future." *Sports Illustrated,* Sept. 3, 1986.

Also invaluable were the individual Browns' season highlight films produced by NFL Films, which also produced two episodes of its *NFL Greatest Games* series on the 1986 and 1987 AFC Championships. Another helpful production was ESPN Classic's *Battle Lines: The 1986 AFC Championship.* Additionally, a shelf full of Browns' media guides from 1978 through 2005 provided much-needed background material.

Thanks to another tradition my dad started shortly after we bought our first VCR in November of 1984 (just in time, I might add), I had at my disposal a library of Browns' games on videotape that helped liven up the research process as well as bring back several wonderful memories.

Index